ALMOST
SISTERS

THE COMPANY OF GOOD WOMEN

ALMOST SISTERS

a novel by

NANCY ANDERSON • LAEL LITTKE
CARROLL HOFELING MORRIS

DESERET
BOOK

SALT LAKE CITY, UTAH

Library of Congress Cataloging-in-Publication Data

Anderson, Nancy.
    Almost sisters / Nancy Anderson, Lael Littke, Carroll Hofeling Morris.
       p. cm. — (The company of good women ; 1)
    ISBN-10 1-59038-576-4 (pbk.)
    ISBN-13 978-1-59038-576-0 (pbk.)
    1. Female friendship—Religious aspects—Christianity. 2. Mormon women—United States. 3. Mormon women—Religious life. I. Littke, Lael. II. Morris, Carroll Hofeling. III. Title. IV. Series: Anderson, Nancy. Company of good women ; 1.
    BX8641.A53 2006
    241'.6762082—dc22   2006007588

Printed in the United States of America
Malloy Lithographing Inc., Ann Arbor, MI

10 9 8 7 6 5 4 3 2 1

To the good women in our lives and to the good men as well, especially Jim, George in memoriam, and Gary

With special thanks to Lori Littke Silfen, who saved us from computer meltdown as we worked on this book

Prologue

2004

They turned heads as they walked along the streets of Moab, Utah, the three older women wearing matching denim jackets with appliquéd fabric art on the back. Around it were embroidered dates and place names, as well as statements such as Dance, Joy, and Hug a Tree. There was something about the women—their obvious enjoyment of life, their confident bearing, the way they linked arms as if they were a set—that attracted attention.

"You must be in town for the Slickrock Rendezvous," a man said with a grin as they passed. "Did you come by Jeep or ride in on your Hogs?"

"Broomsticks," said one of the women, and they all laughed, including the man.

At the pizza place where they stopped for lunch, the young man behind the counter eyed them. "Sisters?" he asked.

"Almost," the tallest of the trio said.

"We qualify," said the one with the soft, round face. "We've been through enough together."

The young man smiled. "Sounds as if you have quite a story."

"We do," the three women said in unison.

Chapter One
1980

JUNEAU

Juneau had just packed one of her Guilty Secrets in her suitcase under a pair of plastic-bagged shoes when the telephone rang. She reached for the bedroom extension at the same time she smelled something burning. Making a split-second decision that in the hierarchy of bad things, burning down the house was worse than missing a phone call, she leaped toward the kitchen, only to stumble over Philip Atwater. The big brown dog lay on the bedroom floor, his head disconsolately resting on his paws, already mourning her impending departure. Pirouetting gracelessly on toward the door, she ignored his yelp at the assault on his doggy dignity.

By now the phone was on its second ring, and the acrid stench of burnt canned corn filled the hallway. So much for the corn chowder, Greg's favorite of her limited cooking repertoire. The plan had been for her to leave it for her family's dinner that night.

The phone rang a third time as she snatched the soup pot from the too-hot gas burner and tossed it into the sink with a clatter that chipped the porcelain. Her mother's constant refrain, "Juneau is our klutzy one," echoed in her ears as she vaulted from the sink to the wall phone before it finished its fourth ring.

"Don't hang up," she said aloud, picking up the handset and gasping, "Hello?"

"Honey?" It was Greg's voice. "Sounds like you've been running."

She laughed. "Not fast enough."

"Meaning what?"

"Meaning I won't be leaving dinner in the fridge. Greg, can you bring home some food from McDonald's? Misty and Nicole would probably prefer that anyway." They were nine and seven, and to them McDonald's was gourmet.

"So what happened?" Greg's tone was indulgent, implying that he was willing to be amused by yet another Juneau-ism.

"You don't want to know."

"Okay. Are you about ready to go?"

"As soon as I soothe Philip Atwater. I figure I'll be pulling out in about half an hour."

"Good. That will put you in St. George before dark." He hesitated a moment. "Are you sure you want to do this, Juney? Drive all the way from Pasadena to Provo by yourself? It's seven hundred desert miles, you know. In August."

She set her jaw. "I can do this." He had no idea how much she wanted to do this. *Needed* to do it. All those hours alone in the car to ponder what had happened to her life.

"Tomorrow will be easier," she continued, "since I'll be stopping to visit Great-Aunt Hattie in Nephi. The next day will be a cinch. I'll be in Provo in time for church."

"Good plan," Greg said. There was a pause. "But don't be a speed demon."

She knew he was smiling. "I won't."

"Stop often to stretch and wake up."

"I will." That one was for sure. She'd be turning into every rest stop. She must have been at the end of the line when bladders were being given out because hers was like a leftover extra-small. Right now, it was even more so. Right now, when she suspected she might be pregnant again. She considered telling him. She pictured a scale in her mind, weighing the pros and cons.

The cons weighed heavy. If Greg knew she might be pregnant, he'd insist on her flying to Utah or maybe try to talk her out of going at all. She'd been miserably sick with both girls, and he'd argue about her traveling alone.

The cons won.

She offered a quick, silent prayer that her nausea was just a touch of stomach flu and then wondered if it was appropriate for a good Mormon wife and mother to hope she wasn't pregnant. Perhaps she'd find the answer to that at BYU Education Week. Would there be classes in Requirements for Mormon Women 101? Or a seminar on how to be happy when you've got what you thought you wanted but it isn't enough?

"Honey? Juney?"

"I'll be fine, Greg. I'll call tonight from St. George when I get settled in my motel."

"The car should be okay," he said. "Just watch the gas gauge. You'll probably have to fill up in Baker."

She shook her head, glad he couldn't see her exasperation. With all the times they'd made the trip from California to Utah, she was quite clear on how far a tank of gas would go.

Changing the subject, she said, "The girls are already over at Marisol's. I can hear all the kids playing something loud in her backyard."

"I'm not worried about them."

"I'll be fine, honey. Really."

"Okay." His voice dripped doubt, but all he said was, "I love you."

"Me, too."

"You mean you love you?"

"I mean I love YOU."

"Drive carefully."

"I will."

"Keep your doors locked."

"I will."

The familiar farewell litany preceded any trip where they would be separated. It was nice. It all said *I Love You*.

After they hung up, she scrubbed the charred soup pot, scraping the bottom to get rid of all the gunky stuff. Symbolic, somehow.

Philip Atwater followed her when she took her suitcase to the car, and she had to pull him by the collar to get him into the backyard. The last thing she saw as she drove away was his morose dog face watching from behind the wrought iron gate, looking the way she'd been feeling—as if she were behind some kind of bars, peering out to see what was going on in the big, wide world.

WILLADENE

Willadene counted casseroles, numbered them, and put them in the freezer. She was one short. "I don't know how that happened," she said apologetically to her husband, Roger. "But I made a lot of the noodle and ham casserole. You can probably stretch it enough for two meals. All you have to do is set the oven for 350 degrees and heat it for 45 minutes."

Roger nodded.

"Remember," Willadene continued, "Bitsy won't eat the ham, just the noodles. Carl won't want the peas but make him eat them anyway. Oh, and don't let Bitsy feed her ham to the dog. The vet said it's too salty and will make him sick."

Roger nodded again, his smile strained.

"Everything's listed right here," Willadene said reassuringly, pointing to her list of instructions. Along with notations on how to prepare the casseroles, she'd written down how many drops of Triaminic each child should receive in the event of colds and the phone numbers of their doctor and the woman with whom she would be staying. She pointed out that number. "If there's anything I forgot to tell you, you can reach me at Sister Farnsworth's early in the morning and in the evening."

"We'll be just fine, Deenie." Roger rounded the kitchen table to give her a squeeze.

Willadene rested her head on his shoulder. "I know I've gone a little overboard, but I've never been away overnight since Paulie was born. Even when I had Bitsy, I was home the same day."

"Come on, Deenie," Roger said kindly. "You've been looking forward to Education Week for months. You know how much you want to take those classes on using gluten."

He was teasing. But it was true. She'd just about run out of new ideas for Homemaking meeting.

"Don't worry," Roger continued. "We've got it covered on this end. Carl and Paul have full-day summer camp this week, and Mom will take the baby while I'm helping Dad on the farm." He looked around. "Are you packed and ready to go?"

"Yipes! Packing!" She dashed to the bedroom to finish. This whole trip was Murphy's Law in action. Whatever could go wrong, did.

When she'd first signed up for BYU Education Week, it had sounded like so much fun. She'd imagined that staying in the dorms with the other Relief Society sisters from her ward would be like a high-school slumber party. But somewhere in all the piles of paper listing things to be done, she'd misplaced her housing request. So instead of bunking with the other sisters, she'd be staying at a private home. She'd been wrong about class schedules, too. She'd had the idea that she and the other ladies from Wellsville would be attending classes together and then sharing sack lunches and notes at the Wilkinson Center. But no. The classes she wanted overlapped the ones they'd signed up for, which meant she'd be on her own.

What if she couldn't find her way from one unfamiliar building to another? What if, with no one to distract her, she got lost in thought worrying about her family and missed something important? There were so many things that could go wrong.

At least she had her packing well organized. Everything was laid out on the bed beside the suitcase. She put in her personal items first and then the full slip with the double shadow panel in the front that she always wore with her summer dresses for modesty's sake. She added two pairs of comfortable shoes, one light and one dark, so her shoes would always be the same color or darker than her hemline. She folded and packed her one good navy poly-ester A-line skirt, three simple blouses and a light cardigan, her favorite pale green dress with the white dots and pique trim, and a blue cotton shift. Finally she added notebooks, sharpened colored pencils, and her scriptures.

After shutting and locking her suitcase, she went through her purse to make sure everything was in it, including the items she'd put in a plastic bag in case someone might need them: Band-Aids for blisters and aspirin she knew she wouldn't take but someone else might need, as well as a tiny sewing kit complete with spare buttons. She had what she thought she needed—except for some sense of control.

"Deenie, your ride's here." Roger's voice came from the front of the house. Willadene grabbed her journal and stuffed it into her tote bag. She snagged her purse and suitcase on her way down the stairs.

In the living room Carl, Paul, and Bitsy waited by the couch to have their family travel prayer. There was a brief conflict as to who should say the blesses. Carl won, but Paul got to shout the "Amen."

Willadene gave both boys a big hug. Then she swooped up Bitsy and buried her nose in the tickle spot of her daughter's neck, drawing a deep breath. The fresh baby smell stirred up a renewed reluctance to leave the safety of her Wellsville home. Small and cluttered as it was, it was hers and she loved it.

Roger stood patiently by the open door holding her suitcase.

"Don't forget to feed the dog," she reminded him as she kissed him on the cheek.

Roger's eyebrows went up. "You're going to be gone a week, and that's all I get? No way!" He put down the suitcase, pulled Willadene into a two-arm hug, and kissed her soundly. When he finally let her go, Willadene felt the heat in her cheeks. Even after eight years of marriage, Roger could still make her blush.

ERIN

"What do you think?" Erin asked her friend Colleen. They were stand-ing in the living room of the apartment Erin shared with fellow hairstylist Rochelle in the artsy enclave of Minneapolis known as Uptown. Before them on the threadbare couch lay the dresses Erin had chosen for her trip to

Education Week at Brigham Young University. She had developed a unique style from years of shopping at Ragstock, estate sales, Goodwill, and vintage clothing stores. She knew she would love wearing these dresses here, but would they do on the BYU campus?

"They look like you." Colleen wiped the sweat off her forehead and folded her arms over her swelling middle.

"Are you okay?" Erin was worried that the heat of her third-floor apartment might be too much for her pregnant friend. "Can I get you some cold water?"

"You sound just like my hubby," said Colleen. "Stop worrying. I'm not *sick,* just pregnant."

Erin was already on her way to the kitchen, where she filled glasses for both of them, going heavy on the ice. She knew she was overprotective of her friend, but it was hard not to feel that way. Although she and Colleen were both twenty-two, Colleen's slight build, pale face, and ponytail made her look much younger and more vulnerable. Especially now.

Colleen held her glass briefly to each cheek in turn before drinking. Then she gestured toward the dresses. "Are these new? I haven't seen them before."

Erin nodded. I've been hitting all my favorite stores."

"They're dramatic, that's for sure. Did you get the short-short haircut to go with them?"

"That wasn't the idea. A stylist friend was supposed to give me a trim, and this is what I ended up with." Erin peered into the mirror over the couch and tweaked her flaming red hair into shape. "Is it awful?"

"Good grief, no. With those great-looking cheekbones and big eyes, you've got the face for it."

"And the dresses?" Erin pressed.

"What can I say? They're you."

"I think I hear a *but* in there somewhere."

"You'll stand out, is all." Colleen flashed a quick smile at Erin. "You know me—I'd do anything to keep from drawing attention to myself."

"Is that a rule for Mormons I don't know about yet? Thou shalt not draw attention to thyself?"

Colleen shook her head, laughing. "It's just me." She touched each short-sleeved dress in turn. There was a white shirtwaist with red polka dots and a flared skirt, a belted brown sheath with large front buttons and white collar, and a simple black dress with a jewel neckline. She held the black dress over her middle. "This is my favorite. It's classy but kind of sexy, too."

That wasn't exactly what Erin had hoped to hear. "But are they okay?"

"Honestly, Erin! Why do you keep asking me that? What are you worried about?"

"You know what it's like out there. I don't."

"You act like Utah is a foreign country."

"It is, to me. There's so much history, with those pioneers struggling across the plains and all. That's where the prophet is, and the Salt Lake Temple. I know there are other temples, but I always think of that one with a capital T. And most everybody there is Mormon. It has to be different."

"It's not as different as you think." With an exasperated sigh, Colleen put her hands on her hips. "Look, if you want to know if these dresses fit the standards at BYU, yes, they do. If you want to know if you'll look like everyone else, no, you won't. But you never give a flying fig about whether you fit in or not, so why ask?"

"That's not true!"

"Then why don't you go shopping at Donaldson's and Dayton's instead of Ragstock?"

Erin offered a rueful grin. "I did. Everything I tried on looked so . . . *boring*. I didn't feel like myself when I looked in the mirror."

"See? You don't really want to look like everybody else." Colleen grabbed Erin by the arms and gave her a little shake. "You know what? I love you dearly, but you're exhausting. There's not a thing I can say that will make you feel okay about this trip."

"You're probably right." Erin could hear an edge to her own voice. She wanted encouragement and support from Colleen, not a reminder of her own insecurity. She made up for her irritation by asking solicitously, "Want more water?"

"I'm okay. I just get so hot and uncomfortable. But I remind myself that there's a baby inside here," Colleen said, patting her tummy. "I'm so excited about being a mom. Steve and I can't wait for this little person to arrive."

"Lucky kid," Erin said with a lightness she didn't feel. "It must be nice to know you're wanted. Not every kid is."

"How can a mother not love her child?"

"I didn't say not loved. I said not *wanted*."

"Is there a difference?"

Oh, yes, thought Erin. *And I know all about it.*

Her first awareness of this distinction was associated with hair. Sitting on her mother's lap, her mother combing her hair. Her grandmother standing in the doorway. Words coming out of her grandmother's mouth that she didn't understand at the time, words like *that red hair . . . , just like that boy's . . . , if you hadn't . . . , if she weren't . . . , things would be different . . . , things would be better . . .* Her mother crying, holding her so tight she couldn't breathe, kissing the top of her head. And later, her grandmother doing the same thing.

Colleen interrupted her thoughts. "I've got to go, Erin. It's time for my nap. Doctor's orders." She stooped awkwardly to pick up her purse and then gave Erin a hug. "While you're in Provo, you really ought to check out the possibility of enrolling at the Y. There are so many interesting subjects to pursue." She winked.

"And hordes of cute single Mormon gals pursuing them. I'd just be one of the many."

"You? Never. Want my advice about these dresses? Take them all."

After Colleen left, Erin packed the suitcase she'd borrowed from her mother. She folded the dresses carefully to minimize wrinkles, added flats to match, and tucked in a drawstring pouch filled with coordinating costume jewelry. She stashed her camera and a notebook in her tote bag. As an afterthought she stuffed in the book she'd been reading. She'd already put the ticket for her flight and other important information in the zippered compartment of her purse, including the address of Gabrielle Farnsworth, the woman she'd be staying with in Provo.

She was carried along on a sense of purpose during her preparations, but once she put her locked suitcase and tote bag by the door, she felt a sudden moment of doubt. Why she was doing this? What did she hope to find in Zion? She was looking for something that she couldn't name, not even to herself. Whatever it was, it held the promise of making her, finally, two years after her baptism, a real Mormon.

Chapter Two

ERIN

Erin sighed with relief as the taxi pulled up to the curb in front of the Farnsworth house. The driver, a BYU student who'd told her he was making a little cash by running a cab service, said, "Here we are, ma'am. I hope you have a pleasant visit in Provo." She smiled at his calling her "ma'am." He was probably the same age as she.

He had entertained her all the way from the bus station, pointing out various sites of interest, including Mt. Timpanogos. "See the shape of it?" he had said. "Legend says it's a sleeping Indian princess."

Used to the rolling terrain of Minnesota, Erin had been awestruck by the towering mountains looming behind the city. Seeing the outline of the sleeping princess in the peaks and slopes of Mt. Timpanogos had made them seem friendlier somehow.

"Thanks," she said as she got out and paid him, including a generous tip. "I feel as if I've been on a really good guided tour."

He smiled and waved as he drove away.

Erin took a deep breath. *I made it,* she congratulated herself. Although everything had gone well, the trip had been a nerve-wracking process. It had included her first flight, her first ride on a Greyhound bus from Salt Lake City to Provo, and various connecting taxi rides.

She stood for a moment looking at the Farnsworth house. It sat on a tree-lined street in an area that showed evidence of decline. In contrast, this two-story brick house was beautifully maintained, with simple white gingerbread trim and a wide front porch lined with rose bushes in bloom.

Old houses and antique furniture had always interested Erin. She was intrigued by what she might find inside but also a little anxious about meeting Sister Farnsworth and the other sisters staying here. Outside of the salon, where she was used to working with strangers, first meetings were not easy for her.

Swallowing her apprehension, she hauled her suitcase up to the porch and rang the doorbell. In the midst of a second ring, the door opened, revealing a tall, gray-haired woman in a pencil-thin gray skirt and a classic lavender shirt.

The woman smiled and extended a hand. "You have to be Erin from

Minnesota. I'm Gabrielle Farnsworth. Just call me Gabby." She ushered Erin into the front hall. "Leave your things by the stairs. You can take them up after you meet my other guests. They're in the kitchen enjoying my famous cowboy cookies."

"Cowboy cookies?" Erin repeated.

"Hunky," Gabby said.

Erin raised her eyebrows, but no further explanation came. "I hope you're inviting me to have some," she said. "I'm starving."

"It's required." Gabby turned, and Erin followed her into a bright kitchen that satisfied her expectations totally. There were gingham-curtained windows, yellow-painted cabinets, appliances that were charmingly out-of-date, an antique work center, and an oak table with matching chairs. Two women were seated at the table on which a plate of cookies and a pitcher of milk sat amidst small plates and glasses.

"Ladies," Gabby said, "this is Erin Larson from Minnesota." After they murmured their greetings, she gestured toward a woman with a pale, pretty face devoid of makeup and framed with long, shapeless blonde hair. "Erin, this is Juneau Caldwell from California. Juneau spelled with an e-a-u," she added.

"Named after the city where I was born," Juneau offered, as if used to explaining it.

"And this," Gabby said, motioning toward a slightly plump woman with a sweet expression and short curly dark hair, "is Willadene Rasmussen from Wellsville, a hundred miles or so north of here. Deenie for short."

Erin's first thought was that these women could both use a good haircut. Her second was, *They're wearing dresses.* She grimaced. She'd wanted to make a good impression, and already she'd goofed. She was the only one in pants.

"Something wrong?" asked Juneau.

"Uh," Erin said, "you're all wearing dresses."

"Of course," said Willadene matter-of-factly. "It's Sunday."

"Don't worry," Juneau said, smiling at Erin. "You'll only have to spend a few months being nursery leader as penance."

There was laughter around the table, and Erin joined in, feeling more at ease.

"Sit, sit," Gabby encouraged. "Do you want milk with your cookies?"

Erin nodded. "Absolutely. Cookies and milk are great comfort food."

"Amen to that!" Juneau said fervently. She helped herself to another cookie and then passed Erin the plate.

Erin took one and bit into its chocolatey richness. Now she knew why the "hunky." The cookies were filled with big hunks of chocolate. She felt herself relaxing as she savored each bite. She'd arrived safely, she'd met her housemates, and she was still alive and feeling welcome.

Gabby set a glass in front of Erin, filled it from the pitcher, and sat down. "Well, we're all here." She looked them over approvingly. "I so much enjoy the company of good women, and I always look forward to meeting a new group of sisters each year. I've never been disappointed."

"You don't know us yet," Juneau said.

Gabby gave her a wise smile. "Oh, I've figured out a few things already. For instance, you drove alone all the way up from Pasadena. That tells me you're independent and self-confident and that you needed to have some time alone to think. Time to rest, too."

A flash of color warmed Juneau's cheeks, which puzzled Erin. But Juneau merely shrugged as she reached for still another cookie. "I'm okay. I took the drive in stages, so it wasn't bad."

Gabby turned to Willadene. "For you, family is everything. You've been away from your kids only a few hours, but you're wishing you were home to tuck them in and give them good-night kisses."

Willadene clapped a hand over her mouth. "Have I been talking too much about them?"

"Not at all, dear," Gabby said. "It's nice to hear."

"It's just that I've never been away from them this long before." Willadene sounded a bit apologetic, but Erin heard a note of pride in her voice. Willadene added, "Being here doesn't feel quite right. I honestly don't know why I thought I could stand it."

Gabby patted Willadene's hand. "Don't worry. Your husband loves them as much as you do. He'll take good care."

Willadene nodded. "I know. But it's not only my husband and kids I miss. I don't like being away from my little sister Sunny. Of course, she lives with our mom and dad, but she calls me almost every day to say, 'Deenie, it's time to come home and play with me.' I hate not being there to take her calls." She looked down at her hands and sighed.

Going by what Deenie had said, Erin imagined Sunny to be in elementary school. "You have a little sister that young?"

"No, she's sixteen."

Willadene offered no explanation, and Erin wished fervently that she had kept her mouth shut. She felt even worse when Juneau said, "Brace yourself, girl. It's your turn to be Gabbied."

Gabby laughed and said, "Don't be afraid. I'm not psychic or anything like that. But turning the pages of more calendars than you can count has some advantages. You learn to read people."

Erin breathed deeply. "Okay. Go for it."

Gabby leaned back, surveying her. "Well, I first read that you can't be much older than twenty."

"Twenty-two," Erin confessed, feeling impossibly young.

Gabby nodded. "I imagine you're wondering what there is to talk about with three 'older' women in skirts."

"Hey," Juneau objected with a grin, "who are you calling 'older?' I'm only thirty-four."

"I'm twenty-eight," Willadene sniffed. "Not exactly skidding into eternity."

Gabby was unruffled. "As I said, 'older.'"

Erin flashed a smile. "It did cross my mind that I'm the youngest one here, but I'm a hairstylist. I have a lot of experience making small talk with women of all ages. But this is different." She paused and then said what was in her heart. "I want my clients to like me as a hairstylist. I want you to like me as a person."

Willadene patted her shoulder. "Of course, we'll like you. You're a good person."

"How do you know that? You've only just met me."

"Well," Willadene said, "we're all here for Education Week, aren't we? That says something."

"Says that very likely you're all Mormons," commented Gabby dryly.

Erin shifted a little uneasily. "I haven't been one all that long. I bet you're all lifers."

Juneau hooted. "That sounds as if we've been tried, convicted, and sentenced. But yes, I'm a lifer."

Willadene raised a hand as if she were in school. "I am, too. A great-great-grandmother of mine drove a wagon from Winter Quarters to the Valley. She was thirteen! And ancestors on both sides of the family were among the first settlers in Wellsville. We've been there ever since."

Erin turned to Gabby. "What about you?"

"My husband's people made the trek, too," she said enigmatically. "Now tell us about you, Erin. How did you become interested in the Mormon Church?"

"I met up with two very attractive sister missionaries who asked me questions I couldn't answer."

"You mean, Where did I come from? Why am I here? Where am I going?" asked Gabby.

"At the time I had a thousand questions, not just three," Erin said. "About Life, the Universe, and Everything."

"*The Hitchhiker's Guide to the Galaxy,*" Juneau murmured.

"Yes," Erin said, delighted that Juneau recognized the campy book that was a favorite of hers. "Well, I liked what the sisters said, and . . ."

"Wait." Willadene held up a hand again. "Rewind. Back to the Hitchhiker's Whatever. Is this something I should be reading?"

"Depends on what you like," Erin said.

"Actually, I don't need another book on my 'to read' list," Willadene said. "I barely have time to read my scriptures and the *Ensign* as it is."

"Me, too." Gabby stood up. "Ladies, I'm old. *Older,*" she amended. "My Sunday afternoon nap is calling."

"I hear the call, too." Erin didn't really want to cut off the conversation, but she suddenly felt the effects of a long travel day. Standing up, she said, "Let me help you clear the table first."

Gabby waved her toward the hall. "This stuff will wait," she said. "Your room is to the left at the top of the stairs. Don't sleep too long. We'll have supper at seven."

Juneau looked surprised. "I wasn't expecting supper."

Gabby shrugged. "You won't get it any other day, but I always fix supper for my guests on Sunday. And I'll provide breakfasts. Just cereal, but that's better than the nothing you'd probably have if I turned you out without making sure you eat."

"Mama Farnsworth," Juneau said. "I appreciate it."

Gabby laughed. "I was young once, too, you know. Always choosing another minute in bed over a decent breakfast."

Gratefully, Erin gave Gabby a little hug and then hauled her luggage up the stairs to her room.

There were three bedrooms on the second floor and one very spartan bathroom with ancient fittings. Erin's bedroom had a single bed with an iron headboard and quilted coverlet, a nightstand, an old oak rocking chair, and an oak chest of drawers with a mirror. She fell in love with it immediately. She smiled as she crawled under the coverlet and fell asleep.

JUNEAU

"I'm going to redd up the kitchen," Juneau said after Gabby and Erin left. "Then I think I'll go for a walk."

Willadene's forehead furrowed. "Redd up? I haven't heard that before."

"Oh, sorry." Juneau began gathering up the plates. "I picked it up when my family lived in the mid-south for a while. It just means to clean up."

Willadene nodded. "I'm beginning to feel well traveled! And speaking of traveling, do you mind if I walk with you?"

Juneau's first thought was that she wanted to be by herself. She wanted to do some thinking about her visit with Great-Aunt Hattie the day before. Besides, she didn't think she'd have anything to talk about with Willadene, or Erin, either, for that matter. With that thought she realized the extent to which she'd already judged the other women. Flamboyant Erin with her short, bright red hair reminded her vaguely of an uninhibited girl named Starette who had been something of an influence on her life a long time ago. And Willadene seemed like a carbon copy of the earnest, efficient Relief Society women who'd kept things running smoothly in the many wards she'd been in. They'd always made Juneau a little uncomfortable because her own family never contributed anything to a ward. They merely passed through.

Ashamed of her early judgment, she said, "Certainly you may come along. Are you like me and can't sleep well at night if you take a nap?"

"Actually," Willadene said, "I haven't had time for a nap for years."

Quickly they set the kitchen to rights and walked out into the late afternoon sunshine. For a few minutes they sauntered along in silence, admiring the shadowed mountains. Then Willadene said, "Juneau, what's it like in California? I've never been there."

"Well," Juneau said, "where I live in Pasadena, it's wonderful. There's a backdrop of high mountains, like here, and I live on the slopes. The weather is great, most of the time. Lots of trees. And traffic. Where the freeway goes past my neighborhood, it's ten lanes wide, and sometimes, at rush hour, it gridlocks."

Willadene shuddered. "Too much for me. Do you like it there?"

"Love it. Wouldn't want to live anywhere else." Juneau wasn't totally sure that was true. She wasn't sure of much of anything any more. But she *did* like living in Pasadena.

Willadene shook her head. "I don't think I could live where there aren't four seasons."

Juneau laughed. "We have four seasons." She ticked them off on her fingers. "Earthquake, fire, mudslide, drought. No, actually, we do have spring, summer, fall, and winter, but the seasons are capricious rather than cyclical. Last year spring was on a Tuesday in January."

Willadene giggled. "You're funny, Juneau. I was hoping my housemates would be easy to get to know, and I think my wish has come true. And I really admire you for driving all that way alone. I wouldn't dare."

Juneau was sorry now that she hadn't wanted Willadene to come along. She was a pleasant little person, even if they didn't see eye to eye on things. "I enjoyed the drive," she said. "I stopped in St. George on Friday, and then last night I stayed with my Great-Aunt Hattie in Nephi."

"That was nice. Is your family close?"

"No." Juneau paused to smell a rose on a bush they were passing. "I'd never seen Aunt Hattie—Harriet—before in my life. I wouldn't even know about her, except that she sends Christmas cards to my parents. Since I got married, she has sent them to me, too. I've always been curious about her, so I wrote to ask if I could stop and see her. I'm glad I did. She's eighty-four and full of old family stories."

"There's always a keeper of stories in a family," Willadene said.

"In normal families." Juneau heard the rueful tone in her own voice. "She gave me a photo that my Great-Grandmother Letitia is in, along with Great-Aunt Hattie. They were sisters. Great-Grandma Letitia raised my mother after my grandparents died in a car crash, but I'd never seen a picture of her before."

Willadene turned to gaze at her. "You're kidding."

Juneau raised her right hand. "Truth." Very likely a family like Juneau's was beyond Willadene's comprehension, living as she apparently did with several generations of her relatives. Probably everyone in Wellsville was related to her, including those resting in the cemetery.

Thinking of cemeteries reminded Juneau of another of the photos Aunt Hattie had given her. It was of a gravestone in the cemetery of the small town of Mink Creek, Idaho, where Juneau's parents had grown up. The names of both her Great-Grandfather Orville and Great-Grandmother Letitia were on the gravestone, but the death date for Letitia was conspicuously absent. When Juneau had asked where Letitia was buried, all Aunt Hattie said was, "Is she dead?"

"Mother always told me she is," Juneau had said.

Aunt Hattie had shrugged and said, "So she must be." Then she'd gone into what Greg called "button-down lip."

Juneau didn't want to explain all that to Willadene, so she just said, "I've told you about Pasadena. Now you tell me about Wellsville."

Later that night, after the tasty soup-and-salad-and-fresh-bread supper Gabby prepared, Juneau lay awake in her room. Great-Aunt Hattie and all the questions that had been stirred up by the visit chased through her mind. Why was Great-Grandmother Letitia's grave empty, and why wouldn't her parents talk about her? Did they know why she'd left that little Idaho town? Was there a connection between her reason for leaving and her parents' reason?

Juneau didn't know what had motivated her parents to become the Peripatetic Paulsens, always on the go, seeking new plots for their popular From *Pillar to Post* mystery series. She and her younger brother, Flint, had been part of their nomadic life, rootless and wandering. Their succession of Airstream trailers and Winnebago motor homes had traveled to every setting they'd ever used, which was what made the novels seem so authentic. But for Juneau it meant never having long-time friends, never finishing a complete school term in one place, never knowing other family members.

She'd been so happy to get married and settle down with two babies. For a while, it had been enough, but recently she had felt a strange restlessness. *Why?* she wondered. Was it in her genes? What scared her most was that she'd recently given in to an inner urge and signed up for a writing class. It had become a vitally important part of her life, something she looked forward to with pleasure each week. Was this interest in writing, not to mention her restlessness, an indication that she was doomed to follow in her parents' wandering footsteps?

Sighing, she slid out of bed. She'd warned the others that she'd be getting up at least twice during the night.

"Just don't flush," Gabby had said. "The thrones in this house rattle and groan like Sherman tanks."

She tiptoed down the hall and took care of her needs quickly. The queasiness she'd experienced two days ago was back, although it had pretty much disappeared during the trip. Maybe it was just all those cowboy cookies she'd eaten.

Or not.

Despite her insomnia, the next morning Juneau felt like a college girl, with limitless possibilities in this day ahead of her. Maybe that was what was wrong at home. The *dailiness* of it all. The feeling that the excitement of life was over.

But today she was headed for the BYU campus, and anything was possible.

Chapter Three

WILLADENE

Willadene stood on the steps of the Wilkinson Center trying to look more confident than she felt. She put down her heavy shoulder bag and redistributed the weight in her tote, shaking her head all the while. Here she was, once again overprepared and overburdened. No one else carried an umbrella attached to her purse—just in case. The summer-weight sweater she wore loosely over her shoulders was a mistake, too.

She smiled at her foolishness. Shrugging off the sweater, she stuffed it into the shoulder bag and then pushed both bag and umbrella into her tote. This was *not* going to be one of those times that left her feeling stupid. So what if her classes didn't have titles like "God, Man and the Universe"? Ways to use powdered milk had a place in the cosmic scheme of things, too.

"Willa-deeeene! Deenie Rassss-moooo-son." Deenie recognized the familiar high-pitched hail easily. It was Sister Billings, the Wellsville First Ward Relief Society president.

"There you are." Sister Billings walked toward Deenie, followed by other members of the board. One sister limped a few steps behind.

"We're so glad we found you," Sister Billings declared. "Kathy has a heel-blister emergency. We all said, 'If you need something, just ask Willadene. She probably has it in her purse.'" She surveyed Willadene. "So where *is* that legendary purse?"

Laughing, Willadene held up the bulging tote bag. Digging into the purse inside it, she retrieved the wanted Band-Aids along with a little disposable foil package of first-aid cream.

Everyone clapped as she took care of the blistered foot.

Way to go, girl, Deenie thought. She liked the feeling she got when she could come to the rescue, even when it was for something as simple as Band-Aiding a blister. It was nice to know people counted on her.

After thanking her soundly, Kathy said, "When today's workshops are over, what do you plan to do the rest of the week? I want to know where to look in case I need you again."

Amidst friendly chuckles, Willadene dug in her tote. "Just a sec. My schedule is here somewhere." But it wasn't. One more item to add to the growing catalog of things she'd missed, forgotten, or had been late to since Bitsy's birth.

To cover up her frustration, she laughed again. "The only thing I'm sure of at the moment is that I have a class on making powdered milk yogurt this afternoon."

The session was more interesting than Willadene had anticipated. By the time the class was over, she had pages of notes on the possibilities the new skill offered. She had added ideas of her own on making the product better and had also outlined four solid possibilities for Homemaking cooking segments.

She was satisfied but tired and sticky, so she headed toward the Wilkinson Center to get something cold to drink before meeting Juneau and Erin. As she walked, she studied the faces of the women she passed. She liked thinking they all were part of each other and part of something bigger. The feeling of being alone and a little lost was gone. It had been a good first day, and she looked forward to tomorrow.

She wondered if Erin had fared as well. She hoped no one had been unkind. Erin's out-of-fashion dress, combined with her short-short hair, could draw a comment that might hurt the feelings of a new convert. Willadene knew the damage that could do. She was a visiting teacher to an inactive sister whose brand-new testimony had been insulted right out of her. She didn't want that to happen to Erin.

Maybe I can find a way to help her, Deenie thought. Refurbishing second-hand clothing was second nature to her. She pictured Erin's old-fashioned pants from last night. They could be updated easily by reducing the break, if she could figure out how to offer help without implying criticism.

She was concerned for Juneau's welfare as well but for a different reason. She knew Juneau was pregnant. Because the topic hadn't come up, she wondered if Juneau herself knew.

Willadene's ability to sense pregnancy, sometimes even before the expectant mother knew, was a gift she'd inherited from Nana Lewis. It was a gift she would rather have done without. Along with the foreknowledge she often hid to avoid awkward situations came the uncanny ability to sense when the mother or baby was at risk. She'd recognized that frisson of warning at breakfast when Juneau sat down beside her but felt helpless, not knowing how to broach the topic or even if she should. Maybe she was wrong. She'd been wrong before.

At least she could pray for Juneau, which she did.

The following days, Deenie was free to take the classes that caught her fancy. On Wednesday morning she went to a class on the proper way to submit family group sheets. In the afternoon she attended the well-recommended class on journal keeping. She was hoping it would inspire her. She loved reading and retelling the stories from the journals of her pioneer ancestors, but she saw little value in keeping a journal herself. When she did, it read more like a grocery or to-do list.

Two hours later Deenie left the classroom discouraged. The teacher had exhorted them to write testimonies that burned across the pages, faith-promoting stories that would inspire future generations. As if anybody would ever look at anything she wrote as scripture.

She also balked at the idea of "recording the path of her own truth." That sounded too much like psychobabble gobbledygook. Deenie was uncomfortable enough even thinking about her deepest feelings. She surely wasn't going to commit them to paper where someone might read them. If anybody wanted to stir around in feelings, they could read a novel.

As soon as that thought occurred, Deenie followed it. She was going to take a break, buy a treat, and find a book with a happy ending. Gabby had mentioned the corner drugstore in town as an easy walk and a good place to find both a Heath candy bar and a good book.

ERIN

Erin walked into her School of the Prophets class on Wednesday eager but a little wary. Of all the classes she'd signed up for, this was her favorite. She felt challenged and inspired. The teacher, a BYU professor, was intense, even fiery. The certainty with which he spoke was like a physical force.

"Finally, I'm getting the meat of the gospel," she had told the other women at Gabby's on Tuesday night. What she didn't tell them was that she was deeply unsettled by the references to sacrifice that came up over and over again. The examples the professor gave were soul-stirring in selflessness and willingness to obey despite the consequences, leaving Erin to wonder if she herself would actually be willing to turn her back on hearth and home for God.

Her fear was that she wouldn't. But then she realized that to some extent she had left her mother and grandmother behind when she joined the Church. She loved The Women, which was what she called the two of them, but her baptism had put a gulf between them that hadn't been there before, even when they were going at each other tooth and nail. Was that separation a big enough sacrifice?

It felt big enough, judging by the sore spot in her heart, but she was afraid of what might yet be required of her by her new faith. What was required, the professor had said the day before, was the sacrifice of all things. The words had both thrilled and frightened her. She'd been grateful to get back to Gabby's that evening, after a pizza dinner with Juneau and Willadene. The discussion of the day's classes, and Gabby's cowboy cookies and milk, had calmed her down. Gabby was full of wry wisdom, and Juneau was insightful. Erin especially appreciated Willadene's steady demeanor. She wouldn't fling herself off a cliff, a sacrifice for some unseen glory. She would trust God, make supper, and put the kids to bed.

The class topic on this day, Wednesday, was following the promptings of the Spirit. As before, the professor gave examples of Saints going against all logic and even common sense in order to fulfill the need of a higher order, sometimes with devastating personal consequences. Erin listened, enthralled but increasingly uncomfortable. Then, from two rows behind her, a young woman asked a question, putting voice to Erin's own pondering.

"How can you know if what you think is the prompting of the Spirit really is?" the young woman asked. "I mean, what about that guy who's gone up the canyon to live a higher order?"

"He *says*," interrupted the professor.

"And taken all those people with him," the young woman continued. "He insists he's following what the Spirit has told him to do. That's what you've been saying today, isn't it, that we should be willing to follow the Spirit no matter what?"

The professor took off his glasses, peered through them, and then polished them on his necktie as he continued speaking. "Yes, if the promptings you're getting really are from the Spirit."

"But how can you know for sure they are?" The young woman was clearly distressed. "I mean, if you really want to serve the Lord and you're praying and asking for direction, and you get an answer to your prayer, and you know in your heart it's from the Spirit, and then someone like your bishop says it isn't, what then?"

"Then you follow what the bishop says. It is his calling and responsibility to guide the members of his ward."

Erin looked over her shoulder at the woman, who was flushed with frustration, blinking back tears. "Now you're saying that no matter how clear your promptings are, if your bishop says they aren't true promptings, they aren't?"

"Generally speaking, that's correct."

"But, but," the woman sputtered, "say your desire is to do good and serve the Lord. Won't God protect you from being deceived if your intentions are good?"

The entire class was captivated by the discussion, all swinging their heads from the woman to the professor as if at a tennis match.

"Not necessarily." The professor gazed out of the window a moment before continuing. "The natural man can create all sorts of manifestations that serve his own purpose."

"You mean I could be deceiving myself and not know it?"

Heads swung to the professor.

"It happens."

"Even when I want more than anything to serve the Lord?" The woman's voice was choked with tears. Erin wished she knew the story behind her question.

The back-and-forth went on and on, taking up the remainder of the class. When Erin left, the young woman was in private conversation with the professor, wringing her hands as she listened to what he was saying. Part of Erin wanted to hear what he had to say, but the other part wanted desperately to get out into the fresh air. She was feeling the distress of the young woman too strongly. She knew that uncertainty and fear.

What if, in spite of her desire to do good, she was misled by other desires, deep and unrecognized? What might her natural self concoct in its own service? How could she know for sure that promptings were of the Spirit? She was afraid that if put to the test, she might not recognize the promptings or might misinterpret them.

Erin's thoughts were still in turmoil when she saw Juneau sitting on the grass under a tree near the Wilkinson Center. She headed in that direction and then stopped, wondering if Juneau would understand her anxiety over the need to know—*to know for sure*—that one could know. *For sure.*

Maybe. Juneau was the kind of woman who thought about things. She obviously had a good education. Erin could tell that from what she said and how she said it. She was also a bit wound up, like some of the clients Erin saw weekly, the ones who had something they needed to talk about but didn't.

Juneau saw her. "Hi, Erin!" she called with a smile and a beckoning gesture.

Erin dropped down beside her, dumping her purse and notebook on the grass. "Taking a break?"

"Uh-huh. Brain overload. I'm considering sluffing the rest of the afternoon to let it sink in."

Erin grinned. She'd felt guilty at the thought of skipping her afternoon classes, but if Juneau, a lifer Latter-day Saint, was playing hooky, then she could, too.

Stretching out on the cool grass, she put an arm over her tired eyes. "Do you think your life is going to be different because you came?"

Juneau was silent for so long that Erin thought she hadn't heard. But then she said, "I don't know. When I decided to come, I guess I hoped I'd hear something that would zap me like a fairy godmother, changing me from Cinderella into a princess." She chuckled. "Never happened! I guess what I've learned here mainly is that there is hope that if I roll up my sleeves and have faith, I can work through my problems."

Erin raised herself up on one elbow. "I thought lifelong membership in the Church might smooth out all the bumps along the highway."

Juneau laughed. "Dream on! No. All it does is keep you close to the Power that can help you work things through." She was quiet again for a time, and then she said, "Maybe I will do some things differently when I get home. Life is full of possibilities."

"I guess that's what scares me a little," Erin said. "I'd like to have fewer possibilities and more structure. I'd like to see where my life is going."

JUNEAU

Juneau hoisted herself to her feet. "Well, it won't happen this afternoon. I was thinking about driving downtown. I know a drugstore where we can get the very best rootbeer floats. Want to come with me?"

The drugstore was at the corner of University Avenue and Center Street. It was cool and dim inside. Juneau sighed with relief as she and Erin sat down at the soda counter and ordered their root beer floats, which came in frosty mugs with scoops of vanilla ice cream filling the top third.

"This is heaven," Erin said, digging in with a long-handled spoon.

Juneau sighed in agreement. She was glad for Erin's company. She was easy to be with, and the difference in their ages and marital status didn't seem to bother her. Juneau glanced sideways at her white dress with red polka dots and a red vinyl belt. She was intrigued by the younger woman's nonchalance about her short-short flaming red hair and outdated dresses.

She'd never felt that she, herself, could pull off anything like that. Maybe it was because she was already so different in less obvious ways from the other girls she'd encountered in school and in Young Women's classes in all the wards her family had briefly attended. She wondered if she might have attracted more friends if she'd had Erin's confidence in being different.

They took their time drinking the floats and then sat at the counter, reluctant to leave the coolness of the drugstore.

"Do they have paperback books here?" asked Erin as she slurped up the last dregs of ice cream.

Juneau pointed. "In the back."

Erin pushed her empty mug away. "I've finished the book I brought with me. I need something to read the next couple of nights and on the plane home."

"I love to read, too. I always have a novel with me." Juneau looked speculatively at Erin. "What kind of books do you like, besides *Hitchhiker's Guide?*"

"All kinds. I just finished *Watership Down*. And I want to read the new Agatha Christie." Erin paused as if considering whether she should continue speaking. "Mostly, I read romance novels."

Juneau couldn't suppress a burst of laughter. "Really? *Romance* novels?"

"I guess you think that's pretty trashy."

"Sweetie," Juneau said, "I couldn't be more delighted. Romance novels are one of my Guilty Secrets. I tucked a new one far down into my suitcase where it wouldn't be easily seen if I'd had to share a room at Gabby's. I never leave them in view when my visiting teachers come. And I never read them in front of my girls. Which makes me feel *enormously* guilty. Not that there is anything particularly wrong with them, but I always feel I should be reading the Book of Mormon or the *Ensign* to set a good example."

Erin grinned. "I like historicals. I always tell myself I'm reading them for the details on the time period. Truth is, I enjoy them, whether I learn anything or not."

Juneau nodded. "I throw a bone to my guilt by saying that I learn a lot about plotting from them." Then realizing she'd said more than she meant to, she added, "In case I ever write a book, you know."

Erin slanted a quizzical look at her. "Do you write?"

"Just a little," Juneau said quickly. "My parents are writers, but it's not really something I want to get into, although I *am* taking a writing class. I heard about this marvelous writing teacher and couldn't resist signing up."

It sounded like an apology, even to her own ears. Not wanting to say any more, she nodded toward the book counter. "What are we waiting for?"

As if choreographed, they turned around on their stools, got off, and headed toward the book section at the back of the store.

"Don't bother with these." Juneau pointed at a row of books by the same author. "Her heroines are all brainless twits. Now, these . . ." She stopped abruptly, looking to the left. "I don't believe it."

Erin turned to look in the same direction. "Willadene!" she exclaimed.

At the end of the row Willadene stood frozen, holding a book in her hands, her mouth an O of surprise.

Juneau waved. "Well, fancy meeting you here! We're looking for a little light reading. How about you?"

It took a moment for Willadene to find her voice. Her face flushing, she said, "I'm just looking for a book with a happy ending. That's what I need at the moment."

"Don't we all!" Juneau said. "Well, you've come to the right place. We should know." She gestured to include herself and Erin.

"You mean . . . ?" Willadene began.

Juneau nodded. "We're romance junkies, too."

Willadene's face crinkled in a smile. "You're kidding!" She put down the book she'd been holding. "You can forget this one. The first paragraph is booooooring. If I'm not pulled in within a few sentences, I toss it aside."

Erin picked up a novel with dramatic cover art featuring a scantily clad heroine and a dark, intense hero. "How about this one?"

Willadene put out her hands as if to ward off evil. "I don't read books like that. Too long, for one thing. And too steamy."

Erin opened the book and flipped though the pages. She stopped to read a passage, immediately slamming the book shut and fanning her face with it. "I see what you mean."

"You can always tell a poultry-counter romance by the cover—too much purple and too much skin. We never put those in the Shoebox."

Juneau was puzzled. Some of the terminology Willadene used was obscure. "What on earth is a poultry-counter romance?"

Leaning toward them, Willadene whispered, "Too many chicken parts." When they didn't respond, she insisted, "Think about it!"

A vision of the poultry counter at Safeway popped into Juneau's head. Chicken parts. Legs and thighs and . . .

She joined Erin in a howl of laughter. "Never heard them described that way, but it's perfect. No, poultry-counter romances would never make it past my Guilt-o-meter. I do have limits!" Laughing again, she said, "You amaze me, Willadene. Imagine you being a connoisseur of romance novels!"

"I get the poultry-counter reference, but what does a shoebox have to do with romance novels?" Erin asked.

Willadene's grin was wide. "I'm not the only one in my ward who reads romance novels. I thought I was, at first. When a few of us discovered that we were all fans, we started passing books around . . . in the parking lot . . . after Relief Society."

"I love it!" Juneau said, clapping her hands.

"We had them in a brown paper bag at first," Willadene continued. "But then one of the sisters covered a shoebox with pretty Contact paper, so now we put the books in that and pass it around. Nothing purple goes in it. Just sweet romances. After all, the bishop's wife takes a turn, too."

"Actually, the purple ones are kind of dumb," Erin said. "All that nipping and grazing."

"Sounds like a goat," commented Willadene.

"How about this?" Juneau had picked up a book and spotted a good passage. "'His dark eyes hung on her full, red lips.' Isn't that a silly picture?"

They laughed, covering their mouths with their hands so as not to attract attention.

Willadene looked over Juneau's shoulder. "I found a good line." Clearing her throat, she read dramatically. "'The impact of the stranger's intense gaze almost stunned her. He coalesced within her vision.'"

Juneau made a gagging sound. "Coalesced! Sounds like grease left in a frying pan after breakfast."

They read passages and laughed until they were giddy.

Finally, Juneau said, "We'd better get back to Gabby's before we're arrested for disorderly conduct."

They each bought one of the "sweet" romances Willadene pointed out. The kind, as she said, that were comforting because you knew everything would work out fine in the end. That statement made Juneau wonder what was going on in Deenie's life that she would need a novel for comfort.

As they left the store and headed for Juneau's car, they linked arms. Juneau couldn't believe the other two shared her Guilty Secret. Just a couple of days ago she'd thought she didn't have anything in common with Erin and Willadene, but something important had happened there in the store. The three of them were no longer just acquaintances. They were friends.

Chapter Four

JUNEAU

Juneau felt guilty driving off alone after dinner that evening. Even though it had been a good day, she could tolerate only so much togetherness. Besides, she had things to think about.

Backing the car out of the driveway, she turned toward Springville. She wouldn't get lost there. It was Greg's hometown, and they'd visited every now and then before his parents moved to Arizona. Her stomach lurched as she turned onto University Avenue. One more thing to think about.

She drove for some time. Off to her right she saw a truck-stop restaurant. The abundant flowers beneath the front window told her somebody cared enough to make it attractive, so it would be okay to stop there. "A clean, well-lighted place." The words came back to her from a Hemingway short story she'd read in one of her English classes in her spotty college career. Not even that had been spent at one place. She'd attended four different colleges altogether, close to wherever her parents were stopped at the time because she wanted to be nearby, part of the family. She'd finally gathered enough credits to graduate from UCLA before she and Greg were married. She'd never been enrolled at any of the Utah universities, which was what made being at BYU so exciting now.

She pulled into the parking lot of the restaurant and got out of the car, pausing after she closed the door. Did she need to lock up here in the heart of Zion? She always did in Pasadena, even in her own driveway.

Out of some kind of defiance, she left the car unlocked. It was supposed to be safe here.

Inside, she chose a table by the window and looked around. In a corner booth, a young couple were kissing. She stifled a sudden impulse to shake a finger at them, a warning that they couldn't begin to know what kind of dilemmas that might lead them to.

There were only three other diners in the room, two older women chatting together, and a lone man eating a hamburger at the table facing hers. She avoided eye contact but felt him looking at her.

When the waitress came over with a menu, Juneau waved it aside. "Just Pepsi, please," she said. "Lots of ice."

"Small, medium, or large?" the waitress asked. She was young, with a look about her that said college girl earning money to keep herself in school.

"Large," Juneau said. "It's so hot."

She immediately regretted her choice, thinking that with a large, she might not be able to get back to Gabby's without a pit stop along the way. But she felt self-conscious about changing her order with the man watching. Why she should care escaped her, but she let it go. She could always drink only half.

The waitress turned to go, but the man held up his hand. As if asking permission, Juneau thought.

"DeeDee," he said, "as long as you're turning on the Pepsi faucet, bring me one, too. Large."

He smiled at Juneau. She nodded slightly and looked out of the window at her car. Her *unlocked* car. She imagined a scene in which the man followed her outside as she hurried to the car. She saw him opening the passenger door before she could get it locked against him. *The dark stranger, smiling wryly, said, "I've been waiting forever to meet you, Regina. You can't run away before we talk." His eyes hung on her full, red lips.*

She smiled at her own foolishness. He was probably a tired grocery clerk or even a BYU professor, stopping by the restaurant to cool off before he went home to his wife and three kids. Eight kids. This was Utah.

She almost giggled.

The man seemed to take her private smile as an invitation. Getting up from his table, he came over to hers. "Want company?" he asked.

Juneau was ashamed that one part of her wanted to say, "Yes, I do. Sit down."

Instead, she said, "No, thank you."

"Okay," he said mildly. "Far from home?"

"Not really."

"No?" He glanced through the window at her car.

She looked out to see her California plates in plain sight under the bright neon lights. She didn't say anything.

"I'm sorry," he said. "Guess I just wanted to talk to somebody on a lonely summer night."

"I'm sorry, too," she said. And she genuinely was. He was nice-looking, probably about her own age. Dark hair. Blue eyes with dark lashes.

His beautifully shaped lips twisted into a wry smile. Reaching out his hand, he said, "You're the only one, Regina. Come with me."

She rose, impelled by something impossible to resist. She would go with him, leaving behind husband, children, responsibilities. Even Philip Atwater.

Regina might, but she, Juneau, wouldn't, not really. But wasn't that in a way what she had done, leaving Greg and the girls—and the dog? As if she could escape her responsibilities, especially now that she had to admit she was pregnant?

She turned away. When DeeDee brought her Pepsi, she drank it quickly and then went to the rest room, hoping the man would leave before she came out.

He had, she realized with relief when she returned. But once outside, she saw him standing by her car. She stopped, her heart thumping.

"Flat tire," he said, pointing. "Want me to change it for you?"

She hesitated. He might have flattened it himself.

He spread out his hands. "It's okay. I'm harmless." He smiled. "My name's Jay," he added, as if that made a difference.

"I'll call the auto club," Juneau said without moving.

"If you wish," he said. "But I could have it changed before they have time to get here."

She pictured him bashing her with the tire iron. But the same perverseness that had made her leave the car unlocked kicked in. "I'll open the trunk."

It was when he took out the spare tire that Juneau saw the envelope. Actually, Jay saw it first. Picking it up, he said, "Is your name . . ." he hesitated. "Juneau?"

"I was born there." Juneau's response was automatic. She plucked the envelope from his fingers and turned it over. "It's my husband's handwriting. I wonder how it got in *there*." She twitched her head toward the spare tire well.

Jay busied himself with taking out the tire and jack and squatting beside the flat.

Juneau slid a fingernail under the flap of the envelope and opened it, scanning the enclosed note quickly. "Dear Juney," it said. "Just in case you ever get a flat with nobody to help you, here are the instructions."

She burst into tears and then choked them back, embarrassed.

Jay stood up, concern on his face. "Is something wrong?"

She held up the note. "From my husband," she said. "How to deal with flat tires."

He smiled. "Nice guy."

She smiled back. "There are a lot of nice guys in the world, Jay. Thanks."

She wept all the way back to Gabby's.

When she entered the lamp-cozy living room, Willadene rose to her feet. "Are you okay, Juneau?" she asked.

Juneau opened her mouth to tell about her adventure, but all that came out was, "I'm pregnant."

"Yes," said Willadene, "I know." She opened her arms, and Juneau ran into them, as if they were the comforting arms she'd always wished her mother would offer.

When the fresh tears had passed, Juneau blew her nose and said, "I'm sorry. Forget that happened."

But Gabby fixed Juneau with a gimlet eye. Or that's how Juneau thought of it. She'd read that somewhere, and it seemed a perfect description. "Unplanned, I take it." Gabby said.

Juneau nodded. "What am I going to do?" she wailed.

"Have it."

"But I don't want it," Juneau blurted out. Then she hurried to amend what she'd said. "I mean not right now."

"You *have* to want it!" Erin said.

Juneau ignored the shocked expression on Erin's face. "What do *you* know about it? You've never been pregnant, have you? You don't know the implications. The commitment that comes with it."

Erin's voice trembled with intensity. "I joined the Church because of Forever Families. Mormons *want* their children. Children are a gift from God. *Aren't they?* Isn't that what Forever Families are all about?"

Juneau saw the fear and need in the young woman's face, and she wondered what pain her words had awakened. She looked to Gabby, hoping the older woman would say something wise, but Gabby was silent.

"I'm sorry," Juneau said. "I misspoke." The word made her sound like a politician trying to wriggle out of something. "What I mean is, I'd *like* to have another child. I *want* at least one more. But not *right now.* I'm not ready for another baby."

"So, Juneau," Erin said bitterly, "since a baby is such an inconvenience at this time, are you going to get rid of it?"

"No!" Juneau put up her hands as if to push away something ugly. "Oh, Erin, no. How can you suggest such a thing?"

"Isn't that what you do when you get a little surprise? Have it 'taken care of?' Or do you go ahead and have it and then tell it that it wasn't wanted?"

Juneau knew she had to weigh her words carefully, because whatever she said, Erin would take it personally. "In answer to your question, no, there will be no abortion. I would never do that! And I wouldn't think of ever telling him that I didn't want him. Nobody will ever know that, except the four of us in this room. He'll be loved and cherished every day of his life. And I'll thank God for sending me such a gift." Juneau gave the younger woman a hug. "I'm sorry I said what I did."

Erin snuffled against her shoulder. Then she said, "Him? You're sure it's a boy?"

"No. But Greg wants a boy really bad, so I'm hoping that's what it is. It really doesn't matter, though."

Juneau could almost hear gears changing in Erin's head as she nodded slowly. "Sorry about what I said earlier. I think I was getting some of my own baggage mixed in with yours. It's been a confusing week. Trying to sort things out. Trying to fit the gospel to real life." She looked around at the others, reaching out her hands. "Are we still friends?"

"Friends," they all echoed.

When they came together for a group hug, Juneau held Erin extra tight.

WILLADENE

On Friday they left campus early, having decided to cook dinner for Gabby.

Willadene had noticed in the newspaper that game hens were on sale at Reams. She knew immediately that she wanted to do something special, and she'd had no trouble getting the others to agree to her plan.

"Stuffed game hens are one fancy dish I can do that's not a family pioneer favorite," she said. *This time when I make it, I won't be getting all those comments about highfalutin' cooking and why aren't chicken and dumplings good enough,* she thought.

They did their shopping and trooped up the steps to Gabby's porch, their arms full of grocery bags. They surprised Gabby, sitting in a lounge chair and reading a novel with a cover that shouted "romance!"

Juneau pointed with an elbow, "She's one of us," she stage-whispered.

"One of what?" asked Gabby.

Juneau gave the others a conspiratorial raise of the eyebrows. "The Society of Secret Romance Readers," she announced.

Gabby grinned sheepishly. "Guilty, but they're so much fun." She set the book aside. "What's going on here?"

"We've come to cook dinner for you!" Willadene shifted the bags of groceries she held into a more secure position. She was pleased to see the happy expression on Gabby's face. Her idea was a good one.

"Wonderful! Here, let me help you." Gabby rose from her chair and took one of the bags Willadene was holding.

"You've had your hair done," said Erin. "It looks great."

Gabby touched her hair, styled in a smooth cap that framed her face. "Looks as good as can be expected with all these streaks."

"Hey, I have clients who pay to get that effect."

"My father's family gets credit for the few remaining strands of red I have. The gray hair came courtesy of my children. And the white, exclusively through my grandsons."

She led the way into the kitchen and watched with interest as they unloaded the bags, placing the unusual mix of ingredients on the table. Picking up a can of coconut milk, she said, "What, no green Jell-O?"

"Not a chance." Willadene patted one of the game hens. "Wait till you see what some wild rice and raisins will do for these little dears."

Erin waved a bunch of green onions in the air. "Willadene is going to show me how to make a seven-layer salad."

"Awkward as I am, I can make flan." Juneau took a deep bow in the crowded kitchen, knocking the rice and raisins to the floor in the process.

"I have something to add that won't take any effort at all." Gabby retrieved two cold bottles of fancy carbonated grape juice from the refrigerator. Holding them up, she added, "I think this calls for dinner in the dining room."

Willadene watched over the cooking in Gabby's kitchen with a twinge of anxiety. How could a perfect meal come out of Juneau's awkwardness, Erin's inexperience, and her own insecurity? She felt as if Grandma Stowell were looking over her shoulder. But then, seeing how much fun Juneau and Erin were having, she gave Grandma the boot.

Two hours and several false starts later, dinner was ready to be served. Taking a deep whiff of the savory aromas, Willadene looked over their offerings. The stuffed game hens were roasted to a golden brown, dripping in their butter and orange-zest glaze. A glass bowl displayed the alluring colors of the seven-layer salad. Juneau's individual flans boasted perfectly toasted coconut and warm caramel topping. But best of all was the fine feeling of friendship and mutual accomplishment that warmed her heart.

As they paraded their offerings into the dining room, Juneau said, "A meal like this deserves a special description." She cleared her throat dramatically. "*Regina waited breathlessly in the flickering candlelight. All her senses were engaged, her eyes searching, her nose quivering, her mouth . . .*"

"*Drooling!*" Willadene finished, surprised and delighted at her own wit.

"If you keep up that up, I'm going to drop this salad," Erin said, laughing.

Gabby poured the bubbly grape juice as they arranged the food on the table. "Thank you, ladies. This is the nicest treat." She took a moment to admire everything and then asked Erin to bless the food.

Erin folded her arms and bowed her head. "Dear Lord, thank . . ."

Willadene started as a mechanical buzz stopped Erin in mid-phrase. Bzzzzzz! Bzzzzt! Bzzzzt! The insistent sound shattered the atmosphere.

Bzzzzzz! Bzzzzt! Bzzzzt! "Gran, are you in there?" Bzzzt! Bzzzt! Bzzzt! "Open up. It's me, Bryan. I need to talk to you!"

"My grandson," Gabby said in a flat voice.

"The one that caused the white hair?" Erin asked.

"One of them." With resignation Gabby rose to her feet, folded her napkin, and laid it on the table.

"Would you like us to leave?" asked Willadene. She could feel her cheeks redden in sympathetic embarrassment for Gabby.

"Please stay and be comfortable," Gabby responded. "These visits never last more than a few minutes. They are usually short—and loud."

She had barely turned the knob on the front door when a young man pushed past her without pause.

"What took ya so long? I've been waiting out there forever!"

"Hello, Bryan. You seem to be in a hurry this evening."

Willadene held her breath as a young man barged into the dining room, stopping with surprise at the sight of the women. "Got boarders?" He sneered as he walked around the table. "Isn't this a little fancy for the paying customers?" He tore a leg from the lovely little hen sitting on Gabby's plate, took a bite, grimaced, and dropped it. "I'll take Colonel Sanders any day."

Into the stunned silence that followed, Gabby said, "You're interrupting my guests, Bryan. Is there something you need?"

"The Caddie!" He spoke loudly and urgently. "The guys from the ward are going to a campout by Utah Lake. Dad took Mom's keys by mistake, and Kenny has the other car. I'm late already. Just give me the keys!"

Willadene ducked her head, wishing she didn't have to witness the shameful scene. In mere seconds the whole wonderful atmosphere had been ruined.

Gabby took the lanky teenager by the arm and moved him forcefully into the kitchen. The closed door muffled their voices, but the words were still clear. "Is it a ward activity?"

"What's the diff? All the guys that are going are from the ward."

"I take it the answer is no, and this outing is without adult supervision."

"Like that matters. We're just going to the lake!"

Willadene thanked heaven that Carl was still a sweet young man who addressed her with respect. "We shouldn't be listening to this," she whispered.

Juneau put a finger to her lips. "Shhh. We don't want to distract Gabby while she's dealing with that brat."

"So, can I have the car?" Bryan's voice grated on Willadene's nerves. She hated the sound of conflict.

"No."

"Why?" he yelled. "You never use that car. You're saying no to be mean. Just like Dad said you would."

Willadene jumped to her feet at the sound of a chair being knocked over. Erin pushed her own chair back from the table, hissing, "Someone ought to smack him." They stood together, waiting, not knowing what to do, ears straining as Gabby spoke.

"Bryan, here is the contract we agreed on when you first asked me for the use of Grandpa's old Caddie." Willadene heard the sound of rustling paper. "Is there anything you can check off?"

"No, but so what? You know Grampa Golden meant for me to have that car."

"But I'm in charge of the Caddie now, Bryan. You'll get it when you earn it."

"You crazy old broad! Thanks for nothing."

Deenie heard the loud slam of the back door, followed by the repeated bounce of the screen door. She and the others quietly waited in the held breath of the house. Gabby entered the dining room and stood quietly for a moment. Then she said, "Ladies, I'm so sorry you had to hear that, but please don't let it destroy our lovely evening." Smiling wryly, she added, "It's a good thing we can choose our friends, because we're stuck with our relatives. Those boys are the rocks in my stream! I guess every life has its share of boulders."

They all sat back down. Willadene was no longer hungry, but she took a tiny bite of her game hen. It was still warm.

Later, as they relaxed in the living room, Gabby apologized again for her grandson's behavior. "Thank heaven I have Sophie. She's his sister, but nothing like him. She spends Saturdays with me. I hope she comes early enough for you to meet her." Gabby smiled wistfully. "She'd never call me a crazy old broad."

Juneau shook her head slowly. "I was amazed that you seemed so calm when he said that. I would have blown my stack."

Gabby sighed. "I was tempted to do just that. But when you've lived as long as I have, you've learned that the two essentials in an argument are a cool head and soft words."

Willadene shuddered. "I still can't believe he said that. It was horrible."

To her surprise, Gabby grinned. "To tell the truth, I don't object to the 'old broad' part. There's something of longevity and strength in those words. It's the choice of adjective I don't like. In fact, with a different modifier, 'old broad' could be considered a well-earned title."

"And what would you consider a more appropriate adjective for 'old broad'?" Willadene asked.

"There is always the oft-used and respected 'crusty,'" suggested Juneau.

Erin nodded. "'Crusty' is good."

"Like a fine sourdough bread," Willadene added. "Warm and nourishing with some real texture."

"Trust Deenie to come up with a food simile," Juneau teased.

Gabby nodded thoughtfully. "'Crusty old broad.' I like it."

"Hey, Juneau," said Willadene, "you could use a crusty old broad in that book you're not going to write."

"Then it can't be a romance," said Erin.

"What makes you think that?" Gabby's smile was arch. "Just 'cause there's snow on the roof, doesn't mean there isn't fire in the furnace. I have a romance novel upstairs that has a heroine older than I am."

"Really?" said Juneau. "That sounds like something we should read aloud."

And they did. They each chose a page to read amidst silly comments and giggles. Willadene was amazed once again that an episode of near-disaster had turned into a moment of lightness and shared laughter. Still, she felt a lingering concern about Juneau and the pregnancy, and she wondered yet again what she should say to Juneau. Or if she should say anything at all. What if she were wrong?

ERIN

Gabby's granddaughter Sophie did come in time to meet them all the next morning. Erin and the others were sitting at the breakfast table when she knocked on the back door.

"You don't need to knock, honey." Gabby waved her granddaughter inside and gave her a huge hug. It was the kind of hug Erin had always longed to get from her own grandmother, the welcome without reservation or expectation, the hug that said, "I'm glad you're here."

With her arm around Sophie, Gabby said, "Come meet my Education Week ladies, dear. I had a special crop this year." She went around the table introducing them.

"This is Juneau. She was brave enough to drive here from California all by herself."

"Do you live anywhere near Disneyland?" Sophie asked.

"Close, but not close enough for my two girls. They're nine and seven. How old are you?"

"Almost eleven. I'm in fifth grade."

Gabby gestured to her right. "This is Erin from Minnesota. She's a new convert with a special sense of style. Erin, stand up and show her your nifty outfit."

"Hi, Sophie." Erin stood and pirouetted in her pleated gray twill slacks and pink silk crossover blouse that tied over her right hip.

"I really like those pants," said Sophie. "I've never seen any like them in the stores. Where can I get a pair?"

"I don't know where you'd find them here. I bought these at a second-hand store back home."

Sophie frowned. "I don't think my mother would let me go into a secondhand store. I wish she would."

Gabby next turned to Willadene. "This is Willadene. She's a *chef magnifique.*" Gabby kissed her bunched fingers and made a sweeping gesture with her hand. Then she lowered her voice. "She reads romance novels!"

Sophie giggled. "Just like you, Grandma." She sat down at the table, and Gabby gave her some French toast and juice.

Erin watched Sophie tuck into her breakfast, envious of her ease in a room full of strangers. She could see that Gabby's love gave Sophie the confidence that comes from having a sense of safety and belonging.

"So, Grandma," Sophie said, looking up slyly. "I saw that neighbor of yours in front of his house when Mom dropped me off. He said to tell you he'll be over soon."

Juneau grinned. "A gentleman friend?"

"A friend—and a gentleman," Gabby said with a brief smile.

Willadene wiggled her eyebrows. "There seems to be more romance around here than just in the novels!"

There was another knock at the door, and a tall, distinguished man with a mane of white hair entered. "Good morning, ladies. Good morning, Gabrielle," he said in a courtly manner.

"Brother Pratt, can we offer you breakfast?"

Gabby was obviously flustered, and Erin was charmed at the blush that rose in her cheeks.

"Thank you, I've already eaten. But I'll take some introductions instead."

Once more Gabby went around the table. Brother Pratt acknowledged the introductions with a smile. "Call me Jonas," he said. "Have you ladies enjoyed your time here?"

After a flurry of yeses from the whole group, Erin said, "More than you know. I for one hate to leave." She couldn't imagine going back to her life in Minnesota with her roommate Rochelle. She would miss the wonderful discussions, the laughter, and the unbelievable moments of togetherness. These women whom she had known barely a week were as dear to her as her mother and even Colleen.

"I guess it's time." Willadene rose, and the others followed suit. Jonas helped them carry their luggage to the porch.

"I have to call a cab," Erin said. She dreaded the shuffle of cab and bus to get to the airport.

"Oh, we'll take you," said Willadene. "My friends and I."

"Really?"

"There's room in the van, and it's only a short detour to the airport."

"Thank you," Erin said gratefully, touched by Deenie's easy offer of service.

Erin, Juneau, and Willadene began their final good-byes while Gabby, with the help of Sophie and Jonas, went inside to fix the bag lunches she insisted they take with them.

"This has been wonderful. I don't think it was a coincidence we ended up here at Gabby's. It was meant to be." Erin bit her lip as tears threatened. "Honestly, I never thought I'd get so emotional. I can't even explain why."

"Whereas I can chalk it up to being pregnant," said Juneau.

"Gabby's the one who brought us together," Willadene said. "She's amazing, crusty old broad or not."

Erin nodded. "If that's what she is, that's what I want to be, too."

"Same here." Juneau glanced at Willadene. "What about you? You up for being a crusty old broad when you grow up?"

"Crumbs and all," Willadene said quite seriously.

Juneau drew an elaborate heart symbol in the air. "I christen us the COBs, Crusty Old Broads—in training, of course. We'll have to earn the title."

"Then until we do, I guess we're COBettes!" Willadene said, grinning.

Gabby came onto the porch and handed each a sack lunch. "Watch out for the reentry syndrome," she said.

"Reentry? Like coming in from outer space?" Erin asked.

"More like rarefied space. You have all changed, but your families will be the same. Don't be surprised if you get the emotional bends."

Juneau told her about their all wanting to be COBs.

Gabby put her arm around Juneau. "Watching the growth you lovely women have made in just these few days has been an absolute delight. I'd say you're well on your way."

"You've already arrived," Erin said to Gabby. "How will we know when we make it?"

Gabby's smile was enigmatic. "You'll know."

After that, things moved quickly. In a blink, Juneau was gone with a final wave and a hollered "Don't forget to write!" As she backed out, the van from Wellsville arrived, and Erin found herself stowed in among Willadene's friends, her luggage at her feet.

She looked back at the house, where Gabby, Jonas, and Sophie stood waving. She wasn't ready to leave. It was too soon. But the van pulled away, and Erin waved as long as she could see them.

Chapter Five

JUNEAU

Juneau had enjoyed Education Week, both the classes and the companionship. The classes had been good and had made her think, especially the one in which the teacher had said, "The gospel is not a destination; it's more like a vehicle, constantly moving you forward to where you can discover the truth."

Another class she'd especially enjoyed was one on self-discovery in which the discussion had been about the "shadow self" that lurks behind what you display at church. That had been on Thursday. It had still been on her mind when she'd driven off alone that evening. And admitted to herself that she really was pregnant. And found the note from Greg, giving instructions on how to change a tire. It had made her realize once again that he was a stable, loving force in her life, despite her present restlessness. Which had all fed into the encounter with Willadene and Erin and Gabby where she'd revealed at least one of her shadow selves—and had been accepted with love.

She didn't stop to visit with Great-Aunt Hattie again in Nephi. She'd shown Gabby and Erin and Willadene the photographs Aunt Hattie had given her, including the one of Great-Grandma and also the one of her apparently empty grave. Gabby had stared at Letitia's likeness in the picture with her sister. "Hmm," Gabby had said. "I wonder what secrets lurk behind that pretty face."

Juneau thought of that as she passed through Nephi on her way south. What indeed was hidden behind that face? What might her story reveal about her granddaughter, Juneau's restless mother? Or for that matter, Juneau herself?

Juneau wasn't much less confused when she got home than she'd been when she left. Nothing had really been solved. She'd found new friends, but very likely they would fade away, just as all the friends over the years had done. She hadn't stayed in contact with any of them.

Well now, that was an interesting realization. *She* hadn't stayed in contact with those transitory friends of the past. That was one thing she could change. She *could* stay in contact with Willadene and Erin and Gabby. They had each one filled some empty space in herself, and it was comforting and good to have them there. So she would make the effort to write, as promised. She would install them as permanent friends, along with her dear neighbor Marisol and friends Donnabeth and Sharma at church. After all, hadn't they formed a club of sorts—the COBs, or COBettes, as Willadene had said? With a goal, frivolous as it might be. But *was* it frivolous? To become like Gabby, a "Crusty Old Broad," was a good goal at this time when her life seemed to be more or less undirected.

In the meantime, it was fine to be back to her good house on the slopes of the San Gabriels. The mountains were shadowed when she arrived in the late afternoon, and she could have fallen into a complicated contemplation of the nature of shadows and shadow-selves—but she didn't. Pushing her thoughts aside, she greeted Greg and the girls and Philip Atwater with joy.

After the girls had been put to bed, Greg asked her if she'd enjoyed Education Week.

"Yes," she said. "More than I can say." She thought about telling him she'd found his note, but then she'd have to explain about having a flat tire and how the man named Jay had changed it for her. Then Greg would go into his watch-out-for-strangers mode, and she'd feel like a little kid. It hadn't been such a big deal anyway, had it? She'd had the tire fixed before she left Provo. Maybe she wouldn't tell him about it at all.

She didn't try to explain about the COBs, either. She didn't think men developed that kind of friendships. She would just add all those things to her ever-lengthening list of Guilty Secrets.

August 17, 1980
Memo to: Willadene, Erin, and Gabby
Subject: Reentry Syndrome

So how was your descent from the rarefied atmosphere of Education Week where everything is not only possible but expected? Any lingering effects? Any carryover? Any regrets?

No regrets on my part. It wasn't the easiest week I've lived, but what I harvested was worth any "rocks in the stream," as Gabby put it. What could be better than finding friends when you're in need?

And Gabby. What can I say? You were an education in yourself. You, of course, are our patron saint and senior member of the COBs. Right, ladies?

I want to thank all of you for being there when I needed to empty out my ugly stuff. I feel as close to you as to anyone I ever met. I can't say that I ever had a really close friend since we never stayed in one place long enough. I didn't stay long in Provo, either, but I feel as if I'm crazy-glued to all of you.

Well, enough mushy. My family was happy to see me, especially Philip Atwater.

Philip jumped to his feet the moment Regina walked into the house. His eyes brimming with joy, he bounded across the room and threw himself at her, bestowing wet kisses all over her face from eyebrows to chin, concentrating on her full, red lips.

Did that get you going, dear romance readers? Maybe I'd better remind you Philip Atwater is big mutty dog. He really was happy to see me.

So were Greg and the girls. They showed me how much by leaving the week's dishes for me to enjoy.

If that sounds sarcastic, maybe it is. Nevertheless, I love my family to distraction and am happy to be back with them. But I haven't yet told them my little secret. I don't know why. Maybe I'm saving it for a special moment.

> With love and fond memories,
> Juneau

WILLADENE

The first thing Deenie noticed on her return home was the absence of a family greeting. No anxious husband, babe in arms, waited on the front porch. No eager little boys rushed down the walk crying, "Mommy, we missed you!"

The second thing she noticed was the flowerbeds bordering each side of the front walkway. The petunias, stocks, and bachelor buttons she had planted haphazardly, hoping to create of profusion of mixed color, had been thinned into neat, precise rows.

A voice floated over the garden wall. "Why, you darling boys! How could your mother stand to be away from you a whole week?" The high clear voice with the assumed English accent and the regimented flowers could mean only one thing: Roberta Jean Rasmussen—better known as Bert, her nearly perfect and perfectly oblivious, well-meaning, soccer-star, college-student sister-in-law—was home from her semester in Europe.

Drat! Deenie hurried to the side yard. She would have to change gears fast. Reentry with a bang. And a ball. A bright patchwork soft ball, one made of leftover quilting pieces stitched and stuffed by the Stowell women landed softly at Deenie's feet.

"It's mine!" Carl slammed out the garden gate.

"No, mine, mine." Paulie scrambled after him. Rauf, the family dog, shambled in his wake, wagging his multicolored tail.

"No, my turn!" Deenie's sixteen-year-old sister, Sonya, loped out the gate next. When she saw Willadene, she cried, "Deenie, you came home!"

"Hey, you guys, take turns." Roger walked through the gate with a squealing Bitsy on his shoulders. "Sunny! Slow down!"

Roberta Jean came after him. Her tall spare frame was well suited to the blue jeans and faded T-shirt she wore. "Let them fight it out. A little competition is good for the soul."

Hurt by the lack of greetings, Deenie said the first thing that came to mind. "They're too young for any competition and never within the family."

Cries of "Mommy!" came from all sides as the children realized Deenie was home. Swooping both boys into her arms, she kissed and snuggled, asked and answered a dozen questions before she had time to swing them around.

"We missed you, Mommy." Carl said. "I'm so glad you're home."

"Me, too," Deenie said. She reached for Bitsy, who was now cradled in Roger's arms. "And how about you, my little rug rat?"

Bitsy took one long look at Deenie and buried her face in Roger's neck.

"She's missed her mommy way too much to be nice about it." Roger hugged Deenie with his empty arm. "So have I," he whispered in her ear. "Okay, folks," he said to the others. "Let's move this love fest inside. I'm sure your mommy wants to get cleaned up before the company gets here."

"Company?" Deenie asked as Bert herded the boys into the house.

Deenie could feel her eyebrows reaching lift-off as Roger explained. "Bert thought you'd like a chance to tell the whole family about your adventures this week and that you'd probably want to do it only once. So she invited the folks over for a late lunch. Besides, she wanted to try out some new recipes and needed guinea pigs. I thought you'd be glad not to have to cook . . ."

Deenie tilted her head, trying to keep her expression neutral as Roger's explanation trailed off.

"Look." Roger shifted Bitsy to his other hip and took Deenie's hand. "I know this wouldn't have been your first choice, but she's been helping out all week, and she did get your mother to let loose of Sunny for a whole day. You gotta admit that's something. Besides, wait till you smell her pork roast. It's out of this world." Roger came to a full stop.

Deenie knew instantly by the oh-drat expression on his face that Roger had realized the implied insult in his words. Her anger over being usurped in her own home softened at Roger's chagrin. "Okay, I give in," she said. "But if your sister has rearranged my spice cupboard again, I may have to strangle her."

Deenie joined arms with Roger as they walked into the house, but her thoughts were in turmoil. *Why can't people get it through their heads that this house is my house and these are my kids? I have to set some boundaries, but how can I do that without hurting someone's feelings? I wonder how the COBs would handle this situation.*

ERIN

Erin was pensive on the trip back from Utah. She didn't know what had happened to her in Provo, but she knew something had. Her heart felt open and rather tender. She had the odd feeling that she had been beamed up but all her molecules hadn't quite come together at the new location.

Images of Willadene, Juneau, and Gabby came to mind, making her smile. Willadene, practical and sweet, with a huge heart. Easy-going Juneau, with hints of California hippie still clinging to her like the fragrance of incense burned long ago. And Gabby, who had seemed rather like a firm but loving schoolteacher.

She sighed, wondering how she could ever explain to people at home the closeness she had felt to those three women—and to the Spirit. The easiest thing would be if no one asked about her trip. Then she wouldn't have to try to figure out what to say.

But everyone did ask. Erin found herself changing her answers depending upon what she thought the audience was open to hearing. She told her roommate Rochelle about the magnificent landscape and the hairdos of the ladies at Gabby's. She regaled people at church with stories about her classes and teachers. She confided to Colleen about the new friends she had made.

"I wish you could meet them. They're *real* Mormon women. They aren't afraid to let you see behind the Sunday smile."

She wasn't sure how much to tell The Women, who had invited her to dinner the Sunday after her return. Neither of them had ever asked her much about the Church, even during the tense months before her baptism.

She arrived at her childhood home with the borrowed suitcase in hand. Her grandmother Ruth Swenson Larson opened the door and greeted Erin with a rare smile. She was shorter than Erin, her back hunching slightly with the beginnings of osteoporosis. Her tightly curled gray hair, the result of a poorly timed home permanent, framed an oval face distinguished by a high forehead, arched eyebrows over very large, pale blue eyes, a long but well-shaped nose, and thin lips whose resting position was turned down.

Erin's mother, Joanna, came from the kitchen, wiping her hands on her apron. She was a younger, taller version of Grams, with the same striking eyes and high cheekbones. Her dishwater-blonde hair curved naturally above her shoulders, and wispy bangs softened her high forehead. She carried twenty extra pounds well, her erect posture making her look thinner than she was.

Joanna hugged Erin. "We're ready to sit down now, if you're hungry. I made your favorite, the Norwegian version of Swedish meatballs."

Erin chuckled at the family joke as she took her seat at the dining room table. It was set for three, as had almost always been the case since Erin's grandfather Alfred had died when she was four. Erin had a faint memory of him in the armchair at the end of the table. It was his chair then, the "empty chair" now.

"You look none the worse for wear," Grams said after the traditional Lutheran blessing on the food. "I guess your trip must have been all right."

Erin nodded, helping herself to the meatballs. "It was. I was a little afraid of flying, but that part turned out to be really neat."

"What about the place you stayed?" Joanna asked.

"I lucked out. I met the nicest sisters at Gabby's . . ." Realizing how Mormon she sounded, she amended, "The nicest women. They were going to Education Week, too. We didn't take the same classes, but we spent a lot of time together."

"Did you enjoy the classes?" asked Joanna.

"A lot. It's funny, but it's hard to remember the specifics. What I remember most is how I felt." Erin laid her hand over her heart, an unconscious gesture. "Expansive. I could see things differently. See what's possible."

"What's possible?" The way Grams said it was a challenge, not a question.

"A way of life that's full of love and service . . . and sacrifice."

Joanna looked at her sharply. "Why sacrifice?"

"Because sometimes you have to give up something you hold dear to gain something of greater value."

"What would that be?" Another challenge from Grams.

"Having the Spirit with you. Being able to go to the temple and receive endowments."

"You don't have to join the Mormon church to live by the Spirit," Grams said. "Lutherans do that as well as Mormons."

"Do you?" Erin blurted out.

Grams grew very still. "What are you trying to say?"

"Nothing. I'm sorry."

"No, you meant something. Might as well spit it out."

Erin looked at her mother and then back at Grams. This was not how she'd imagined dinner with The Women going.

"Sometimes it seems like there's not much love in this house. If the Spirit is present, it seems to me love would be present, too."

"Well! Sitting in judgment now, are we? Guess being a Mormon makes you high and mighty."

Joanna said quietly, "Erin's right, Mom. Where the Spirit is present, love is present." She paused, and Erin held her breath, wondering what was coming. "Where love is present, forgiveness is present."

"Who are you saying needs to forgive?"

"I'm asking you to forgive me. It's been a long time."

Her mother's pleading look angered Erin. She set down her fork. "No way, Mom. Grams should ask you for forgiveness after the way she's treated you. And me."

Ruth shoved her chair back with an angry scraping sound.

"I should ask for forgiveness? I know I've never mollycoddled either one of you, and I've always said what was on my mind, but I've given my life for you two, Miss Uppity. You can talk all you want about spirit and the Mormon temple and . . . what was it?"

"Endowment," Erin whispered.

"Endowment. But I show my love with action. You can put that up against any Mormon idea of sacrifice any day of the week!"

Ruth walked into the kitchen, the picture of offended dignity. Moments later, Erin heard the sounds of cupboards being opened and dishes being placed on the counter. She pushed her own chair back. "I moved out so I wouldn't have to hear Grams do her drama," she said. "I think I'll take off before she comes back."

"Don't leave, please." Joanna put a hand on Erin's arm. "She doesn't realize how she sounds when she gets like that. Besides, she made her famous apricot cream cake. Your favorite."

Erin shook her head. "I don't understand her."

She sat back down, and in the silence that followed, Ruth appeared in the kitchen door with a large cake frosted in whipped cream and decorated with apricot halves and slivered almonds. As if the harsh words had vanished completely from the air and from her mind, she asked, "Anyone want dessert?"

Sunday, August 24, 1980
Dear Gabby, Juneau, and Willadene,

Would you believe this is the first letter I've every written in my life? My old Remington typewriter is in shock and my fingers are smudged with carbon-paper goop. I'll have to get used to it, because when I said I would write you guys, I meant it.

You were right about reentry, Gabby. It's almost impossible to tell people about an experience like we had. They can hear the words, but they don't feel the feelings. When I tried to tell my mom and grandma (The Women, I call them), Grams took something I said wrong, and we ended up in an argument. How's that for re-entry? Right now, it's hard to think the week was real, when nobody here understands what it meant to me. At least with you guys, I don't have to explain myself.

I'm back at work, but I've got my application in at Stefani's, an upscale salon in Wayzata. If I'm going to be doing this the rest of my life, I might as well get the big bucks.

Juneau, I really wish you had let me cut your hair while we were at Gabby's. I can just see how you would look in a short cut—sooo cute! And you wouldn't believe how much weight that would take off your mind, ha! ha! (That's the only place you could take off weight. You're thin enough, for sure. Although some of my clients are always saying you can't be too thin or too rich!)

That's all for now.
Erin

Chapter Six

JUNEAU

Juneau had been home from Utah for two weeks when she received a phone call from her mother.

"Juney," her mother said without preamble. "Bad news. It's Daddy's heart." She paused, and the phone line hummed.

Even as fear for her father swept over her, Juneau felt a familiar irritation at her mother. She was so used to building suspense in her novels that she did it in real life, too. Generally Juneau waited until her mother was ready to go on, but this sounded serious.

Clutching the phone so tightly her hand cramped, she said, "What is it, Mama? Has Daddy had a heart attack or something? Is he all right?"

"He's not all right," her mother said ominously. "But no, it's not an attack."

Again the phone line hummed. Suspense built up like water behind a dam.

Much as Juneau loved her mother, she wished she could rewrite her character. Make her as strong and decisive and forthcoming as the lady detectives in her mystery novels. There were more memories than she could count in which her mother flip-flopped around until people guessed what she was holding back and offered it to her just to get life started up again.

How would Gabby deal with someone like her mother?

Juneau gritted her teeth. "Mama!" she said so loudly that Philip Atwater, snoring at her feet, raised his head to stare at her. Giving him a reassuring pat, she lowered her voice. "Mama, you're scaring me. Just tell me what's wrong."

"He's been so tired lately," her mother said. "So out of breath."

Water was overflowing the dam.

"Mama!"

"He has to have one of those bypass operations," her mother said.

Well, at last it was out. Juneau's thoughts skittered like a mouse in a maze, trying to find the right solution. "So do you need money for the hospital?" She felt as if she were dropping into a pit. She and Greg were already stretched to the limit. She'd have to get a job. But how could she do that with the baby coming?

"No, no," her mother said. "You know we have more money than we need. And Daddy has always insisted on maintaining a health insurance plan. No, Blue Cross will pay for the operation."

If money wasn't the problem, what was it? What else was there?

"You need a place for him to recuperate." That had to be it.

"Yes," her mother confessed. "You know how small the motor home is. He'll be a caged lion when we can't be moving along for a while."

She frequently spoke in metaphors. She wrote that way, too. But she was right. Juneau thought frantically how she might accommodate two more people in the small house. She could move her typewriter and filing cabinet and all the office stuff out of the middle bedroom and rent a queen-size bed for them. Or maybe her father would need a hospital bed. Okay, there was room for that and a twin bed if the big bookcase came out, too. She could store her books in the garage. In boxes. She'd have to go digging every time she wanted a thesaurus or a book of quotations, but that was workable.

"Mama," she said, "you know you're welcome here. When is the operation going to be?"

"Bless you, Juney," her mother said. "It will be nice to be with family at a time like this."

"When?" Juneau repeated.

"Friday," her mother said. "Here in Omaha."

Juneau knew that's where they'd been for the past six weeks. Their new mystery involved some of the Mormon history sites around Winter Quarters. Old graves and wagon trails. They liked writing about old graves. Juneau thought briefly of asking about the old grave Aunt Hattie had given her a picture of. The mystery of the missing great-grandmother. But why do it on the phone? She could bring up the subject while her mother was right there in the house. Not that she expected to get any real information. Her mother would most likely polish up one of her well-worn evasions. The only thing she'd ever said about Letitia was that the woman had raised her after her parents died in an accident. And that she was dead.

"So how soon will you be here?" Juneau asked.

"The doctor says Daddy shouldn't travel for a while. So maybe around the end of the month?" Her mother's voice went up at the end in a question.

"I'm sure we can arrange it," Juneau said. The kids would be back in school then, so the house would be quiet during the day. Greg's teaching schedule at Cal State L.A. would be starting about that time. He was spending a lot of time at the computer lab on campus these days, anyway.

"We don't want to be a burden," her mother said.

"Mama, it's okay," Juneau said.

It had to be okay. Wasn't this what families were for? Willadene came to mind. Willadene, who would go out of her way to do things for people, especially family. Juneau could do it, too. It would work out. Fortunately, Misty and Nicole were still happy to share a room. As for her typewriter, it could sit on the kitchen table. She supposed she'd have to tell her parents that she was taking a writing class. The machine would be a clue, and they dealt with clues every day of their lives.

She hadn't told them she was going into motherhood again, so she'd have to tell them that, too. But first she'd have to tell Greg. She should have done it already.

Now that the housing problem was settled, Juneau's mother chattered on about Omaha and their research and how well the new book was doing. And Juneau thought about what she'd do with the middle room after her parents left, which would be as soon as her father felt able to travel. They were far too restless to stay a day longer than was absolutely necessary and would want to be off to track down a new plot. She might as well go ahead and make the room into a nursery as soon as her parents left, since her writing stuff would already be moved out of there.

Would they be moved out of her life, as well? Would having her parents there be enough to convince her that the writing life was not for her?

That evening at dinner Juneau told Greg and the girls about the phone call. "How would you feel about Grandpa and Grandma coming to live with us for a while?" she asked right after the blessing on the food.

The girls cheered. They loved their elusive grandparents, who always brought gifts and stories to entertain them. But Greg raised puzzled eyes from the pork chop he was cutting, and Juneau wished she'd told him privately before she involved the girls. Too late now.

Quickly she explained the situation.

"Will Grandpa be okay?" Misty asked, and Juneau promised he would be, although she had no real basis for such positive assurance.

Sensitive little Nicole saw past that part. "Are *you* going to be okay, Mom?" she said. "You love your office with the typewriter and all."

Juneau reached out to ruffle her hair. "I'll write right here in the kitchen while they're visiting."

"How long will it be?" Greg asked.

She noticed the use of *will* rather than *would*, which indicated that Greg accepted the idea.

She patted his hand, as she'd patted Philip Atwater earlier. "You know how my parents are."

Greg nodded. "So you won't be displaced for long."

She loved him for realizing how much her little office meant to her. He didn't know she wouldn't be moving back into it.

After the girls went to bed, she said she needed to talk with him. "Greg," she said, "I have some other news to tell you."

He looked at her apprehensively. "Don't tell me Flint is getting out of the Marines and coming here to live, too." He said it lightly.

She smiled. "No. You know well enough my brother is a career Marine. No, it's somebody else. I don't know his name. Actually, I'm not even totally sure it's a him, but I feel that it is."

For a couple of seconds he looked at her blankly. Then understanding made his face glow like a searchlight at a Kmart grand opening.

"Are you sure?" he asked.

"I'm sure *somebody's* coming," she said.

"Have you been to the doctor?"

"I plan to call tomorrow."

He wrapped his arms around her in an enormous hug.

His arms were like bands of steel, imprisoning her within his joyful embrace. He kissed her, first on the forehead, grazing then across her cheeks until he came to her full, red lips.

"Juneau, honey, sweetheart," Greg said, "I can't tell you how happy I am about this."

"Me, too," Juneau said. And she was. Greg's obvious joy boosted her up into the happy zone.

He pulled back to look into her face. "Where will we put him?"

She shrugged. "My typewriter's moveable."

"Can you give up your office? Permanently, I mean? Or at least for the next eighteen years, until he goes away to college?"

"Priorities," Juneau said simply.

"Maybe I can get a carport built," Greg said, "and frame in a room for you in the garage like we talked about."

They'd talked about creating that room after Nicole's birth, so the girls could have separate bedrooms and she could have a place to keep her sewing machine and fabrics. She'd been in a learning-to-sew phase at the time. The room had never materialized, however. Not then, and not now. She was quite sure Greg would never get around to it.

A *round tuit*. She'd seen those buttons at stationery store checkout counters with bold printing that commanded "Get a round tuit."

"That would be nice." She smiled in spite of her doubts.

"Let's wake the girls and tell them the news," Greg suggested.

Juneau shook her head. "I don't want to tell them yet."

Greg's eyebrows raised. "Why not?"

She didn't know why not. "Just let me pick the time."

"I don't see why we can't . . ." Greg stopped, his eyes searching her face. "Okay, Juney," he said. "It's your call."

September 27, 1980
Dear COBs,

Well, I lived through it. My parents' visit, I mean. I must admit it was a mixed blessing. In one way I loved having them here. Dad was docile for the first two weeks, poor lamb. He's a sweetie. Mom was . . . What can I say? Mom was Mom. I love her, but I'm glad I don't have to live with her anymore. I tried to ask her about our ancestors back in Idaho, especially Great-Grandma Letitia, who raised her after her parents died. I thought for a little while she was going to launch into an information moment, but then she buttoned down and said, "There are some things better left buried, Juneau, and that's one of them." I'll just have to go to Idaho sometime and see what I can uncover.

The girls were hyper the whole time my parents were here because the Peripatetic Paulsens are quite a show. Stories on demand. Love and kisses. Candy and cakes. McDonald's and the Colonel. I could have written the script ahead of time.

Am I sounding cynical again? It's just that I've been there, done that. Mom and Dad are mercurial; they're here and then they're gone, even though their physical bodies might still be in your presence.

I shouldn't be mean. They did the best they could with Flint and me. Other kids used to envy us because we lived in this cool motor home and traveled all over the continent. Gabby, O Woman of Wisdom, why is it we always envy what we don't have? I guess it's the Grass-Is-Greener Syndrome.

On the other hand, why am I not happy with what I do have now? I thought it was what I wanted.

Actually, I am quite happy at the moment. Mom and Dad were thrilled about the impending (well, several months away) arrival of Max (that's what Greg and I are calling him) and Mom, who is a first-class knitter, promised she'd whip up a bunch of baby items when they get back on the road. She was annoyed that we couldn't talk about him around the girls. I haven't told them about their brother-to-be yet. I don't know why. Mom says I always did like to keep secrets. Which is true, considering all my Guilty Secrets. Greg was sweet about it, telling Mom I like to do things in my own good time. She agreed to leave it alone.

Anyway, I asked her to make all the baby stuff in blue. So what if it's a girl? Don't even think it. This is a boy. Greg asks each day how his little quarterback is doing. If it's Maxine instead of Max, she's going to have to love football. And blue.

In a week or so I'll begin redecorating my former office. Make it into Babyland. My IBM Selectric resides now on the kitchen counter, to be moved each day to the table after breakfast. And so I type while stew simmers in the Crock-Pot and Philip Atwater snores at my feet. Not a bad scene, eh?

Mrs. Jarvis invited "the famous Paulsens" to come to her writing class and speak about how they do their books. Everyone in the class was dazzled, and actually I was proud because they do an impressive presentation. Besides that, Mom gave me some really good writing pointers while she was here. Dad read through my collection of short stories produced in Mrs. Jarvis's class before he got too restless and wanted to be on the road again. He declared them good. As for my part, I fed them balanced (though uninspiring) meals for the three weeks they were here, probably the only balanced ones they'll have until they come again. Willadene, I even tried game hens! They were a little dry, but delicious. Everyone was impressed!

So good to hear from all of you.

Love,
Juneau

Chapter Seven

ERIN

On the second of September, Colleen Harrington gave birth to a six-pound, five-ounce dark-haired little girl she named Erin Joy. She told Erin the news over the phone. "I think our moms are disappointed we didn't name the baby after one of them, but this little girl is definitely not a Frances. Or a Lillian."

"I guess that means I'm her godmother."

"Mormons don't have godmothers and godfathers, but you can be her Auntie Erin."

Erin chuckled. The idea pleased her immensely. "I'd love to. I don't know anything about taking care of a baby, though."

"Neither do I, and I'm her mother."

Once Colleen came home with the baby, whom she called EJ for short, Erin began stopping by a couple of times a week after work. She often arrived just in time to take care of EJ while Colleen prepared supper. She was afraid she was making a nuisance of herself, but Colleen said, "I'd rather have you here than my mom or Lillian. They drive me crazy fussing."

Three weeks after EJ was born, Colleen opened the door looking a mess. Her hair was tangled and dull, and her eyes were red-rimmed. The bathrobe she wore was wrinkled and stained. EJ was straining in her arms, wailing.

"Here, you take her," Colleen said without even a hello. "She's been like this all afternoon. I've had it."

She pushed the baby, red-faced and stiff with either fury or distress, into Erin's arms. Erin panicked. "What's the matter with her?"

"I don't know, but she's yours. I'm going to have a good cry."

There was nothing for Erin to do but to take EJ, who immediately arched her back against Erin's hands and howled. Terrified, Erin walked from one end of Colleen's living room to the other, patting EJ's back and making noises of comfort. She hoped her voice didn't sound as scared as she felt.

"There, there, little Erin," she sang. "You're okay. That's right. Just relax and be good for Auntie Erin." Another turn of the room, another round of patting and cooing. "Please, EJ. Stop crying, or Auntie Erin is going to cry, too. Then all three of us can have hysterics in the bedroom. And your daddy will come home and commit the bunch of us."

Finally, she changed the baby's diaper, dressed her in a clean cotton sleeper and washed her face and hands with a cool cloth, crooning and pleading as she worked. Then she wrapped her snugly in a receiving blanket and began doing what she thought of as "The Relief Society Sway."

Miraculously, EJ's little body began to soften, her cries dwindled, and she fell asleep. Holding the warm body of such a helpless little person against her heart, Erin felt fiercely protective. She realized that she would do anything in the world to make sure this child was loved and safe. *This must be what it feels like to be a mother,* she thought. She looked down into the now peaceful face and whispered, "I love you."

When she looked up, she saw Colleen leaning against the sofa, watching her. "You're a natural," Colleen said.

Erin smiled shyly. "You think so?"

EJ wasn't the only reason Erin loved spending time with the Harringtons. The idea of Forever Families had drawn her to the Mormon Church, but she had no idea how one created such a family. Her grandfather had died when she was young, and she had grown up in a household of women. She had never seen the dance of give and take between a husband and wife until now.

She sometimes felt like a voyeur as she watched Steve and Colleen's casual gestures of affection. But they knew she had a clear view of their relationship, and they didn't pull the blinds. She saw them moving easily together as they cared for Erin Joy or fixed a meal. She saw them on edge, their communications sharp or even caustic. She once saw them both make a sudden, palpable shift from mutual irritation to forgiveness and laughter. "Kiss and make up" looked anything but trite at that moment.

Watching them, Erin felt a deep yearning to have a family of her own. She wanted to be loved by someone the way Steve loved Colleen. She wanted a child of her own to hold to her breast. It was a yearning like none she had ever felt before, one that was with her day and night, demanding to be filled.

When she finally confessed her longing to Colleen, her friend said, "Well, you can't find a man hanging out with me and Steve. You've got to get out there."

The idea of "getting out there" was distinctly unappealing to Erin. She had had very few dates in high school and none since. She didn't know how to make small talk outside the salon—chatting with clients was far different from socializing. "I don't know . . ." she began.

"Listen, here's what you have to do." Colleen dragged Erin over to the table in their apartment. She grabbed pencil and paper and sat down, all business. Within minutes she had written out a three-point plan, which included attending the University Branch, going to singles functions, and joining a singles family home evening group.

"Do you really think this will work?"

"You won't know until you try it."

Erin was doubtful, but the longing she felt was stronger than the resistance. "Okay," she said. "Here goes nothing."

The next Sunday, Erin attended the University Branch, where she was invited to join a singles family home evening group. It was a long way from Uptown to Dinkytown, as the shopping area near the University Branch was called, but she drove the distance Sundays and Monday nights, hoping to meet someone who was as interested in knowing her as she was in knowing him.

She also attended a singles dance at the Minneapolis Stake Center in Golden Valley. She stayed at the dance less time than it had taken her to get ready for it, and she drove home very discouraged. Once in her apartment, she kicked off her high heels and dialed the Harringtons' number.

"I quit," she said when Colleen answered the phone. "Your plan looked good on paper, but it will only work if there actually are some guys out there worth meeting. The ones my age seemed too young. The older ones—well, let's just say they're single for a reason. Besides, most of the guys at the singles dance were interested in one very beautiful girl from the Crystal Ward."

"Are you telling me you've already written off every single guy in the Twin Cities?"

"Listen, if you'd been out there with me, you would have come to the same conclusion. You got the last good one, I think."

"Steve is the best." Colleen paused. "So what are you going to do? Give up?"

"Yes." Erin hesitated. "No. I don't want to, but this beating the bushes is wearing me out."

"Well, maybe you don't have to beat the bushes. Steve's best friend Cory Johnson is coming back from his mission next week."

Sunday, September 28, 1980
Dear Ladies,

Guess what? I've finally experienced a little of what it's like to be a mother! My friend Colleen had a little girl, and she named her Erin Joy after me. I play momma to EJ a couple of evenings a week so Colleen can have a break. It didn't take long for that sweet thing to wrap me around her little finger but good.

My roommate, Rochelle, is convinced I've lost my marbles, because I think babysitting is more fun than bar hopping. Rochelle lives for weekends—she and her friends do a lot of partying. We do okay as roomies, though, because we both think it's important to keep the bathroom and kitchen reasonably clean. That smooths over a lot of differences.

Anyway, for the first time in my life, I catch myself thinking about what it would be like to have a family. Yes, I know. I have to find a husband first!

More good news: I got the job at Stefani's! There really is a Stefani, in case you're wondering. He's one part easygoing flamboyant man of the world and three parts drill sergeant. He paired me up with a buddy, who's supposed to answer all my questions while I get settled in.

My buddy's name is Angela Dunmeyer, Angie for short. She doesn't look like an Angie. Imagine a tall, rather masculine woman with a large face, broad shoulders, bandy legs, and a head of dead black hair in a style best described as "artfully wild." She sounds rather homely, but she's quite attractive in person. I think it's her big smile, nice green eyes, and great sense of humor.

She's been with Stefani the longest, and she mothers and bullies everyone, including him. The receptionist told me he lets Angie get away with everything because she's the best in town.

I'm going to love working at this new salon. The only downside is that now I'll have to drive my car every day. It's an old rust bucket, but it still has a good heater and reliable motor, so I think I'll be okay. Knock on wood.

That's all for now.

Erin

WILLADENE

September 30, 1980
Dear Ladies in Triplicate,

I yogurt, I yogurted, tomorrow I will yogurt again. I am swimming in yogurt! We have yogurt spread with herbs, yogurt cheese, yogurt-based icing, casseroles, puddings, sandwich spreads, etc., etc., etc. Juneau, maybe you can tell me if I've conjugated yogurt correctly. By the way, I'm happy to hear you're back in your writing class.

I like writing letters, especially when other people are doing them and sending them to me in the mail. It's better than journal writing—with letters, you get payback. In fact, if you keep my letters and then send me copies at the end of the year, that will be my journal. I've had more mail in the last two weeks than I've had in months. Many thanks! My poor mailman must think I have a crush on him since I run out to the mailbox as soon as I see him coming.

Juneau, you weren't being unreasonable keeping this pregnancy to yourself for a while. Once the announcement is made, privacy goes out the window. Moms need some time to get comfortable with what's happening to their bodies before everyone else gets on the bandwagon. Even husbands.

We were living in an apartment over my father's store when I was pregnant with Carl. I was working as a clerk and started each shift with a mad dash for the bathroom. Everyone guessed I was pregnant before I ever made it to the obstetrician's office. It wasn't long before it felt like the pregnancy belonged to everyone else, and the fact that it was happening in my body was only incidental.

What you're feeling is pretty normal. However, I am uneasy about your not seeing an ob-gyn yet. My Great-Granny Min, who was a practicing midwife, always said the sooner known, the better cured. Not that there is anything here to cure, but sometimes hormones get the best of us, and a chat with an understanding practitioner can help. So Mother Willadene is poking her nose in from so many miles away. If you haven't been to the doctor yet, please go!

I sent a box of peanut butter fudge and the latest Shoebox novel to Gabby, along with a thank-you card. I signed all our names. I just wanted you to know about it, so in case Gabby writes, you'll know what she's talking about.

Keep in touch!

Love,
Deenie

Deenie raced home from mailing her letter to Juneau, pushing Bitsy in front of her. Bitsy always protested strolling in a stroller. She wanted warp speed ahead, and today was the perfect day to indulge her. Deenie came to a squealing stop in front of the house and unbuckled her happy toddler. Then she noticed her father stretching out his long body on the steps of the porch in the morning sun.

"Daddy, this is a surprise." Deenie handed Bitsy over to her grandfather.

John Stowell snuggled Bitsy close. "How's my little Snowdrop?" he asked.

Deenie collapsed the stroller and carried it inside the front door. "Where are Mom and Sunny?"

"Can't I visit my girl by myself?" John asked. Bitsy began to wiggle, and he put her in her playpen.

"Daddy, you can come any time at all. I'm always glad to see you." Deenie hugged her father, but she wondered at his visiting on a work day. Alone. He always came in tandem with her mother. Even when Deenie visited their home, her mother never left the two of them alone. She would always pop into the room, sooner rather than later.

"What brings you out on a work day?"

John made himself comfortable on the couch. "I wanted to talk to you about your mother."

"Is she all right?" Deenie asked, frightened by the possibility of something being wrong with the indomitable and dignified Margaret Stowell.

John's mouth twisted around as though he had something unpleasant to say. "She's as all right as she can be at the moment. Your Aunt Stella says it's the change, and it's hit your mother like a ton of bricks. She can't sleep at night for the sweats and says she feels like someone took a cheese grater to her nerves during the day."

Deenie sagged with relief. "Is there anything I can do to help?" she asked.

"I don't think so. I'm taking extra time off to spend with Sunny in the afternoons so your mom can catch up on her rest and have some time to herself. Besides, Maggie would, er . . . have my guts for garters if she knew I'd been out here talking about her behind her back. Could you be a little extra careful around your mother, Deenie? Just for now?"

Deenie looked solemnly at her father, the father she had always counted on to take her side, and said, "Sure, Daddy, anything you say." But that wasn't what she was thinking as she walked him to the door.

"*Just for now, Deenie.*" Her nostrils flared as she was flooded with memories. "*I know you don't want to be at Grandma Hunter's while you're sick, Deenie, but it's just for now.*" "*It's almost the same as the outfit you picked out at ZCMI, and we couldn't afford that. The budget's a little tight. It's just for now.*" "*You can put off your education until Roger's through school. It's just for now.*" "*The original part of the house is in great shape and perfect for a small family. When the men find time, they can finish the addition Uncle Marty started when he had the house. It's just for now.*"

Bitsy began to fuss in her playpen. Deenie picked her up and patted her on the back. "I bet you're ready for your nap." She took Bitsy through the naptime routine automatically. After conversations like the one she'd had with her father a moment ago, she often felt as though she were caught in an unending version of the old comedy routine "Who's on First." Was she ever first position in anybody's life? She knew she had felt deliciously first when she and Roger were courting; however, that feeling had slowly faded when Roger went back to school and she had gone to work to support him. Would she ever be first again with anyone? The most important? Or was her life calling to be the pinch hitter, significant only when needed?

Deenie shrugged as she always did when such uncomfortable feelings surfaced. *It doesn't matter much who's the star in the long run,* she thought to herself. *Everyone's on a team, and the game has to be played.* For Deenie that meant putting in a load of wash, weeding the tomatoes, getting Bitsy up and fed before collecting the boys from a play date with their cousins. She was way too busy to be bothered with such thoughts. And she was glad of it.

Two hours later Deenie pulled her van of squabbling children into the driveway. "Quiet!" she snapped at the boys in the back. She usually parked in front of the house so she could ignore the two-story skeleton that attached the garage to the original section of the house. Getting a broadside view of the neighborhood eyesore always shortened her temper. Seeing her sister-in-law sitting in the middle of the twelve-year-old framing only raised it a notch. *Wonderful!* Deenie thought grimly.

Bert came toward her as she hoisted Bitsy and her carrier out of the middle seat of the van. She looked even grimmer than Deenie felt. *Oh boy,* Deenie thought.

"Hi," she greeted Bert as she ushered the children into the house. Without speaking, Bert followed. "We're having PB&J for lunch. Would you like to join us?"

"Okay," Bert answered. Her tone was neutral, but her body language said she was anything but. She took out a loaf of bread and opened it. Stopped. Twisted the tie shut and then sat down at the table with her hands in her lap.

I don't have time for nineteen-year-old drama, Deenie thought, grabbing the bag and hastily assembling the sandwiches. The meal was managed in silence, punctuated by the boys looking back and forth between Bert and her, waiting for someone to break the mood.

After the kitchen had been put to rights, Bitsy put down for her afternoon nap, and the boys settled to play quietly in the bedroom, Deenie rejoined Bert at the table. "What's with the silent treatment?" she asked.

Bert lifted her chin. "I knew if I tried to talk, I would start to cry, and I didn't want to cry in front of the kids."

"Sounds serious," Deenie said, her response only a tiny bit flippant.

"I overheard Roger asking my mom to request that I quit interfering in your lives. He said I was getting on your nerves but you were too *nice* to tell me to my face. So you went behind my back."

"Oh, my. I'm sorry you overheard, and I'm so sorry you were hurt," Deenie said. She meant it. Although she hated Bert's tendency to take over things in her house without asking her, she never wanted family conflict because of it.

"Well, is it true?" Bert asked tersely. "Do you think I meddle in your life?"

Deenie had no idea how to respond. *If there's a guardian angel for COBettes anywhere out there, I could use some help,* she thought.

Before she could come up with an answer, Bert continued. "I never meant to. I was only trying to help, to be part of the family."

"You do help," Deenie hastily assured her. "You help a lot—" she stopped mid-sentence, registering the complete content of Bert's response. "Do *I* ever make you feel like you're not part of this family?"

"Along with everybody else." Bert rubbed one eye with the back of her hand. "Mom has Dad, Gordon has Charlotte and the boys, Keith has Jenny and the girls, and Roger has you and your kids. Where do I fit in?"

Deenie repented of every mean thing she had ever thought about her sister-in-law. "You fit in right here, doing what you always do, being a part of our family. If I'd been straight with you and everyone else from the beginning, none of this would have happened."

"Straight about what?"

"Setting boundaries."

"You mean like Rauf marking his territory?" Bert asked with a faint grin.

"Pretty much. When we first moved in and I had Carl, everyone showed up to help. I needed the help, and I appreciated it. I still do. But your mom still had a key to this house and came right in without knocking. She often had the laundry in the washing machine before I even realized she was here. My mom was almost as bad, but at least she and my visiting teachers knocked. They were kind and helpful, determined to make me feel as if I belonged. But they never asked. They barged in and took over."

"Kind of like I do?" Bert asked.

"Well, you did pull up half of my flower bed."

"I was trying to straighten the rows," Bert said defensively.

"I didn't plant them in rows. I wanted the colors all jumbled together."

"Oh."

A crash came from down the hall, followed by a thump, a squawk, and a howl from Rauf. "Mommmm!" came the unison cry.

Deenie jumped to her feet and raced down the hall. After a few stern words to the boys, a redivision of toys, and a pat for the pooch, she returned to the kitchen.

"Another boundary issue," she said as she sat down.

Bert looked unconcerned. "My dad would have let them fight it out on their own."

"Nine-year-old boys don't 'fight it out' with four-year-old little brothers. They beat them up." Deenie was exasperated. "I don't want my boys growing up thinking the way to settle a problem is to pound on somebody!"

"But Dad . . ."

Willadene held up her hand. "No buts. My home, my kids, and my rules."

"Well, that pretty much puts me in my place." Bert leaned away from the table. "And Mom and Dad."

"Wait a minute. Bert, I love your mom and dad and your whole family. I love it that you're all so close and know each other so well you can finish each other's sentences—and projects. But I'm not part of that circle. I don't plant my petunias in straight rows. I put herbs in the flower garden and marigolds with the vegetables. I like cornbread stuffing better than sage. I don't believe lard is the answer to a flakier piecrust." Deenie took a deep breath to calm herself. "And I want to raise my children the way Roger and I have decided is best for our family."

"We didn't mean to cause a problem," Bert said in a sad voice.

"I *know!* I know," Deenie repeated more softly. "But if your family doesn't start asking before they march in and take over, they are going to *help* me right over the edge."

Bert raised her hands in a "What can I say?" gesture. "We are kind of a charge-right-in-there-and-get-the-job-done kind of family."

"Exactly like my family. There is a lot to be said for that attitude, Bert. Unless you're at the other end of the charge and don't know what's coming."

"So the bottom line is, ask first?"

Deenie nodded.

"I can still come and play house at your house as long as . . . ?"

"You ask first."

"That's it?"

Deenie nodded again, but this time she was smiling broadly.

"I can do that," Bert said. In a formal voice, she asked, "In fact, I will. Deenie, is there anything you would like me to help you with?"

Deenie knew what a powerhouse Bert could be. She had the Rasmussen men wrapped around her little finger. What they wouldn't take time to do for Deenie, they would do for Bert. *You don't waste that kind of leverage,* Deenie thought. *What do I want done the most?*

Finally she spoke. "You can flick your Bic under the Rasmussen men and get them to finish the addition. There are owls nesting out there."

"I can do that!" Bert said in her "project voice."

They cemented their new understanding by spending the afternoon playing with the children, Bert careful to observe and follow the rules.

Sunday after sacrament meeting brought the first fruits of Deenie's "flick your Bic" request when Gordy cornered her in the church foyer.

"I understand from my baby sister that you have owls nesting in your rafters," he said.

"Yes, we do." Deenie was floored by his comment, thinking of all the times she had mentioned the same thing over the past half dozen years.

"Well, we can't have that. Messy things, owls." He gave her a hug and turned the conversation to the annual Fourth of July picnic at the Rasmussen homestead.

Early Monday morning Deenie was awakened by a tap, tap, tap from the rear of the house. *Great*, she thought. *Now we have woodpeckers as well as owls.* She pulled on her robe on the run, snagged the broom by the back door and raced out, ready to wreak havoc on the intruders. No downy feathered fiend was going to add to the mess attached to the back of her house. She found Wilford Rasmussen instead, hammer in hand, tapping firmly into the framing.

"Just checking for water rot." He pointed at the broom she still held at the ready. "Say, now, I know we've been making some mistakes but is that necessary?"

Deenie quickly lowered her broom. She was so embarrassed. "Stay for breakfast?" she offered weakly.

"No can do. Mother's waiting the Cream of Wheat for me, and I'm finished here." With a smile and a nod, Wilford pocketed his hammer and left, whistling a cheery tune.

If that wasn't enough, Monday night after family home evening, Keith appeared out of the blue with two large measuring tapes in hand, grabbed Roger, and disappeared around the house.

Deenie was amazed. Bert hadn't just flicked her Bic under the Rasmussen men; she'd lit a four-alarm fire! The morning after the big family picnic, the first truckload of lumber showed up with her sister-in-law Jenny driving and Bert standing on the passenger side runner, waving as they came.

Deenie turned to Roger, who was standing beside her. "Did you know this was going to happen?"

He grinned. "Looks like you have yourself a real first-class advocate."

"Sure do," Deenie answered, all the while thinking, *I gotta figure out how she does that!*

JUNEAU

October 6, 1980
Dear COBettes,

Deenie, I loved your letter about making yogurt.

Regina watched him approach the house, her knees quivering like the molded cherry Jell-O she loved to make for him. Everything was ready. She had spent the whole afternoon making yogurt, and the pristine jars sat now upon the kitchen counter, awaiting his passionate embrace. Her heartbeat snare drummed as she thought of how he would lift one jar after another to pour the contents down his grateful throat. Then he would turn to her, his burning eyes hanging on her full, red lips. After a resounding burp, he would say, his voice heavy with desire, "What's for dinner, babe?"

Hmmmm. Maybe I should take up yogurt making.

I wrote a story for my writing class about a pregnant woman who takes her male cat in to be neutered. Is that symbolic? It was very well received by Mrs. Jarvis and the class. They thought it was hilarious. I guess they would have thought it was even more so if they'd known I'm expecting.

I've tried to give up writing, but then I get all these ideas. So I have to face it. I want to be a writer. I seem to be able to work at the kitchen table as well as I did in my former little office, so I can't use that as an excuse not to do it.

Things are more or less fine with the family at the moment. Greg, as I think I told you in one of our discussions in Provo, teaches computer science at Cal State L.A. and is hoping for a grant to research artificial intelligence. He's in the bishopric at church and enjoys that calling. Misty is moody, but her grades are good, and she's cooperative—most of the time. Nicole is always sweet. She and Beto, Marisol's younger son, announced that they are going to get married—on October 31 (they like Halloween) in the year 2000 and then go to Egypt, where they'll dig up mummies.

Philip Atwater is his usual doggy self.

I've been called to teach the Social Relations class in Relief Society. I don't like to give up my little seven-year-olds in Primary, but I've accepted. I think I'll enjoy it.

Well, that's all for now. Just wanted to stay in touch.

Love,
Juneau

Chapter Eight

ERIN

"What do you think?" Colleen whispered in Erin's ear. It was sacrament meeting, and Cory Johnson was at the pulpit giving his mission report. Colleen had insisted they sit toward the front of the chapel so Erin could get a good look at him.

Without taking her eyes off Cory Johnson, Erin poked Colleen lightly in the ribs, hoping the Do Not Disturb message got through to her. Tall, blond, and handsome, Cory had the Scandinavian good looks often seen in Minnesota. His grin showed teeth that were very white against the tan she knew he had acquired going door-to-door in Arizona. It gave him the look of a surfer or tennis player, but when he spoke of things close to his heart, his eyes glistened and his face shone.

Looking at him, Erin felt something she had been hoping to feel in her forays into the world of Mormon singles: a sense of recognition and faint but distinct warmth in her heart. Mesmerized, she couldn't turn away from him, even when his gaze rested on her face. His eyes, which radiated kindness and a hint of humor, were very, very blue.

What does this mean? part of her wondered. *Is he the right one? Maybe it doesn't mean anything,* another part countered. *Except wishful thinking.*

That brought to mind the class she had attended at Education Week. How could she really, truly know what those feelings meant? And what difference would it make either way, if he wasn't equally interested in her?

Oh, boy. I've got a lot to write Juneau and Willadene about, she thought.

After the meeting was over, Erin and the Harringtons stayed in their seats, waiting for the crowd of people around Cory to dissipate before approaching him. EJ rested in her baby carrier next to them.

"You be nice to him," Steve said to Erin, grinning. "Returned missionaries are in a vulnerable state. They're likely to fall for the first good-looking Mormon girl they see."

"Is that why you fell in love with me?" Colleen asked with a saucy grin. "Because I was the first on the scene?"

"I fell in love with you because you were the prettiest girl in town."

When Cory was finally free, he waved and called, "Hi, there!" Moments later, he and Steve were hugging each other. Then he turned to get a hug from Colleen. "It's so good to see you. You look great."

"Thanks. You didn't see me when I was pregnant out to here." Colleen's hand measured a foot out in front of her.

"And who is this?" Cory asked, bending over the baby carrier to touch EJ's cheek lightly.

"Erin Joy. Named after my friend Erin." Colleen drew Erin forward. "She's a convert to the Church. She's been in our ward since she moved to the Uptown area a year ago."

Erin thrust out her hand, feeling awkward and eager at the same time. "Nice to meet you."

"Same here. I was afraid I'd come home to a ward with no one my age except Colleen and Steve."

"What are your plans now that you're back?" Colleen asked the question, but when Cory answered it, he was looking at Erin.

"I'm not sure. I was thinking of going for a master's degree at the U of M or at BYU, but Dad says I ought to try to get into the PR department of one of the big corporations headquartered here—Pillsbury, General Mills, Cargill. There are a lot of Mormon executives in those companies I can use as contacts." He made a self-deprecating gesture. "Dad's already been scouting for me here, and my Grandpa Harold is doing the same in the Chicago area. He and my Grandma Trina live in Naperville."

"Must be nice to have them rooting for you," Erin said.

Before he could answer, Cory's parents joined them. They were an impressive couple, fit, immaculately groomed, and handsomely dressed. Looking at them, Erin could see that Cory got his intense blue eyes from his mother, Linda, and his height and strong chin from his father, Skipp.

"Cory, how would you like to have your friends join us for dinner?" Linda asked. "I wouldn't want you to be bored your first Sunday home."

"I'd love it," he said. "You'll come, won't you?" His question included Erin.

Sunday, October 12, 1980
Dear COBettes,

I bet you didn't think you'd hear from me so soon after the last short note, but something interesting has happened. Cory Johnson gave his mission report in sacrament meeting today. Colleen told me he was good looking, and I can tell you now that she wasn't exaggerating!

I felt an immediate connection with him, something I've never experienced before. I've been wondering what that was all about ever since. Maybe it was the Spirit that was present when he was giving his report. If so, everybody felt the same thing I did.

His parents invited me and the Harringtons to Sunday dinner afterward. I was a bit surprised. They've been polite enough since I moved into this ward, but that's all. I was glad Steve and Colleen were there. They've both known Cory forever, and they are perfectly comfortable with Skipp and Linda (Cory's parents).

Sometimes I really get sick of the voices inside my head. All through dinner I could hear part of me singing the same old song: They really don't like me; they only asked me because I'm Colleen's friend. I don't belong here; I'm from the other side of the tracks. What would they think if they knew all about me? I'm an imposter, a fraud. Blah, blah, blah.

We sure had fun, though, laughing and talking for the longest time. Colleen and Steve have already come up with an agenda of things for the four of us to do together. Cory seems willing, and I'm all for it. So who knows?

Regina picked a daisy and slowly pulled the petals off, one by one. He loves me, he loves me not, he loves me . . . , completely ignoring the frog waiting to be kissed.

Love you guys,
Erin

The Sunday dinner after Cory gave his mission report was the first of many such dinners at the Johnsons' the fall of 1980. Before dessert was served, it was clear that there was good chemistry among Cory, Erin, Colleen, and Steve. They talked and laughed long after Cory's parents had finished washing the dishes and retired to their master suite. Before the evening was over, Colleen had issued Cory and Erin a standing invitation to their apartment for family home evening, and the four of them had made plans to drive up the St. Croix River to see the colors, which were changing early that year.

After that, it was easy for Erin and Cory to fall into step together. They sat with the Harringtons during sacrament meetings and had family home evening with them on Monday nights. The four of them often did things together on the Saturday afternoons when Erin was off work. The time they spent together was easy and comfortable, with lots of laughter.

Whenever she was with Cory, Erin experienced an intense attraction; when they were apart, she was filled with longing. She waited for Cory to call, just so she could hear his voice. His face was the last thing she saw behind closed eyes before falling asleep. *Is this love?* she wondered. *It must be. I've never felt like this before.*

But was he interested in her? She couldn't tell. While he always seemed pleased to be in her company, several days often passed when she didn't see or talk to him. When they were together, the physical contact between them was limited to social kisses accompanied by brief hugs, comfortable hand-holding while walking together, and friendly snuggles when watching TV.

"How are things going with you and Cory?" Colleen asked Erin. They were walking EJ through Cordelia Park on a crisp fall Saturday afternoon; Steve and Cory were at a Vikings game.

"What can I say? Cory's a perfect gentleman and a good friend."

"Don't worry," Colleen said. "He's just taking his time."

JUNEAU

Misty and Nicole were excited and mystified when Juneau finally told them about the coming baby. Or at least Nicole was. At seven, she still believed in the mysteries of Santa Claus and the Tooth Fairy and the stork. Juneau would have thought Misty, nine, knew little more and was startled when she said slyly, "I know where babies come from."

Juneau felt her face reddening and was embarrassed that she couldn't control it. One day she was going to have to speak to the girls about the facts of life. Like perhaps today. Maybe she'd already waited too long. Maybe that was why she'd delayed telling them about Max, because she'd known she'd have to get into things that were difficult for her to talk about.

She remembered a discussion—maybe it was in a Relief Society class—where the advice was given that you should not give children any more information than they specifically ask for when they bring up the subject. Maybe she wouldn't have to supply too many details. Maybe Misty was not referring to what she thought she was.

Juneau looked at the upturned face, trying to read what was behind Misty's statement. The knowing eyes, the slightly tipped head, told her what she hadn't even suspected. Somebody had been telling Misty things that she might not be ready to know. No, that was a cop-out. This was 1980. The subject was all over the billboards and TV. She, Juneau, should already have put down a factual foundation for the girls to build their knowledge on, so they'd get it right.

Nicole had been watching her and Misty, her innocent little face puzzled. "Where *do* babies come from, Mom?"

Juneau put her arms around the girls. Smiling, she said, "Tell you what. Let's have a dish of ice cream and sit down at the table. I want to tell you all about the wonderful, clever way Heavenly Father created for mamas and daddies to have babies."

She decided to give them the full course. She forced herself to tell it accurately, factually. The girls listened quietly, the only sound being the clink of spoons against the pretty pink glass dishes she'd put the ice cream in.

Nicole was enchanted. "Is the baby really there inside your tummy right now?" she asked.

Juneau nodded. "It really, truly is. It's only about this big." She measured with her thumb and forefinger.

Nicole's eyes widened. "That's itty-bitty." Her voice lowered to a whisper. "Can it hear us?"

"Maybe," Juneau said. "Do you want to say something to it?"

"Yes." She leaned close to Juneau's midsection and then looked up at her. "Does it have a name?"

"Not yet," Juneau said. "But your daddy and I think it might be Max."

Nicole leaned in closer. "Hello, itty, bitty, tiny Max," she whispered. "I love you."

Quick tears sprang to Juneau's eyes. "I love you, too," she said silently. That's what she should have said when she first suspected she was pregnant. How could she ever have resented its presence?

Misty turned to face Nicole. "It'll be this big when it's born." She held her hands about thirty inches apart.

Juneau couldn't help smiling to herself. But her amusement was tempered by the thought that somebody had definitely been talking to Misty.

Keeping her voice light, she said, "And who, may I ask, has been telling you all about babies?"

Misty elaborately scraped the bottom of her ice cream dish and then licked the spoon. "Just somebody," she said. She raised her eyes to meet Juneau's, and there was defiance in them.

Where had that come from? Juneau had noticed a trace of it before in Misty, and it frightened her. She wanted to grip her daughter's thin little shoulders and demand to know the source of her information. Who, and when, and where? But she restrained herself. She would seek a better time, without Nicole present, to find out who'd been telling her daughter things that were her responsibility to tell.

Greg didn't consider it a big deal. When she told him about the incident, he shrugged and said, "Kids pick these things up everywhere. How did you learn about the birds and the bees?"

It was hard to find that right moment to bring up the subject again. In the meantime Juneau decided just to be watchful. So she looked at the crowds of kids when she took the girls to school, watching for one that might look too knowledgeable. How about neighborhood playmates? She was alert around them, too.

On the next Sunday at church she even looked around the chapel but then immediately felt guilty suspecting any of the good people in her ward. Her mind straying from the low-key speaker at the pulpit, Juneau remembered the girl in one of the many trailer parks her parents had stopped at during her early years.

Starette, her name was, with wild black hair and bold eyes. She and her mother had lived in a colorful gypsy-looking trailer, a fascinating lure to every kid in the trailer park. And ten-year-old Juneau, with inadequate supervision at all times, had been willingly lured in. Starette had unloaded all the information she'd gathered from who knew where.

Actually, Juneau had always been grateful to Starette because otherwise she would have been totally horrified the day, at age eleven, she'd awakened to find she'd begun menstruating before her mother had gotten around to telling her what it was all about.

A ripple of laughter from the congregation brought her back to the present, sitting there in the chapel on the padded bench with Nicole on one side and Misty on the other. Greg, second counselor to the bishop, sat on the stand, as always. For a while Juneau concentrated on the speaker, but then her thoughts strayed again, this time to the Felton family on the pew ahead of her, whose first-counselor father also sat on the stand. Seven children they had, and another on the way. Did Camilla Felton have a dream, as Juneau did (even though she tried to suppress it), of accomplishing something besides raising kids? Or perhaps that *was* her dream. She certainly seemed happy enough, although always a bit harassed.

Like now, when her full attention was on trying to keep the two smallest boys, four and two, from squabbling, while occasionally reaching to the bench ahead to touch the shoulder of the oldest girl, Tiffany, who was whispering to her girlfriend. Twelve-year-old Reggie, suddenly so long-boned that his wrists stretched far beyond his sleeves, had passed the sacrament for the first time that day. He sat solemnly now at the end of the pew with two sisters, ten and seven. Five-year-old Jane, she of the plain name, the quiet one, the one who always seemed lost in the crowd, sat at the wall end of the bench. She was looking backward, watching Nicole, who slowly flipped through the hymnbook.

When Nicole noticed, she invited Jane to slip under the bench and join her, which she did, after failing to attract her mother's attention to ask if it was okay. She slid in between Nicole and Juneau, and for a few minutes she observed the pages of the hymnbook with Nicole. Then she shifted almost imperceptively closer to Juneau, laying her head with its hastily combed hair against Juneau's arm.

Poor little scrap, Juneau thought. Didn't Sister Felton realize that sometimes the quiet, undemanding one needed attention as much as the noisy ones?

Suddenly Juneau was ashamed of herself, sitting there in judgment of someone else when it was she who was found wanting. Wanting in sense for not informing her children of the facts of life before someone else did. Wanting in humanity for putting the possibility of a writing career (which she'd been trying to avoid) over bringing up another child of God. That was twisted. She should be ashamed of herself for being critical of Sister Felton.

She was reminded of the hymn they'd sung last Sunday, the one titled "Truth Reflects upon Our Senses," in which one person sees a mote in the eye of the other but cannot see it well because of her own eye containing a beam.

Once again she was guilty.

But sitting there, with little Jane snuggled warmly against her side, Juneau got the idea for a story.

October 20, 1980
Dear COBs,

I told the girls about the baby, and they, of course, are excited. And so am I!

I've finally got into the nesting mode. The girls have been helping me make my former office into a nursery. I borrowed a crib (I gave away the old one after Nicole's birth—always a mistake, I've heard). The girls and I painted the room—sky blue walls with darker blue trim. Greg joined us one Saturday and sketched in an apple tree on one wall. The girls are carefully coloring in brown bark, green leaves, and red apples. Soon I'll pull out my long-neglected sewing machine and make some blue-and-white-striped curtains. I bought a changing table at a garage sale, and it's now a startling shade of red to match the apples. Max is going to love it!

I'm so happy that the girls are occupied this way. Misty has been becoming a bit rebellious lately, not wanting to go to Primary and refusing to sit still for family home evening. Her grades are good, but she likes to hang out after school with her friends, some of whom I'm none too happy about. But she's really into this getting-ready-for-Max project. So there is hope.

I'm feeling very well this time (with each of the girls I had the nine-month barfs). I enjoy an occasional nap, and I like to settle down into Greg's big recliner chair with a romance novel now and then, but overall I'm fine!

Hope you are all the same.

Love,
Juneau

Chapter Nine

WILLADENE

October 27, 1980
Dear COBs, Cobbletes, Cobbits, and/or COBettes,

Here's some shocking news! The first Sunday of this month I was released—you got it—from my calling in Relief Society. All those notes on yogurt and no place to teach them. Do you think the Stowell Family Tree can stand the shock?

Roger has also been released from his longtime calling with the Boy Scouts since he will be starting night classes soon for his master of education program at the University of Utah. Big changes all around.

Bert has become my biggest supporter and new best friend. She has a "flick your Bic" technique for getting things done that is amazing. Her motto is still, "If there is anything to be done, it's my job to do it." But she is asking first now and spending a lot of time getting details right before she dives in. It's great to be able to trust her to respect our family boundaries but still be part of our family.

In case Gabby hasn't passed on the news, we enjoyed a fun Saturday visit from her and Sophie. Sophie hit it off with Sunny right from the beginning. It was fun to watch them together. Sunny is so fragile and requires some special care. Sophie seemed to know exactly how to be her friend. Sunny doesn't have a lot of friends her own age. So this visit was very special for her and for us. Thank you, Gabby and Sophie, for the lovely visit. Come again soon.

Juneau, I love the idea of the artist's apple tree, so much more convenient than the real thing. If you add names to the apples, it can be your family tree with roots and everything.

For the rest, keep on writing to me.

Willadene

November 5, 1980
Dear Ladies in Triplicate,

I have been called as a stake advisor to help establish a pilot program to meet the needs of the physically and mentally handi-
capped young adults in Cache Valley.

There are no words.

Willadene

ERIN

That fall Erin had more fun than she could ever remember having. She
was a part of a group, and she could always count on having something to do
over the weekends and on Monday nights. Being with the Harringtons and
Cory took precedence over visiting The Women on weekends, and days
went by when she didn't call them, either. It never occurred to her that they
would miss her company until Joanna called to see if everything was okay.

When Erin told Joanna what she had been doing, her mother said,
"You're spending a lot of time with this Cory Johnson. Are you serious about
him?"

"It's not like that, Mom," Erin said. "We're good friends, and we enjoy
doing things with Colleen and Steve. That's all."

"That seems like a lot of time to spend with a boy you're just friends
with." Joanna's pause was eloquent. "I don't want you to get hurt waiting for
something that might not happen."

An explosion of feelings wiped all of Erin's caution away. She said the
first thing that came to mind. "Why would you say that? I'm not you, and
Cory's not That Catholic Boy!" She had never before called her father that,
and it gave her surprising satisfaction to form the words.

"You're right," Joanna said softly. "I hope things turn out the way you
want them to."

Angie Dunmeyer, the senior stylist at Stefani's assigned to be her buddy,
was also curious about what Erin was up to. "You're always talking about this
Cory guy," Angie said to Erin one day when they had a break at the same
time. They were sitting at a picnic table under a tree at the edge of the parking lot, faces turned to the sun. Angie was dressed in black tights that made
her legs look even thinner and a colorful print top with wide sleeves.
"What's the deal? Do you two have a thing going?"

"Maybe," Erin said enigmatically.

"So tell!"

Erin described the dinners at the Johnsons', family home evenings and outings with the Harringtons, and long talks on the phone in the evening. She smiled as she spoke. Her life had never been so rich and full.

Angie snorted, unimpressed. "What's with dinner at his parents' house and this family home evening thing with friends? Don't you two ever go on a real date?"

A real date? The words shocked Erin into reality. She'd been pretending that the times she was with Cory were dates, but they weren't really. Even when the two of them met for lunch or went to a singles' event together, it was just as friends.

"Ah, baby girl, I didn't mean to make you feel bad." Angie scooted next to Erin and put her arm around her shoulder. "If you want this guy, you've got to put some romance in the quotient. Let him know how you feel about him. You know what I mean?"

"How do I do that?"

"Flirt, of course. Don't tell me you don't know how. I see you do it all the time with the boys here."

"But they're safe," Erin said. And wondered, Now what did that mean?

On Sunday in mid-November, the bishop asked every adult in the ward to fill out four generations of family group sheets. When Erin heard the word genealogy, she stiffened and stopped listening. What was the point? She wasn't going to fill out any family group sheet. Not now, not ever. She glanced at Cory to see how he was responding to what the bishop was saying. His head was bent, his eyes were closed, and he was breathing deeply.

He's asleep! she thought with relief. With any kind of luck, she could avoid the conversation about her family a little longer. She fervently hoped so. She didn't want to have to admit—even to herself—that she had lied to everyone around the table one Sunday when Skipp had asked her what her father did. Taken by surprise and feeling put on the spot, she did something she hadn't done since her gradeschool days. She had smiled and told them he was a dentist.

Cory might have slept through the bishop's talk, but Linda hadn't. As they were finishing a simple supper of shepherd's pie and salad, Linda said, "After hearing the bishop's talk today, I brought home some blank group sheets for us. I thought we could each fill one out tonight." She looked at Erin. "Unless you've already done yours."

"No," she said. "I'm not very interested in genealogy."

"Me, either," said Cory. "So we might as well get it over with. Mom's already put what we need on the game table."

Skipp rose. "You two go get started. I'll help Linda with the dishes."

In the family room Cory pulled out a chair for her and handed her an empty group sheet and pen. *Why not?* she thought. *I can at least fill in some of the blanks.*

She started with her own name and information and then went on to her mother's. When she came to the blank for the date of marriage, she stopped, the old bitterness welling up. There was nothing she could write in that space, and the only blank she could fill in for her father was the familiar yet mysterious name: Andrew J. McGee. She wrote the name in a quick, jabbing motion and then tossed down the pen with a deep sigh. "I'm done," she said.

Cory turned her sheet around and studied it. "You've still got blanks."

"No kidding."

"What about your father?" He glanced at her, and she could see that he was wondering why her last name wasn't also McGee. "You can at least fill in his date of birth, can't you?

"I could, if I knew it." She pushed her chair back from the table. She couldn't keep the irritation from her voice. "I told you I didn't want to do this. I'm going home."

"Erin, honey, wait."

She stopped stock still, her eyes searching his face. It was the first time he had used an endearment when addressing her. He surprised her again by pulling her into a hug that was distinctly not social. His arms were strong, the smell of his cologne and warm body a heady combination. "I'm sorry. I didn't mean to upset you."

"I'm not upset."

"Yes, you are. What is it?"

"Why do you want to know?"

"Because I care about you. A lot."

She had yearned to hear him say something like that, but now that he had, she felt trapped by her lie. Tilting her chin defiantly, she said, "My father got my mom pregnant, and he left her high and dry. I don't know anything about him, not where he lives and not what he does." Her voice was harsh in her ears as she added, "I made it up when I told you guys he was a dentist. Are you satisfied?"

"I'm sorry. I didn't know."

Mortified by the look of surprise and disappointment on his face, she picked up her purse and went to get her coat in the entryway closet. "Say good-bye to your mom and dad for me."

"Don't leave yet." He pulled her down onto the entryway bench. "Listen, I'm sorry you felt you had to lie about your dad. Whatever happened between him and your mom doesn't change who you are."

"Don't kid yourself. It changes everything."

He patted her on the back, as if comforting a child. "It must be hard, never knowing your father. Never hearing his voice."

His words conjured up a memory. "I heard it once. I think. When I was eleven, I was obsessed with finding him. I knew Mom and Grams wouldn't help me, so I called all the Andrew J. McGees in the St. Paul phone book."

"Why St. Paul?"

"Because Grams calls him That Catholic Boy from St. Paul."

"Were there a lot of listings?"

"Three. The first two, I got the phone slammed down in my ear. The last one, a man answered. When I said Joanna Larson was my mom and I was his daughter, he didn't hang up."

"What did he say?"

"Nothing for the longest time. Finally, he said it was probably better if we didn't talk. That was the end of that."

"You don't happen to remember the address of that Andrew McGee, do you?"

Erin's eyes narrowed. "Why do you want to know?"

"It's a clue. We can find him, if he's still alive. Dad has lots of contacts."

"You don't get it, do you?" Her voice was shrill. She jerked away from him and pulled on her coat. "I don't want to find him! I got over that a long time ago!"

"Okay, okay. I was just trying to help."

"No, you weren't. You were trying to make me do and feel what you thought was right. Fill out my group sheet. Care about some, some . . ." she sputtered, not wanting to swear in Cory's presence. "Some *sperm donor* who has never, ever cared about me." Against her will, she burst into tears.

"Ah, Erin. I'm so sorry." Cory embraced her tightly. "Don't you know how much you mean to me? I'd never do anything to knowingly hurt you." He kissed her forehead. "Will you forgive me? Please?"

She had thought it would be over between them when she admitted to her lie, and now here he was asking for her forgiveness. "Yes," she said, the word as soft as a sigh. She wrapped her arms around him and rested her head on his shoulder, heedless of the mess her mascara was making on his white Sunday shirt.

Not long after that, Colleen called Erin to ask a favor. "Can you watch EJ on Friday night? Steve and I haven't been out for the longest time. We need to be a couple again, not always a family."

Erin hesitated. "I don't know. Cory and I were thinking of having a video night at his parents' place."

"You're the only one I trust with EJ beside her grandmas, and neither of them can help me out. Besides, if all you guys are going to do is watch videos, you might was well do it here while babysitting. You'd have a lot more privacy here than with his parents in the next room."

"Hmmm. I'll think I'll ask him," Erin said, grinning.

To her surprise, Cory thought it was a great idea. "Steve's my best friend. If he needs a night out with his wife, that's the least I can do."

Erin figured he would plop himself on the couch and commandeer the remote control, but Cory surprised her again. After Steve and Colleen left on Friday night, he took over. He popped popcorn for them to enjoy while watching TV, he took phone messages, and he even helped Erin with EJ.

"I know why you agreed to this," Erin said as she settled down on the couch. "You like playing house."

"You got me." He sat down beside her and flipped through the TV channels until he found something they could both agree on. Then he put his feet up on the coffee table and reached into the bowl for a big handful of popcorn. "This is nice. Just like a couple of old married folk."

She smiled at him, wondering what he was thinking.

The second time Cory and Erin watched EJ, the Harringtons left in a flurry, with the kitchen a mess and EJ crying. "She's ready for her bottle," Colleen called over her shoulder as she hurried out to the car. "Don't worry about the kitchen, okay?"

Cory jiggled EJ in an attempt to comfort her while Erin warmed a bottle. When it was ready, Erin held it out. "Do you want to do the honors?"

"Why not?"

He sat down on the couch, and moments later, EJ's wails were replaced by sucking and smacking sounds. While Erin loaded the dishwasher and wiped the counters, Cory finished feeding EJ, changed her diaper, and then patted her back until she burped hugely.

"Success!" he crowed.

Erin started the dishwasher and came to sit beside him on the couch. "How do you know what to do for her?"

"I ask her, and she tells me."

"Really?"

"Yeah. Like this." He held EJ so they were face to face and let go with a stream of baby talk. EJ gooed and widened her eyes in response.

He can work his magic on babies, too, Erin thought. She was solemn when Cory came back from putting EJ in her playpen.

"What are you thinking?" he asked.

"That you will be a wonderful father. I'm amazed at how easy you are with EJ. I was scared to death the first time I had to take care of her alone."

He sat beside her and leaned back, crossing one leg over the other. "I have a knack, I guess." Then he grinned sheepishly. "Actually, I have had some experience. Some of the contacts I worked with in Phoenix had little kids. On some visits I spent as much time playing with them as I did teaching the gospel."

"How did your companion feel about that?"

"He was okay with it. When the kids were happy, the parents were more receptive."

"Ah."

"Do you want children?"

She looked briefly at him and then down to the bowl of popcorn. "I used to think I didn't, but taking care of EJ has made me a sucker for babies."

"Is that a yes?"

She flashed him a grin. "Um-hmm. How about you?"

"A houseful."

She guffawed. "Really! You'll have to talk that over with the bride, I think."

"Oh, I will."

His voice and his expression were intense, and she was suddenly afraid of the direction the conversation was taking. As much as she wanted more than friendship between them, the intimacy she longed for frightened her. She got up and walked over to the shelf of videos under the Harringtons' TV. "Let's see what they have here."

He stood behind her, looking over her shoulder as she read off the names of the videos. She felt his closeness as intensely as if he had touched her. She grabbed the closest tape and turned to show it to him. The movement brought them face-to-face. "How about this one? *Love Story* with

Ali McGraw and Ryan O'Neal. "It's sappy, I know, but it's Colleen's favorite."

"Romance isn't bad. I'm all for romance." He put the video in the player and started it while she went to check on EJ. When they sat down on the couch together, he draped his arm casually around her.

They had sat so before many times, but this time, there was something different. Erin experienced an acute awareness of where his body touched hers. She could hear her heart thumping, as her own body—without her agreement—relaxed into him. She shivered as she felt his warm breath on her ear, flushing with shame that her reaction to his nearness was so obvious. It didn't help that the movie was about a boy and a girl finding true love.

What is he thinking? What is he going to do next? she wondered. She sat so still, she was hardly breathing.

Her question was answered when his arm tightened around her shoulders. He turned her face toward him, and the tenderness she saw in his eyes thrilled and frightened her at the same time. He drew her to him, murmuring her name as he kissed her forehead and her temple and then left a trail of kisses on her cheek. When he finally found her lips with his, they were warm, soft, and insistent. Something in Erin told her to run, run! But her mouth opened slightly as she returned his kiss.

Sunday, November 16, 1980
Dear Ladies,

Regina stood at the top of her tower, watching as Reginald galloped toward her on his white steed.

"I've come to claim you," he cried. "Let down your hair, Rapunzel."

Regina ran her fingers through her short, red tresses. "Sorry. You've got the wrong tower."

Are you wondering why Regina and Reginald are showing up in this letter? Romance! For the longest time, Cory and I were just friends. My friend Angie said I wasn't letting him know I was open to a different kind of relationship. I didn't realize until then that I've been playing it safe, probably because I was scared of making a mistake like my mother did. I was almost ready to show him how I felt, when he beat me to it.

Ladies, Cory is one great kisser! He's also a romantic right down to his bones. If our romance were a novel, it would be one of the sweet ones, Deenie. No purple cover, no poultry parts.

I'm walking on cloud nine right now, but I'm also trying to keep my feet on the ground. There's nothing predictable about romance except in the books.

Love,
Erin

Chapter Ten

JUNEAU

Juneau realized in the next few weeks that the attitude of Mrs. Jarvis's class members had changed subtly since her parents had been there and spoken to them. Somehow her status had been ratcheted up a few notches. It was the first time she personally had been affected by their fame as authors of the *Pillar to Post* mystery series.

It gave her new respect for her parents, and she wished she'd taken the opportunity to learn more from them when she was young. But during those years it hadn't mattered to her that they were famous or that they knew their craft well. What had mattered was that they so often were not "there" for her when she needed them. She had frequently felt neglected, unheard. Even unseen.

That fit right in with the story idea she'd had in church. She wouldn't tell her own story directly, nor even little Jane's. She'd give it a shift, as she knew writers so often did, and people the story with characters fresh from her mind.

The plot came easily, once she got to thinking about it, and as she usually did, she managed to put in some humor. She typed it at the kitchen table. She had not moved her typewriter back to the little room after her parents left because that would make it doubly hard to give it up again. Besides, the room was all decorated now and ready for the baby, even though that event was still months away.

At class the week after she handed in the story, Juneau was nervous. Maybe it was frivolous. Maybe it didn't say what she'd intended, after all. What *had* she intended to say? She wasn't even sure of that.

She watched Mrs. Jarvis shuffle through the stack of manuscripts that had been turned in at the last class session. Here was the raw material from which she would extract the nugget of writing wisdom she would present to the class this week. Juneau alternately hoped her own offering would be picked and then prayed it wouldn't. Mrs. J pulled no punches. If your ego was too fragile to take honest criticism, you had no business being in her class.

With an expression that said she'd found what she was looking for, Mrs. J pulled a manuscript from the pile, and Juneau's heart thudded. She recognized her story, typed on the blank side of various colors of junk paper and old flyers from church. *Oh, be kind,* she cried silently. She wanted to slide down in her seat, run out to the rest room, disappear into thin air before Mrs. J and the class members pulled the feathers from her poor little bird. Wasn't that what her story was, a living thing, the creature of her mind as surely as the baby growing within her was the child of her body?

Oh, for Pete's sake, Juneau, she scolded herself. *It's just a dumb story.*

She settled back, trying for nonchalance so as not to reveal that it was her story. Mrs. J never identified the author until after a manuscript had been read, so the class would thankfully be judging her story without knowing that the daughter of the famous Paulsens had produced it.

"This story," Mrs. Jarvis said in her soft, deceptively benign voice, "will be the basis of tonight's discussion of theme."

Meaning what? That the story had no theme?

Mrs. J was big on theme. A story must be structured around a theme, she said. You can't write a story without knowing the theme, she said. The theme is the reason for a story's existence, she said.

Juneau shifted nervously, and the baby within her shifted, too, reminding her there were things more important than stories. Max, for instance. She'd named the little boy in the story Max in honor of the coming baby Max.

Mrs. J began to read: "Nobody worried much that Max didn't speak. He was only five and wouldn't have had a lot to say even if his seven older siblings and dozens of cousins hadn't taken up all the air time."

Juneau groaned silently. Somebody in the class would surely have something to say about such a large family. She should have cut that down to maybe four siblings. No, then Max wouldn't be so totally lost in the forest, so to speak.

Mrs. J read on, her voice revealing nothing. Occasionally there was a chuckle from the class and then a gasp when little Max tumbled out of the back of a pickup truck "full of more people than he could count," and nobody noticed he was gone. Juneau heard a ripple of worry from the class when the family got to their destination and Max wasn't there. Another chuckle when they drove back to find him, only he wasn't there, either, which caused one of the siblings to wail that maybe he was dead, to which the mother replied, "Hush. If he was dead, he'd still be here, wouldn't he?"

Then an outright laugh from the group when the sheriff showed up with an unhurt Max in his car, and one of the kids worried that maybe it was against the law to fall out of a truck. More laughter when the sheriff told how Max had talked nonstop ever since being picked up, "as if he'd never get another chance," and had revealed all the family secrets. An almost unheard sigh of relief when, with all siblings absolutely quiet, the mother asked Max if he was okay and how he felt, and he, after looking around and listening to the silence, grinned at all of them and said, "Thwell."

The class applauded when it was over. As soon as Mrs. Jarvis looked up from the manuscript, someone asked, "Who wrote that story?"

Mrs. J smiled. "Let's talk about it first. Do you see a theme?"

"Loud and clear," a man named Clyde said. "It's advocating population control."

"Can you put it into a sentence?" Mrs. Jarvis asked. She always made them state themes in the form of a sentence.

Clyde grinned. "It's way past time for population control."

A woman named Flory voiced the no that Juneau was saying to herself. "That's not at all what I got from it," Flory said. "To me it says little pitchers have big ears."

Mrs. J nodded approvingly. "Any other ideas?"

An older woman named Norma raised her hand. "What it says to me is that very often the one who most needs love is overlooked in the busy-ness of our lives."

"Bingo," said a male voice from the other side of the room.

Juneau listened to the answers with interest. She wasn't certain she'd had a theme in mind when she wrote the story and felt even less certain that a reader would be able to find one in her words.

Mrs. Jarvis nodded again. "Different people see different themes," she said, "but I think this is probably closer to what the author had in mind. Would you like to tell us, Juneau?"

All eyes turned toward Juneau, and she felt her face flame. "Yes," she said. "That's what I had in mind." Well, wasn't that the truth? She'd felt sorry for poor little inoffensive, unnoticed Jane and had transferred that feeling to fictional Max. Suddenly she felt a rush of love for the innocent little thing that rode there beneath her ribs, silent and uncomplaining. Before she had to say anything further about theme, the bell rang, signaling the end of the session.

Amidst the noise of people gathering their belongings to leave, several voices said, "Way to go, Juneau," and "Great story," and "You're going to sell that one, girl." Flory came over to hug her, and Clyde gave her a thumbs-up sign.

Above the commotion, Mrs. Jarvis called, "Juneau! Juneau! Can you stay for a few minutes?"

Juneau told Greg about it later, after she'd checked on the sleeping girls.

"Mrs. Jarvis said I've been doing some really good stuff and that I'm ready to submit to big-time markets," she said.

He looked up from where he sat at the small desk in the family room. "That's great, honey." She wasn't sure whether he was as interested in what she had to say as he was in the papers spread out in front of him. But he reached out to pull her close. "Happy for ya, babe. And how's my little Tiger doing?" He rubbed the bulge that was his "little Tiger."

"He's doing fine," Juneau said. "I can't wait to hold him in my arms. And pass him on to you when his diaper needs changing."

He grinned. "Your job," he said implacably.

Oh, sure, Juneau thought, and immediately she was back to seeing all the ways this baby was going to cut into her new interest—the classes, the hours at the typewriter, the quiet times when she just sat in contemplation.

Then the fictional Max wavered before her mind's eye, the one who needed love the most. She sighed. "It's going to be all right, Tiger," she reassured her baby-to-be.

Exactly a week later she miscarried.

She knew what was happening as soon as she felt the first pain. It was a good thing the girls were in school. She called Greg, but he was away from his desk. "Tell him to meet me at the hospital," she told the office secretary who'd answered the phone.

"Mrs. Caldwell, is something wrong?" The girl's voice was tense with concern.

"I'm not sure," Juneau said. "Just tell him to come, please."

Next she called Marisol next door to ask for a ride to the hospital. Marisol came immediately, solicitous and efficient. "Hang on," she said as she settled Juneau in the passenger seat and buckled the seat belt.

Juneau wasn't sure whether she meant to hang onto the baby, her nerves, or the car seat. It didn't matter. Why was she thinking of all these dumb things? *Oh, Lord,* she prayed silently as Marisol expertly navigated the freeway, *let this be just a false alarm. It's too soon. I want this baby.* As the pain increased, she settled for repeating *please, please, please* over and over in her mind. Until, at the hospital, there was no more reason to say anything at all.

The doctor was sympathetic. "I'm sorry, Juneau," he said.

She nodded numbly. This wasn't her own OB, who was out of town at the moment, but she was acquainted with him. He was LDS and lived in her stake. Dr. Timothy Hart. Brother Hart. She'd even worked with him on a stake fair the summer before.

She was blurry from whatever anesthesia they'd given her. Or from the guilt that numbed her senses. She'd wished this baby away. Not so much in recent weeks, no, not at all, but at first. Back when she'd first realized it was on the way. She'd even stated it in words, loud and clear, to Gabby and Erin and Willadene in Provo. The baby had heard and had honored her wishes.

She thought of a song an elderly lady in one of the wards they'd been in used to sing to her and Flint when she'd babysat them. Something titled "Babes in the Woods," a sad little dirge about two children who get lost in the woods and then lie down and die. "And when they were dead, the robins so red brought strawberry leaves and over them spread." She remembered those words, and the ending, "Poor babes in the woods, oh, poor little babes."

What would be spread over her lost baby?

"Was it a boy?" she asked.

Dr. Hart, somewhere behind a sheet that covered her elevated legs, answered. "Yes. A boy." He paused and then said, "It wasn't your fault, you know. Sometimes these things just happen."

She knew what had made it happen. "May I see him?" she asked.

"Maybe not," Dr. Hart said, and she didn't ask again.

He said she could go home, but not until she'd rested for a couple of hours. Greg came, his face drooping with concern for her and grief for little Max, who would never be. Marisol checked in, saying she'd gather up Misty and Nicole from school and take them home for a sleepover with her kids that night.

"Thanks, good friend," Juneau whispered. "What would I do without you?"

"Probably drive yourself to the hospital," Marisol said matter-of-factly. "Then rise from your bed of pain to hobble home and cook dinner. I know you strong Mormon women."

Juneau wanted to protest. It was Willadene, not her, who was that kind of strong Mormon woman. But she was too tired.

"You'll get through this, Juneau," Marisol said. "But right now, take it easy. Let me earn a star in my crown for helping you out." She kissed Juneau's cheek gently and was gone.

Juneau turned to Greg. "I'm so sorry." She wished she could tell him how sorry she was that she'd caused this to happen, but she'd never mentioned to him that at first she hadn't wanted the baby. She hadn't said anything to Marisol, either.

She wished she could tell Willadene. That's who she wanted to talk to.

Gabby and Erin, too. They had been there when she'd admitted she was upset about being pregnant. She wouldn't have to explain her guilt to them.

Maybe she'd write to them tonight.

Overcome by emotion, she clutched Greg's hand and sobbed for the first time since the pains had started.

WILLADENE

Sunday, November 23, 1980
Dear Ladies in Triplicate,

Great news! Thanks to Bert, the Rasmussen men have stepped up to the plate and finished the addition to our house (it's been in progress for twelve years, but that is a whole other story). Now the house and the garage meet, and we have a roomy gathering space and a guest room to boot. The new part of the house will get its test run this weekend. As part of my first assignment in my new calling, we are hosting a "Cooking Thanksgiving Dinner" Party for our special needs young adults. We've divided them in groups with parental help where needed. Each group in the stake will prepare part of the dinner. Sunny will be in the group I help, and we will cook two turkeys here.

The men will set up tables in the new family room, and my mother has volunteered to help with the table settings. She finds whatever reason she can to stay close to Sunny. Sunny has an enlarged heart along with a package of other congenital birth defects, and she is struggling more than usual in the colder weather.

The ward Shoebox no longer makes stops here. I've been busy with my new calling and keeping an eye out for the building inspectors, as well as hunting down treasures that can be redone to furnish the new part of the house. What with all of that, Roger being gone to the university three nights a week and me gone one other night, there just isn't time for reading romances. I could really use a good dose of my Ladies in Triplicate and a midnight read.

> Missing Adult Conversation,
> Yours in COBhood,
> Willadene

ERIN

As Thanksgiving approached, Erin found herself getting short-tempered and moody. She was putting in extra hours, and she was bone tired by the end of the day, wanting to do nothing more than go home, flop on the couch, and watch TV. She had no patience with Cory's upbeat attitude and need to be on the go.

"What's up with you?" Cory asked one night when she snapped at him for no reason. They were waiting for dessert after enjoying a wonderful meal at Leanne Chin's.

"Sorry. I'm not very good company this time of year. I'm sick and tired of picky customers, my feet hurt, and I'm suffering from PHS."

"PHS?"

"Pre-holiday stress. I'm not a great fan of either Thanksgiving or Christmas."

"Really? I love the holidays."

"That's a surprise." She didn't mean to sound so sarcastic, and she hastened to explain, "I would too, if I didn't have The Women to deal with. My mother and grandmother get into it every Christmas. They always promise me they won't, but they always do. It's tradition."

There was more than PHS bothering Erin. Rochelle's behavior had been changing ever since she started going out with a guy named Al. She came home in the wee hours of the night, spaced out and smelling of grass. She got up late and had missed at least one early appointment, resulting in an irate call from her salon. She was getting sloppy in her dress and house-keeping.

Most disconcerting, Erin sometimes had the feeling in the morning that Al was with Rochelle behind her closed bedroom door. Rochelle had agreed at the beginning that neither of them would bring a guy home, but Erin was certain that agreement was being broken. She could sense something icky in the air those times and could hardly wait to get out the door.

She was silent so long that Cory said, "There's something else on your mind. What is it?"

When she told him her suspicions about Rochelle and Al, he blew his stack. "You've got to get out of there as soon as possible. I never did like you living with her. Or in Uptown, for that matter."

"Good grief, Cory. I know I need to find a new roommate, but there's nothing wrong with Uptown."

"Except that it's where the hippies and potheads live."

"Hippies and potheads and a whole lot of ordinary people like me."

"Maybe, but I'd rather you lived in a better part of town."

"Why?"

The frown lines on his forehead softened. "Because I worry about you."

She smiled and touched his cheek. "Why?"

He dropped a kiss in the palm of her hand. "Because I love you."

She leaned over to kiss him across the table. Then she sighed. "I hate the idea of moving, especially when the weather's so nasty. 'Course, if I could find a place like Gabby Farnsworth's and roommates like Willadene and Juneau, I'd take it in a minute."

After her conversation with Cory, Erin knew she had to talk to Rochelle, but she kept putting it off. She hated confrontation. She was hoping to find an opening where she could slide in her concerns. She found it one evening in early December when she and Rochelle were home at the same time. Rochelle was cutting carrot sticks and complaining about an argument she'd had with her boss.

"Did you get into trouble when you missed that appointment last week?" asked Erin.

"It's not just that. He's getting on my case about everything these days. Drives me crazy."

Now's the time, Erin thought. "Maybe he's trying to help you,"

"Help me?" Rochelle set the knife down on the countertop with a clang. "What makes you think I need help?"

Erin shrugged, avoiding her gaze. "I don't know. It seems like you've changed since you started dating Al."

"If I have, what's it to you?"

"I'm worried about you. I don't think he's good for you."

"Thanks, but it's not your business."

"It is as long as I'm your roommate."

"That can change anytime." Rochelle's voice was cold. "I'm thinking about asking Al to move in."

Erin drew in a surprised breath. "When?"

"As soon as you move out."

Erin was stunned at the swiftness with which her situation was changing. She had known she needed to find a new place, but she wasn't ready to do it yet. "I'm not going anywhere until I've found a new place. I'm for sure not leaving until the end of the month."

Rochelle shrugged. "Don't wait too long."

On Saturday, Erin came home from work early to dress for a special evening. It had come up in conversation with Cory that she had never been to a performance of A *Christmas Carol* at the Guthrie Theater. He had immediately gone to the phone to purchase tickets for them. "Dress up," he had said. "And be ready around six. We'll go early enough to have supper there before the performance."

She put on a burgundy dress with hints of medieval styling and jewelry she had purchased at the Renaissance Fair. She was especially careful with her makeup and hair, going for a look that was dramatic without being overdone. Her efforts were rewarded when Cory gave a low whistle the moment he saw her.

From that moment on, it was the evening she had always dreamed about. She felt beautiful, Cory treated her like a queen, and the performance was delightful. Everything was perfect up until Cory opened the door to her apartment building late that night. The smell of pot was immediately obvious though faint, as were the sounds of murmured conversation and zither music. "Nice neighbors you have here," he said.

"This hasn't happened before." Erin's frown deepened as they climbed the stairs. "I think that music is coming from my place."

She dashed up the last steps and flung open the door to her apartment. People were everywhere, draped over the couch and chairs, sitting on the floor, huddled in the corners. Rochelle was standing in the kitchen doorway. Next to her stood a scruffy, skinny man with a ratty goatee. His arm was draped around her shoulder, and they were sharing a joint. Al.

"What's going on here?" Erin demanded.

Rochelle gave her a long, slow smile. "What does it look like? We're having a party."

"Who are these people?"

Al answered her question. "Friends of mine. You going to be a friend?" He held out a joint.

"Put that thing out!" Cory put a protective arm around Erin. She could tell he was furious.

"Who's the pretty boy?" asked Rochelle. "Do you mind sharing him?"

Now Erin was furious. "That's disgusting!" She turned to a couple sprawled on the couch. "The party's over. Time to leave."

The only movement they made was to look at Rochelle.

"Right on, Erin. Time to leave." Rochelle's grin was loopy, and her eyes glazed. "Only you're the one who's leaving. I'm kicking you out." She picked up a duffel bag and thrust it at Erin. "Here's some of your stuff. Come back tomorrow for the rest."

"You can't do that!"

"Sure, I can. I'm the one who signed the lease."

"We had an agreement. I'm not leaving."

"Erin." Cory gripped her arm tightly to get her attention. "Let's get out of here. You can come back for the rest of your things tomorrow."

"Listen to pretty boy," sneered Al. As they went out the door, he called, "Merry Chrissssstmas!"

Erin let Cory lead her down the stairs and out to the parking area. Halfway there she began to cry.

"Why are you crying?" Cory asked. "This isn't the best way to get you out of that place, but I'm glad it happened."

When she started for her battered Escort, saying she was going to drive home to St. Paul, he insisted she come home with him instead. "It's too late. The Women would have a heart attack if you pounded on the door at this time of night."

"I have a key," she protested. Then she realized that Grams would probably bean her with the rolling pin if she came in so late, thinking she was an intruder.

In the end, going to the Johnsons' was the best thing to do. Cory's mother got a bed ready in the guestroom and laid out a nightgown and robe in case there wasn't one in the duffel. She, Skipp, and Cory fussed over her, said family prayer with her, and tucked her in bed as if she were a child.

When she woke up in the morning, the memory of the night before seemed like a bad dream. But the wonderfully comfortable bed and lovely surroundings were real. She lay back down, burrowing into the soft pillows and warm comforter. She didn't want to get up yet, didn't want to disturb the wonderful feeling of peace and security. She closed her eyes and slept until a knock woke her up again.

She sat up in bed, pulling the covers up to her chin. "Come in," she called, suddenly embarrassed to have been in bed so long.

Cory and his parents all trooped into the room, Linda carrying a breakfast tray with eggs, toast, and juice. "Good morning, sleepyhead," she said brightly. She was always bright. It could be a little wearing at times, but on this morning, it was nice. "You had a good long sleep, didn't you?"

"The best I've ever had. What time is it?" Erin asked.

"Almost 1:00. We've already been to church, but we thought you needed sleep more than you needed a sermon. Here, have some breakfast, dear." She chuckled. "Or lunch, I should say."

Erin took the offered tray. "Thank you for letting me stay over. I can't believe what happened last night. I honestly didn't think Rochelle would pull something like that. We've gotten along great up to now."

"Do you have a contract with her?" asked Skipp.

"Not a written one. We didn't think it was necessary."

Skipp shook his head. "If you have any problems working things out, I'll do what I can to help."

"Thanks. We'll have it out when I go back this afternoon."

"You don't need to go back," Cory said. "I've already been over there. I woke up Rochelle, which she didn't appreciate, I can tell you. I had to step over potheads sacked out on the living room floor to get to your room, but I put all your things in boxes and brought them home. I even made her tell me what kitchen equipment was yours. If I missed anything, we can go back and get it later."

"What?" Erin's abrupt reaction sloshed orange juice from her glass. "Why would you do that when I didn't ask you to?"

"I'm sorry if I overstepped my bounds, but after what I saw, it never occurred to me that you would want to go back to that apartment."

"It's better than being out on the street. It won't be easy to find a place that I can afford. And I have to stay somewhere while I look."

"Stay here, if you want to," Skipp said. "For as long as you want to. Mother and I have had a soft spot in our hearts for you ever since you joined our ward. And since Cory's been bringing you for visits, we think of you as part of the family."

Erin looked at Cory with a startled expression.

"Don't worry," he said, grinning. "It's not a proposal."

Later that afternoon Erin left for Uptown. Her key still fit the lock of the apartment, which surprised her. The living room was a wreck but empty of the messy humanity that had filled it the night before. As she surveyed the destruction, Rochelle came out of the bedroom. She looked wiped out, with pasty skin, bleary eyes, and wild hair.

They eyed each other silently for a moment, and then Rochelle said, "Sorry about last night. You really moving out?"

"That wasn't my plan until you kicked me out."

"That was the pot talking. I didn't really mean it."

"How was I supposed to know?"

"I told that guy you sent over. I said you could bring your stuff back. Al's out of the picture. Jerk."

Erin regarded her silently, wondering if she could trust what Rochelle was saying.

Rochelle cleared her throat. She was twisting the bottom of her shirt in an anxious, repetitive movement. "Look, if I promise something like that will never happen again, will you stay?"

"As long as you're hanging out with Al and smoking pot, you can't promise."

"I told you, Al's gone."

"And the pot?"

Rochelle hesitated. "I can't promise I won't smoke a joint now and then."

"I guess that does it." Erin made a sweep through the bedroom, bathroom, and kitchen, looking for items Cory might have missed. She found only a few, which she put in her tote.

"Got it all?" asked Rochelle, still wringing her shirt.

"Except for what you owe me. I'm paid up until the end of the month. You owe me seventy-five bucks rent at least, plus my deposit."

"You'll have to wait until I get my paycheck."

"Don't even think about stiffing me on this," Erin said angrily. She left without a word of good-bye or a backward look, wondering why she had ever thought rooming with Rochelle was a good idea.

"Well, Erin, you've really got yourself in a mess," she muttered as she went down the stairs and out to her car. "No apartment, no security deposit, hardly any money in the bank, and you haven't even gone Christmas shopping. Wait until The Women hear about this."

Chapter Eleven

JUNEAU

Life had no guarantees, Juneau decided. Right when you thought you were heading for one place, one destination, it was apt to throw you a detour. It was like planning a trip to Hawaii, and packing and being all excited about it, but then suddenly finding yourself landing in Peoria. What did you do with all those clothes you'd packed for the sun and fun of Waikiki?

Now she wasn't going to Babyland. Her ticket had been altered. But Max stayed, not a reality, less than a memory, but *there*, something like a wisp of smoke that lingers after the fire is gone.

What was she to do with all the tiny shirts and nightgowns she'd brought out from dark closets and washed and stacked carefully in the white chest of drawers in Max's room? That's what they'd called the middle bedroom after her parents left. She and the girls had made such a cozy nursery out of the room. In preparation for the baby. Thank goodness the women in the ward hadn't given her a baby shower as they did for every new arrival.

In the end, she didn't move her typewriter back into the third bedroom. Instead, one day she told Nicole she could have the room, if she wanted.

"Really, Mom?" Nicole's eyes widened. "My very own? You mean to put my bed in and have all to myself?"

"Well," Juneau said, "you might have to share it with Philip Atwater every third night or so."

At present the dog was meticulous about dividing himself fairly between the girls' room and the one occupied by Greg and Juneau. One night with the girls, and the next with the parents. Juneau had the feeling that he preferred staying with the girls, who allowed him on one or the other of their beds, whereas in her and Greg's room he was confined to the floor. He'd probably be able to handle a three-way arrangement with added benefits.

"I don't mind, Mom," Nicole said quickly. "He can stay with me every night if he wants to. In Max's room." She paused, and some of the light that had pinked her cheeks dimmed briefly. "But what about your typewriter? And your desk and bookcase and filing cabinet and stuff? Aren't you going to put them back in there?"

Juneau shrugged. "What's wrong with where they are?" What, indeed? The typewriter on the kitchen counter and the other things in the garage? Never again in the cozy middle room, all handy and close by as she spent the days writing.

But what was the big deal? If Max had been born, she wouldn't have had the room anyway. So why not give it up now? Why not give up writing, too? Maybe she'd been sent to Peoria to do other things. If only she knew what.

"Besides," she told Nicole, "Daddy's going to build me a little room in the garage. As soon as he gets around to it." That round tuit again. She wondered where she might find one of those buttons to give to Greg.

Then again, why bother? It didn't matter that he was slow to get started on the project. If she wasn't going to write anymore, she didn't need a writing room.

She didn't go to Mrs. Jarvis's class the first week after the miscarriage, nor the second, nor the third. One day Mrs. J called.

"Juneau," she said, "are you all right?"

"Yes," Juneau said. Then, anticipating the next question, she said, "I don't think I'll be coming to class anymore."

There was a silence, and Juneau could almost see Mrs. J's eyebrows rising in consternation.

"Juneau?" she said. "Tell me about it."

Her voice was so kind, so concerned, that Juneau had a hard time not bursting into tears. And so she told about Max—but not all. Not the part about having wished the baby away.

"Juneau," Mrs. J said when she finished. "Take some time off, if you must. But then come back. You're one of my most promising students, and you're so close to selling. That Max story is saleable, Juneau. Have you sent it out?"

"I wouldn't know where to send it," Juneau said. She didn't say that she didn't want to send it out. How could she offer life to Max in a *story* when she'd done away with him in reality?

"Juneau, I want you to send the story to my agent. I'll call and tell him it's coming. If he can sell it, he'll probably offer to represent you for future stories. And books."

Juneau tried to put some enthusiasm in her voice when she said "Thank you," but she knew it came out dull and listless.

"Promise you'll send it to him?" Mrs. J was nothing if not persistent.

"Promise," Juneau said.

She did send it, but she didn't go back to class.

WILLADENE

December 20, 1980
Dear Ladies in Triplicate,

Today the house smells like oranges, just like my mother's did when I was little. Oranges made Christmas at our house. Mom would stick cloves in oranges to make pomanders to put in drawers and in the guest closet. There were always orange slices and cinnamon sticks to spice cider. There was orange zest for nut breads, steamed pudding, and fresh orange juice for Christmas Eve punch. She even put orange peel in her oatmeal coconut cookies. They were always my favorite.

This year I am making the clove-stuck oranges to take to my mother. Usually that is Sunny's job, but she has been sick for the last month and in the hospital for the last two weeks. The doctors have limited visits to family and close friends and only a few at a time. Sunny is really restless if she is left alone, so Mom is spending most of each day with her. If we are lucky we will have her home by Christmas Eve. But for now she has a room with a view of the snow-covered mountains and a tiny Christmas tree on her nightstand.

Despite Sunny's illness—or maybe even because of it—this has been a month-long Christmas celebration. I don't think there could be a party or a concert or a program that could fill our hearts with thoughts of Christmas more than have these acts of kindness. We all feel as though God has filled our lives with tender mercies.

There are two LDS elders who attend at the hospital for those who need priesthood blessings. They assisted my father in giving Sunny a blessing one evening and have been stopping by Sunny's room to sing her a Christmas carol before her nighttime meds. Sunny considers them her very own Christmas choir.

My sister-in-law Bert, home for the holidays, has quietly slipped into place as a backup mommy for me and has kept the household running smoothly and the children content. She stopped in at the hospital the other day with a soft baby-blue sweater with white snowflakes worked into it for Sunny.

Her actions endeared her to the whole family, especially me. She later confided that she is going to transfer to the Y and take summer school so she can get lots of religion classes in and be finished with her degree by the time she is twenty-one and can qualify to go on a mission.

Leila Jeffrey, an acquaintance of Mother Rasmussen's, gave Sunny a multicolored smiley face quilt she'd been making for her granddaughter. And Gabby even made the trip to the Logan hospital twice through the snow with Sophie in tow.

Sunny loved their visits. That they would brave the weather and Sardine Canyon this time of year to cheer up Sunny has warmed my heart and opened my eyes. There's a lot more to COBhood, ladies, than being crusty and wise. There is the giving of self and doing it selflessly without any expectation of reward. Gabby, you have been a blessing. Sophie, too.

What were the chances that we would meet when we did and mean so much to each other so quickly? It has strengthened my belief that our Heavenly Father always has us within his sight.

If there is any wishing on stars this Christmas season, I'm going to slip a little extra one in that we can all get together soon.

I'm with Tiny Tim. May God Bless Us, Every One.

> Love,
> Willadene

ERIN

Erin thought The Women were glad to have her back home, but she had to content herself with small expressions of welcome and love—the inevitable Christmas depression was upon them. It had always been this way. Even as a child, Erin had realized that although her home had the trappings of a celebration, the spirit of celebration was missing.

Thank heaven for holiday specials on TV, she thought as the day approached. Specials kept her grandmother going the month of December. "Borrowing Christmas cheer," was the way Ruth put it. Except for *It's a Wonderful Life.* That holiday favorite was poison to Grams.

On Christmas Eve, Erin pushed her Escort unmercifully, weaving in and out through traffic. She wanted to get home in time for them all to go to the eight o'clock service at the neighborhood church of her childhood. She was looking forward to it; those services had seemed like magic to her when she was a girl. She had been awestruck by the lighted Christmas trees so tall the stars on top almost touched the peaked ceiling of the foyer and the pageantry of the processions to organ music so loud she could feel the vibrations through the soles of her shoes. Just thinking about it on the way home brought a smile to her face. She burst through the front door hollering, "I'm here. Just give me a minute, and I'll be ready."

"Are you sure you want to go?" Grams called up the stairs after her. "Being a Mormon and all?"

Erin turned with a grin. "Why wouldn't I? Mormons believe in Christ. Besides, it's a Larson family tradition."

A half hour later, they started out, bundled up against the cold of a clear night. The sidewalk hadn't been shoveled since the last snow, so they walked in the street most of the way to the church, elbows interlocked to help them keep their balance on the icy surface.

It was an unaccountably sweet moment for Erin, arms tucked tightly against her mother on one side, her grandmother on the other. They giggled like girls as they negotiated the icy patches, calling greetings to others converging on the brightly lit church for the Nine Lessons and Carols service. She was moved by the service, especially when the audience was asked to join in singing her favorite Christmas hymn not found in the LDS hymnbook, "Come, Thou Long Expected Jesus." Her heart brimming, she leaned over to kiss the cheeks of her mom and grandmother. The tenderness she felt lasted through the evening. It was nothing short of miraculous to Erin, and she knew The Women felt it too.

When Erin awoke in the morning, she immediately knew something had changed. There was a certain quality in the silence that made her shiver and draw the covers up around her neck. She knew what that silence meant. The night before, she had dared to hope they might make it through Christmas Day without the usual holiday upset. Now she knew they wouldn't. The only question was how long would it take Grams to blow and what would set her off.

When she finally gathered the courage to go downstairs, The Women were already in the kitchen, coffee cups in hand. She greeted them with tentative hugs and then poured some orange juice. "Anybody want toast?" she asked.

Neither one did, so Erin fixed some for herself and joined them at the table. She was trying to be cheerful and positive, but the atmosphere made the back of her neck crawl. They were all too careful with each other as they ate breakfast. Too cheerful as they went about making the dressing and getting the turkey in the oven. Too effusive in their thanks for the gifts they exchanged. And too precise when they folded the wrapping paper so it could be used another year. It was as if they were all on the edge of a major migraine, fearful that any fast movement or sharp tone would set it off.

When the doorbell rang, Erin felt it like a shock through her body. She opened the door to see Cory, arms laden with gifts. "Merry Christmas!" he said heartily.

"Cory! What are you doing here?" She was paralyzed, not knowing whether to invite him in or join him on the steps. It was Christmas morning, and one just didn't barge in without notice. Especially not on Grams, who tended to regard Cory with suspicion. He had used all his charms on The Women when they had gone to dinner at his invitation, but Grams had remained determinedly unimpressed.

Now Grams surprised her by saying, "Don't just stand there. Invite him in."

Erin grinned, realizing that for Grams, having the neighbors see a handsome young man standing on their doorstep bearing gifts was worse than having their morning interrupted. She stepped back and waved Cory in.

"Merry Christmas, Mrs. Larson," he said to Ruth. "I hope you don't mind me intruding on your celebration, but I wanted to make sure Erin got her presents on Christmas. I'm a last-minute shopper," he added apologetically. He handed Ruth the gift basket. "This is for you and Joanna. It's from me and my parents."

Grams hefted it and peered through the amber cellophane. "Looks like it could feed a family for a week. Thank you. And thank your parents for us."

"And these are for you," he said to Erin, handing over two beautifully wrapped packages.

Erin stroked the rich foil wrapping paper. "Gosh, they're so pretty, I'm not sure I want to unwrap them."

"I didn't wrap them. I'm all thumbs," he said with a self-deprecating smile. "That's Mom's touch." At Joanna's invitation to take a seat, he plopped himself down in the old leather chair that had been her grandfather's favorite place to smoke while reading the paper. Erin nearly gasped aloud. It was another chair that had been only rarely used since his death. She held her breath, but Grams simply sat down on the couch facing Cory and asked, "How was your Christmas Eve?"

Erin didn't hear a word of his response. Her ears were buzzing, and her cheeks felt too hot. Why did he have to sit in that chair! Why did he have to talk so loud? Why was he so oblivious to the strained atmosphere? She wanted nothing more than to get him out the door, but he was clearly in no hurry.

When she finally had the opportunity, she handed him his present. He unceremoniously tore off the wrapping paper, dropping it on the floor next to the paper Erin and The Women had folded carefully. "A backpack!" he cried, holding it up so the women could see it. "Just the kind I like, with tons of zippers and compartments." He gave her a brilliant smile. "I'll use it every day and think of you."

She could feel his desire to pull her into his arms and thank her with a kiss. She deflected it by opening her own presents: a red cashmere cardigan and an illustrated book on fashions of the 40s.

"Do you like them?" he asked. "I tried to think of what you'd really want."

"I love them. They're perfect." Her eyes stung, and her heart was brimming, but she held back her emotions. It wouldn't do for The Women to see how much these gifts, so perfectly chosen, meant to her. The warm fleece bathrobe from Grams and the gift certificate to Musicland from her mother were appreciated but predictable and practical. These presents were neither.

"Oh, my," said Grams, running her fingers over the soft cashmere. "How luxurious."

"Why don't you go put it on?" suggested Joanna.

Erin went up to her room two steps at a time and pulled on a long black skirt and then the silky soft sweater. It was like nothing she had ever worn before. She walked down the stairs to the living room with dramatic slow-ness. At the landing, she turned around once with what she thought was model grace.

"Wow," Cory said. Admiration—and more—was plain on his face. The Women exchanged glances and then looked at Erin, their thoughts also plain to read. "Watch out," their expressions said. "Be careful. Don't do anything you'll regret."

So she walked right into his arms and thanked him with the kiss he had wanted earlier.

After Cory left, Grams stopped Erin in the middle of the living room. "What haven't you been telling us?"

"What do you mean?"

"How involved are you with that boy?"

What Erin heard was "That Mormon Boy," said with the same intonation Grams used when saying "That Catholic Boy." She gripped her hands together to help control her sudden flash of anger. "If you're asking whether we're sleeping together, the answer is no."

Grams's expression lightened. "Well. That's good." She patted Erin's shoulder and strode briskly toward the kitchen. "Let's get dinner on the table."

The blowup came that evening. As Grams was flicking through stations, she came across *It's a Wonderful Life.*

Oh, no! thought Erin. In the movie, Jimmy Stewart's character, George Bailey, gives up his dreams and desires to do what he feels he has to do, which seems to lead only to despair and hopelessness. Grams had always identified strongly with Bailey in that part, but she never made the shift with him to discovering the meaning and blessing of his sacrifices. For her, there never was a happy ending.

Erin and Joanna exchanged despairing glances as Grams settled in to watch. "You've seen this one so many times, Mom. Why don't we find something else?" asked Joanna.

Grams's chin rose in determination. "I like it. It's a good reality check."

"Yes, it is." Joanna's voice was bright. "It makes you grateful for all you have, doesn't it?"

"Makes me think how much I've given up for others." Grams's eyes roamed the room, and Erin knew Ruth wasn't seeing the walls Joanna had recently painted, the valances she had sewn and installed, or even the Christmas decorations. She was seeing the worn furniture (which she refused to let Joanna replace), the outdated carpet, and years of unhappiness.

"We've done pretty well, Momma," said Joanna. "We have a roof over our head, two cars, enough food to eat. And we've done a good job of raising Erin." She flashed Erin a hopeful smile.

"We've survived, is what you're saying. That's not saying much."

"That's not what I'm saying. I really do believe we have a lot to be thankful for. Each other. Friends. Good neighbors we've known for years, like the ones at church last night."

"They're not friends; they're gossips." Ruth's voice was bitter. "They're always looking for something juicy to talk about."

Joanna sighed. "Well, then. It's good we don't have anything for them to gossip about."

"Nothing to gossip about? Hah! Don't pretend you don't know what they've been talking about for the past twenty-two years." Ruth's eyes flicked quickly in Erin's direction and then back to Joanna.

"Don't say that. Please," Joanna said quietly.

"It could have been different." Ruth's voice rose. She pointed at the large chair. "Your father could have been sitting right there today instead of Mr. Cory Ain't-Life-Grand Johnson."

"You don't know that for sure. Dad had been having health problems for a long time before he died."

"I beg your pardon. I know exactly what broke your father's heart, and so do you. If you and that boy hadn't put your own pleasure before the honor of your families . . ."

"I should think that after all this time you'd give up on that old story, Mother. Andrew and I were just kids. We made a mistake. And we've both paid for it, believe me. So has Erin, and she's the one innocent in this whole business." Joanna paused. "If you didn't want me and Erin here, you should have let Andy and me try to work it out."

"And have you living with a Catholic and raising your child Catholic? That would have killed your father!"

"Would you rather I had had an abortion?"

Grams shook her index finger in Joanna's face. "How can you say such a thing? That would have killed your . . ."

"Stop!" Erin cried. The mention of abortion brought up all the emotions that had flared when Juneau had said she didn't want her baby. "Stop, both of you!"

The Women turned to face her, shocked into silence.

"Have you ever thought about what listening to the two of you go at it does to me? It makes me feel like I'm a mistake. Like every breath I take steals something from you. Do you really hate me that much?"

"Oh, Erin, honey!" Joanna reached for her, but Erin flung her hand away.

"Colleen keeps asking me why I put up with these, these . . . fits of yours, and I keep telling her I hope that someday it will be different. I want to love you. I want you to love me, but now I think that will never happen."

"We do love you," Grams said.

"How can you think we don't?" Joanna added.

Memories of Willadene, Juneau, and Gabby around the kitchen table in Provo flashed in Erin's mind's eye, replaced by memories of Cory and his parents bringing her breakfast in bed, doing everything they could to make her comfortable and safe. She looked from her mother to her grandmother, feeling no pity for their fearful expressions.

"I've experienced lately what it's really like to be loved, and believe me, it's nothing like this. After Rochelle kicked me out, Cory's mom and dad invited me to stay in their guestroom until I could find an apartment. I'm going to take them up on their invitation."

"Erin . . ." Joanna pleaded.

"I didn't mean it," Ruth said at the same time.

"I don't believe either of you. If you really love me, you'll have to prove it."

Sunday, December 28, 1980
Hello, Ladies,

Merry Christmas and Bah! Humbug!

If I'm not in a holiday mood, I have good reason. I've been kicked out of my apartment, The Women had a huge fight Christmas Day, and I stomped out after telling them they had to prove that they love me. Lovely way to start the New Year, huh?

For now, I'm staying with Cory's folks. I thought about not telling The Women where I'm staying, but that was too mean. They seem relieved to know I'm okay. Maybe I do matter to them a little. Cory says I need to forgive them. He quoted the Lord's Prayer to me, of all things! "And forgive us our trespasses, as we forgive them that trespass against us."

I told him that's not the way I learned it. He said it's the *Book of Common Prayer* version, which he learned from a contact in Phoenix. Anyway, it got me thinking.

Juneau, if you were plotting this soap opera, what would happen next?

Missing you guys,
Erin

JUNEAU

Juneau had kept busy during the weeks before Christmas, repainting the middle room in the soft cream color Nicole had picked and making curtains from Nicole's choice of material. What she picked was not pink, as Juneau had expected because that was her favorite color, but blue, with cartoony drawings of children. "Max would like that," Nicole had said the day they'd gone to the fabric store.

So Max stayed on. Juneau took to thinking about him when she was alone in the house. Sometimes she sang to him, lullabies remembered from when Misty and Nicole were babies. She spent a lot of time in his room—in Nicole's room—lying on the bed, with Philip Atwater snuffling and snoring on the blue rug at its side. She liked it there. Sometimes she had a hard time rousing herself to prepare a snack for when the girls were coming home from school.

Greg noticed her behavior. "Are you okay, Juney?" he asked one day.

"Yes. Why do you ask?"

"Well," he said, "I never hear your typewriter clacking away any more. And you seem so kind of . . ." He hesitated, looking at her as if he hoped she would fill in the blank. When she didn't, he said, "Kind of spaced out."

When she still didn't offer any enlightenment, he grinned and said, "Maybe you're just hatching new stories."

She smiled. "Maybe."

They left it at that.

Misty and Nicole noticed, too. "Why don't you cook pancake animals on Saturday anymore?" Misty wanted to know. It was Nicole who made the right guess. "You're thinking about Max, aren't you?" she whispered one day. And when Juneau nodded, Nicole said, "Me, too."

That distressed Juneau. It was all right for *her* to wander around in never-never land, but Nicole should be thinking kid things. Then again, kids never quite knew where the boundary was between fact and fancy, so Juneau said nothing. She wished there were at least a grave they could visit to help them know Max was gone. But he had left nothing behind, except for the sad little wraith of almost-memory.

Then Christmas came rolling down the tracks, and Juneau knew she had to rise up or forever lie flattened on the landscape. So she went to Relief Society on the day the women were making felt Christmas stockings. She bought enough felt to make five—for Misty, Nicole, Greg, and herself, plus she planned to make a paw-shaped one for Philip Atwater. She didn't really feel up to doing them that day, so she brought the felt home and asked Misty and Nicole if they'd like to help by pasting on bright glitter and little plastic Santa faces.

Nicole counted how many they'd need. "Daddy, Mom, Misty, Nicole, Philip Atwater—" She stopped, looking up. "Where's Max's?" she asked. "We have to have one for Max."

"That's dumb, Nicole," declared Misty.

But was it? Couldn't you hang up a stocking for someone who had *almost* been part of your family?

By judicious cutting of the felt, Juneau made a small stocking for Max. Nicole cut the cartoony figures from leftover pieces of her curtain material and pasted them onto it. She glued glitter around the top to form the name. Max.

And so the stocking hung there on the mantel all through the holidays. Nicole bought a small red plastic truck one day and put it inside on Christmas Eve.

It was Juneau who suggested that they bury the stocking under the pomegranate tree in the backyard after Christmas was over. It was a pretty spot, especially in spring when it was graced with brilliant red blossoms. Max would have liked it.

Chapter Twelve
1981

JUNEAU

Juneau and her family had a ceremony for Max on New Year's Day. They folded the stocking, with the little truck inside, in layers of white tissue paper and laid it gently in a shoebox that Nicole decorated, again with figures from her curtains. Greg, not quite sure he approved of the whole thing, dug a hole. They sang Nicole's favorite Primary song, "I Am a Child of God," as they lowered the box into it. Philip Atwater barked a farewell, and it was done. They had somewhere to visit now, where they could remember Max.

It was soon afterward that Juneau noticed the door to Max's room had sprouted a new sign. It said, "Nicole's Room."

And so it was over. Max had not quite come and not quite gone. He no longer had a room assigned to him in their house, but now there was a big, spacious one in Juneau's heart, and she found herself retreating there more and more. It was then she realized how spaced out she was.

Somewhere during her college years she'd read a piece of literature that talked about somebody's soul being harrowed up. She thought of that phrase many times in the days following the miscarriage. She hadn't really known what it meant when she was twenty, but now she did. She knew what a harrow was and that its purpose was to break up the clods of dirt with all those six-inch-long spikes to make the ground smooth for planting seeds. There were days when she felt the bite of every one of those spikes. There were days when she knew the clods in her soul were being attacked because she hurt so much. There were days when she wondered what kind of bitter, noxious weeds were being planted in her soil.

"Depression," her doctor said. Not Dr. Timothy Hart, the obstetrician. *Brother* Hart. This one was Dr. Randall Reeves, an older man with an abundance of graying hair and a reassuring confidence about him. "I'll prescribe something for you, Juneau," he said. "We'll try Elavil to begin with."

"No," Juneau said. "No Elavil. I won't take it." She didn't tell him she wanted to suffer. *Deserved* to suffer.

But in the long run she took the Elavil because it was Misty, Nicole, and Greg who suffered. That was her fault, too, because she neglected them, sometimes even forgot they existed. Forgot that it was her job to keep them comfortable, fed, and clean.

Once she'd wanted more, wanted success as a writer. It seemed like a long time ago now that she'd sent off the story about the little boy nobody really saw until the day he was lost. How prophetic that story had been! But in real life she didn't get a second chance to really see the lost boy.

And so her thoughts carouseled around and around and around. On some days she wished for Willadene's calm, motherly presence with a fervor that, when it was spent, pushed her further into her depression. In the pits. She knew now what the pits were, where they were, what they looked like, how they smelled.

Greg tried his best to understand what she was going through. But he was a man. He'd never carried a child under his heart. And lost it.

There was a day when with great effort she pulled herself together enough to look for an envelope. She didn't know where things were any more. They skated away from their assigned places and reappeared somewhere else. But that day she located an envelope. On it she wrote "Willadene Rasmussen." She sat looking at it for a long time. She hadn't really talked yet about losing the baby. Not with Greg. Not with her parents, although she'd informed them about it. Not with Marisol. Not even with Dr. Randall Reeves. Now she yearned for Willadene's warmth and comfort.

Everybody needed a safe refuge like Willadene. Her *daughters* needed such a refuge. A mother. So that day, before she wrote the letter, she made graham cracker sandwiches with powdered sugar frosting dripping down the sides. They were sitting on the counter when the girls came home from school. Juneau was rewarded by hearing Nicole whisper, "Mom's back!" as she and Misty ate the offering with delight.

She didn't get to the letter again until that night when the girls were in bed. Greg was off to a bishopric meeting, so she didn't need to feel guilty about taking time away from anybody.

"Dear Willadene," she wrote before the ballpoint pen ran out of ink. Symbolic, that's what it was.

Well, she wasn't going to let that defeat her. Shifting over to her typewriter, she rolled in three sheets of paper with carbons. "Dear Willadene, Erin, and Gabby," she typed. "I lost Max." She wrote a long letter, including her thoughts about setting off for Hawaii and ending up in Peoria.

The responses came quickly. Erin called first, offering sincere words of consolation. Then Willadene. "I knew there was something wrong,"

Willadene said, "because you haven't written any Regina stuff lately. You need to come here to Wellsville for a visit sometime after the snow melts. How about May when the orchard is in full bloom. That's good for whatever ails you."

"I'll come," Juneau said simply. "Thank you, Willadene."

It was Gabby who, as usual, put things into order. "I'm sure you must have encountered Tennyson sometime in your college career," she said when she called.

"An entire semester," Juneau said.

"*Ulysses?*"

"Oh, yes."

"One of my favorite quotes is there," Gabby said. "'Tho' much is taken, much abides.' I can offer no better words, dear."

They were sufficient.

ERIN

January 15, 1981
Happy New Year!

Are you ready for the next installment in the Erin Larson saga? I have a new apartment, thanks to my buddy Angie. She lives in one of those places built on Lake Minnetonka as a summer cottage for city people, way back before the suburbs spread west and surrounded it. The cottage belonged to her grandfather, and it came first to her mother and then to her, lucky lady. There's an apartment over the detached garage that wasn't rented, so she offered it to me.

I'm so excited about it! It's got two small bedrooms, one teeny bathroom with fittings that remind me of the bathroom at Gabby's, and a huge great room with windows all the way around. In the summer when the trees are leafed out, I'll feel like I'm in a tree house. Now, all I see is gray lake and leafless branches. It makes me shiver, but I'm going to put up curtains first thing. (All Angie has up are blinds.)

The best thing is, it's furnished. In "early attic, late basement," according to Angie. I told her that's just my style. If I want to use my bedroom furniture (it's all I have), Norm, Angie's husband, will store what's in the apartment down in the garage. There's room for me to park my car inside, too!

The only negative I can see in the whole situation is the heating bill. Angie says it's horrendous in the winter, with all those windows, but there's a small Franklin stove that will keep me toasty if I want to use it. Norm cuts wood up north every year, so he has a big woodpile stacked against the side of the garage. Angie's giving me a discount on the rent for now, because I'm the only one nuts enough to move into a place that's all windows in the dead of winter!

The Women are relieved. They didn't like me staying at the Johnsons'. Cory thinks I've made a huge mistake because driving to and from work will be a pain, especially during the winter. The roads are two-lane only and crowded at rush hour. They're dangerous, too, because they snake around bays and inlets. He also pointed out that every time I go grocery shopping, I'll have to haul everything up a steep flight of stairs. And he's been lecturing me on the dangers of a wood stove!

He and Steve were great, though. They moved my stuff over last weekend, when it was zero degrees with minus fifteen wind chill. We stoked up the stove and made hot chocolate to toast my new place. I am so excited! Now, when clients ask me where I live, I can say, "On the lake!"

Love to you all. Don't make too many New Year's resolutions.

Erin

P.S. Juneau, I've thought about you and Max a lot lately. My visiting teacher is sure that babies who are stillborn or who die shortly after birth have spirits so evolved that they don't have to go through earth life. I don't know if that's true—who can know?— but I like to think it was true for Max. That way, his leaving was his choice and not for the reason you might be thinking.

WILLADENE

Bitsy's favorite Christmas present was the potty chair Santa had brought her. It had fancy little ducky handles and her name scrolled across the back. From Christmas Day on, she dragged it with her from room to room, and it sat in a place of honor at the foot of her bed at night. Deenie was delighted. She kept her daughter close by during the day, along with a bag of frosted animal crackers, Bitsy's favorite treat for a job well done. There were step stools at every sink in the house for the post-success handwashing ritual. Deenie could see the end of diapers in sight. *Glory hallelujah!* she thought when the number of emergency diapers dwindled to one. Bitsy started staying dry though the night, announcing to anyone who would listen, "I a big girl." After the first triumphant all-dry week Deenie wrote:

Dear Ladies,

Bitsy has taken to toilet training like a duck to water. The whole process fascinates her. In fact she owns it all, potty, treats and product! If anyone tries to empty the potty or flush the toilet without her present, she gets very upset. Grandma Rasmussen says she thinks Bitsy will be ready for the big potty in no time at all. We have had a pair of fancy panties hanging on a little hanger in her room as a reminder that when she stays dry a whole week she gets to wear them and get all dressed up and celebrate with Grandma NeVae and Aunt Bert. That is one Rasmussen family tradition I really like—The Fancy Panty Party. Bert will come up from the Y for the occasion. She and her mother will give Bitsy a Fancy Panty Princess outing. Sunny wants to join the group. She would be welcome, but she is still too frail to go out.

Carl turned eight in the middle of December and had his baptism interview with the bishop. We made all the plans for the baptism, but he insisted we wait until his Aunt Sunny could be there. Grandma NeVae was a bit upset. She had already planned big doings for afterward, and most of the Rasmussen clan had already been invited. But Grandpa Will calmed her down and reminded her that it is Carl's baptism and he should be able to have it the way he wants. Bless his everlovin' heart! So we are waiting until the weather warms a bit and Sunny is well enough to go out. We are hoping the end of April will suit.

Love,
Deenie

When Deenie learned about Baby Max, she was devastated. She mourned for the little boy as if she had already known him. Underneath her sorrow for Juneau was an ugly cloud of guilt. Should she have mentioned the danger she had felt for Juneau while they were at Gabby's? Would it have made a difference, or was it only a coincidence? She was filled with questions and had no one to give her the answers except her Aunt Stella, who was a nurse and midwife and swore by The Sight. She was the one person Deenie couldn't or wouldn't ask.

She finally decided there was nothing to be done about the past. But both Erin and Juneau had accepted her invitation to visit in May, and she was determined that nothing would be left undone that could uplift or comfort Juneau.

Deenie scoured the family attics and local secondhand stores for small bits and pieces that would turn the guest room and bath in the new addition into the perfect refuge. She cleaned and refurbished a looped oval rug she had rescued from a thrift shop. It was a warm cream color vined with faded pastel flowers that fit perfectly between the single beds. Her mother offered a rocking chair for the corner by the window, and her father revamped a set of old cherry oval mirrors to go over the painted dressers.

Bert suggested wrapped chocolates on the pillows like the ones in the hotels where she had stayed on her visit to England and fresh daisies to fill out the bouquets of garden flowers Deenie had in mind.

Deenie's calendar had each task written in at the date and time it needed to be done. She checked them off gleefully on days with Bert and more solemnly when she was alone and thinking only of Juneau. When the guest room was finished and the new towels for the bathroom were purchased, fluffed, and hung, Deenie cleaned house as she had never cleaned it before. Roger teased that if she could find a way to autoclave the whole property, she would. Deenie only laughed and pulled out her collection of cookbooks and began planning meals to cook and freeze beforehand and list ingredients for the meals she would cook fresh.

JUNEAU

Juneau was surprised when Greg invited her out for a Valentine's Day date.

"We'll go to dinner and a movie," he said. "Is there one you'd like to see?"

Juneau was pleased. Usually it was she who had to suggest a night out, and she hadn't done that since the loss of Max. "Yes, there are some good ones around right now," she said. "How about you? Did you have a particular one in mind?"

He shook his head. "Your pick. Where would you like to go to dinner?"

Juneau felt a prickle of annoyance. If he was asking for a date, why didn't he just tell her where they were going? On the other hand, he *had* brought up the subject. Wasn't that enough? Well, no, it wasn't. "I'll choose the movie; you pick the restaurant," she said.

"Okay."

She waited. "So?"

"So what?"

"So where will it be?"

He smirked. "I'm not going to tell."

"But," she objected, "how will I know how to dress?"

"Wear something nice," was all he would say.

The girls were excited about the pending date. Misty was pleased because Isobel, Marisol's fourteen-year-old daughter, would be coming to baby-sit. Isobel loved experimenting with hairstyles and makeup, and Misty was always a most willing model. Nicole was excited about the date itself.

"Wear your red dress, Mom," she said. "For Valentine's Day."

The "red" dress was actually maroon. And velvet. Juneau had bought it a couple of years before for a Christmas ball she and Greg had been invited to as a result of his serving on a city commission. It was too much for a dinner and movie date. But when she started to object, Nicole's face drooped so alarmingly that Juneau hurried to say she'd wear it.

On the night of the date, Nicole hovered over her. "You have to polish your fingernails, Mom," she said. "And your toenails, too."

"Toenails? Nobody's going to see *them*."

"They will if you wear your high-heeled black sandals," Nicole insisted.

"Nicky, honey, I can't wear high-heeled black sandals to a movie."

Nicole's eyebrows rose. "Why not?"

Why not indeed?

So Juneau polished her nails, both finger and toe, and put on her maroon velvet dress and high-heeled black sandals, hoping Greg would pick a restaurant a step up from Denny's.

He did. Juneau was excited when he stopped the car in front of the Hilton Hotel and signaled for valet parking. She saw a couple of heads turn as the two of them walked to the elevators. She giggled. "They think we're movie stars, dressed this way," she whispered to Greg.

He grinned down at her, tucking her left hand into the crook of his right arm. "Naw," he said. "Movie stars would be dressed in blue jeans and tank tops."

"Okay, you're right. They probably think we're Halloween leftovers." She was enjoying herself. She hadn't felt this lighthearted since before she'd lost Max. Greg looked great in his best dark blue "bishopric" suit and maroon tie, which matched her dress. His freshly shampooed blond hair had a slight wave to it, and his grin had a boyish charm that she hadn't seen for some time. At six feet tall, he was a good-looking man, and she felt proud to be at his side. Maybe, she thought, a woman needed a little glamour now and then to dispel the fixing-three-meals-a-day and scrubbing-the-bathroom blues.

The maître d' at the rooftop restaurant seated them at a table by the window where they could look out and see the sparkling city, with the towering San Gabriels behind. It was magical, sitting there in their fine clothes, being served by an attentive and good-natured waiter.

After they'd ordered—filet mignon with carmelized onions for Greg, duck à l'Orange with new potatoes and blanched asparagus for Juneau—she thought back to when she'd met him at the institute of religion at UCLA. She'd been attracted the first time she saw him in a Book of Mormon class. She hadn't been the only one who'd been interested. There'd been a girl named Felice, who'd had no reluctance about showing she liked him, unlike Juneau, who'd more or less hung back in the shadows. But Greg, who turned out to be almost as shy and studious as Juneau, had sought her out, probably because she was nonthreatening and nonaggressive, and he could pursue her rather than the other way around.

They'd dated for several months. Then one night he'd driven over to the Santa Monica beach where he'd proposed. She, with the stars over the ocean in her eyes, had accepted, foreseeing a future as magical as this night at the rooftop restaurant. She was more convinced of it when Greg had driven back along Santa Monica Boulevard so they could look at the Los Angeles Temple, where later they were married.

She'd been young and naïve at the time, and she knew it. But it was lovely to recapture that magic, even for just an hour or two, after twelve years of marriage.

"I love you, Greg," she said. "It was so sweet of you to suggest such an enchanted evening."

Across the table, he reached for her hand. "I love you, too, Juney. But

I'm not the only one you should thank. It was all Nicole's idea. She said we should have a Valentine's date, and I agreed."

So it hadn't been his romantic idea after all. Suddenly the magic dimmed. It was like swiping an eraser across a chalkboard full of beautiful poetry and leaving instead an expanse scribbled with Real Life, including frustrations and disappointments and the depression over Max.

Well, so what? she chided herself. *Who could live every day in the heady atmosphere of velvet maroon dresses and high-heeled black sandals?*

She looked out at the mountains, at Mount Wilson topped with its twinkling television towers endlessly broadcasting the fake, fictional lives of the sitcom and soap opera characters. Real Life was better than that. And a night out was a night out. Did it have to be a downer to know it hadn't been Greg's idea?

"Tell me about your project at the university," she said. "Your study of computers and artificial intelligence."

His gray-green eyes behind the black-rimmed glasses lit up even more than they had when she, coached by Nicole, had walked out into the living room in all her evening's finery. He leaned over the table, almost dipping his tie in his food. "Juney," he said, "things are going great. Just yesterday one of my students made a suggestion that was a giant leap forward." He stopped. "Hey, I sound like Neil Armstrong on the moon! But anyway, I'm excited not only about the suggestion but also because this guy, taught by me, was the one who made it."

Juneau knew how much he loved teaching. And how much he loved computers. And she knew he loved her, somewhere down the line. He was a good husband and a fine father to their girls. Who needed magic?

"So what movie are we going to?" Greg asked as they waited for dessert, which was called Decadent Chocolate Cake.

Juneau clapped her hand over her mouth. "I forgot to look in the *Times*, but I think *Chariots of Fire* may be on at the Hastings."

"It doesn't matter," Greg said. "We can drive around and look at the marquees. Or would you rather take a ride up Angeles Crest and stop somewhere with a view and I'll get fresh and kiss you?" He gave her a friendly leer.

"Sounds fun," she said. "But we'd probably get picked up by the somewhere-with-a-view police. Think what a scandal that would be for a distinguished professor doing research on artificial intelligence."

"I'd get fired, and we'd lose our home, and I'd have to get one of those 'Will Work for Food' signs."

The teasing went on until the Decadent Chocolate Cake came. It was sinfully good. As they left the hotel with a piece of the cake in a small cardboard restaurant box, Juneau suggested that they walk up to Colorado Boulevard and pick up some ice cream to go with the cake for the girls.

"That means we'll have to go right home," Greg said. "It would melt if we go to a movie."

"Didn't think of that. I guess I just wanted to reward Nicole for getting us out for this nice date."

"Let's go for it," Greg said, tucking her arm in his again. "The girls have been pretty cute lately. I kind of like their company." He looked down at her. "As well as yours."

So they went home. The girls were still up. After Isobel had been paid and gone home, they filled four dishes with ice cream and divided the sliver of Decadent Cake between Misty and Nicole.

"Was it fun?" Nicole asked as they ate. "Your date, I mean? Was it romantic?"

"It was," Juneau assured her. "We felt like movie stars."

When Juneau returned to the family room after seeing that both girls were in bed, she found Greg poring over the papers on his desk. She put the ice cream dishes in the sink and then lifted her typewriter from the counter to the kitchen table.

In her mind she saw the surface of a lake, smooth and undisturbed just after something has sunk down into it. A story formulated in her mind. She pulled up a chair and sat down, retreating to her own magical world of fiction.

ERIN

Sunday, February 8, 1981
Dear Ladies,

It is COLD in my apartment, especially when the wind comes howling in off the lake! I bought some cheapie thermal drapes for the windows. They look ugly as sin, but they help some. I turn down the thermostat when I'm gone, and I keep the wood stove going when I'm home. Norm hauls the wood up the stairs for me. He brings me birch to start the fire because it burns fast and oak to keep it going, because it's hard and burns slow and clean. So he says.

Cory comes over a lot. He doesn't invite me to his folks' place any more because he doesn't want me driving these roads at night. I'm not sure it's such a good idea for us to be alone here so much. Not that anything inappropriate happens, but just having him close when there's the possibility makes me nervous. I can hear Grams yelling to Mom about getting "carried away" and the conse- quences of premarital sex. It sounds really weird, but the phrase that keeps echoing in my head is, "The wages of sin is death." (Wherever did that come from, and how can I get it gone?)

Steve and Colleen came over the other night. I was worried about having it warm enough for EJ, so I cranked up the heat and loaded the Franklin stove. It was almost too warm! I fed them and Cory sloppy joes and coleslaw, and we played games and made s'mores, toasting the marshmallows over the fire. It was a lot of fun. (I feel like a pioneer when I stoke my stove, Willadene. It always makes me think of your ancestors. Such resourceful women.)

I was so glad to see EJ. I don't get to see her nearly as much as I used to, because now I have to drive the opposite direction to get home. I get to hold her at church, though. Angie can't understand why I spend so much time at church. (She thinks the three-hour schedule is nutzoid.) She's convinced it's only because I see Cory there. She's very curious about what's going on between us, espe- cially after the big red and white bouquet he had delivered to Stefani's for me.

Love,
Erin

Sunday, March 8, 1981
Hi, Ladies,

I'm really looking forward to visiting you and your family in Wellsville, Deenie! Thanks again for inviting us. It's a good thing the rent on my little apartment is so low. I've been able to save some money, so buying a ticket won't be a problem. I can't wait to see both of you!

Will Gabby be able to come up? I'd love to see her again, too.

March in Minnesota can be cold, especially when it rains. I still use the wood stove, because the damp cold really gets into my bones. When I reminded Angie of what she said about the rent going up in the spring, she just laughed and said the rent won't go up until Cory moves in! I told her Mormons don't believe in living together before marriage, and she said, "After you get married. And you will get married. I can read the signs." Sometimes, I think she has some gypsy in her. Maybe she's related to Starette, Juneau!

To be honest, Cory and I have talked some about marriage but only theoretically. It's been very interesting to hear what he thinks about money and children and stay-at-home moms. We got in a bit of an argument over what is meant by men being the head of the household. When I told him I don't think I'd ever do something just because my husband told me I should, he got upset. He said wives are supposed to take counsel from their husbands. I said, "How about husbands are supposed to counsel *with* their wives?"

Steve and Colleen have the kind of marriage Cory would like. It seems to me that Colleen always defers to what Steve says, even when she doesn't want to. I think if I had a marriage like that, I'd blow a gasket!

Looking forward to seeing you soon!

Love,
Erin

JUNEAU

March 10, 1981
Dear COBs,

I can't wait to see both of you in May. In the meantime, I feel a lot better just having it to look forward to. At least I'm able to function again. I was asked to write this year's road show, and it's been a blessing. I get to work with a dream team made up of Brother Waite, who used to be an actor; Sister Waite, who is a genius at costuming; Brother Martin, who can't read a note of music but can play absolutely anything on the piano in any key if you hum the tune to him; and Brother Hansen, who builds fantastic sets;

to say nothing of the most delightful group of kids anywhere. And guess what? The stake overall director is none other than Dr. Timothy Hart, he who helped me through the Max ordeal. I was a little embarrassed at the first planning meeting when he asked how I was. But doctors are used to seeing people in all kinds of conditions, so I'll get over it.

I was frantic when I was called to this job because I had no idea how to do it. I was in two road shows several years ago in wards where we happened to stay for a few months. But to create one? How?

Then I saw an ad in the *Los Angeles Times* about a sale of new but "as is" furniture. I knew I had a title! *As Is!* And the ideas began to come together. So now we're ready to begin rehearsals on a show about some girls who are doing a road show but don't have any boys to be in it! So they go to the Road Show Rent-A-Rama to get some. That lends itself to some great sets featuring shelves and cabinets holding costumes and kids. There are some really scruffy boys on display, but the storekeeper says the girls won't want them because they are As Is. Of course, through the action of the show, they become acceptable and all shined up for the finale.

One of the production numbers is a tap dance, and Misty asked if she could be one of the dancers. She's only ten, but our rules allow us to use younger kids. I'm so thrilled she wants to be in it because, as I've mentioned, she's been a bit withdrawn and sassy lately, and it's so good to see her really interested in something.

Looking forward to Wellsville,
Juneau

WILLADENE

April 8, 1981
Dear Ladies,

Carl's baptism was beautiful. Roger looked so handsome in his whites. He was so pleased to be baptizing his first child. Carl looked like an angel with a cowlick. I was so proud of my man and my son. The Rasmussens set the standard for all future baptisms with the feed they put on afterwards.

The Stowells and kin were invited too. The resulting mix was a very strange thing to see. The Rasmussens celebrate with food, games, and gifts. The Stowells, on the other hand, mark the occasion with a dinner and reverent conversation. Can we say oil and water?

Sunny was able to attend the baptism, for which we were all grateful, but not the celebration afterward. We took servings of all the different desserts over later in the day to tempt her sweet tooth, but she didn't seem interested. That frightened Mom and me. Dad always says that the only way Sunny would ever pass up a sweet is if she were asleep, and even then it's doubtful. We all hope warmer weather will cheer her up. I okayed it with Mom for Sunny to come and meet you, if she is up to it. That pleased her more than the sweets. I talk about you so often she feels like she knows you.

Juneau, she wanted me to tell you especially that she is sorry about Max and that if she gets to heaven first, she will take care of him.

Popcorn is starting to pop on the apricot trees in the orchard. Apple blossoms are on their way as well. We are all ready and waiting for your arrival with love.

Deenie

Chapter Thirteen

WILLADENE

The stove timer in the kitchen ticked down the final hours before the expected arrival of the other two COBettes. Deenie stood in the doorway of the guest room, consulting her list and silently approving all the extra touches she'd done to make the room welcoming. With a final smoothing of the patchwork quilts folded over the foot of each bed, a fluff of the pillows, and a tweak at the yellow and blue spring flowers gracing the dresser top, she considered the job well done.

Way to go, Deenie, she congratulated herself. The handmade chocolates, courtesy of the Bluebird Cafe in Logan, resting on the pillow shams pleased her. She was proud of the way the homestead looked, with its finally completed addition and "found" treasures, as Erin called previously owned purchases. Not puffed-up proud—oh, no, that wouldn't do at all—but gratefully-humbly-appreciatively proud that the old house finally felt as if it belonged to her and she to it.

The internal chaos that had plagued her the summer before had faded as Roger predicted it would. Her lists had become longer with the tasks surrounding completing the addition to the house and finding and refurbishing furnishings. But the structure of the job itself seemed to help her gain control of the wriggling threads of her life.

That's how she felt now as she finished preparations for the COBs' welcome luncheon. In control. Just like Great-Great-Grandmother Stowell had been in control of the team of horses she'd driven across the plains with one of the first companies of Saints to come to Utah. As if she held those reins herself, Deenie felt her hands clench. Whoa, she said silently, then wasn't sure whether she was addressing those phantom horses or herself.

Hurrying back to the kitchen, she surveyed it with pleasure. Numbered casseroles for the week filled the back porch freezer. Two quiches sat on the counter, ready to pop into the oven. There was a traditional one for the company and one made with hot dogs and cheap cheese, which the kids preferred.

The kids. They'd promised to be on their best behavior, Scout's honor, cross-my-heart-and-hope-to-die. And believe it or not, her mother had agreed to let Sunny spend one night while the COBs were there, the evening Gabby and Jonas were invited to dinner, which she was keeping a secret from Juneau and Erin.

She checked on the children in the family room, making sure they were still engrossed in the rarely allowed Saturday cartoons. She freshened her lipstick, put away her apron, and then opened the living room windows to let in the sweet spring breeze scented with apple blossoms and newly mown grass. That done, she picked a selection from the romance novel Shoebox that was hers for the week. Once the work on the addition and her preparations for the visit were well underway, she had allowed herself the indulgence of a romance novel now and then.

Book in hand, Deenie moved to the front porch where she sat down on her favorite lavender-painted wicker rocker. From where she sat, she could see across the street to the two square blocks that were the heart of Wellsville. There was the playground with the grass freshly groomed. The churchyard, tabernacle grounds, and beyond looked as if they had been dressed especially for her guests. Deenie loved living where she did, in the center of things. That's the way she liked it. Sinking gratefully into the rocker, she concentrated on forcing her fingers to unclench and waited for her friends to arrive.

JUNEAU

Juneau stared out the window as the airplane circled, preparing to land at the Salt Lake City airport. Down below, the city sparkled in the bright spring sunshine. Beyond it, the still snow-covered mountains towered, contrasting with the cerulean blue of the sky, a color seldom seen in Pasadena except on the loveliest sunlit days of winter when the hot-weather smog had abated.

Juneau's spirits lifted as the plane settled into its final approach. She was grateful to Willadene for inviting her to come to Wellsville. She was grateful, too, that Greg had seconded the motion and volunteered to man the home front until she returned, with the help of Marisol next door, who also urged her to go. "You need to get away," they both had said.

Greg had predicted that snow was a possibility in northern Utah in May and so had insisted she fly rather than drive, as she'd done the summer before. She hadn't objected. She didn't have the energy to object. Nor to drive all those miles. She was a different person from that independent, headstrong woman she'd been then. Different in that she'd fallen all the way into the pit that had been merely a lurking shadow when she'd gone to BYU Education Week seeking . . . what? She didn't remember.

What she did remember was Willadene and Erin and Gabby. They loomed like lighthouses in the darkness after Max.

Willadene had invited Erin to Wellsville, as well. Erin had written to both of them regarding her confusion about a guy named Cory. She needed some Willadene-brand advice, too. Maybe that apple orchard in bloom would do the trick for both of them.

Erin's plane from Minneapolis was due about half an hour after Juneau deplaned, giving her time to make arrangements for a rental car. She'd insisted on renting a car, even though Willadene had offered to drive to Salt Lake to pick them up. But Juneau had a claustrophobic feeling about spending a week in an unfamiliar place without an escape route. She needed a car. Just as she had last summer when she'd felt she had to get away from Gabby's.

Erin found her at the rental counter and greeted her with a big hug. *How young she looks,* thought Juneau. Young and every bit as flamboyant as she'd been the summer before in Provo. Her hair was still bright red, and she wore slim slacks and a collared shirt right out of a 1940s movie.

What could Erin possibly have in common with a married, stay-at-home, dull, depressed, thirty-five-year-old woman like her? Juneau wondered. *Erin is probably wondering that too,* she thought. They hadn't said much as they got into the rental car, a snappy little red Pontiac, after stowing their luggage in the trunk. And their conversation, as they got out onto I-15 North, was mostly, "So how have you been?"

"Fine."

"And how are the kids?"

"Growing fast."

It was as if they didn't even want to mention the serious stuff that had brought them there.

Then Erin asked about Philip Atwater.

"Well, he's fine, now," Juneau said. "He had to have stitches last week after an encounter with a nasty-tempered raccoon."

"Poor fella," Erin murmured. "Will he be all right?"

Juneau laughed. "You should have seen him yesterday. He was still a little draggy when I took him to the vet for the removal of the stitches. There was a tasty little female poodle in the waiting room, and that totally energized Mr. Atwater. He sat up, straightened his tie, lifted his ears, puffed out his chest, and was the picture of male pride and machismo."

Erin hooted. "Speaking of machismo, I was thinking on the plane about your adventure last summer. You know, when you went out for a Pepsi and met the handsome stranger at the cafe."

"Oh," Juneau said, "Jay wasn't all that macho. He was just a tired professor kind of guy."

"Aha, so you remember his name," Erin teased. "Maybe you'll see him again this year."

"Erin!" Juneau tried to sound shocked. "I'm quite happy with Greg, thank you very much. As much machismo as I can handle."

Erin laughed and leaned back into her seat, seeming to relax. "I wasn't suggesting anything," she said. "I was merely working up to saying I'd like to stop for a Pepsi."

"Sure." Juneau flashed a grin. "Maybe we could scare up a handsome stranger for *you*."

Erin grinned back. "I can only hope."

Juneau cleared her throat and intoned in a low, throbbing voice, "'*She'd been watching for him every day, in all the old familiar places . . .*'"

"'*That this heart of mine embraces,*'" Erin sang, "'*all day through.*' You're cheating, my friend. That isn't Regina; those words come from a World War II song. I know because Grams has a pile of seventy-eights she plays when she's cleaning house."

Juneau sniffed. "I plagiarize from only the very best sources."

Erin laughed and pointed ahead. "There's a Denny's." As Juneau turned off onto the exit, she said, "Let's see if 'he's' there."

He wasn't. They sipped their Pepsis, keeping an eye on the front door, but the only male they saw was a pimply-faced high school kid whose eyes slid quickly past them as he glanced around the dining room.

"*Regina knew she'd lost him,*" Erin whispered, "*when his eyes locked onto another girl, younger, prettier . . .*"

"*Richer,*" Juneau added. "*She knew then that she'd gone over the hill.*"

"*But that was all right,*" Erin went on, "*because she'd always wanted to travel.*"

They finished their Pepsis. Then, friendship back in place, they chatted pleasantly all the way to Wellsville.

Wellsville wasn't a city. Hardly even a town. It stretched out along the base of the western mountains in a cozy valley they entered after passing through a narrow but spectacular canyon. Juneau had the odd feeling that it was like reentry into the womb. A welcoming, safe place.

And there was Willadene, standing in front of the kind of house every weary, battered life traveler dreams of returning home to. *All is well,* Juneau thought. *All is well.*

The first order of business, after happy greetings, was a tour of Willadene's house and yard. Juneau's feeling of well-being increased with each step taken. The kitchen smelled as kitchens should, redolent of cinnamon and baking, with a firm foundation of something still in the oven. It could be a casserole, or it could be a haunch of beef. Juneau couldn't tell.

"It's quiche," Deenie said when Juneau asked about it.

Quiche. Something her mother might put in a novel but never in the oven of the Winnebago. Juneau and Flint had grown up on Hamburger Helper and any other quick-fix food that happened to be available in whatever city or town or village they might be in.

She herself had never made quiche. Too much trouble, she'd always told herself. And there in Deenie's fragrant kitchen, Juneau had the first of several realizations that would come to her on this trip. It was that she hadn't really given the white-picket-fence life a chance because she'd done very few of the things she'd accused her mother of not doing.

She wondered if Greg liked quiche. She was a little amazed that she'd been married to him for more than twelve years and she didn't know that. The subject had never come up. Why should it? Does quiche matter?

A good title for a story, Juneau decided. If she were still writing stories.

There seemed to be an unspoken agreement that they wouldn't talk until later about the problems that had brought Juneau and Erin there. In the meantime, they had a pleasant Sunday with church and a blue-ribbon pot roast dinner. That's the way Willadene did things. That's the way Juneau wanted to do things. She was glad now that she'd given up writing. From here on she'd concentrate instead on being a truly fine homemaker. She had Willadene as a model to follow. Pamela Paulsen, her mother, had never made any pretense of being a homemaker.

Juneau and Erin and Willadene had planned to get down to serious discussions right after breakfast, but the brilliant skies lured them into a bit of exploration. They walked around the beautiful old tabernacle across the road from Willadene's yard. Then Willadene took them over to Logan where they admired the temple and toured the campus of Utah State University where Old Main, oozing tradition, presided over Cache Valley. Juneau loved it all. It was the kind of place she'd always dreamed of having deep roots.

Willadene even took them to the Logan cemetery to show how many generations of her family, and Roger's too, were there. Juneau was fascinated by the clusters of family gravestones. "It must give you such a wonderful sense of permanence to know how many of your family and Roger's have walked this same land. No wonder you're so well-grounded, Willadene. No pun intended."

Willadene nodded. "It does give me a sense of permanence. Sometimes almost too much. Now and then I wonder what it might be like if we moved somewhere else, but I don't think we could survive away from all this. It tells us who and what we are."

"The ties that bind," Juneau said.

Erin murmured, "Tevya had it right when he sang about tradition."

Juneau knew Erin was speaking of the musical *Fiddler on the Roof.* She loved that show, the family feel of it, and the fact that even when the people were forced to leave the little town of Anatevka, they took their traditions with them.

"I have no traditions," she said. "No firm foundation. No ties that bind. Not to past generations, anyway. I've never visited an ancestor's grave. The only thing I have from my way past is a recipe for Danish rhubarb pudding that came from Great-Grandma Letitia."

"Well, that's *something*," Willadene commented.

Juneau thought briefly of Great-Grandmother Letitia's name on the tombstone over an empty grave and then went on. "I thought I had put down roots when I married Greg and had my girls. But then I got side-tracked with writing, and when I knew Max was coming along, I wished him away." She looked from Willadene to Erin, back to Willadene again, and all of the old unresolved feelings came sloshing up again.

Willadene put her arm around Juneau and led her over to a shady spot under a tree. "There's some nice shade here. Let's sit and talk a bit."

Juneau gazed around the cemetery. "Here?"

Willadene shrugged. "Hey, why not? We're in good company, and none of them is going to interrupt us."

The three of them sat on the grass, close to a crumbling tombstone that said, "Maren Larsen Petersen. Born February 22, 1853, Alborg, Denmark. Died July 8, 1919, Logan, Utah."

Willadene made a "gimme" gesture with her hands. "Okay, Juneau. Let's hear it."

Once Juneau started talking, it all poured out. She spoke of meeting Greg and being thrilled when she'd realized he was interested in her. She hadn't known if she loved him, but it was enough that he'd loved her. She'd wanted to settle down. Make babies. Send down roots—the old and persist-ent dream. So they'd gotten married, young and full of hope for the future.

"Just as a matter of curiosity, what were you majoring in?" Erin asked.

"I started out in human biology," Juneau said.

Erin raised her eyebrows. "Not English? Not writing?"

"The last thing I wanted to do," Juneau said, "was to be like my parents. But within six months I slid right into English lit as if it called me. I got into writing later, when I was going to take a cooking class at Pasadena City College. I thought every good Mormon mother should be able to cook up a storm. Besides, Greg recommended it." She paused to grin at the others. "But when I went to enroll, I spotted a writing class on the list and some-how ended up signing on for that. And fell right into the trap."

Now it was Willadene's turn to raise her eyebrows. "Trap?"

Juneau nodded. "Writing. Living in a world of fiction. Neglecting one's family." She paused. "Wishing away another baby because it would interfere with my writing schedule."

Erin leaned closer and put an arm around Juneau. "You've got to stop torturing yourself with that, Juneau. If a baby could be wished away, I wouldn't be here now."

Juneau pulled back. "But I did wish him away. I said flat out that I didn't want him. I'm guilty."

"Only of being human," Erin said. "You weren't planning on having a baby, but after you knew he was coming, you wanted him. I know you did."

Juneau swiped at her eyes with the back of her hand to discourage unwanted tears. "You're right, Erin. I did. Actually, after I got used to the idea, I pinned a lot of hopes on Max. Hopes that at last I'd find the stability and roots I'd yearned for, with another baby, and especially a boy. Who would carry on the name, you know. That was important to Greg." She took a deep breath. "It was a boy. But he turned out to be only a dream."

Willadene, who'd been gazing thoughtfully into the distance, said, "It's just about as hard to lose a dream as to lose a child, Juneau. You have a right to grieve."

"And to feel guilty," Juneau added.

Willadene shook her head. "Only for a purpose and to a point. You're taking way too much onto yourself."

"And what about forgiveness?" Erin said. "The principle of forgiveness was one of the things that attracted me so much to the gospel. If you believe in the gospel, you have to believe that God has forgiven you, even if you really weren't all that happy about the baby at first. And if He's forgiven you, you should forgive yourself."

Juneau sniffed back the tears that still threatened. "Never."

Abruptly Willadene stood up. "Listen to me, Juneau," she said. "Bad things happen. You lost Max. You don't have to take on the guilt of the world for it. Come with me."

Juneau put out her hand, and Willadene took it, pulling her to her feet. She allowed herself to be led to a tiny headstone with outlines of a lamb chiseled into it and a name. Bonnie Olsen. Age three years, two months. Died October 27, 1918.

There were other tiny headstones nearby. And a row of small ones, five of them, all from one family. Juneau saw that they had all died within two weeks of one another.

"Diphtheria," Willadene said. "My great-grandma knew the family. She said the mother turned away from the fifth coffin, saying, 'I have no tears left.'"

Juneau put a hand over her mouth. She couldn't speak.

"You see what I mean. Bad things happen in life, dear," Willadene said. "God doesn't want us to break down under a load of guilt because we're human and somewhere along the line maybe did or didn't do something we could have. Did that mother of five do all she could to prevent her little ones from contracting diphtheria? I don't know. But I doubt she had the luxury of collapsing from guilt after they were all dead. She had others to care for and bread to bake and quilts to make and gardens to grow. I know she went on, because several descendants of her later children still live here in the valley." Deenie gave Juneau a hard hug. "Sweetie, even Christ passed through the valley of the shadow of death, but he didn't buy a lot and build a house there, and neither should we."

Juneau was weeping now, her shoulders shaking with great sobs. Willadene's words made her think beyond her own small world. And Gabby's quote came back to her: "Tho' much is taken, much abides."

It was time for her to shape up. But she couldn't stop crying.

Willadene stepped forward, and so did Erin. They put their arms around her and let her weep out all the barbed things that had been harrowing her soul.

"Thank you," she said when she could. "This is the first time I've really been able to talk about this. Every time I'd bring it up to my ward friends someone would say, 'Sometimes miscarriages are just nature's way of taking care of a defective fetus,' or 'Just be glad you've got your two healthy girls.'

And Greg. All he said was, 'We'll have another baby.'" Juneau snuffled, and Willadene, always prepared, handed her a tissue. Juneau used it and then said, "All of that was meant to make me feel better, but it made me feel worse. As if Max didn't matter."

Willadene shook her head. "Max did matter. You know that. Even Nicole knows that. You wrote about how she hung up a stocking for him."

"Yes," Juneau said. "And we buried it on New Year's Day, under the pomegranate tree in the backyard. The memory of Max."

"So now you have roots there," Willadene said. "You've started a tradition."

Juneau had never thought of it in quite that way. "Thanks, Willadene," she said. "You get the COBette award of the day." She stretched. "You know, I feel so much better that if I were still ten years old, I'd leapfrog over that tombstone over there." She pointed at a stone that was just the right height.

"Go ahead," Erin said. "Do it. I double-dog-dare you."

Juneau laughed. "Oho," she said. "You don't know that you're talking to the double-dog-dare queen of the trailer parks!" Without another word she sized up the stone, squared off, and took a run at it, soaring over it with the ease of that long-ago ten-year-old—and then was totally embarrassed when she saw that an elderly couple strolling through the cemetery had stopped to stare.

Laughing, she and Erin and Willadene ran for the car.

When they were driving out the gate, Willadene said, "Juneau, didn't you say that your parents grew up in Idaho?"

"Yes. A little village named Mink Creek, just north of Preston."

"That's only about forty-five miles or so from here, at the upper end of Cache Valley. Want to go there? See if any of your family roots are still hanging around?"

"You mean right now?"

"Right now."

Juneau thought about actually standing on the soil where her ancestors had lived. Seeing Great-Grandma Letitia's empty grave. The idea intrigued her, but she'd had enough of graves for a while. She'd go to Mink Creek the next time she came this way. Right now she wanted to enjoy being ten years old again.

Chapter Fourteen

ERIN

Erin sat in the shade of an apple tree watching Juneau draw lazy circles in the water of the irrigation ditch with the bare toes of her right foot. On the other side of Juneau, Willadene lay back on the prickly orchard grass half-asleep.

It seemed to Erin as if she had been there in Wellsville for weeks rather than scant days. She had listened more, laughed more, hugged more, and cried more during those days than she had since being at Gabby's the summer before. Yet she hadn't told Juneau and Willadene about the things that were bothering her, with Cory's proposal on top of the list. In the face of Juneau's problem and Willadene's contentment, her concerns had seemed unimportant.

She wished she were back home with Colleen. She could tell Colleen everything that was on her mind without feeling so . . . young. That was how she felt, in spite of the amazing level of intimacy the three of them had reached as Juneau shared her deepest, rawest feelings. Young and inexperienced, as if she were a little girl tagging along after the big girls, who tolerated her presence with amused affection.

But the thing was, she *hadn't* told Colleen about her concerns. Instead she'd brought them along with her, trundling them along like so many pieces of baggage. Her left temple began to throb, and she pressed her thumb against it, hoping to forestall a full-blown headache.

"You okay?" asked Juneau. "You've been awfully quiet."

"I'm fine," Erin said. *Liar, liar, pants on fire*, a voice in her head accused.

Juneau playfully splashed some water toward Erin. "I don't know if you guys realize how much being here with you has meant to me. I was in real trouble until we talked the other day."

"And now?" asked Willadene.

"I feel so much better. For the first time in ages, I can sense a future out there that isn't all grief and guilt."

"And you got that just by being here?" asked Erin.

"By being here with the two of you," Juneau said.

"If I had known that Willadene and I could work such magic, I'd have

brought The Women in my suitcase. Between the two of them, they've suffered enough G & G for a whole ward of women."

"G & G?" asked Willadene.

"Grief and Guilt." Erin grinned. "I just made it up."

Juneau cocked her head in thought. "I'll have to figure out how to use
that in a story."

"Are you writing again?" Willadene asked.

"I mean, if I ever decide to write another story." Lowering her voice,
Juneau said, *"They stood there in the corral of the G & G Ranch. Regina
watched as he turned away and swung himself into the saddle. He leaned forward,
and she noted breathlessly how the crisp hair on his arms glinted in the sunlight.
Reaching for her hand, he said . . ."*

Juneau gestured to Erin, who said in a John Wayne voice, *"Coming with
me, little missie?"* Then she handed it off to Willadene.

Deenie clasped her hands in front of her like the heroine of a melo-
drama. *"She felt her yearning rise like bread dough left too long in the sun. Then
it collapsed as she realized that no matter how handsome Randy was,"* she paused
dramatically, *"you just didn't marry your brother."*

Erin fell against Juneau, clutching her sides as she laughed. Willadene
passed it on to Juneau, who had to catch her breath before saying in a little-
girl voice, *"Randy, darlin', Momma always wanted a fork in the family tree.
Forgive me, but I'm going to marry Uncle Jim."'*

After more laughter, Willadene said, "That's a little twisted but would
make for great drama."

Juneau nodded. "And drama, ladies, is what keeps the reader from being
bored. And me, too, I guess," she admitted sheepishly. "I've been indulging
in enough drama to fuel a jet plane. And ignoring what it did to everyone
else. Maybe that's why I liked writing. I could indulge in more drama without
having to live it."

"I should recommend writing to The Women," Erin said. "They've
made an art form of drama, and they don't seem to care a bit if it affects me."

"I kind of guessed that, from your letter after Christmas," Willadene
said.

Erin breathed in deeply and let out a long sigh, pressing her thumb on
her temple again.

"Okay, Erin. Spit it out," Juneau commanded. "You've been aching to
say something ever since you got here, but you've been shut up like a clam."

"I haven't either. I told you guys all about the Christmas blowout."

"Old news," said Juneau. "And you told it for laughs. There's something else."

"It's no big deal." Erin looked from Willadene to Juneau, laughing nervously. "I've just been wondering how you know you're in love and that getting married is the right thing to do."

"I knew it!" cried Willadene, clapping her hands. "Cory's asked you to marry him, hasn't he?"

Erin held up her hands to fend off the explosion of congratulations. "Wait a minute. I haven't said yes. I told him I had to talk to you first."

Juneau shook her head. "I hate to tell you, Erin honey, but that's not how it's done."

"Oh, I know how it's done," said Erin bitterly. "You pray, asking if marrying the guy is the right thing to do. You get the confirmation of the Spirit. And then you say yes and live happily ever after."

"What went wrong?" asked Willadene.

"I didn't get confirmation." Erin looked away from them, not wanting to meet their eyes. "I didn't get anything. No signs, no 'burning in the bosom,' no feeling of peace or rightness. Nothing. That's when I told Cory he'd have to wait for an answer until I talked to you. He doesn't understand why I would put the opinion of two people who have never met him before the opinion of God, but at least I can hear you guys."

"Wow. And you said this was no big deal," said Juneau.

"The worst of it is, I don't know if what I'm feeling is love. To tell the truth, I'm not sure I know what love is."

"Shades of Prince Charlie and Lady Di. Wasn't that awful what he said, when a reporter asked if he was in love?" She paused and then said in a nasal Eton accent, "'Whatever in love is.'"

"Poor Diana," said Willadene. "If Roger had said something like that, I would have run in the opposite direction."

Erin looked down at the grass she was twisting between her fingers. "I understand why he said that. I can't imagine life without Cory, but I'm not sure myself if what I'm feeling is love. I don't want to say yes if I don't know for sure that it's the right thing to do."

"Women get married all the time with a lot less going for them," said Juneau. "I don't think 'knowing for sure' before getting married is all that it's made out to be. It's how you live afterward that matters."

"Amen to that," said Willadene. Erin got to her feet and put an arm around the gnarly trunk of an apple tree. "How did you know Roger was the right one for you?" she asked Deenie.

"I didn't, not the way you think. I've known Roger all my life. He was my brother Jerry's best friend. They went on their missions at the same time, and when they got back, they went to Utah State together. When Jerry told him that my boyfriend had broken up with me right before senior prom, Roger said he'd go with me. Up until then, he'd thought of me as a pesky little sister and I'd thought of him as another big brother." Willadene paused, grinning broadly. "Until the first slow dance. Then everything changed."

Juneau laughed with delight. "Slow dancing can do that for you."

"Neither of us had a question after that. Sorry I can't come up with anything more spiritual, Erin."

How can that be? thought Erin. *What about love? What about fasting and prayer?* She turned a questioning gaze on Juneau, who shook her head ruefully.

"You heard my story when we were in the cemetery. I didn't have any revelation about Greg being the right one either, and I wasn't even sure I was in love with him when we got married."

"You don't love him?" Erin's voice revealed her shock.

"I didn't say that. Love sneaked up on me. I knew I loved him the day he blessed our first baby. When he held her up for the ward to see, I felt an amazing flood of warmth inside. I felt like the Grinch when his heart 'grew three sizes that day.' I try to remember that when things are tough and I'm wondering why I ever got married in the first place."

"You wonder even now?" The idyllic notion of Forever Families to which Erin had clung was taking a big hit.

"Sometimes. Marriage is no easy ride. It's hard work, with lots of ups and downs. I've fallen out of love with Greg a dozen times since we got married. So far, I've made it through the dry spells until I fall in love with him again. Knock on wood." Juneau tapped the trunk of the apple tree she was leaning against. "Things like that note about the spare tire when we were in Provo remind me of what a good man he is and how much he loves me."

"But what about the confirmation of the Spirit?" Erin asked.

"Listen, dear," said Juneau, "the Spirit isn't like a fairy godmother waving her wand, changing everything with a magic incantation. The real confirmation of the Spirit comes as couples live their commitment to each other and the gospel."

"That's true," Willadene said, nodding.

Erin sighed. "I guess was hoping for the fairy godmother version. I wanted to know for sure."

"Sometimes we don't get the handwriting on the wall," Juneau said. "Then we have to do what seems right at the time. We just throw ourselves off the cliff—so to speak—and pray on the way down."

"I guess I'll be doing a lot of praying, then," said Erin, "because what I do know for sure is that I'll regret it forever if I don't marry Cory."

Willadene smiled. "Sounds like love to me."

WILLADENE

Thursday morning over breakfast, Deenie said, "You've got a couple of choices for today. You can either go hiking up one of the canyons or horseback riding at the farm. Or you can just sit around and be lazy while I do a bit of catching up around the house. What do you think?"

"I vote for lazy," Juneau said.

Erin stretched her arms and yawned luxuriously. "Me, too, but I don't mind helping out a bit, if you'd like."

"That would be nice," said Deenie, who'd been hoping they would want to stay at the house. She was a little tired and didn't feel like hiking or horseback riding, but she would have gone with them because she didn't want to be left behind.

It turned out to be a lovely day. Deenie and Erin dusted and vacuumed the whole house, with breaks for hanging freshly washed clothes on the line. Juneau spent her time in the flower gardens, pulling weeds and deadheading early spring blooms that had faded.

During the afternoon Juneau did something surprising. "Erin," she said. "I've decided I want to go home a new woman, now that I've unloaded my guilt and other garbage. I'd like you to cut my hair, if you will."

"I will!" exclaimed Erin. "I'd love to."

Juneau looked delighted. "I don't even care what it costs. I just want to look different."

"Different it is," Erin said. "No charge. I'll do it just for the pleasure." She waved aside Juneau's objections and went to her room, bringing back a small leather packet containing her hairstyling tools, which she said she always carried with her. "For emergencies," she said.

Juneau nodded. "This qualifies."

Deenie ran for a towel to put around Juneau's shoulders and then stood back to watch the transformation. It was amazing. Erin was like an artist creating a painting. And Juneau did indeed look like a different person when Erin was finished. One moment she was a flower child with long flowing locks; the next she looked uptown, almost corporate, with the short neckline style Erin had expertly cut. The layers swirled as Juneau turned her head back and forth and then rested perfected, exactly where Erin intended. Deenie tried not to look as jealous as she felt.

"I owe you one," Juneau told Erin.

After dinner they all sprawled in the living room for a game night. Juneau played Go Fish with Bitsy, and Erin took on Carl for a mean game of Monopoly. Deenie smiled to herself as she saw how relaxed Erin and Juneau were. Each day, it seemed, had gone better than the day before.

When Deenie crawled into bed later that evening, she was exhausted but happy. She'd been able to hold everything together well. So far.

Roger tucked her under his arm so that her head rested on his shoulder. "Is it going as well as you hoped?" he asked.

"Yes. It's been wonderful. *You've* been wonderful, riding herd on the kids and playing backup." She kissed his scratchy cheek. "Thank you so much."

He hugged her close. "Are you all set for tomorrow's big surprise?"

"Sure am," she said.

She could tell he was proud of her. And, to tell the truth, she was proud of herself. So far her lists hadn't failed her.

Dinner the next night was a smashing success. The Ladies were as surprised and excited as she had hoped they would be at the arrival of Gabby and Jonas. Sunny was thrilled to be included, and Willadene was pleased that the color had returned to her cheeks. Even so, the girl appeared thin and fragile.

Everyone raved about the food, heaping compliments on Deenie, who told them that the recipe for the stuffed pork chops was from the Lion House cookbook and that the layered salad was her mother's own concoction.

"Time for dessert," she announced to groans of "I couldn't possibly" and "Where will I put it?"

Deenie laughed. "You'll find room. It's only a little puff pastry with homemade apple filling and fresh sweet cream from the dairy farm."

The groans turned to moans of pleasure.

Later that evening, while the men and The Ladies did the dishes, Deenie excused herself to settle the children and an overtired Sunny into bed.

"Thanks for helping with Bitsy and the boys," she said as she kissed her sister goodnight.

"I like to help," Sunny said. "It's fun. I like pretending to be a mother."

"You're a true second mother to my kids, sweet girl. I love you." Deenie turned out the light and closed the door, pausing for a moment as the old sadness filled her heart. She knew the only children Sunny would ever mother would be hers—Willadene's.

When she returned to the kitchen, it was abuzz with industry. The table had been cleared, food put away, and the dishwasher loaded. "What did I miss?" she asked. "Besides all the work."

"Nothing we couldn't say in front of the men." Gabby laughed, wiping her hands and folding a dishtowel over the edge of the sink. "We saved the good stuff for the ladies only." She grinned at Jonas and Roger. "So if you gentlemen will excuse us?"

Jonas shrugged good-naturedly. "I know when I'm not wanted. Roger, I'd like to see that new home office you mentioned building."

"My pleasure," Roger said, leading Jonas out.

"Take your time, gentlemen," Deenie teased as they passed and then turned to the women. "There are some soft chairs in the family room that are calling our names."

When they were settled, Deenie provided them all with afghans crocheted by the Stowell women. "It may be spring, but when the sun goes down, it's still cold in the mountains."

Juneau snuggled under hers and said, "Okay, let's get to the good stuff. What's new with the snow-on-the-roof-but-fire-in-the-furnace crowd, Gabby?"

"Not a thing, if you're asking about me and Jonas." Gabby put her feet on an ottoman and leaned back with her hands over her head. "We're just good and faithful friends."

Deenie noticed a bit of tension in Gabby's voice. "Besides you and Jonas, then."

Gabby shook her head. "Well, I am so blessedly vexed with Cecilia at the moment!"

"Cecilia," Erin said. "That's your daughter-in-law, right?"

"Right," Gabby said.

"Sophie is nearly thirteen now and coming of age. I know that Cecilia has told her the facts of life—as she says, it's her *duty*—but she's made it all so technical and sterile that she's taken all the joy and wonder out of becoming a woman. Sophie is embarrassed and self-conscious about it all."

"I know what that feels like," said Erin in an undertone. "When I first started to menstruate, all my grandmother said was, 'Well, I guess you'll be running off now and getting pregnant like your mother did.'"

"My Aunt Stell told me the facts of life," Deenie said. "She was practical and no-nonsense about the technical stuff, but she made becoming a woman and having children seem like a special gift and responsibility from God. Comes from being a Mormon midwife, I guess." For some reason her voice sounded faraway to her own ears. And kind of hollow. Odd, she thought.

Gabby nodded. "Too bad your Aunt Stell wasn't on hand for Sophie."

"What exactly did Cecilia say to her?" asked Juneau.

Deenie leaned forward to hear. Now it was the other voices that sounded faraway and hollow. And it seemed as if the lights were dimming. Deenie felt herself tipping off the chair.

"Willadene!" Gabby cried.

Willadene wasn't sure how she got onto the floor, but there she was. With several anxious faces hanging over her. One of them disappeared and then was back with more faces. Roger and Jonas.

Roger fell to his knees beside her. "Somebody call 911," he shouted.

"No!" Deenie said. "No! No 911." Her tongue felt too big for her mouth, but she was able to say the words.

"But you fainted," Roger said. "You're going to the hospital."

With great effort, Deenie raised her head. "Don't be silly," she said. "I fainted because I didn't take time to eat."

Roger looked up to the others and then back to Deenie. "Okay. I'll wait a while, but if you aren't feeling better, I'm calling."

"People faint," Willadene said, feeling embarrassed at having caused such a fuss. "It's no big deal. Help me back into the chair, please."

"I'll help you into bed," Roger said. "If you won't go to the hospital, that's where you belong. You're totally exhausted. You've been working too hard."

"And we've just gone ahead and let you do it," said Juneau, who was hunkered down beside Roger.

"I did what I wanted to do. Don't go hoisting a whole new batch of guilt onto your baggage cart," Willadene said.

Everybody laughed, sounding relieved.

"Well," Juneau said, "it's true. I think it was Robert Frost who said, 'The world is full of willing people, some willing to work, the rest willing to let them.'"

Gabby nodded in agreement. "Remember what it says in the Doctrine and Covenants: 'Do not run faster or labor more than you have strength.'"

"That was aimed at Joseph Smith when he was translating the Book of Mormon," Deenie objected.

"It was aimed at all of us," Gabby said implacably.

There were too many of them to resist. Deenie allowed herself to be helped upstairs and tucked into bed by her husband and good friends. Just before she fell asleep, she realized she never did hear what Cecilia had said to Sophie.

JUNEAU

Juneau was embarrassed that she and Erin had accepted all that Willadene had been doing for them without considering the toll it might be taking on her. She talked to Erin about it, and they decided that they would get up early and make breakfast for the family the next morning. That was the least they could do.

They had already fed Roger and the children and were cleaning up the kitchen when Willadene came downstairs. She bustled into the kitchen, saying she was sorry she had slept so long and she'd have breakfast ready in a jiffy.

"Not this morning, friend," Juneau said, leading Deenie to a chair. "Erin and I have already fed the troops, with Sunny's help. They've scattered to the four winds. All you have to do is have breakfast and rest some more."

"You sweet things," Deenie said. "I was going to do something spectacular for your last meal here, but I see you know spectacular, too."

"Right," Juneau chuckled. The food wasn't that spectacular, but Erin had run out to the orchard while Juneau cooked and brought back a bouquet of apple blossoms, which now graced the table in a pretty blue vase. And Juneau had put the scrambled eggs into a chafing dish she'd found in the cupboard, complete with a flickering flame from a can of Sterno underneath. The kids were impressed. It was a trick she sometimes used at home when the fare was uninspiringly plain. She'd make it memorable by the way she served it or with pretty dishes on the table.

Juneau enjoyed being able to do something for Deenie. She and Erin waited on her hand and foot, paying no attention to her protests. By the time Deenie was finished with breakfast, there wasn't much time left to visit before the two of them would need to load the car and head for Salt Lake.

"Did Gabby ever tell you what Cecelia said to Sophie?" Deenie asked.

"Nope," Erin said. "After the scare you gave us, we forgot to ask her about it. She and Jonas left not too long after you went to bed."

Willadene looked regretful. "Too bad. I really wanted to hear what Gabby is losing sleep about." She smiled. "I hope you didn't lose any sleep over *me*."

"Actually," Juneau said, "I did. I lost several hours thinking about you, and Erin, and me. And Gabby. We all have so much going on in our lives. So many threads. Makes me wonder how everything will work out."

"Me, too," Willadene confessed. "But I do know things tend to work out *somehow*."

"I'd like to know how our life stories progress," Juneau said. "How about we make a pact to get together in twenty-five years to see how we've all done?"

Erin's eyes widened. "Good grief, if we get together in twenty-five years, we'll all be *old*."

Juneau grinned. "We'll all be old then even if we *don't* get together. How about it? Are you guys up to having a reunion in the year 2005?"

"That's not twenty-five years; it's twenty-four," Willadene said, ever the practical one.

"I'm figuring from the time we met, in 1980," Juneau said. "Nice round numbers."

Erin frowned. "Are we going to have to become Blood Sisters to make a pact? I go wobbly at the sight of blood."

Juneau did a Regina pose. "*Regina gazed with fright at the small folding knife he pulled from his pocket. 'Do we have to do this?' she asked as he opened it up. 'Yes.' His eyes feasted on her full, red lips. 'We do if we want to be blood brothers. Blood sisters. Blood brother and sister,' he amended. 'Oh, but I faint at the sight of blood,' she cried. He pushed the point of the knife into his finger and watched as a bead of blood oozed out. 'So do I,' he murmured as he collapsed onto the floor.*"

They laughed together and then Erin said, "How about Spit Sisters? I could manage that."

"No need," Juneau said. "We can make The Pact with just hand contact."

She put out a hand. Erin and Willadene put theirs on top of it.

"Okay," Juneau said. "I don't really know how it's done, but this is the way Starette showed me back in that memorable year when I was ten."

Willadene looked curious. "What were you making a pact with her about?"

Juneau thought back. "I think I was promising I'd never tell who put the Doublemint in another girl's hair. I like this pact better. Now, repeat after me:

"'I'—say your name."

"I—say your name," Erin and Willadene said together, and the whole thing broke down in giggles, as if they were *all* ten years old. But The Pact was made.

Chapter Fifteen

JUNEAU

May 30, 1981
Dear Erin, Willadene, and Gabby,

I can't believe how much better I feel since I returned home after a few days of COB therapy. I'm a new woman! Literally, what with the short haircut and all. Greg was a bit dismayed by it since I've had long hair ever since he met me.

Regina approached the door with trepidation. What would he say when he saw that her long tresses were gone? Why had she had them shorn? He might not even recognize her! Then what? Would he turn her away and dash off to campus where he would approach the first long-haired coed, whimpering softly as he reached out to caress her long mane of golden curls?

If he did, it would be Regina's fault when he was fired from his job!

Actually, what Greg did was stare at me for a moment and then say, "I hope you weren't hurt too much." When I asked what he meant, he said, "You apparently had a losing encounter with a lawnmower." Oh, well.

Nicole wasn't sure she was happy about such a big change in her mom, but Misty loved it, especially when she saw the picture of the three of us that Roger took. She pointed at you, Erin, and said, "Can I have hair just like that?"

I said we could get it cut, if she wanted, but we couldn't do much about the color, which is blonder than mine. She was so excited that I took her to the beauty salon the next day for a cut. She kept asking for it shorter, shorter. Ended up with a cute pixie cut, which is very flattering.

The day after that she went over to her friend Capri's house and came home a fiery redhead. Seems she spent her allowance on a bottle of Lady Clairol. I tried not to be upset. I remember there was a scene in *Anne of Green Gables* in which Anne wants to change the color of her hair, so she and Diana do something or other that turns it green! So I've decided things could be worse and am just letting Misty enjoy her redheadhood. Greg, after muttering, "Now look what you've started," pretty much has let it go, too, so all is calm.

Lately, I've been wondering if Misty takes after Great-Grandma Letitia, the unknown quantity. Was it rebelliousness that took her out of Mink Creek? Is Misty taking after her, even though she never knew her? Stay tuned for further adventures of Letitia (if I ever find out anything more).

Thanks again, dear COBettes, for making my life interesting, and I mean that sincerely.

> Loving my short hair,
> Juneau

ERIN

Sunday, May 24, 1981
Hi, Ladies,

I had such a great time at your place, Willadene. You and Roger are really amazing. The way you support each other is great. What touched me the most was watching you two with your children. Lucky kids. They know they are loved.

I've never told you this before, but I don't know anything about my father except his name: Andrew J. McGee. My parents never married, and the extent of his involvement in my life was paying child support.

Cory knows about my situation. He's fascinated with it, for some reason. He's always on me to ask my mom for information about my father. What a laugh that is! All my life, my father has been the biggest part of what can't be talked about. I can't just walk up to Mom and say, "Tell me about Father." Okay, I can. I just don't want to.

Juneau, thanks for letting me cut your hair. You looked great! I'm so excited about the writing you're doing. Sharing it with us makes me feel like I'm part of the process. And I love the Regina shtick you do.

Regina cut her way through the underbrush with her trusty machete. She had to make it through to the other side. "Father, hang on! I'm coming!" she cried. From far off came a voice that chilled her to the bone. "Daughter, don't bother. I'm busy!"

Okay, I know it's corny, but it's the best I can do.

Love to you both and to your families,
Erin

On Memorial Day, Cory formally asked Erin to marry him. He got down on one knee and wooed her with promises that made her heart sing. Then he slid a one-third-carat diamond engagement ring onto her finger.

"I know you said you liked emeralds, but a good quality emerald is hard to come by. I wanted to get you something that was perfect." He tilted her hand in the light so the diamond caught fire. "This is perfect."

Erin gave him a fierce hug. "It is perfect."

The Johnsons were thrilled when Erin and Cory told them. She was officially welcomed into their family with hugs and kisses and toasts made with sparkling grape juice. "We knew he was going to ask you," Skipp said, "and we were 99 percent certain you would say yes, but it's nice to have it all settled."

The Women were split in their reaction. Joanna hugged them both, tears in her eyes. Grams held back, as if a joyful reaction would bring bad luck. "Aren't you glad for me?" Erin asked her when Joanna and Cory were busy talking.

"I hope you'll be happy," Grams said. "I hope That Mormon Boy will take care of you."

"Grams! When did Cory become That Mormon Boy?"

"Wasn't he always?" Ruth said.

"I . . . yes, I guess he was," Erin said soberly. Whatever the phrase meant to Grams, it was the truth.

When fellow stylist Angie saw the ring, she shrieked. "Oh, my gosh! Look at that. It's beautiful." She moved Erin's hand this way and that while she inspected the diamond. Then she gave a low whistle. "It's got it all—clarity, color, and cut. You hit the jackpot, baby."

Erin flushed with embarrassment, glad that the doors to the salon weren't yet open and few stylists were on the floor. "What do you know about diamonds?"

"A lot. When I was your age, I worked at Hudson's Jewelry downtown. I had to know what makes one diamond ordinary and another special. This is definitely a treasure, girl." She pursed her lips, thinking. "Did he pay for it, or did his parents?"

Erin jerked her hand away. "Why do you ask?"

"If I were you, I'd want to know if I was engaged to that Ken doll of yours or his parents."

"What did you call him?"

Angie had the grace to look embarrassed. "A Ken doll. Sorry, but he does look like one. Think of it. He's blond, blue-eyed, and handsome. And he's got this great body. Right? "

"I don't know if that's a compliment or not."

"Don't get me wrong. I'd be hot for him if I were single and your age. Just one thing. Don't let him turn you into a matching Barbie doll."

"What, me?" Erin laughed. "With my short red hair and flat chest, there's no way I'll ever look like Barbie."

Colleen and Steve were their biggest supporters. They had a wonderful dinner together, talking and laughing nonstop. Colleen kept grinning at Erin as if to say, See? Didn't I tell you? Ever the planner, Colleen purchased a whole pile of bridal magazines full of glossy photographs of weddings and receptions that were hugely extravagant. "You can get a lot of ideas from them," she assured Erin. "And there's always a checklist of things to take care of before the happy occasion."

"But we're getting married in the temple."

Colleen looked at her oddly. "You really are clueless as to what this will take, aren't you? You'll want to get reservations for supper the night before you go to the temple and make arrangements for the breakfast the next morning. And the reception here will be a very big deal."

"What do you mean?"

"Skipp and Linda know everybody. They'll have a huge guest list, not just ward members and your family."

"I can't afford something like that. I've been wondering how I'm going to manage a reception in the church cultural hall."

"The cultural hall?" Colleen shook her head. "Oh, honey, I don't think that idea is going to fly. You'd better talk to Cory and his parents."

"I'd better elope."

JUNEAU

Juneau lost no time in instituting the changes she meant to make in her life after returning from the visit to Willadene's. Remembering how the aroma of Deenie's kitchen had been so welcoming and comforting, she decided that the first area to address was food. As a child she'd always liked to watch the *Donna Reed Show* on TV and had wished for that kind of homey house to return to each day rather than the crowded Airstream trailer her family had lived in at the time. It wasn't too late to create that kind of atmosphere, now that Deenie had shown her how it was done. That would help to quell her mysterious restlessness.

So on Monday after she returned, she baked cookies, timing them so they'd be coming out of the oven just as Misty and Nicole arrived home from school. Chocolate chip cookies, everybody's favorite. The smell would linger long enough for Greg to get a whiff, too, although by the time he came it would be overwhelmed by the smell of a roast finishing up in the oven, after a long, slow cook. They could sit down to dinner right away without questions of "When are we going to eat?" She would preside over it all in a crisp cotton housedress and apron, a la Donna Reed in that old TV show. She had such things in her closet somewhere, gifts from Greg's mother a long time ago.

Her family would be amazed at the new mom, and memories and traditions would start abuilding.

It didn't work out quite as planned. She used the cookie recipe Willadene had given her and measured all the ingredients carefully. But instead of baking up plump and round and brown, the cookies flattened out on the baking sheet, thin and pallid, the chips rising up out of them like pimples on a teenager's pasty face.

Still, they smelled good, and Juneau scooped them onto a cooling rack, expecting Misty and Nicole to fall onto them with cries of pleasure.

They didn't. They peered at them briefly as they came into the kitchen.

"What's that?" Misty asked, pointing. "Pancakes?"

"Cookies," Juneau said. "Have some. I'll pour milk to dip them in."

"I don't think so." Misty went on to her room.

Juneau peered at Nicole, who stood there looking as if she knew something was expected of her. "How about you, pal?"

"I'd like one," Nicole said politely. Gingerly she picked up a cookie, peering at its lumpy surface.

Juneau rushed to the refrigerator and snatched the milk carton. "Here," she said, grabbing a glass. "Sit down at the table." Quickly she poured, reminding herself not to hover.

Nicole sat down. Dutifully she dipped the pale, brittle cookie into the milk and chewed obediently. "You know what I'd really like, Mom? One of those graham cracker sandwiches you make. You know, with the powdered sugar frosting dripping out of it."

"You got it," Juneau said, reaching into a cupboard for the ingredients. Quickly she dumped powdered sugar into a bowl and mixed in a little milk, being careful to leave it slightly runny since Nicole had specified she liked the frosting to drip out. She made four squares and put them on a small plate.

Nicole gave her a sweet smile. "Thank you, Mom. I love these." She stood up. "May I take them to my room?"

"Certainly," Juneau said.

Philip Atwater stood there beside her, a long slime of drool hanging from his mouth.

Juneau laughed. "Well, I'm glad somebody appreciates my efforts," she told him. Picking up the remainder of Nicole's cookie, she flicked out the chips, since the dog shouldn't have chocolate, and gave the rest to him. He munched happily.

The rest of the mess she deposited in the garbage can. So much for her cookie baking efforts.

The dinner didn't work out much better. She'd taken so long to bake the cookies that there wasn't time to slow-cook the roast and be finished by 5:30. So she turned up the heat, thus eventually producing the same tough hunk of beef that she usually did. And she'd never gotten around to changing into a crisp cotton housedress and perky apron.

But her family accepted the dinner with gratitude, glad, as always, to get any kind of food.

"That was good, Mom," Nicole said as she finished her last bite.

"Yes, it was," Greg agreed, dropping a couple of scraps into Philip Atwater's eager maw. "Going to make pot pie with the leftovers tomorrow?"

"Mmmm, yes," Nicole said enthusiastically.

Misty said nothing, but at least she'd cleaned her plate.

It was the next day that the phone call came from Larry Steers, the literary agent Mrs. Jarvis had told Juneau to send her story to.

"Great news, Mrs. Caldwell," he said. "The editor at *Ladies' Home Journal* loves your story. She's buying it."

"My story! She's buying it?" Juneau felt stupid, but she'd scarcely thought of the story since she'd mailed it. She'd been afraid to hope and even more afraid to find out that she carried her parents' writing genes.

"Yes," the agent said. "Congratulations! There'll be a check coming along soon. It will probably be out some time this fall."

"Oh," Juneau said. Then "Oh! OH! Oh, thank you, Mr. Steers. Thank you."

"Call me Larry," he said. "Do you have more stories you'd like to send me?"

More stories? Without even thinking, she said, "Yes. Yes, I do."

"Send them along," she heard him say. "I'll see what I can do with them."

It wasn't until she hung up that Juneau remembered she wasn't writing anymore. She wondered if she should call him back and tell him that. No, she decided. She'd talk to Greg first. Right now she needed to run next door and tell Marisol that she'd sold a story! Then she had to call Mrs. Jarvis, who, she was sure, would tell her she must come back to the class.

"Of course you should keep writing," Greg said that night after the girls were in bed, after they'd all celebrated the good news by going out for McDonald's hamburgers, which in Misty's and Nicole's eyes was the ultimate celebration. "Why would you ever think of stopping?"

"I just thought I need to take better care of my family," she said lamely. She didn't want to go into the whole thing about Max and her decision not to write anymore.

"There's time for both," Greg said. "I thought you'd just lost interest or something."

No, she hadn't lost interest. Hardly. It lurked there in her blood, inherited from the Peripatetic Paulsens, her parents. She needed to write. And maybe to wander. Was that what her restlessness was all about?

She tried the Willadene Effect one last time when the check for her story arrived. She took the girls out shopping.

"We're going to buy quilts for your beds," she told them. "Patchwork quilts. Then we'll throw out those ratty bedspreads we've been using for so long."

"Throw them out?" gasped Misty. "Why?"

Nicole wailed, "I love my bedspread!"

From the look on their faces, you'd have thought she'd suggested dumping Philip Atwater into the garbage.

"I just want to make our house look better," Juneau said.

"Our house looks fine," Nicole said. "What's wrong with it?"

"You wait and see how much better it can look," Juneau said. "Just be willing to try this, okay?"

After promises of ice cream cones at the mall, the girls settled back, muttering to each other all the way to the store. Juneau had to buy the cones right off and then a bag of popcorn at a mobile cart by J. C. Penney's to sustain them through the arduous task of selecting the right patchwork quilts. Even then, Misty resisted.

"I don't want patchwork, Mom," she said. "The only spread I like in the whole store is that one." She pointed at a heavy, dark denim spread that had pockets along the side, like those on jeans. It was expensive.

"We can bring these back if you don't like them," Juneau said as she picked two twin-size quilts and then a queen-size one for Greg's and her bed. "You'll love them once you see them on your beds."

Again she was wrong. In Misty's messy room the patchwork quilt looked like an attempt to bring a sweet old grandma into a garbage dump. In Nicole's neat little chamber, the quilt clashed with the curtains Nicole had so carefully chosen, the ones with the cartoony characters she'd said Max would have liked.

Even in her and Greg's room, the patchwork was all wrong. Juneau was not sure why. Apparently she wasn't a patchwork person. What had worked so perfectly in Willadene's house was totally uneasy in hers.

She took the quilts back to the store, and the next day when the girls came home from school, she was seated at the kitchen table, pounding away on her typewriter.

"Oh, good," Nicole said. "I thought maybe your typewriter was broken."

Juneau didn't say it was she who'd been broken.

"Girls," she said, "I want you to help me out here. Tell me some things you like to remember about our family. About our home."

Looking bewildered, they both came over.

"I like to remember Philip Atwater," Misty said right away, reaching down to pat the head of the big dog that pressed against her leg.

Nicole's face was thoughtful. "I like to remember how you used to sing that song to wake us up in the morning."

Juneau felt a pang. Why had she ever stopped singing "that song," a silly ditty about how it's nice to wake up in the morning when the sun begins to shine? She'd thought the girls didn't like it because they'd always groaned so much about getting out of bed.

"Anything else?" she asked.

"I like to remember how we used to toast marshmallows in the fireplace," Misty said.

"We'll do that again in the wintertime," Juneau told her. "No, we'll do it tonight. Okay?" Who needed to wait for winter?

"I like to remember how I used to hear your typewriter whacking away when I was going to sleep," Nicole said. "And . . ." She hesitated.

"And?" Juneau prompted.

"And I like to remember Max and how we buried his Christmas stocking under the pomegranate tree," Nicole finished.

Quick tears sprang to Juneau's eyes. Not for lost Max but for time lost wishing for something that had been there all along. The girls had been gathering good memories during all the years of their lives. Why had she ever thought they had to be the same as those Willadene was creating for her family?

Perhaps she hadn't been as inadequate as she thought. The girls had never complained. Neither had Greg.

A line from an old college class came to her. A Shakespeare class, when they'd been reading *King Lear.* Regan, one of the daughters, said about her father, "He hath ever but slenderly known himself." Mentally, Juneau applied it to herself. She said aloud, "I have but slenderly known myself."

The girls looked puzzled. "What did you say, Mom?" Nicole asked.

"Nothing," she said. "Let's go visit Max's stocking's grave, then we'll come in and have a snack."

Traditions, she thought. Each family has its own. They don't have to be like anybody else's. She smiled as she recognized the thought as a good theme for a story. She was well into the story, typing it at the kitchen table after the girls had gone to bed, when Greg came home from teaching his Tuesday night graduate seminar. He came over to lean down and kiss her cheek. "The clackety-clack sounds good," he said. "I'm glad you're back."

She stopped typing and looked up at him. "I'm not sure what you mean."

"Well," Greg said comfortably, "you're back to what you were before."

"Before what?"

Greg was silent for a moment. Then he said, "I guess before the baby.

Or actually, before you went to Education Week. I think that's when you changed."

Was she really back to being that person? That confused, lackluster woman who'd gone to hear lectures that she'd hoped would let her know who she was? "I don't think so," she said.

"So how do you think you're different?"

She couldn't believe he was so dense. If he didn't realize that you can't go through being harrowed without coming out changed, then she couldn't explain it to him. She raised a hand to point at her head. "New hairdo," she said.

He reached over to touch her hair. "Cute. I'm beginning to think I like you with short hair. Of course, I'd like you even with no hair at all."

He was sweet. She remembered thinking the same thing when she'd found the note in the spare tire well last August. Had she ever thanked him for that?

When she asked if she had, he said, "You didn't tell me you'd had a flat tire." She remembered now how she'd decided not to tell him about it. But why not? She told him now, emphasizing how loved and protected she'd felt when she found the note. She didn't mention Jay. Why should she? He'd merely been another nice man who'd helped her out. If she told about him, she'd have to confess she'd been driving around alone, late at night.

"It was no big deal," she said. "Easily taken care of. But I liked the note. Sorry I didn't tell you sooner." She paused. "I was pretty messed up last summer."

"That's why I'm so happy to have you back to what you were before," he said.

Something stirred down deep inside her, like a small trapped thing that didn't have enough room to move around. After all these years of marriage, Juneau thought, he but slenderly knows me. Then to be honest, she admitted that she didn't know him any better.

June 16, 1981

Dear Erin, Willadene, and Gabby,

I found out something important. I'm not Willadene. If that sounds mysterious, tune in for the next thrilling episode. But let me assure you, Willadene, it is highly complimentary to you. Not so much to me!

My big news is that I sold a story! It's true! Somebody is paying me for something I wrote! Can you imagine! Actually, it was that check which indirectly brought about my realization that I am not Willadene. I'll tell you the full story next time we get together, which I hope is soon. Let's not wait twenty-four years for The Pact to come due.

Love,
Juneau

Chapter Sixteen

ERIN

Saturday, July 6, 1981
Dear Ladies,

News flash! I told Cory yes! You can't imagine how hard it was to get the word out of my mouth. Well, yes, you can. You know me . . .

He was like a little puppy waiting for his master to give him a treat. I was like the master, holding the treat just out of reach. Finally, he reached out and snapped it up. Metaphorically speaking. (Is that right, Juneau?)

He said something like, "Is that a yes I can see on the tip of your tongue? Come on, now tell me. It is, isn't it?" If he had a tail, it would have been wagging.

When I actually said the word, he whirled me around the room, shouting at the top of his lungs. He called his parents and Steve and Colleen. He was about to call The Women when I snatched the phone from his hand. I wanted to break the news in person. Cory says I'm a masochist. I looked it up in the dictionary. Maybe I am, when it comes to Mom and Grams.

When I told them I was going to marry Cory, Grams said, "At least he's not Catholic." Mom hugged me and said how happy she was. She whispered in my ear that I should follow my heart, no matter what. It made me sad to see her cry.

The hardest part was telling them that we wanted to get married in October in Salt Lake City. In the temple. Seeing the look on their faces when they realized they couldn't be there was horrible. The fact that we'll be having a reception here in the Twin Cities didn't make up for it. They feel left out, and I don't blame them.

So I told them I wanted them to help me with the planning. Announcements, cake, dress. The very next day, Cory's mom said she's got a whole notebook of ideas she's just been waiting to use for "Cory's reception!"

Angie laughed when I told her. She said, "Watch out, girl. That's just the beginning."

Is life ever simple? Is there ever a time when you feel like you've reached the goal? And here I thought the time between getting engaged and getting married would be a prelude to bliss.

Say a prayer for me, please.

> Love,
> Erin

P.S. Cory is already dropping hints that he doesn't want to move into my little tree house when we get married. It's old and there's no elevator or heated parking, but it has so much more character than the kind of places Cory is thinking of. I pretend I don't know what he's talking about.

July 12, 1981
Dear Juneau, Willadene, and Gabby,

I invited Mom and my friend Colleen to lunch, and we created a whole flow chart of what has to happen between now and October 29th. Yes, we've actually set the date! I have to have a heart-to-heart with Linda. Not only does she want to plan the reception here but she wants to direct everything in Salt Lake, too.

Is it at all possible that you can come? I would love having you with me. If you don't, I'll be all by myself, surrounded by Johnsons. As much as I love Cory and his parents, I don't like feeling managed. If that makes any sense.

> Holding my breath,
> Erin

JUNEAU

July 15, 1981
Dear, dear Erin,

Shades of Prince Charles and Lady Di! Romance is in the air! I am so thrilled about your news, as I said in my phone call. It sent me tumbling into a contemplation of the conundrums of life (hey, I've been reading the *Reader's Digest* "It Pays to Enrich Your Word Power" page) and how the decisions we make mysteriously lead us to the paths we are meant to take. You and Cory were meant to be together. The only way that could happen was if you joined the Church so you could meet him.

I can't help but think about how confused we both were back there in Willadene's orchard and how we all wept together. Which brings me to one of my favorite scriptures from Psalms: "Weeping may endure for a night, but joy cometh in the morning." Your joy has come, and my wish to you is that it may ever increase. I'll end with yet another scripture, from the Doctrine and Covenants: "Wherefore, lift up thy heart and rejoice, and cleave unto the covenants which thou hast made."

Cory sounds like the absolute tops in guys and worthy of being the husband of a COBette. I send heaps of good wishes to both of you.

Love,
Juneau

WILLADENE

July 20, 1981
Dear Erin,

Congratulations! Cory sounds like one romantic and eager fellow. And Yes! Yes! Yes! It will be COB and COBettes to the rescue. We can't have a bride without backup wandering around Temple Square.

The Johnsons' plans for the big reception sound impressive. What a way to start married life . . . mingling with the movers and shakers. I wonder if you'll be expected to actually remember the names of all the people you'll meet.

But I have to agree with your buddy Angie. "Mother" Johnson sounds like a take-charge kind of gal. The advice my Nana Lewis always used to give to newlyweds was "Begin as you mean to go on." And if Cory's mom gets to be in charge of everything now, maybe she'll think that it will be okay to do the same thing later.

Not to worry. Gabby will hold the fort in Salt Lake City, and The Women sound like they can handle anybody in Minnesota!

Anything we can do from this end, just ask and we'll get right on it.

And Erin, about the temple. I am so excited for you. I love to go there, and I love knowing that you will be able to share that joy. Maybe someday you will be able to have the work done for your grandfather. Wouldn't that be great?

We are making the most of summer in the garden and at the farm. Now that Bitsy is diaper-free, I feel a lot easier about letting her spend a day with her grandmothers and her Aunt Sunny. She is loving it and making the most of being a "big girl" and getting praised and rewarded for it. I already have prickly feelings in the back of my neck about her as a teenager.

Looking forward to October (but I bet not as much as you are!).

Love,
Deenie

P.S. I called Gabby about Cecilia and Sophie. She said Cecilia had made becoming a woman a messy threat more than a promise. Gabby says it's become a full-time activity trying to reeducate Sophie. She finished our conversation by telling me she couldn't be in the same room with Cecilia without wanting to smack her.

JUNEAU

August 3, 1981
Dear Deenie and Erin,

Did you see The Wedding in London? Wasn't Lady Diana (now Princess Di) right out of fairyland in that big-sleeved dress? And Charles looked fine in his elegant uniform. Do you think they are truly in love?

Regina, in a cloud of white, walked regally down the aisle of the cathedral. Up ahead she saw her husband-to-be waiting for her, standing there beside the Best Man. Her heart leaped as she realized he really was the Best Man. She was marrying the wrong guy. Or was she? She slid her eyes to her groom, whose eyes, she saw, were on the Maid of

Honor. She stopped short, her attendants piling up behind her. "Author,"
she cried. "Please rewrite this scene!"

I wonder what lies in store for the Prince and Princess of Wales.

I wonder what lies in store for us. Erin, hang in there with the
wedding plans. Everything will work out and be beautiful.

Love,
Juneau

ERIN

Erin's concern about having enough money to cover her wedding
expenses drove her to take on as many clients as she could, so she was at
the salon from early until late. Cory often stayed late at his work, too.
Sunday rides after church became a special time for them.

They started by exploring the tree-lined streets of Edina, Hopkins, and
Minnetonka. Once they drove out to Excelsior on Lake Minnetonka, arriving
just in time to buy tickets and board the *Queen of Excelsior* for a two-hour
cruise.

Another time, they ventured further out to Buffalo, where they poked
around in antique shops. In one of the shops Erin saw a piece of Red Wing
pottery that she wanted. "Wait for me, Cory," she called to him. "I want to
buy something."

Cory was instantly at her side. "We don't buy things on Sunday."

She was about to argue with him, but seeing the look on his face, she
waited until they were out on the sidewalk. "I don't get it. What's the difference between buying a piece of pottery and buying a ticket for the *Queen of
Excelsior?* Or an ice cream cone?" They had just enjoyed double-decker cones
and the creamy sweet taste of strawberry ice cream was still in Erin's mouth.

"Is the pottery important enough to make an issue of it?"

"No," she said, feeling perverse. "But I would like to know the reason why
it's okay for you to buy what you want on the Sabbath but it's not for me."

"There isn't any reason, okay? From now on, I won't buy anything on a
Sunday. Period."

"Don't yap at me. I just asked a question."

"Sorry." He ruffled her hair and then put his arm around her. "I like to
do things right."

"No kidding. That seems to be a big thing for you."

"And it isn't for you?"

"Not the same way."

"What do you mean by that?"

Erin frowned. She had boxed herself into a corner, and she wasn't exactly clear why she had said what she did.

"You look at the little things. They're not as important to me as they are to you."

"What is important to you?"

"Being kind to others. Love."

"That's a short list."

"I could add a few things more. Doing my work well. The Women. You, too. That goes without saying."

He shook his head.

"What?" she asked. "You don't believe you're important to me?"

"I don't believe The Women are important to you. If they are, you sure aren't showing it."

She pulled away from him. "What do you mean?"

"You never take the first step, you know. We see them when I make reservations at a restaurant, or when your mother invites us over."

"Are you suggesting I go to them?"

"I am. You told them to prove they love you, but now you're not giving them much chance to do that."

Erin felt an urge to stamp her foot. "I don't want to. I want them to come to me."

"Groveling all the way, I assume."

He was right. It took Erin a long time to come to that conclusion, and when she did, she was ashamed to realize she was treating The Women the same way they had treated each other—and her—for so many years.

The next Sunday found Erin and Cory on the doorstep of her old house. Her heart pounded as she rang the doorbell. She hadn't told them she and Cory were coming. Would they be glad to see her, or would they close the door in her face?

She was weak with relief when her mother's reaction to seeing them was a huge smile. "Erin! Cory! It's so good to see you. Come in." She ushered them into the living room, calling, "Mom! Come see who's here!"

When Ruth came out of the back bedroom, Erin saw the flash of joy on her face. It was immediately replaced by a clamped-down look, but it was there long enough for Erin to know that Grams did care about her.

They chatted about neutral subjects for a few minutes, and then the topic turned to wedding plans. "Oh! You'll never guess what my friend Gabby from Provo is going to do!" Erin didn't notice the soft touch of Cory's hand on her arm. "When I told her you wouldn't be coming to Salt Lake City, she said she'd be my 'Utah mom.' And I think Juneau and Willadene are going to come, too. Isn't that neat?"

She was smiling, expecting an enthusiastic response. When she saw the sadness in their faces she rushed to Joanna's side and hugged her. "I'm sorry, Mom. I didn't mean that the way it sounded. I'd rather have you there when I get married, really I would."

"Well, I can't." Joanna said and sat up straight. "But there is one thing I can do. I'd like to make your wedding dress. Unless you want something really fancy. I'm not sure I'm up to that."

"Would you? That would be great." Erin didn't realize until that moment that this was why she had been resisting going dress shopping with Linda: She wanted to be married in a dress her mother had made.

She turned to Cory. "Did I ever tell you my mom's a great seamstress? When I was little, she made me five new dresses before the start of every school year."

"Until she stopped wearing dresses," Joanna said with a smile. "Do you have some ideas about the style you want?"

A quarter hour later, Erin and Cory said their good-byes and walked to the car. The moment Erin shut the car door behind her, she burst into tears.

"Hey, what's the matter?" Cory asked. "I thought everything went really well."

"It did," Erin said, smiling through her tears. "That's why I'm crying."

Wednesday, August 13, 1981
Dear Gabby, Juneau, and Willadene,

Gabby Farnsworth, you are an angel! I am so thrilled that you will be my Utah "mom" and take over the planning on that end. You should have seen Linda when I told her. You'd think I was depriving her of life and limb.

Juneau and Willadene, you'll never know how much it means to me that we will all be together. Now I feel tons better.

Mom and I found a pattern for my dress. It has a draped neck, flowing sleeves, a fitted waist, and a slightly flared skirt with a short train. If you can't imagine it, think of Katharine Hepburn in *Philadelphia*

Story. You'll get an idea, at least. Mom and I are looking at fabrics now. We're leaning toward silk and chiffon in a shade off dead white.

Poor Linda is in a tizzy about the dress. She agreed that the style was suitable for the temple and the reception, but it's not what she was expecting. Even though I told her Mom's an expert seamstress, I get the idea she's afraid the dress will look homemade. She'll probably hate it no matter how it turns out.

I'm taking the class for people getting ready to go to the temple. We've already talked about the sorts of questions the bishop will ask when we go to get a temple recommend. Just thinking about that makes my hands sweaty. I'm glad Cory and I haven't done anything that we wouldn't want to tell the bishop.

The other news is that I finally decided Cory was right about the apartment. If we lived here, he'd have to use a headbolt heater on his car and dig it out every time it snowed, which would be a real pain. Angie and Norm were disappointed when I told them, but they totally understood. They are such wonderful people!

Love,
Erin

WILLADENE

September 1, 1981
Dear Gabby and Juneau,

Gabby, your plans for the wedding weekend in Salt Lake City sound perfect. I've never stayed in a big hotel before, and I've always wanted to stay at Hotel Utah. That's where my parents went on their honeymoon.

I have the edging crocheted on the temple hankie for Erin, and Leila Jeffrey is going to do the monogram on her fancy sewing machine. But I am going to do the rosettes on the peignoir by hand.

My mother says this is all way too much—being so involved with people who are almost strangers. I don't feel we're the least bit like strangers. Grandma Streeter says it's affinity. Some people have it the minute they meet, and some don't have it even within their own families. Even though my mother doesn't understand why we are doing this, she takes Bitsy and watches the boys when I'm sewing. Bitsy is glad to go with her grandma. I have kept her inside quite often this summer so I could finish working on the lingerie. She stands at the front door, puts up her arms, and says "Go. Go." whenever anyone leaves the house.

The whole thing made me realize how my mother's life has been limited by the responsibility of Sunny. I remember when she used to wear business suits and go to community functions, give talks on education, and attend Daughters of the Utah Pioneers meetings. On top of keeping the books for Dad's store, she went back to teaching high school English when I started first grade. That all stopped cold when Sunny was born. What with Sunny's care, she simply doesn't have the time or energy to make or keep up close friendships anymore. That makes me sad.

I've been wondering about Sister Johnson. From what Erin has said, she sounds like she's a mother who likes to be in control. What do you think? I told Roger I was a little concerned about how she might react to our making these plans for her daughter-in-law-to-be. Roger said not to worry, that there wasn't anything she could dish out that you, Gabby, couldn't handle.

I got a new "store bought" suit for the wedding, soft ecru linen with an apricot blouse. I feel very uptown in it. It's the kind of suit my Great-Grandma Lofgren would have called "right snooty."

Sunny has been asking about getting married. It happens whenever she hears about a wedding. My dad tells her that Heavenly Father will handle all that for her. She accepts the idea readily but will have to be reminded when the next wedding comes along.

This is all so romantic! And speaking of romance, did you and Jonas get the tickets to the opera you were talking about, Gabby?

This has been quite the summer for all of us, what with Erin getting married and you, Juneau, getting a story published. I feel like I'm trailing behind. Roger asked me if there was something I would rather be doing. I couldn't think of a thing. I see a future filled with kids and canning jars.

> Keep me up to date,
> Deenie

Chapter Seventeen

ERIN

After seeing how glad Grams and her mother were that she had come to see them, Erin made a point of driving over to their place as often as she could. Whenever she and Cory visited, Grams always had a cake or strudel ready to serve them. That told Erin volumes. Grams baked only for special occasions.

One day after visiting The Women, Cory turned east on I-94 instead of west. "Where are you going?" she asked when he took the Cretin Avenue exit.

"I thought you'd like to see the houses on Summit Avenue."

"Great," she said. Summit Avenue, the grand street of St. Paul, was lined with gracious homes, including the mansion of railroad magnet James J. Hill and the Governor's Mansion. They cruised the avenue slowly, pointing out the houses they liked best and the landscaping features that pleased them most.

Before they reached the St. Paul Cathedral, Cory turned right and a block later right again, so that they ended up driving in the direction they had come from, but on another street, this one with homes only slightly less imposing. "I can't imagine what it would be like to live in one of these places," Erin was saying when Cory suddenly pulled over to the curb. "What are we stopping for?" she asked.

"See that house over there?" She looked where he was pointing to see a large two-story house set back from the road, with a brick and wrought iron fence surrounding meticulously landscaped grounds. The circular drive was full of late model cars, and the smell of grilling and the sound of easy-listening music wafted toward them.

"Somebody's having a party." Erin grinned. "If we're invited, I don't think we're dressed appropriately."

He chuckled. "We're not invited."

"Are you considering this house for us?" she joked. "Sorry, dear, it's out of our price range."

This time he didn't laugh. "Do you know who lives here?"

"No. Do you?"

He nodded. "Your father. Andrew J. McGee. I know you asked me not to, Erin, but I did some poking around. Dad helped. Having a lawyer for a father has its advantages." He smiled at her, pleased with himself and obviously hoping she would be pleased, too.

For a moment, Erin was too shocked to speak. "You investigated my father without asking me? Why?"

"It's obvious that you carry some pretty heavy baggage from your childhood, Erin. A lot of it having to do with your father. I thought it might help if you knew he was alive and well, living in St. Paul. Think of this as an early wedding present."

Now Erin was furious. She crossed her arms and sat pressed up to the door, trying to get as far away from him as she could. "You've got to be kidding. Unless the man who lives in that house confesses or agrees to a paternity test, there's no way to know for sure that he is related to me."

"That's true, but the chance is good—"

"Even if he is, I told you I didn't want to have anything to do with him."

"Erin, he's your father."

"No. He's the sperm donor, remember?"

He rested his head against the steering wheel, not looking at her. "I guess I made a big mistake. I thought I was doing something nice for you."

"Don't ever do something like that again. I mean it."

ERIN

September 6, 1981
Dear COBs,

I had a huge argument with Cory. What happened was Cory and Skipp checked out everyone named Andrew McGee in St. Paul. Can you believe it!

What really makes me mad is that I specifically asked him not to poke his nose in my business. He said if we were going to get married, my business was his business. He wanted to know what I was going to tell our kids when they asked about their grandfather. I said, "Ask me again when we have some."

I was still fuming when I told Colleen about it. She said that I needed to practice taking deep breaths and counting to ten, because marriage is all about misunderstandings, compromise, and making up. I think Steve must have said pretty much the same thing to Cory.

I guess you guys would have given us the same advice. And you probably know that it's not easy to let go when you're furious—and right! (ha, ha!) It took a couple of days for us both to decide that being right wasn't worth it. So, I admitted that I overreact to anything having to do with you-know-who, and Cory admitted he should have asked before acting. Then we made up! That was the best part.

Love,
Erin

Sunday, September 21, 1981
Dear COBs,

I'm getting cold feet. It isn't Cory. It's going to the temple. The things I've been told about it are strange and beautiful—and scary. When I get my endowments, I'll be making covenants on a higher level. I don't think I can, even if the bishop gives me a recommend. I don't feel like I'm a good Mormon as it is.

Colleen says I should stop thinking so much. She says the feeling you get in the temple is the most important. Angie says she's heard Mormons who go to the temple wear funny underwear and do strange things. I told her she should maybe talk to the missionaries to get things straight. She just hooted. She does that a lot. I'm so glad she isn't mad at me because I had to move.

Love,
Erin

WILLADENE

The October Harvest Festival was a Wellsville specialty, held every other year in the center of town, which was directly across the street from the Rasmussens. This year was a festival year, and the weather promised to be perfect. On Friday evening the men of the community set up booths and constructed temporary barriers for old-fashioned games for the younger children, volleyball and softball for the older ones. Even a section of the parking lot was set aside for music and dancing.

On Saturday morning the ladies took over. The booths were decorated and filled with homemade goods to taste, trade, or sell. Quilts were hung for viewing inside the tabernacle, and wood for a huge blaze was laid in the bowery fireplace.

By four o'clock that afternoon, the smell of simmering barbecue had drifted all the way to the Rasmussen front porch. Deenie inhaled it as she packed the donated salads for the potluck into coolers by the front door. She was tired and wired and ready to be fed. But there were still four loads to haul to the picnic area before she could relax and claim a spot for the family.

Bert showed up just in time to help. "I knew you'd be up to your eyeballs in all this stuff," she said, gazing at the array of food Deenie had gathered. "Let me help you get it across the street."

"Roberta Jean, you are a welcome sight. You can start with that." Deenie pointed to a large red cooler that was packed and ready to go.

"Where are the kids?" Bert asked as she picked it up. "I didn't see them when I came in."

"The weather is so nice, Mom and Dad drove out from Logan with Sunny. They offered to take the kids over to get started playing games."

"Then why don't you get ready, and I'll finish up here?" Bert pushed the screen open with her hip and headed across the street.

The last chore on Deenie's list was to gather coats for the family, in case the weather turned, and a blanket to sit on. To her surprise, they were already stacked on the table in the kitchen. Roger had done it without her even asking. She smiled, thinking, *A good man in a good mood is a fine thing.*

Since she now had a moment to spare, she decided to fix up a little extra. The summer had been so busy, she had seldom taken the time for more than Chapstick. Roger always appreciated it when she went the full makeup and pressed-pants routine, and even the kids noticed. So she pressed a neat plaid shirt and slipped into a newer and less comfortable pair of jeans, took time to put on a going-out face, and brushed her random curls into better order. As she closed the front door behind her, she wondered why it always took an occasion before she was willing to take care of herself.

The festival was in full swing when she arrived. Roger and Bert had already set out the salads for her. So she checked on the children and then worked her way down the line of stalls. After she gathered the few treasures she had promised herself, she joined Bert, Sunny, and Bitsy sitting on their blanket waiting for the potluck to start.

The conversation was lazy and friendly. Sunny teased Bitsy with a dolly made of empty spools of thread that Bert had purchased for her. Bitsy teased back by trying to catch the autumn-colored ribbons flowing down Sunny's back from a headdress made of silk chrysanthemums.

"What did you get?" Sunny asked as Deenie stuffed her goods into the laundry basket.

"Treasures for Thanksgiving," Deenie answered in a low, secret-filled voice. "If you promise not to tell, I'll show you."

Sunny nodded with excitement twinkling in her eyes. Slowly, Deenie began to unveil the jars in the basket, looking suspiciously one way and then the other, as if searching for prying eyes.

"What is it?" Sunny cried.

"Grandma Streeter's Dilly Beans," Deenie growled in her pirate voice and flashed a quick view of the jar. Then there was Leila Jeffrey's authentic mincemeat, and Jenny Rasmussen's tomato conserve to ooh and ah over.

"That's quite a haul," Bert said.

Looking pointedly at the paper bag next to Bert, Deenie said, "Looks like you found a treasure of your own."

Bert opened the bag and displayed a beautiful box-cut, patchwork jacket embellished with cording and satin ribbon embroidery. "It's not usually my style," Bert said, turning the jacket first one way and then the other. "But it was too beautiful to pass up, and it looks like BYU. Maybe it will help me fit in better."

"Looks like romance to me," Deenie said, admiring the handwork. "Any news in that department?"

"You sound like Mom and Dad. They never let up on the subject. It's always the first thing they ask when I come home."

"They're only asking because they want you to be happy."

"I know, but I wish they would stop. I suppose I could tell them I'm not looking, but that would open a whole new can of worms." Bert took hold of Deenie's arm and leaned forward. "Deenie," she whispered intensely, "I'm going on a mission."

"You're too young for a mission!"

"I won't be by the time I graduate."

"But what about marriage and a family?"

Bert shrugged. "I want that too, but I want to go on a mission first. That's why I'm not looking."

Bert's attitude was a complete surprise to Deenie. Her own contemporaries had made marriage and family first on their life plan list, from Beehive years on. Everyone she knew who was Bert's age had those same priorities, too. She shook her head.

"Hey, don't go doing a NeVae on me," Bert said.

Before Deenie could explain her thoughts, Roger showed up and offered to take Sunny and Bitsy for a turn on the swings.

When they were alone again, Bert apologized. "Sorry. I should have never spoken about my mother like that."

"It's okay. Sometimes my mom gets to me, too. But I thought your mom really supported you transferring to the Y and switching your major from English lit to early childhood development."

"That's another thing. I heard a life strategies speaker talk about how the happiest people are the ones who make careers out of the things they have a passion for. So I followed his advice and changed my major to anthropology and my minor to sociology."

"Good grief," Deenie said. "Your parents don't know any of this, do they?"

Bert shook her head. "Not yet. I know how they'll react, so I'm putting off telling them until I absolutely have to. You're the only one who knows."

Bert was filling Deenie in on the details when Roger returned. Sunny followed, carrying Bitsy.

"Bitsy needs a change," Sunny said, scrunching up her nose.

"The line in the bathroom was far too long," Roger said with an apologetic shake of his head.

Bert stood and opened her arms. "Let me take her. We'll run home and get cleaned up. Then Bitsy can pick out a clean pair of panties all on her own."

With Bitsy taken care of, Roger and the boys headed for the softball game. Deenie and Sunny sat enjoying the fading warmth of the setting sun.

"Good evening, you two." NeVae Rasmussen greeted them as she pulled a lawn chair up next to the blanket. "Enjoying the last bit of the day?"

Deenie smiled and hugged Sunny to her side. "We certainly are. It's great that it's been warm enough for Sunny to be here, too."

NeVae smiled briefly at Sunny and then looked back to Deenie. "I thought I saw Bert with you a moment ago. You two were huddled so close together I had to wonder what all the secrecy was about."

"It was just girl talk," Deenie said lightly.

"I guessed as much," NeVae said. "Bert always comes to me when she has something serious on her mind." There was an odd undertone to her voice.

"No one can take your place with Bert," Deenie said with a smile. When NeVae looked unconvinced, she added, "I thought you were glad the two of us were becoming good friends."

NeVae reached over and patted Deenie on the shoulder. "Oh, we're all pleased about that."

"I'm actually beginning to think of Bert as a sister."

"But, Deenie," NeVae said, "you already have a sister."

Deenie heard the warning in NeVae's voice. "Are you asking me not to be friends with Bert?"

"Of course not, dear. You're part of the family." NeVae paused, and her smile was anything but warm. "But you did ask Roger to ask us and Bert not to interfere with the way you ran your family. Now I'm asking the same of you."

Coming on the heels of the conversation with Bert, NeVae's words struck Deenie speechless. All she could do was nod.

NeVae gave her a quick kiss on the cheek. "Thank you, dear. I knew you'd understand."

But Deenie didn't understand at all. She was confused, hurt, and a little scared. In the ten years she and Roger had been married and living close to the Rasmussens, there had never been a true conflict between NeVae and herself. She had trusted Roger to communicate her request about boundaries to his parents in such a way that they wouldn't be offended, but clearly, they were.

"That lady was mad," Sunny said. "Did you and Bert say something bad?"

"No, honey," Deenie reassured her. "We were talking about Bert's school. She's graduating from the Y next May. Isn't that exciting?"

Sunny fidgeted for a moment with Bitsy's dolly. "I wish I could go to a school that graduates," she said. "We always do the same old thing. Every day we do."

"Maybe we can talk to Mom about that."

"Well, okay," Sunny said, sounding doubtful.

Later that evening as the games wound down and the dance music got louder, a chilly wind persuaded most of the folks to gather at the festival bonfire. Deenie rounded up her family and handed out sweaters and sweatshirts. Margaret Stowell arrived as they finished, Sunny's warm coat draped over her arm. John followed with gloves, a scarf, and earmuffs.

"Oh, boy," Sunny groused as her mother bundled her to her ears.

"Wow, Mom," Deenie said. "It's not snowing."

Margaret's mouth compressed into a thin, well-known warning line. Deenie changed tack immediately. "Bert's graduating in May. Sunny says she'd like to go to a school that isn't so boring, somewhere she could graduate from, too. I thought that sounded like something you might want to know."

Her father, standing behind Margaret, gave Deenie a look that said, "Did you forget what I told you about treading softly?"

Margaret gave Sunny a quick hug and sent her off to find Roger and the kids. When she was out of earshot, Margaret turned to Deenie. "There isn't anything you can tell me about Sunny that your father and I don't already know," she said shortly. "For your information, we've been looking into other schools for months. Your father has decided on private tutoring. It'll start in the spring."

"Great," was all Deenie could say.

"You don't need to protect Sunny from me, Deenie," Margaret added in a tone Deenie had never heard before. "And I wish you would stop trying."

Deenie walked away, feeling as if she had been buffeted in a windstorm. She went through the rest of the evening lost in her own thoughts. *Am I meddling where I shouldn't? No! I am Bert's friend. And I am Sunny's big sister. I was only taking care of the people I care about, the same as I always do. That was one of the things NeVae used to say made her love me. When did that change? And tonight Mom sounded like she didn't even like me!*

Deenie felt as if everyone was suddenly playing by a new set of rules, and she had no idea what they were. She needed to talk to somebody, but because of what NeVae had said, it wouldn't be Roger. Deenie promised herself she would never put him in the middle again, especially since he'd demonstrated that he felt free to repeat things she thought were said in confidence.

She wished Gabby was right there beside her for comfort and guidance. She couldn't wait until the wedding. *I'll write her as soon as I get the chance,* she thought.

When the chance came later in the evening, Deenie struggled to find the words. After three false starts she gave up. The whole idea of putting down such personal feelings of doubt and pain reminded her too much of the journaling class she had taken at Education Week. She couldn't, wouldn't commit them to paper when they were so new and raw. Maybe she would write later, when enough time had passed that she could make a funny story of the incident. Maybe then she'd write: Hey, guess what? I'm on the outs with my mother, again, and an outlaw to my in-laws. But not now. Not when her feelings were so real.

Chapter Eighteen

ERIN

Sunday, October 18, 1981
Dear Gabby, Juneau, and Willadene,

I guess I really am getting married, because I have my temple rec-ommend! Right up until the stake president signed his name and gave me his blessing, I was sure I would say something that would be an immediate fail.

Everything is falling into place. My dress and veil are finished. I can't wait to show them to you! Grams bought me a new suitcase as a wedding present. It's about time I had one of my own. The way Cory and his parents talk about travel, I'll probably be doing a lot more of it. I've already packed the suitcase (it's a Samsonite!) with vacation clothes and lingerie I got at my showers. Between the sisters in the ward and Angie and my friends at work, I'm well taken care of.

The reception here has been almost entirely taken over by Linda and Skipp. Cory is their only child, and they want to celebrate his marriage with all the people they know—social and business acquaintances as well as church and family. It's going to be at a new hotel in Minnetonka with a fabulous dessert buffet. My part is paying for the floral arrangements, so I got to choose them! One of my clients gave me the card of a small florist in Golden Valley who does great work at a good price.

Mom is busy sewing dresses for herself and Grams. She's worried sick that they will embarrass me. I'm worried that I'll embarrass Cory. Cory isn't worried about anything.

Counting the days until it's over with,
Erin

During all the months of preparation for her wedding, Erin had been dutifully checking off her to-do list while never quite believing it would actually happen. The reality of it hit her as she walked off the plane at the

Salt Lake City airport. She was getting married. For time and—please God—for all eternity. A Forever Family.

As she, Cory, and his parents went down the escalators to the baggage claim level, Erin noticed a uniformed chauffeur holding a card with a name on it. She did a double take when she realized the name was her own. "That's me!" She looked at Cory, amazed and flustered.

He gave her an encouraging nudge. "Don't leave the man standing there."

When she identified herself, the chauffeur handed her a note from Gabby. She had engaged him to drive Erin to Hotel Utah, where she, Willadene, Juneau, and Sophie were waiting.

"I guess I'm going with him," Erin said. She couldn't keep from grinning. "Unless you and your folks want to ride with me?" The Johnsons were also staying at the hotel.

"This is for you. But tell your friends I thank them for convincing you to marry me."

"You did the convincing. They just gave me their blessing."

"Then thank them for that."

"I will. Don't forget dessert at the Lion House tonight. Gabby's treat."

Erin sought out the spires of the temple as the limo headed toward downtown Salt Lake City. Tomorrow morning she would be getting her endowment there, with dear Gabby as her escort. Cory would be going through at the same time—he wanted to meet her in the celestial room when she had completed the session.

Am I really ready? she wondered.

She was still pondering that question when the limo slid into a space in front of an elegant hotel just across the street from Temple Square. The chauffeur opened the door and extended his hand to help her out. Gabby, Juneau, Deenie, and Sophie immediately surrounded her. They tipped the chauffeur, told the bellboy where to take Erin's luggage, and whisked her through the lobby and into the elevator.

Erin had never seen anything as beautiful as the suite Gabby ushered her into. She slowly looked around, taking in the rich carpet, the gleaming antique tables and chairs, the brocade camelback couch and loveseat in the sitting room. In the master bedroom the four-poster bed was dressed in a rich comforter and puffy pillows. Even the bathroom was luxurious, with marble floor and tub surround, piles of thick towels, and fancy bottles of complimentary toiletries.

"This is fantastic," she said. "It's more beautiful than I ever imagined."

"It's Hotel Utah," Gabby said simply. "This room is yours, and here is where Sophie and I are staying." She opened a door to a smaller but equally beautiful bedroom. "Willadene and Juneau are across the hall."

Sophie tugged on Erin's arm. She was fairly dancing with excitement. "Do you have your dress? Can I see it?"

"Why not? I need to hang it up anyway." Erin carefully unpacked the dress. She felt a surge of pride in her mother's work as she laid it on the bed, the veil next to it.

"Ohhhh," said Sophie, touching the dress reverently.

Willadene looked over Sophie's shoulder. "It's even more beautiful than I imagined."

"It *is* Katharine Hepburn-ish," said Juneau. "And I can just see Audrey Hepburn in the veil."

"I think they both are pure Erin Larson," Gabby pronounced.

Erin flashed her a grin. "Mom did a good job on them, didn't she?"

"She did a fabulous job." Juneau ran her fingers lightly over the dress. "They're exquisite."

"I'm glad you have something to wear that represents your mother," said Gabby.

"Me, too. She put a lot of love into this dress," Erin said.

"I know what it's like not having your mother with you at such an important event." Juneau looked pensive. Then she brightened. "But you have us."

Erin's smile included all of them. "You're the next best thing."

The COBs and Sophie were the first to arrive at the Lion House. Sophie entertained the others while they waited, but Erin hardly heard a word she said. She was too anxious about how this meeting would go. A few minutes later, the Johnsons walked through the door, Cory in the lead. They were dressed casually, but they gave the impression of refinement and polish.

"You must be the famous Sister Farnsworth," said Cory, holding out his hand to Gabby. "I'm so delighted to meet you."

Gabby smiled and took his offered hand. "Call me Gabby. This is Willadene, and here's Juneau, and Sophie, my granddaughter."

Cory shook their hands in turn and then introduced them to his parents.

"Cory's parents look like those pictures of mission presidents in the *Church News*," whispered Willadene to Erin.

Erin nodded. "They do, don't they?"

Once they were seated and had ordered from the tray of elegant desserts the waiter offered them, conversation centered on the order of events in the coming days. In the morning, Erin would be getting her endowment, after which her friends were giving her an intimate lunch and shower.

"Perhaps you'd like to join us?" Gabby asked Linda.

"I'd love to, but it's your time with Erin." She flashed a smile. "We had quite a shower at our home for her before we left. Didn't we, Erin?"

"I think the whole Relief Society was there," said Erin. "Plus The Women and some of my friends from the salon. We played all those silly shower games, and I had to get my picture taken in a goofy hat Colleen made out of a paper plate and all the ribbons from the presents."

"Oh, that sounds fun!" Sophie said. "I hope I have a big shower when I get married."

"You will, dear," Gabby assured her.

"Now, dinner tomorrow . . ." Linda led them through the arrangements. The dinner, which the Johnsons were hosting, was at the restaurant on the top floor of the hotel. The wedding itself was scheduled for the day after the endowment. Afterward, there would be photos on the steps of the temple and a wedding breakfast at Little America, which Erin had insisted on paying for herself. She and Cory were to leave for Florida and Disney World immediately afterward.

"The honeymoon is our gift to Erin and Cory." Linda was looking directly at Gabby when she spoke. "We had Cancun or Kauai in mind, but Cory insisted on Disney World."

Erin and Cory exchanged a grin. Gabby chuckled. "From what Erin has told us of Cory, I think that's the perfect choice. There's so much to see and do."

"You're giving our Erin quite a gift as well," Linda said. "The hotel, the limo. She's lucky to have such a good friend."

Gabby's smile held a hint of frost. "We're all lucky in that regard."

Skipp leaned back in his chair. He seemed larger than his actual physical presence. "It's a wonderful thing to have people around who have your best interests at heart. You know, we had the privilege of looking after Erin during her troubles at Christmas. I think that's when Linda and I grew to love her. She's part of our family, now."

"But she's a COB, too!" There was a hint of anxiety in Sophie's voice. "Aren't you?"

Erin had the awful feeling of being tugged at from both sides of the table. It reminded her in a sickening way of being between Grams and her mother. She summoned a smile and said reassuringly, "Of course I am, sweetie. That will never change."

Cory must have heard something in her voice, because he gripped her hand under the table and gave her an encouraging smile. "Juneau," he said, "I've been dying to ask you how you got that unusual name."

He couldn't have asked a better question, Erin thought. Juneau launched into her story of the Peripatetic Paulsens, much to the amusement of everyone around the table.

Dessert finally came, and Erin was relieved when, as Gabby had predicted, a large dose of sugar took the tension down a few notches. But it was Cory who had turned the tide, Erin knew. Even as he had shifted the tenor of the evening, he had kept Erin's hand in his, squeezing it gently now and then, as if wanting to let her know that everything he was doing was for her.

When the party broke up, Erin and Cory walked together across the street and into Temple Square. Peace settled on her shoulders as she walked through the gate. Everywhere she looked was beauty—the temple itself, the sculptures. Even the bare trees had a certain spare elegance. Her heart warmed as the evening air cooled her cheeks.

"Everything will be different after tomorrow," Cory said.

"I know. It's a little scary."

He pulled her close as they strolled down the main promenade. "You'll be fine. I'm really glad your friends are going through the temple with you. They're wonderful women."

"I'm glad you think so. Things were getting a little strange before you stepped in. What do you think that was all about?"

"Mom's a little jealous of your friends. She's not used to feeling left out."

"If anyone's left out, it's my mom." Erin was suddenly overwhelmed with longing. "Here I am surrounded by people who love me, and I want my mother!" With surprise, she realized that she wanted her father, too. Was he really the Andrew McGee who lived in the fancy house off Summit Avenue? Would he be happy to know she was going to be married?

She fumbled in her purse for a tissue. "I better not cry, or I'll end up with puffy eyes and a red nose."

"Even if you did, you'd look beautiful to me."

When Erin saw the dramatically lighted statue of Christ through the large window of the Visitors' Center, she pulled him to a bench facing it. They sat in silence for a few moments gazing at the impressive sight, and then Erin asked, "Why do you love me?"

"What kind of a question is that? Of course I love you. Why else would I have asked you to marry me?"

"I didn't ask *if* you love me. What I'm asking is *why* you love me."

He flung his arms wide and declaimed, "Why do I love thee? Let me count the ways!" He paused. "Actually, I think it's supposed to be 'How do I love thee?'"

"Be serious, will you? For once?"

He took both her hands in his and said, "I love you because you're funny and smart and courageous and have a go-for-it attitude. I love you because you're fun to be with. But I think I love you most of all because you are so committed to family and the gospel. You're my inspiration."

"I am?" It had never occurred to her that she, Erin Larson, could inspire anyone. She snuggled close to him. "Well, are you going to ask me?"

"What?"

"Why I love you."

"Sure. Why do you love me?"

"Because you are a truly good person. You always look for the best in others. You help me see the positive side of things, and I feel wanted and safe when we're together."

"You'll always be safe with me. I promise you that."

Back in the hotel, Erin opened the door to the suite carefully, thinking that Gabby and Sophie might already be in bed. The dark room burst into light, and voices shouted, "Surprise!"

"We didn't want to wait for the shower, so we're having it now!" crowed Sophie. "Isn't that neat?"

Juneau grabbed a stunned Erin by the arm and drew her into the room. When Cory began to follow, she held up her other hand to stop him. "Ladies only."

"I can tell when I'm not wanted," he said laughingly. He kissed Erin lightly. "See you in the morning. Good-bye, ladies. Take good care of my sweetheart."

"We will," Sophie promised, beaming. Watching her, Erin wondered if these days together with the COBs would be the basis for Sophie's dreams of love and romance.

"Come on," urged Sophie when the door shut behind Cory. She pulled Erin to the center of the room, where a circle of chairs had been placed, and motioned for her to sit. There was a pile of presents in the middle.

"You didn't need to do this," Erin said.

"Yes, we did," Willadene said. "You only get married once—it's a celebration."

"Here's my present." Sophie thrust a gaily wrapped package into Erin's
hands. "I've been waiting forever to give it to you."

Erin unwrapped it, handing the ribbon to Willadene, who stapled it
onto a paper dessert plate.

"Oh, no. Not again. I've already had my picture taken with one of those
cheesy headdresses."

Willadene grinned. "You can't escape it. It's tradition."

Erin sighed, and she then opened the box to see a gift pack of elegant
Shalimar-scented bubble bath, bath oil, and powder. "Thank you, Sophie,"
she said. "How did you know I love Shalimar?"

"I guessed," Sophie said proudly. "I paid for them myself with the
allowance I had saved up."

Erin hugged Sophie. "They're perfect."

"Grandma said we're supposed to give advice with our presents. So
here's mine: Brush your teeth, say your prayers, and have fun."

"That's good advice for all of us," Erin said.

"Let's have a toast," Gabby said. "Then, Miss Sophie, it's time for you to
go to bed." Sophie tried to wheedle her way out of it, but after the toast with
nonalcoholic bubbly, Gabby moved her gently but firmly into her bedroom.

With Sophie tucked in, the women turned to their own gifts and advice.

Willadene's gift was a frothy full-length white nightgown and peignoir
set. The nightgown had a modest bodice decorated with embroidery and
lace. On the inside back was a tag saying: *Handmade by Willadene.* "You
really made these? They're gorgeous."

"With my very own hands."

"You do fabulous work."

"Thanks. My Aunt Stell gave me some advice when I got married that's
worth passing on. Trust each other. Talk to each other. Remember that men
don't automatically become mind readers once they're married."

"Hear, hear," said Juneau.

"One more bit: Physical intimacy in marriage is meant to be enjoyed.
It's a gift."

"Here's to the unwrapping!'" Juneau raised her glass in a toast.

Next, Erin opened Juneau's gift, which was a knee-length gown and
robe in soft pink. When she held it up, Gabby looked from it to Deenie's

full-length peignoir set and said, "Looks like you have the long and short of it covered, Erin."

"My advice is short, too," said Juneau. "Don't go to bed mad."

"The key to a successful marriage," said Deenie, grinning.

"What's your advice, Gabby?" asked Erin.

"Celebrate life's moments when they come, dear, the small as well as the significant."

Erin gave them each a heartfelt hug. "I don't know how to thank you for everything you've done for me."

"Our pleasure," said Gabby.

"One thing's for sure. I'm set for the honeymoon." She blushed a little, which made the others smile.

"How long do you have at Disney World?" Gabby asked.

"A whole week. "

"That's nice. You'll have plenty of time to relax and get to know each other."

Juneau stepped forward and said, "*Regina clasped her hands to her bosom as she watched him approach. He came to stand over her, his eyes darkly gleaming, the smell of a strong, athletic man who didn't believe in deodorants rolling off him like waves. 'You're mine,' he said, reaching for her. She drew a quavering breath. 'Prove it to me. Show me the winning lottery ticket.'*"

When the appreciative chuckles died down, Juneau turned to Erin, a twinkle in her eyes. "Since we're stand-ins for your mother, is there anything you need to know? Any questions you want answered?"

That struck Erin as terribly funny, because her mother would never have asked that, even if she had been there. "I know everything I need to know," she said with a saucy grin. Then she turned sober. There was something she needed to say. She could feel it rising, pressing her to speak. "There's a part of me that's a little scared of intimacy. It's like I'm afraid that if I enjoy it—"

"Heaven forbid," murmured Gabby.

"—something awful will happen."

"That's just your Grams speaking," Juneau said shortly. "Whatever you do, Erin, don't take her along on your honeymoon. A threesome will ruin the whole thing."

Their explosion of laughter was like a quick and hard cloudburst, leaving Erin feeling giddy and somehow fresh, open and clean inside.

Sophie appeared in the doorway, rubbing her eyes. "What's happening?" she asked sleepily.

"Sorry we woke you," Gabby said. "Go on back to bed. I'll be joining you soon."

Juneau looked at her clock. "It's almost midnight."

"Then it's time for our final surprise."

When Gabby handed Erin a small white suitcase, she knew immediately what was inside. "You got me my very own temple clothing!" Tears stung her eyelids as she carefully opened the suitcase. Inside were an elegantly simple white dress, a beautiful lace-trimmed handkerchief with the initials EJ, and the other items used in the temple ceremony.

It was too much. Erin's heart was full of things she wanted to share, but she couldn't find the words.

"Looks like we've reached overload," said Juneau.

Willadene took the suitcase from Erin's lap and set it on the coffee table. "Time for beddy-bye," she said. "A lot's happened today, dear. You need to sleep on it."

There were hugs all around, and then Juneau and Willadene went across the hall and Gabby disappeared into the adjoining room. In the welcome dark and silence, Erin undressed, crept gratefully onto the luxurious bed, and pulled the silky sheets up around her shoulders. Then she dropped into a sleep as deep as a well.

Sunday, November 23, 1980
Dear Gabby, Juneau, and Willadene,

Thank you, thank you, thank you for all that you wonderful ladies did when I got married. I love you all so much. Gabby, your generosity still amazes me. I wonder how I ever deserved such a gift as you gave me—having you all with me made everything perfect. I only wish Mom and Grams could have been there, too.

I'll always remember how it felt to kneel across the altar from Cory. Over his shoulder I could see into one of the infinity mirrors, but what I saw in his eyes was better by far. I hope I will see it in his eyes for the rest of our lives.

The pictures taken on the steps of the temple turned out great. I'll be sending you each a copy of the best one and some of the pictures Cory and I took on our honeymoon.

The HONEYMOON! At first, I thought Cory's idea of going to

Disney World was really goofy, but it was so much fun! We were like a couple of kids, laughing and playing all day long.

As for the nights . . . I think I married the most romantic man in the world. He was so sweet. He always put me first and gave me all the time I needed. I thought I loved him before, but I'm learning that love can always grow larger and stronger.

I came back to earth with a clunk when the plane landed in Minneapolis—the big reception was in two days! I'm glad now that Linda handled it all. It would have been too much for Mom and Grams, especially financially. There were at least two hundred people there. Many of them were friends or business acquaintances of Linda and Skipp, so they were complete strangers to both Cory and me. I could feel how relieved Mom and Grams were when someone from our old neighborhood came through the line. It made me wish we had family in Minnesota. When Grams and Gramps moved here from Michigan for his railroad job, they left all of their relatives behind. Cory has scads of relatives and both sets of grandparents there.

I was surprised that Linda's parents, Frank and Gladys Wagner, came. We visited them while we were in Orlando. They are in poor health, and I think they came just because Cory is Linda's only child.

Skipp's parents, Harold and Trina, are from Naperville, a suburb of Chicago. They're really active for their age. They've got their papers in for their second couple's mission.

Now it's back to real life. Work, church, getting our little apartment set up. It's your basic two-bedroom, two-bath in an older complex in St. Louis Park. It has a heated underground garage, and it backs onto wetlands, so we have a nice view from our balcony. We can start moving in this Saturday. Yeah!

I'll be so glad to get out of the Johnsons' guest room. I appreciate everything they're doing for us, but I want to be alone with my husband!

> Love to you all,
> Mrs. Cory Johnson

P.S. I've discovered Cory likes to eat cereal and milk for supper!

Chapter Nineteen

WILLADENE

December 5, 1981

Dear Ladies and Jonas ('cause I'm pretty sure he'll end up reading this!),

We are decking the halls around here something fierce. Sunny will spend this Christmas doing all the things she missed last year, and we are all determined to be a part of it. My parents have deigned (how do you like that word, Juneau? I looked it up especially for you!) to spend Christmas Eve night here with Sunny. Will, NeVae, and Bert will join us for the evening.

We will have snacks at 5:00, soup supper at 7:00, and desserts before the family toast at 9:00. Bert is working with the kids to put on a Nativity scene for us with Rauf as a sheep, the boys and Bitsy as the shepherds/wise men, and her mom and dad as Mary and Joseph. NeVae is making a special Baby Jesus for the occasion and to use in coming years. Mom has made an angel dress for Sunny, who has carefully memorized the "good tidings" message from the Bible.

The audience has been cast as the heavenly host. It will be a joyful, if not completely on pitch, sound. Like Grandma Stowell says, "Count your blessings, and thank the Lord." We are all doing both.

Christmas morning we will open presents and have a special breakfast with Mom and Dad and Sunny. I am planning to try a breakfast casserole recipe I saw in the *Parade* section of the Sunday newspaper. It has a crust of thinly sliced potatoes and a quiche-like filling of eggs, browned onions, sausage, peppers, pimientos, and cream (so thick you have to spoon it from the jar) from the farm. I'll add a bowl of fresh fruit to make it look like a balanced meal.

At 2:00 we will head for Grandpa and Grandma Rasmussen's for Christmas dinner. Bert has her own set of recipes she wants to try out but won't tell what they are. We are looking forward to the surprise. Grandpa Will has promised to hitch Dot and Belle, his two draft horses, to a sledge and take everyone for a ride. We will have to bundle up and over to survive the cold. But Grandma NeVae heats blankets in the dryer and bricks by the fire so at least we start out toasty. The boys really look forward to this—that includes Grandpa Will, all his sons, and all their sons. The girls go along mostly to prove that they can do it.

Christmas evening we will drag ourselves to my folks for a light supper and a quiet evening of Christmas music and visiting. I know the kids will be asleep before they finish eating. But then I get to snuggle with my hubby and talk to my family. It is the part of our family traditions that I love the best. And it is the most peaceful time we have together all year.

We have family prayer in a circle in front of the fire before we leave. It is sweet, and the Spirit fills the room.

Wishing you equal sweetness for the season,
Deenie and all of us here

JUNEAU

December 15, 1981
Dear Christmas COBs,

I'm dreaming of a white Christmas . . . You know the rest. Well, the grass is green here, and the orange and palm trees are swaying. I've never quite got used to southern California Christmases. But I sure can't complain about the weather. It's perfect. Nicole was asking if we could go to the beach on Christmas. We told her maybe not, and she settled for a promise that we'll go down and sit along Colorado Boulevard on New Year's Eve so we can watch the Tournament of Roses parade right up close. The girls are both excited about that. Frankly, I don't look forward to sitting there for all those hours, but you have to stake out a spot early and then occupy it in order to keep it. I've been there, done that. But it's an experience every true Pasadenan and anyone else who loves parades should do at least two or three times! So if you watch the parade, you can imagine us there. I asked Misty and Nicole if they still want to sit there all night if it's raining. Nicole, our Fearless

Fact Finder, informed me that the last time it rained on the Parade was 1955. So I guess statistics are in their favor.

Well, good friends, have a wonderful Christmas. My household, including Philip Atwater, sends the very best of wishes. Our family photo card is enclosed. (Philip Atwater is the one with the bow tie and shades.)

Love,
Juneau

ERIN

Sunday, December 27, 1981
Merry Christmas, Gabby, Juneau, and Willadene,

I hope you all had a wonderful Christmas. I can just see what Christmas looks like at your houses, Gabby and Willadene. Sorry, Juneau, but I can't begin to imagine what Christmas is like in a place where there are palm trees and warm weather in the month of December!

Sorry it took me so long to get these pictures sent, but at least I got my thank-you notes written. (It was pretty strange writing all those notes to people I don't know and will probably never see again.) As you can see, Cory and I had a ball at Disney World. We were on our own with nothing to do but have fun.

Christmas this year was much better than last year. We solved the where-to-go dilemma by attending Christmas Eve services with The Women and Christmas Day dinner with Skipp and Linda. I'm so glad Cory agreed with the compromise. It really meant a lot to Grams.

Our apartment is starting to look good. It took a while for us to agree on what to buy. We ended up at Slumberland, where we bought a basic couch and loveseat in a blue/brick red/cream plaid and a blue recliner for Cory to watch sports in. For the bedroom, we bought a queen bed, two nightstands, and two dressers in red oak with antique brass fittings.

Cory wanted to buy the table for the dining area there, too, but I held out for something more fun. Are you ready? I bought a 1950s dinette set in chrome and red from an antiques store on 50th and

France! He wasn't sure about it, but I promised him that it would look great, and it does, now that I've got some other 50s accents in blue and red and cream in the kitchen area. Colleen and Steve love it. Even Skipp and Linda like it!

My biggest find was an antique oak armoire. Bless Cory, he didn't flip out when I told him what it cost. It's now the focal point of our living room. Whoever had it before had installed a sturdy shelf at just the right level to hold a TV. We keep our videos in the drawer at the bottom.

Furnishing the house brought up a bunch of issues about money. Most of the time, I'd rather save it than spend it. Cory spends happily and assumes more will come our way. I offered to do the finances, but Cory thinks it's his job as head of the household. That makes me nervous!

On a different note, the bishop asked me to teach the Sunday School class for seven-year-olds. I was so surprised! I guess now that I am a respectable married woman, the bishopric trusts me not to lead the kiddies astray!

I'm so glad I said yes. (As if I could have said no.) The kids in this class are getting ready for baptism. They are so sweet. Guileless, says Cory. I looked up the word. It means innocent or naive. That fits.

The father of one of the kids stopped me in the hall this week to thank me for teaching his daughter. According to him, I had said something the week before that really touched her heart. I have no idea what that might have been. I just taught the lesson the way it was in the book.

Cory is teaching the investigators class, so on Saturday night, we're both at the kitchen table with our books spread out. There's something very special about that time together.

Here's wishing you a Happy New Year!

Love,
Erin

P.S. Cory's parents invited us and The Women for Thanksgiving dinner. Mom said they already had plans, but I didn't believe that for one minute. They probably ate at Denny's.

Chapter Twenty
1982

WILLADENE

January 21, 1982
Dear Ladies All,

Hello from Heckuba! Is there anything grayer than a gray day in January? We are suffering from one of the awful air inversions we get this time of year. The clouds are gray, the snow is gray, the cars look gray, and the air even tastes gray when you breathe in. It's a good thing it's bright inside, or we would all be going bats!

Erin, congratulations on your new calling. I have never taught that age group, but I've raised one son through it. You're absolutely right about how endearing they are, but they can be equally naughty. Try checking out pictures from the ward library and let the kids tell the story that goes with it. Both my sons loved doing that when they were that age, and I think they learned a lot, too.

Not much else to tell; we're all hiding inside unless we absolutely have to brave the cold. I did go out for one extra errand Roger said was silly, but I said was an absolutely-have-to. When the Shoebox stopped at my house, it was EMPTY. I took my rainy-day money and made the slippery trek to Logan in the van. Deseret Industries had a good selection of Shoebox-type books for a quarter apiece so I bought a bagful. When I got home I divided them up with plenty for me and enough to fill the Shoebox and sent it on.

Waiting out winter with Regina,
Deenie

ERIN

Sunday, February 7, 1982
Hi, Ladies,

I can't believe it's already February. Last year at this time, I had no idea I would be married before the year ended. It's amazing to me how fast things can change. Cory and I went dancing New Year's Eve. I'm not much of a dancer, but we had a ball. We're decided to sign up for swing dance lessons at the health club. Won't that be fun?

I made a New Year's resolution to be a better housekeeper, but I'm having trouble keeping it. When I told my friend Angie how frustrated I was, she asked me why I was making such a big deal out of it. She said, "As far as I know, being messy isn't a moral failure." A couple of days later, she brought me in a little plaque she and Norm had made. It had a quote on it from A. A. Milne: "One of the advantages of being disorderly is that one is constantly making exciting discoveries." I love it, and Cory laughed out loud when he saw it. He helped me hang it in the kitchen, one of the places where I make the most discoveries. That made me feel better, but I know he wishes I would keep house like his mother.

He also wishes I were like his mother when it comes to entertaining. He loves to have people over, especially the guys from Pillsbury. It's a good thing we got so many fancy dishes for entertaining from Skipp's business friends. We're going to be doing a lot of it. When I use those dishes, I put a pad on the dinette set and cover it with one of our fancy tablecloths. So long, Fifties Funk.

By the way, a client of mine was looking at the pictures of my kitchen the other day, and she went wild. She had all sorts of questions about where I found the 50s dinette set and especially the fabric for the curtains. When I told her Colleen and I seemed to have a knack for finding the good stuff, she asked if we would be willing to find some things for her family room!

We're going to take a Polaroid of whatever we think she might like and put it on hold. Then she'll stop by Stefani's to see if she wants it or not. She said she'd pay us a finder's fee for everything she decides to buy!

Isn't that just a blast? We won't make any money by the time we've paid for gas, but we'll have fun. I'm really going to have to keep up on the housework, though, because I'll be out and about on my day off. Who knows? Maybe it will turn into something.

                    Love and kisses,
                    Erin

JUNEAU

February 14, 1982
Dear Erin:

Your quote, "One of the advantages of being disorderly is that one is constantly making exciting discoveries," reminds me of one I have which says, "A messy desk is a sign of a creative mind." It has become my motto!

Love,
Juneau

P.S. Happy Valentine's Day to you and Cory. Did you have a Valentine Box at school when you were a kid? We always did, wherever we were, and I never got more than four or five valentines because nobody knew me since we moved around so much. Or maybe they just didn't like me!

Sometimes people asked Juneau where she got the ideas for the weekly stories she produced in Mrs. Jarvis's class. The man named Clyde said he did well to come up with an idea a month. "I get lots of magnificent ideas when I'm drunk," he said, "but when I sober up, they don't seem all that good." He paused to grin at Juneau. "But you don't drink, do you?"

"No," she said.

"Well, then," he continued, "where *do* you get all those ideas?"

"I don't know," she said. "They just seem to come from observing life."

She'd always been an observer. She assumed it had started during those years of traveling around, never really being part of what was going on anywhere. So she watched and recorded what she saw, somewhere in her mind. It was all there to be used—situations, characters, bits of philosophy, and place names like Beetdigger Lane and Mutton Hollow Drive and Skunks Misery Road. Mrs. Jarvis liked to quote a line from a writer named Jessamyn West that said, "Fiction reveals truths that reality obscures." Someday Juneau hoped to write meaningful fiction that would shine a light on obscured truths.

The thing was, in a story you could change things, twist them around to fit the needs of fiction. In real life things refused to twist to serve anybody's needs. It was the needs that had to adjust.

She had tried to make a story from an incident between her and Misty. She'd wanted Misty to clean up her room, which was an unkempt slough of clothing on the floor, half-eaten sandwiches under the bed that even Philip Atwater wouldn't eat, and pictures of hairy rock stars on the walls. Juneau wasn't sure which area she considered the worst.

"Tidy it up," she told Misty one day. "It makes me sick to look in there."

Misty shrugged. "So don't look in there."

It reminded Juneau of the old joke about the man who goes to the doctor, raises his arm up high, and says, "It hurts when I do this." The doctor says, "So don't do that."

But this wasn't funny. It was annoying. It was unhealthy. It was slovenly.

"Misty," she said, "how can you live that way?"

"I like it," Misty said.

"You like living in a swamp?"

"I'm a swamp creature." Misty's tone was flippant.

"I'm serious," Juneau said.

"So am I."

Juneau realized she was in a contest of wills with an eleven-year-old girl, and the girl was winning. She'd have to try another tack.

"Misty," she said, "this is *my* house. It is not very big, and it gets smaller the more clutter there is. It is important to me to have things fairly neat. I really would appreciate it if you'd bring your room up to some kind of neatness standard. It doesn't have to be perfect. Just the clothes picked up and the dirty ones sorted out and the maggoty food thrown away. Would you do that for me?"

"No," Misty said.

Juneau suppressed an urge to shake her daughter. "Why?" she asked.

Misty faced her squarely. "I live here, too, Mom. You have to let me be here even if I don't keep my room neat."

Absurdly, Juneau thought of the line from a Robert Frost poem that said, "Home is where, when you go there, they have to take you in."

Juneau nodded. "Yes, I do. But I don't *have* to let you live in a pit."

"It's *my* pit, Mom."

Juneau didn't want to start another round of "but it's *my* house." So she said, "Sweetie, please cooperate just a little bit, maybe?"

"Okay," Misty said. "I'll keep the door shut."

Later, Juneau tried to build a story around the conflict. But she couldn't even make her fictional character clean up her room. So she twisted her own needs around to fit Misty's idea of cooperation, thinking that Misty would go off to college in about seven years. She hoped. In the meantime,

Juneau figured she'd better resign from her Church calling of teaching the Social Relations lessons. Just the month before she'd taught the lesson "Love within the Family," in which she'd made the point that a family should provide a place where each individual can grow and develop to his or her highest potential. She felt like a hypocrite.

Since that story didn't work out, Juneau worked instead on an idea she got from Nicole, who'd long been enamored of Cinderella. One day she came home from school and said, "Mom, they don't make glass slippers any more, do they?"

A *great title*, Juneau thought. She wrote a light little story to fit it and sent it out. It sold to a preteen magazine. It was the second story she sold that year. The man named Clyde in Mrs. Jarvis's class pronounced it one of her best.

ERIN

Erin sat at the red and chrome dinette, her Sunday School manual before her, wondering. Only the day before she had been talking to Colleen about how hard it was to adjust to living with Cory. Colleen had said, "You didn't expect it to be easy, did you? Before you got married, you had stuff to deal with, right? Now you're married, you have twice the stuff to deal with."

Now Erin thought, *I not only wanted it to be easy, I wanted it to be perfect!* It was important to her to show The Women that by joining the Church and marrying in the temple she would be able to create an ideal family.

"What's going on, babycakes?" Angie asked a few days later. She was leaning against the client chair in front of her station, watching Erin sweep up the hair from her last cut.

"What?" Erin asked.

"Something's up. You've only laughed four times today. Four laughs, seven chuckles, fifteen smiles. Way below your normal count."

"You keep track?"

"Not usually. So what is it?"

"Hey, I'm still in the honeymoon phase, Angie. I have noooo complaints."

Angie gave her the look that said she wasn't buying it. "We haven't gone over to Dockside after work for months. We're due. What do you think?"

It seemed to Erin that she was always obligated to someone or something after work. Tonight, however, there was nothing on her schedule except fixing supper for Cory when she got home. Looking at Angie's open

face with its big grin, she realized she had missed her friend's companionship and blunt humor. "Sure," she said. "I'd love to."

They asked the hostess at Dockside for a booth by the fireplace and next
to the windows so they could look out on Lake Minnetonka. As they
nibbled on appetizers, Angie entertained Erin with stories about Norm's new
hobby of carving and painting duck decoys and what her children and
grandchildren were up to. When the crab cakes and teriyaki wings were
gone, Angie sat back, crossed her arms, and said, "Enough with the chitchat. Tell momma all about it."

Erin sighed. "Your kids must have had a tough time getting things by
you."

"They never could fool my . . . baloney detector." She didn't say it, but
Erin could see she was thinking, *You, either.*

"What do you think is going on?" Erin asked.

"I think the reality of marriage is setting in."

Erin gazed pensively out at the gray lake with wind-driven whitecaps.
"It's not so much being married to Cory. It's being married to his family. You
know what I mean?"

"I have an idea."

"All my life, I've wanted to be part of a family. Now that I am, I feel like
I've been swallowed by a whale."

Angie's uninhibited laugh drew the attention of nearby diners. "I love
it! That's such a great description."

"A very big whale named Johnson," Erin added, grinning. "Before the
wedding, I was so thrilled to be accepted and wanted by Skipp and Linda."

"Skip. That's a nickname, right?"

"No. It's a family name. Skipp with two ps."

Angie raised her eyebrows but made no comment.

"Now I feel smothered by them. They're always planning something for
us to do together. They expect us to go to their place or meet them somewhere for supper a couple of times a week, not counting Sunday."

Suddenly it all welled up, and Erin could hear her voice vibrate with
intensity. "I am so sick of living my life in public. I want some time for myself.
Is there anything wrong with that?"

"Does Cory think there is?"

"He loves being with people, so he can't understand why I can only take
so much, especially when I've had to socialize all day long with my clients.

He promises to talk to his parents, but every time they invite us to their place, Cory says yes. Most of the time without asking me."

"Tell him to go by himself."

"I do, but then he says, 'What do you want me to tell Mom and Dad? That you've had enough of them?' So I end up going, and then I'm so ticked off at Cory, I give him the silent treatment."

"Oh, honey, you've got yourself a situation. You have to stand up for yourself, or you'll be dealing with this for the rest of your life."

"But I don't want to hurt Linda and Skipp."

"*Linda* and *Skipp* won't die if you decline an invitation."

Erin smiled a little. "Listening to Cory, you'd think they would." She paused. "What would you do?"

Angie sat back in the booth. "If I'd been swallowed by a whale? Well, if I were Jonah, I'd promise God I'd do what he asked me to do."

"That's no help. God says to honor your father and mother. Cory would interpret that as letting his parents have their way in everything."

"Okay, no pass." Angie pursed her lips in thought. "If I were Captain Ahab . . . no, never mind that. Ahab made an enemy of that whale, and he got what he deserved."

"How about Geppetto, Pinocchio's father. He got out of the whale by lighting a fire."

"There you go, girl. But it wasn't the fire that got the whale to cough old Geppetto out. It was the smoke. The irritation."

"Then that doesn't work, either. I don't want to be seen as the source of irritation in the Johnson family. I don't want to be spat out. I just want some time to myself. I want some time alone with my husband."

Angie wasn't the only one who had noticed Erin had stopped smiling. Cory kept asking her what was wrong, but she saw no point in telling him. It wouldn't make any difference anyway. But several days after she talked to Angie, he confronted her in the kitchen.

"Mom and Dad say we need to have a long talk. They're worried about you," he told Erin.

She stood, arms akimbo, in front of the kitchen sink. "Great. I'm worried about me." She should have been grateful that he was finally willing to talk, but her ire was raised by the fact that he was only doing it because his parents had told him he should.

"I thought we were doing okay," he said.

"You may be, but I'm not."

"What's wrong?"

She lifted her chin defiantly. "What's wrong is that ever since we were married, everything has been going your way. We do what you want to do. We buy the things you want to eat and cook them the way you like them. We spend way too much time at your parents' place and hardly any with The Women."

"Grams isn't that much fun to be with."

"That's beside the point. I felt like a person when I married you. Now I feel like a possession."

He made a disparaging sound. "That sounds like a line from a B movie. Or one of those romance novels you like to read."

"You're missing the point. I feel like I'm turning into—"

"A Johnson?"

There it was, out in the open. "Well, yes. I hate it. I want to do what I want to do sometimes. I want to do things my way and know it's okay. I want to be me, Cory, not your mother."

Cory reached out to take her hand. "You know I love you, don't you?"

She jerked her hand away. "Don't try to change the subject! I'm sick of never having a say in what goes on here. Do you get that? I want a life of my own. I want to be Erin Larson, who just happens to also be a Johnson."

"I have no idea what that means." Cory's voice was cool. "And I hate it when you get hysterical."

"I'm not hysterical. I'm furious!"

"Then why are you crying?"

"I always cry when I'm mad!" She ran into the bedroom and slammed the door. For some time there was silence on the other side. Then she heard the rise and fall of his voice, but the words were unclear. *He's probably talking to his dad,* she thought. *Or Steve.* She hated the idea of his revealing their private business to others, but didn't she do the same?

Later, she heard a soft knock on the bedroom door, and Cory slipped into the room. "Can we talk?"

She was lying on her side, her face in her pillow. She sniffled and nodded, without changing position.

He sat down on the side of the bed and smoothed her hair back from her forehead. "I talked to Steve. I hope you don't mind."

"It depends on what you said."

"I said something was wrong between us, and it was probably my fault."

She rolled over so she could look into his face. "Really?"

"He gave me the plain and pure word, Erin. He said I've been acting like I'm still single. I do what I want to do and expect you to come along as my cheering squad."

"Yay, Cory. Rah-rah-rah." She smiled faintly.

"He said I should stop hanging around my parents so much. He quoted scripture to me. Something from the Bible exhorting men to leave their parents and cleave unto their wives."

"Yay, Steve!" she said, her voice more animated.

"It hasn't been much fun for you, has it?"

"Some of it has."

"How about we have family home evening by ourselves Monday night? We can talk about what's important to us both and work out some compromises. Sound good?"

"Sounds great." She pulled him down into a kiss. He lay down beside her, and she rested her head on his shoulder. "Cory?" She stroked his cheek and gave him what she hoped was a seductive smile. "What did that scripture say about cleaving?"

Chapter Twenty-One

WILLADENE

April 7, 1982
Dear Ladies,

Bert came home last weekend. She announced to the whole family that she has talked to her bishop and is planning to go on a mission when she graduates in May. Everyone starting laughing, because they thought it was her April Fool's joke. Everyone except Roger and me, since she had confided in us some time ago. When the Rasmussens saw how serious Bert was, things changed rapidly. Grandpa Will got weepy, and Grandma NeVae got worried. She was afraid Bert would be called to some place far away without running water and doctors.

I was so proud of Bert. She handled herself as I imagine Gabby would have in like circumstances. She kept her dignity up and her voice down.

Then the topic of graduation came up. When Bert finally told her parents she had switched her course of study to anthropology and sociology, I thought NeVae was going to pass out on the spot. Her first reaction was, "Who would ever want to marry an anthropologist?"

Bert reminded her gently that she didn't have to worry about that for at least a year and a half.

She is planning to take out her endowment as soon as she can and has asked us especially to join her.

Everything is spring here. Snowdrops have followed crocuses in the side garden, and the first shoots of lettuce and greens I planted in the cold frame last winter are starting to show. The farm has lambs and calves in the barn, and Belle is due to foal by the end of May. I think it is the perfect time to make new resolutions and changes in our lives. Much better than New Years!

Hopefully,
Deenie

P.S. Bert brought home a Sony compact disk player with some disks that are supposed to replace vinyl records. She's sure I'll be converted to this new kind of sound—no scratches, no phantoms, no skipping needles. But I'm so used to the scratches on my LPs, they seem like part of the music.

ERIN

April 7, 1982
Dear COBettes,

I think I would like your sister-in-law Bert, Willadene. She sounds like a very strong young woman with a mind of her own. It's great she's going on a mission. I know how much Cory's mission meant to him. Did I tell you that Cory's grandparents Harold and Trina were called to the California San Diego mission? They're assigned to the mission home, where Harold manages the finances and Trina mothers the missionaries.

Francine Ralston, the client who asked me and Colleen to do some shopping for her, has been giving our numbers to all her friends. Colleen and I got two calls this week! Neither of the jobs is big, but we're very excited. Cory calls our little enterprise a "kitchen business." He and Steve laugh at us, but I think they like that we've got something going.

I'm glad to say that Cory and I are getting some issues worked out. We spend more time at home, and he sometimes goes over to his parents' place without me. That works out well, because I've been visiting The Women without him!

Everybody at work has had the flu. It hit me hard, and I gave it to Cory. Two people sick at the same time is way more than twice the misery! But we're feeling lots better now.

Love to all,
Erin

When Erin stopped mid-haircut for her third rest room break, her customer asked, "Not completely over the flu yet?"

"More like too much soda," Erin answered apologetically and then began to razor in the layers of the cut as requested. As she was cleaning up her area afterwards, Juneau and her numerous pit stops in Provo popped into her mind.

Could I be pregnant? She wondered. She was flooded with warmth at the possibility. Then panic set in. *What is Cory going to say? We weren't thinking of having a baby yet.*

That night for the first time in weeks she drove to Colleen's after leaving work. Colleen opened the door, wearing an apron, spatula in hand. The minute Erin stepped inside, the smell of cooking onions assailed her nostrils and sent her stomach into flip-flops. With a cry, she dashed for the bathroom, grateful to make it before the retching got serious.

When she came out of the bathroom, shaky and embarrassed, Colleen handed her a glass of water. "You're pregnant, aren't you." It was more a statement than a question.

"Is that the sure sign?" Erin attempted a grin.

Colleen nodded, laughing. "I'd say so. I've turned the stove off and put the frying pan in the oven. I hope that helps."

Erin nodded gratefully and took a sip of water.

"Come sit down. EJ's having her power nap, so we've got a few minutes to ourselves."

They talked about maternity clothes and when Erin was going to tell Cory. Then Erin asked, "Colleen, how did you feel—emotionally, I mean—when you found out you were going to have a baby?"

"Ecstatic. For as long as I can remember, I wanted to be a mother. I loved playing with my baby dolls. When I got old enough to baby-sit, I took every job that was offered me. I got to earn money and play mommy." Colleen smiled. "And now I am one."

"Did you ever wonder if you would be a good mother?"

"Not then." Colleen leaned across the kitchen table to pat Erin's arm. "Listen, I've seen how you love EJ and how tender you are with her. You'll be a great mother. And Cory will be the best dad."

Erin smiled. "He will be, won't he? I guess I'd better tell him. But not until after I've seen my gynecologist."

When Cory heard the news, he gave a whoop of joy and twirled her around the room. "Really? Are you sure?"

"My gynecologist is sure." She hugged him fiercely. "I'm so glad you aren't upset."

"How could I be upset? We're in good shape financially, and my job is going well." He smiled hugely. "Let's call Mom and Dad."

She grabbed him by the arm. "Let's not. I'd like to have some time for us to get used to the idea."

Cory was willing to wait, but he couldn't sit still. She could see he had to be doing something, so they finally ended up going to a B Dalton bookstore where Cory bought a pile of books on pregnancy and childbirth, some on parenthood, and a large-format book with full-color pictures of developing fetuses in every stage. Standing in an aisle of the bookstore, he found the image corresponding to the estimated age of their baby.

Pointing at the tiny dot in a sea of darkness, he said, "That's what he looks like right now." His voice was full of awe.

Erin grinned. "It could be a she, you know."

The look on Cory's face was one she hadn't seen for a long time: adoration. "If it is, I hope she looks just like you."

That night when they crawled into bed after their prayers, Cory put his hand on Erin's abdomen. "Hi, little person," he said tenderly. "We're so glad you're coming to us. We love you. We'll take such good care of you. You grow now and get strong and beautiful. Love, Dad."

Erin turned to him. "That was so sweet." She held him and kissed him, the love she felt overflowing.

Cory couldn't keep a secret. Erin had wanted to tell The Women first— they always seemed to take second place—but Linda read it on his face when she and Skipp dropped by to lend Cory a reference book for his Sunday School lesson.

The Johnsons were delighted. Skipp pounded Cory on the back, and Linda hugged Erin and then held her at arm's length to give her the once-over. "You don't look too peaked. Are you able to keep food down in the morning? No? Well, I found that . . ."

She was off and running. Skipp wasn't far behind, wondering aloud what denomination of CD he should purchase for his yet-to-be-born grandchild. Erin felt a dull pain in her temple as Cory and his parents filled the room with enthusiastic conversation.

Sunday afternoon, Erin awoke from a nap certain that it was time to tell The Women. When Cory turned off the TV to go with her, she said, "You don't have to come. In fact, I think it would be better if you didn't."

"Why?" He was hurt and offended; she could hear it in his voice.

"I think it's important that I tell them myself."

"If you say so. But you aren't driving that old Escort anymore. It's not safe."

All the way from Minnetonka to Nordeast, Erin prayed. *Dear Lord, please make them glad about this baby. Especially Grams.* She wished she were driving to Gabby's instead. She wanted to be surrounded by love when she told her news. She wanted Grams and Joanna to react the way she knew Gabby and Juneau and Willadene would.

Joanna met her at the door, welcoming her in. "It's so nice to have you come for a visit." She looked past Erin. "Where's Cory? Isn't he coming?"

"I wanted to have some time with you alone. Girl time," she added with a grin.

"Grams is on the patio catching the last of the sun. I just made some lemonade. Or would you rather have something else?'

"That'll be fine." *I think,* Erin added to herself. She never knew these days what might give her the heaves.

She joined Grams at the patio table and looked around the yard. Early tulips, hyacinths, and daffodils lined the flower borders that were Grams's pride and joy. The work she put into them showed in the lush growth and beautiful blossoms.

"You've really been busy, Grams. The flower gardens look great."

Grams shook her head. "They don't look the way they should. I can't work in them the way I used to—my knees and hips hurt too much."

Erin shook her head. Grams was definitely not Gabby.

Joanna brought the lemonade and sat down beside Erin. As they sipped the drink, they made small talk about what was going on in the neighborhood and Joanna's job. All the time, Erin was aware of Joanna's scrutiny. Then Grams gave her a questioning look. Feeling their probing gaze, Erin blurted it out. "I'm going to have a baby."

"Oh, Erin!" Joanna leaned close to hug her. "Oh, my dear. This is such good news. Are you feeling okay?"

"Not bad, after I throw up in the morning."

"Ugh. I remember that stage." Joanna turned to Grams. "Isn't this wonderful? You're going to be a great-grandmother!"

"I suppose you're going to raise it Mormon."

"Y-yes," stuttered Erin.

"Well, don't overwork or get too carried away trying to be perfect."

Erin was about to make a sharp reply when she noticed that the corners of Ruth's mouth were turned up and there was a glint of humor in her eyes. She was trying to make a joke!

"Don't worry, Grams. I'll take good care of myself. Cory will make sure of that."

Grams rose to go inside. She paused as she passed, resting her hand on Erin's shoulder. Erin looked up into her face. There was a connection in that moment like none she had ever experienced with her grandmother.

After Grams left, Joanna shifted her chair closer. "I'm so proud of you, Erin. You and Cory are doing so well, and now . . ." She hesitated. "I think you made the right choice when you joined the Mormon Church."

"Really?"

"I see you and Cory making a life for yourselves." She looked away from Erin, her lips trembling. "Your baby will have the life I always wanted for you. A real family. A loving family."

"Mom, don't cry."

"It's okay. I'm not crying because I'm sad. I'm crying because this baby is my second chance." She looked into Erin's eyes, and Erin could see how much she was loved. "Be happy, dear."

Erin left half an hour later, tired but content. She never understood why she took the entrance ramp east on I-94 instead of west. Why she took the Cretin Avenue exit and then turned left onto Summit Avenue. She followed the route she thought Cory had taken all those months ago until she came to the house where—if Cory and his father were right—the redheaded Catholic boy lived.

June 7, 1982
Dear Gabby, Juneau, and Deenie,

Sorry I haven't written for a while. I'm pregnant and sick as a dog. I'm about three months along. My doctor says that I should be feeling better soon, but Angie says, "Being pregnant isn't bad. It's just the first four months—and the last five months!"

Cory is thrilled, although he isn't much for holding my hand when I'm hugging the toilet. He talks to the baby every night after we say our prayers. He tells it that it's loved and wanted and we'll take good care of it. It brings tears to my eyes.

Mom cried when I told her. She sees the baby as her second chance. She'll be free to love him (or her) in a way she wasn't free to love me, not with everything else that was going on at the time. Grams told me not to overwork, which is her way of showing concern. Linda went shopping right away, so I've already got receiving blankets and little fleece sleepers in soft yellow and green. She's now researching car seats to find out which ones are the safest.

Juneau, my dear friend, I've been thinking a lot about the conversations we had at Gabby's in 1980. You know which ones I mean. Now that I'm pregnant, things don't seem so simple to me. I'm not always happy about being pregnant. I'm alternately thrilled, touched, terrified, or tearful. So please forgive me for being so judgmental back then. I had no idea.

I'm really missing you all right now.

> Love,
> Erin

JUNEAU

June 14, 1982
Dear COBettes,

Erin, I'm sorry you're so barfy at the moment, but this will pass. Actually, I'm envious. I've been hoping for almost two years now to have another baby, but it hasn't happened. In my weak moments I fall back into the pit about being punished for having wished Max away, but then I think of all the support and help I got from you and I pull myself out of it. I'm still hoping . . .

I've been working hard on my writing. It's funny, but before I sold anything, my goal was to sell a story. Now that I've done that, my goal has moved on. I want to sell more stories. I'm even thinking of trying a book. The carrot always seems to be far up ahead. I wonder if I'll ever reach a final destination!

We've had a busy summer so far. Right now I'm keeping an eye on Marisol's kids while she and Manny are on a trip to Mexico City. You remember, the Sanchez family lives next door, and Marisol is my wonderful and dependable friend who has done so much for me. Manny (Manuel, that is) is in the import business and gone a lot. This time Marisol got to go with him. I'm happy to watch their kids to repay her for so many similar services. Isabel at fifteen doesn't want to admit she needs a "baby-sitter," but she checks in regularly with me. Misty is in awe of her since Isabel is really into doing makeup. Misty is a willing model. Vincent is twelve and so sweet I could eat him! (Too bad the Sanchezes aren't Mormons—he'd be such a cute deacon now.) Beto is nine, same as Nicole, and they've been the best of friends since they were toddlers. Right now they have a big project going. They've had this thing about Egypt for some time and plan to go there after they are married in the year 2000 (?!), but now they're convinced they can find mummies in our back yards if they dig deep enough. So whenever Marisol or I need a flower bed dug up, we kind of hint that there might be a mummy about a foot or two down. I told Marisol maybe I should have them look for Great-Grandma Letitia while they're digging. She has to be buried somewhere!

Manny and Marisol threw a wonderful Cinco de Mayo party for the neighborhood. Their whole backyard was hung with pinatas, which absolutely dazzled all the kids. I thought at least one or two of them would have to be rushed to the hospital, what with all those sticks swinging wildly to break the pinatas open. But Greg took charge of making sure nobody bled. He's good with over-enthusiastic kids. (I'm predicting he'll be made Scoutmaster after he's released from the bishopric.) It all turned out fine. We gorged ourselves silly on Marisol's tamales and enchiladas and chile rel-lenos. I know the thoughts of such things won't agree with your poor stomach at the present time, Erin. Sorry!

Buenos noches,
Juneau

WILLADENE

The news that Erin had a baby on the way set Deenie into fast forward. She bought flannel to make receiving blankets and began to send Erin every coupon for disposable diapers that came her way. She put them in cards and notes of encouragement. In the warm, early summer evenings she sat on the front porch and crocheted edging with piquet points on the finished blan-kets. It filled the time while Roger was at school, and she could watch the kids while they played. On June 29 she wrote:

Dear Erin,

Congratulations again, little mother! Try B_{12} shots and lots of fresh air for the nausea. It worked for me.

Goodies on the way.

Love,
Deenie

Chapter Twenty-Two

WILLADENE

On July 1, Grandpa Will called and asked everyone to meet at the farm. Bert had received her mission call and wanted the whole family present when she opened it. Since Roger was already there, Deenie and the kids piled into the car without a thought for sticky hands or uncombed hair.

As expected, she found the Rasmussens gathered in the grove of cottonwoods that surrounded a small spring behind the barn. It was the place where all major discussions were held, weather permitting.

Roger sat with Will and NeVae, saving a place for Deenie and the kids. The rest of the family was seated at various picnic tables. Bert stood at the head of the circle, an envelope held tightly to her chest.

As soon as Deenie and the kids sat down next to Roger, Bert took a deep breath and slowly tore open the letter. She peeked inside the flap and then peeked a little farther as though she wanted to savor every moment of delicious suspense she could get. Finally she opened the letter all the way, read for a moment, closed her eyes, and said in a stunned voice. "The Scotland Edinburgh Mission. I've been called to the Scotland Edinburgh Mission!"

After that, everything was pandemonium. The complete letter was read aloud and passed around over and over again. Then the questions flew. Did Bert need new luggage? When was she going into the Missionary Training Center? Was her passport still good? What was she supposed to wear and would they buy it or make it? The grove was filled with energy and excitement and support. And it was all focused rightly on Bert.

After offering to sew anything Bert wanted her to, Deenie sat back and watched the show. It was a good one. The Rasmussens did everything in a big way. Even their voices and gestures were oversized. Except for Roger. He was more restrained in everything he did, more like the Stowells. As she watched, Deenie wondered what it would be like to have something more exciting to look forward to than Bitsy's Fancy Panty celebration. Even that had been for Bitsy and not really for her. *What would it be like to have something new and unexpected happen just to me?*

She had occasion to regret that prophetic thought two weeks later. She

was cutting out jumpers for Bert in three different colors of washable wool
when the second counselor in the bishopric came by to ask if she would take
on being assistant den mother for the Cub Scouts.

WILLADENE

August 10, 1982
Dear Ladies,

Hang on to your hats! Sit down tight! I am in for one heck of a
ride—as assistant den mother! I don't think a Stowell gal has ever
been a den mother before. Hmmm . . . Are there any known appli-
cations for the use of yogurt in Cub Scouts?

We have had only four boys Carl's age in our ward up to now. But
in one month our membership has grown to eight, hence the need
for an assistant to the den mother.

Two of the newcomers seem like nice boys. The other two are a bit
of a handful. Sister Streeter (Grandma Streeter to everyone in the
ward) is taking in her twin ten-year-old grandsons, Reece and
Ryan. It seems her daughter, Patience, who lives in the Chicago
area, has been having marital problems with her husband, Vance.
The twins are "acting out," whatever that means, and their
fifteen-year-old brother, Stan, is in trouble with the juvenile
authorities. I guess that even in the nicest neighborhoods there is
always someone to encourage a restless boy to go bad.

Ryan and Reece are trying to prove they're tough guys, so they're
constantly in one scrape or another, with Carl following devotedly
behind. When I try to bring up the subject with Carl, he says, "But
nobody messes with them, Mom." I am appalled, but Roger is
understanding. He insists it is perfectly natural for Carl, who is the
smallest in his class and often the object of bullying, to be
attracted to boys with power, boys nobody messes with. Grandma
Streeter hopes a few months of hard work and hard play in mountain air will straighten them out. I sure hope she's right.

> Mystified in the mountains,
> Deenie

P.S. I'm a world away from the romance of the wedding. Sigh. Oh,
to be a newlywed again.

ERIN

August 11, 1982
Hi, Ladies,

I'm feeling much better, hallelujah! I'm wearing maternity clothes now. There's none to be found in vintage shops, so Mom made me a couple of cute dresses, and I bought some tops and pants at Donaldson's. I look like every other pregnant woman in town, but maybe that's not all bad. Willadene, my doctor said I wasn't urpy enough to get vitamin B_{12} shots, but your suggestion about fresh air worked! Thanks.

Cory's been taking good care of me. He insists that I drive his car because it's safer. He makes sure I take my prenatal vitamins and eat properly. He's even taken over some of the housework because he wants to make sure I get enough rest.

Every night before we go to sleep, he talks to our baby. I close my eyes and pretend he's talking to me, too. Those are sweet moments. I love to see Cory so enthusiastic, not just about the baby but about life. He gets down once in a while, but he doesn't stay there for long. Before I met Cory, I didn't really understand "Man is that he might have joy." Living with him is teaching me that it's all right to be happy.

Love and kisses,
Erin

WILLADENE

August 17, 1982
Dear Ladies,

I am beginning to have a greater sympathy for Grandma Streeter's Chicago daughter. Single parenting is the pits! With Roger pushing to complete his master's degree at the University of Utah, we seldom see him and then only very early or very late. I don't know how he can stand all that classroom time, but he loves learning and being with people who share his interests. He's so wrapped up in it that it's all he talks about, even to me. It gives me a queer feeling in the pit of my stomach to have him so enthusiastic about

something I have no part in. It's like he lives a separate life at the
university.

*Regina sat quietly by the parlor window gazing hungrily at the passing
traffic. Would he come today? She ran her long, slender finger caress-
ingly across the envelope that lay on her lap—his name and her address.
Could this be the letter that would bring an end to his patient longing?*

*Suddenly he was there, windswept and wonderful. "Is it come at last?"
he gasped, kneeling at her feet.*

"Yes, my darling, at last!"

*He tore the letter from her hands and ripped it open. Surging to his feet
in one feline motion, he read the letter quickly, clasped it to his bosom,
and groaned in ecstasy. Then in one fell motion he dropped the letter
and ran from the room.*

*Bewildered and bereft, Regina knelt beside the letter and read:
"Permission granted. Original records for research at your disposal. The
National Historic Society."*

In contrast to Roger's endeavors, my newest reading project is
"100 Ways to Use Popsicle Sticks." Sunny has designed the clever-
est pioneer cabin the boys are making for the July pack meeting.
Paulie is our product tester. Then there is Rauf, who has taken an
unhealthy interest in the taste of craft glue on wood. He chews up
everything we drop or leave within reach. Bitsy helps by feeding
them to him. So far it hasn't made him sick, but I am expecting a
major after-doggie-cleanup any day.

Bitsy is my bright spot, Mommy's Sunshine Girl.

> Hanging on and hanging in there,
> Deenie

August 28, 1982
Dear Ladies,

Ryan and Reece have returned to Chicago and not a moment too
soon. Their latest venture into nastydom was last Saturday. Carl
begged me to invite them to our traditional first-of-fall picnic on
the farm. I said yes.

Sunny was with us, and they zeroed in on her immediately, calling her a retard in front of the whole family. I was furious. The worst part of the whole thing was that Carl didn't stand up for his Aunt Sunny. All he had to say was, "Well, Mom, she is a retard."

It's only been a year and a half since he refused to be baptized unless his Aunt Sunny could be there. Now he's calling her names. He should know better. Roger went into his wise father mode and said Carl does know better, that he's just going through a phase. I said that wasn't good enough for me.

Grandma Streeter came over after they left to apologize for their behavior and asked me to pray for them. I am ashamed to admit that praying for them will be a lot easier now they are in Chicago.

Gabby and Jonas came Sunday afternoon. They brought Sophie along to visit with Sunny and cheer her up. Roger and Jonas spent most of the afternoon closeted in Roger's office.

Imagine how I felt to discover Jonas was encouraging Roger to pursue his doctorate in education with an emphasis on administration. He thinks Robert's master's thesis has enough questions and interesting research to move into a doctoral dissertation. So does Roger's adviser at the University of Utah.

That, ladies, is not good news. When I told Roger he has been away from the family too much already, he said not to worry and that we'll find a way to make it all work out. What he means is that he expects me to find a way to manage it all.

It is no wonder he is so drawn to Jonas. Jonas understands his need to achieve, which is more than I can say for myself.

> Done to a crisp and smoldering,
> Deenie

P.S. With the twins gone, I am no longer needed as assistant den mother and have been released.

ERIN

Erin stood looking out the balcony door, watching for Colleen's car to come into the parking lot. Light snow coated the trees, and the sun glinted off it in a million bright sparkles. When she saw the car, she grabbed the overcoat she had purchased at Ragstock when she found she couldn't button up her winter coat and moved down the stairs as fast as she could. She and Colleen were on their way to scout stores in Anoka where they hadn't been for some time. Their small notebook had several pages of client requests, some for furniture pieces and some for smaller items such as antique frames and jade or red and white Oven King kitchenware.

From her car seat in the back, EJ clamored for attention. Erin looked over her shoulder to play with her for a minute. When she turned back, she said, "I can't believe I'm going to have one of those. Only three months to go." Her lips curved up in a secretive smile. "It's so amazing that I can go about life as usual, and all the while, a little person is growing inside. All I have to do is keep breathing."

Colleen chuckled. "Enjoy it while you can, friend. You don't believe it now, but this is the easy part."

They spent the next two hours going from shop to shop on the quaint Anoka main street. They found several items they were looking for. They purchased the smaller ones outright and took Polaroids of larger items which they thought Jake or one of the clients might be interested in.

On the way home, they stopped by Finishing Touches to check in with Jake, who had done more than any other shopkeeper to teach them what to look for on their forays.

They found Jake in one of the last rooms of his rabbit warren of a shop. A mountain of a man with a bald pate and neatly trimmed gray beard, he was wearing a plaid, short-sleeved shirt and chinos held in place around his middle by both red suspenders and belt. He greeted them with a booming voice. "Well, look who's here. What have you been up to, dear ladies?"

He listened with interest, scanning the Polaroids they handed him. A business card was clipped to each, indicating the store where the item was and the price. "I'll hang onto all of these and make some phone calls. You should be getting a check soon." He crossed his arms over his girth. "Have you girls decided on a name yet? I think it's time you set up a business account."

"Do you have a suggestion?" Colleen asked.

"You're finders, aren't you? Call yourself Finders, Inc."

In November, Finders brought in $260 each for Colleen and Erin. It was their best month yet, due to several high-ticket furniture items they found for clients. The Friday after Thanksgiving they chortled over their good fortune, and while they decorated the Harringtons' Christmas tree, they had fun talking about how they would spend their money. Then Colleen surprised Erin by saying, "I'm not sure we should keep going in December."

"Why should we stop when we're picking up steam?"

Colleen took a Christmas ornament out of EJ's hand and offered her a toy instead. "That should be obvious. Any free time you have, you should be resting up for when the baby comes."

Erin looked down at her midsection, wishing she had a harness to help hold it up. She was getting very uncomfortable—the baby was due in early January—and in recent days her feet and ankles had begun swelling markedly. Still, she was reluctant to put Finders on hold. "Do you think we really need to?" she asked.

"I think *you* need to. I also think you should quit working at Stefani's. Look at your feet."

Erin shifted as the baby did a somersault. "I'm not ready to quit. I've worked ever since I was fourteen, Colleen. I wouldn't know what to do with myself if I didn't have a job to go to. Besides, I like making money of my own." She paused, looking at her hands. "I feel better if I have some stashed away for a rainy day."

Colleen looked at her sharply, her eyebrows drawn together in a frown. "Is there a problem?"

"Not the way you're thinking."

"Then you better consider quitting. Soon."

Only a few days later, Erin cancelled her late afternoon appointments because she could no longer stand to be on her feet. Once home, she put on holiday music and plugged in the Christmas tree lights before lying down on the couch with her feet on a pillow. She was dozing lightly when Cory got home.

"Merry Christmas," he said, kneeling down to stroke her cheek. "How long have you been home?"

"Since two o'clock. My feet were killing me."

He sat down on the end of the couch to give her a foot rub. "I've been telling you it's time to stop working, sweetie."

Erin groaned. "Not you, too."

"She didn't want to admit it, but she knew he was right. The needs of her body and the child she would soon birth took precedence now.

"Okay," she said, making her decision. "Hand me the phone."

She told the receptionist at Stefani's she wouldn't be coming in the rest of the year and asked her to do what she could to reschedule her clients with other stylists. "I'll call the manager in the morning," she promised.

She handed the receiver back to Cory, who took it with a disapproving glance. "What now?" she asked.

"You made it sound like you'll be coming back. I thought we had agreed that you'd be a stay-at-home mother."

Erin stood, a laborious process, and went into the kitchen to start setting the table. "I don't see why I can't work part time. Just because I'm having a baby doesn't mean my whole life has to change."

"Yes, it does. You're a mother now. Your main concern should be that our baby grows up healthy and happy. Of all people, you should know how important that is."

She stopped stock still. "What do you mean by that?"

"You know what it feels like when a child doesn't get its needs met. I don't want our baby to suffer the way you've had to."

"Cory, what went on when I was little didn't have anything to do with my mom working."

"Maybe not, but I want to do what's right for this little guy."

With a whack she put down the package of hamburger she was holding and turned to face him. "You don't know any more about being a father than I know about being a mother. I do know one thing, though. The best we can do for our baby is love it—and each other."

His stance softened.

"I do love you, and I know you love me." He stroked her cheek and then gently patted her stomach. "Let's not fight about this. We can talk about it later, after you and the baby have been home for a while."

Erin watched him as he went into the bedroom to change clothes.

We haven't solved a thing, she thought. *He expects me to change my mind.*

WILLADENE

December 15, 1982
Merry Christmas, Ladies,

I have been called as Spiritual Living teacher for Relief Society.

> Wondering why,
> Deenie

ERIN

December 28, 1982
Dear Ladies,

We made it through another Christmas, hurrah! We kept to the tried-and-true, going to the Nine Lessons and Carols service with The Women Christmas Eve and spending part of Christmas Day with the Johnsons. Seems to make everybody happy.

I'm feeling pretty good, considering the fact that I waddle when I walk and can't get out of a chair without help. I've discovered I like being home. Imagine that! In the morning, I putter around the apartment. In the afternoon, I fix Cory a nice supper and then sit in the rocking chair and read the Book of Mormon or the lesson for my Sunday School class. I used to think feeling the Spirit was an unusual experience, but I sense it more and more these days. Maybe it's because I'm about to become a mother, and mothers need all the help they can get.

The baby is due in three weeks. I think I'm as ready as any new mother can be. The idea of giving birth scares me, but as Angie says, "Girl, there's no other way out!"

I wish you could all be here, and we could sit on a bed and talk the way we did at Hotel Utah. You could tell me everything I need to know, and we could have a good laugh or two. And some good hugs.

> The Almost Momma,
> Erin

Chapter Twenty-Three
1983

WILLADENE

"Sister Rasmussen, I have to tell you, that was one of the most professional presentations I've ever seen in a Relief Society lesson."

"Wonderful lesson, Deenie."

"I loved the way you had so many sisters participate . . ."

The compliments flowed over Deenie as she packed away the visual aids from her very first Spiritual Living lesson. She'd pulled out all the stops—a picture for each point, a choral reading for the scripture, preassigned questions so there would always be at least one answer from the class, and even treats to sweeten the deal—and it had paid off. Everything had gone as planned. Even her timing had been spot on. She had managed to close at exactly five minutes to the hour. And now the room was filled with praise.

Why does it seem like something is missing? Deenie wondered. She could feel the answer just out of reach, and it didn't feel good. So she tried harder.

In February she added music. In March, a discussion panel. By April the answer was staring her in the face. Her painstakingly prepared and flawlessly delivered lessons were spiritually flat—flat as a pancake. Any light that infused the enlightened words of the text came from the sisters in the class, not from her.

Her father said, "Have patience." Her mother told her to look at what her intent was when she taught. Everyone she asked seemed to have reams of advice on how to bring her own spirituality into the lessons—except Roger. He had little patience with what seemed to him to be her endless need for reassurance and approval.

Frustrated, she decided to call her brother Nathan in Salt Lake City. *If a seminary teacher can't give me the answers I need, who can?* she wondered as she dialed his home phone. After the usual pleasantries Deenie got straight to the point. "And before you ask," she finished her narrative, "I do close each lesson by bearing my testimony."

"About what?" Nathan asked.

"What do you mean, 'about what?' The usual, of course."

"What I'm asking," Nathan said in a tone Deenie called his patiently impatient voice, "is do you have and bear testimony to the individual principles in each lesson? Do you experiment on that word when you prepare your lessons?"

Of all the exasperating advice Deenie had been given, this topped the list. "That takes a lifetime," she said.

"Now's as good a time as any to get started, Deenie. I know you're busy, but if you want to teach by the Spirit, you'll make the time. Just like you do for anything else you really want to do."

Deenie hung up the phone, thinking of all the things she would rather not do that she had to make time for at the moment. Like taking out the garbage, getting the cars serviced, picking up the dry cleaning, and taking care of a dozen other small irritating jobs she did now to allow Roger extra time to prepare to defend his master's thesis. She had taken on the bigger tasks, too. Time-consuming and energy-eating tasks like tilling the garden beds and getting a head start on pruning the apple orchard.

As far as Deenie was concerned, experimenting on the word was on the same to-do list as genealogy, the one you started when you turned the age of Leila Jeffrey or Grandma Streeter. For now, any spiritual dynamics in her lessons would have to come from the sisters in Relief Society.

In this, Deenie accepted that she was doing the best she could and that would have to be good enough. In all other things, she kept to the usual stringent standards she expected of herself. As the days marched closer toward May and Roger's graduation, Deenie kept going by promising herself that times were extra hard "just for now."

After Roger graduated, everything would get back to normal.

ERIN

The first week of January Erin went to three different showers: one hosted by Linda and Colleen for her church friends, one by Grams for the neighborhood women, and one by Angie for her Stefani's friends. "I think we have everything the baby could possibly need," Cory said as he helped Erin find places for the items in the nursery.

Erin had to agree. The dresser was full of baby clothing from newborn to toddler, the closet held toys and accessories, the changing table was fully stocked, and the two-shelf bookcase held a cassette player and several soft books for babies. Watching over the crib and oak rocker was a framed print of Christ with the children. Erin loved to sit in the rocker when she was reading her scriptures. She had the feeling that Christ was watching over her, too.

Erin surveyed it all, supporting her stomach from below with both hands. "The room's ready, and I'm ready," she said. "All that's missing is the baby."

Two days later, on January 12, Kayla Marie Johnson was born after a nine-hour labor. A little girl with reddish-blonde hair, she was a mystery and a miracle to Erin, who loved touching Kayla's rosy lips, tiny fingernails, and perfect pink ears. When Kayla first latched onto her painfully swollen breasts, Erin felt the pain lessen as she gazed at the sweet little face topped by wispy hair.

Once they were home, a parade of visitors came, bringing food and offers to help out. Erin was overwhelmed by the outpouring of love but also disconcerted by it. She couldn't help wondering who had come to celebrate her own birth. Had friends and neighbors exclaimed over her tiny hands and feet? Had they brought gifts and food for the family? Those unanswered questions left Erin feeling vaguely unsettled, a feeling that was intensified whenever her mother visited.

"I'm probably coming over too often," Joanna said apologetically one Thursday evening. "I just get so hungry for this little sweetheart."

Erin felt a great yearning as she watched Joanna lift Kayla out of her baby seat and plant little kisses on her cheek. She sighed deeply.

"Are you okay?" Joanna asked.

They were alone; Cory had gone on splits with the missionaries. Erin knew that if she wanted more information about her birth, now was the time to ask. "I was just wondering . . . Were you glad when I was born?"

"Of course. But it was a difficult time. You know the circumstances."

"Actually, I know very little about the circumstances except what I've heard you and Grams say when you're yelling at each other."

Joanna opened her mouth to protest and then closed it.

Erin sat down where she could look into her mother's face. "I've never asked about you and my father, because I didn't want to bring up painful things. But now that I have Kayla, I need to know. Who is he? How did you meet him? What made you fall in love with him? What happened that you didn't get married?"

Joanna's smile was tinged with sadness. "I've been wondering when you would ask. You father's name, as you know from your birth certificate and your grandmother's yelling, is Andrew McGee. I met him at a fireworks display on Harriet Island. We were standing in a very long line waiting to get corn dogs."

Erin nodded. She had gone to fairs and musical events on the island in the Mississippi River and knew that corn dogs were a must on such occasions.

"I was seventeen that summer," Joanna continued. "I had a year to go before graduating from high school. He was nineteen and headed for his sophomore year at the University of Chicago in the fall."

"What made you fall in love with him?"

"His impish smile and sense of humor. While we waited, he kept me entertained with magic tricks, like taking a quarter out of my ear. By the time we got to the front of the line, we were more interested in each other than in the food."

"Did Grams and Gramps know you were going out with him?"

"Good grief, no. They would have locked me up rather than let me date a Catholic."

"They were that prejudiced against Catholics?"

Joanna nodded. "Unfortunately, yes. When I told them I was pregnant, they exiled me to Aunt Helen's in Brainerd—home of Paul Bunyan and Babe the Blue Ox. His parents exiled him to Chicago, with the threat that if he saw me again, they would stop paying for his studies. And cut him out of their will."

"Why?"

"They had their plans for him, and it didn't include a wife and child. At least not then."

"How do you know that?"

Joanna rose and began to pace the room. "I overheard a conversation between my parents and Sean and Margaret McGee." She made a bitter sound. "I listened from upstairs while the four of them reached an agreement about my future. And yours. We would stay out of Andy's life, and his parents would make sure child support checks came regularly until you were eighteen."

Erin couldn't believe what she was hearing. "Mom! You let them buy you off!"

"What choice did I have? Even if Andy had been willing to go against his parents, it wouldn't have worked."

"How do you know? You gave up."

"You don't know what you're talking about," snapped Joanna. "You asked me to tell you the truth, but what you really want to hear is a fairy tale. Real life isn't like the storybooks."

"Do you think you need to tell me that?"

Joanna sat back down and leaned forward, resting her arms on her knees. "Listen, Erin. Andy and I didn't have the kind of relationship that you and Cory have. We didn't know each other, not in a way that counts. We weren't in love; we were infatuated. We liked the added excitement that came from knowing that our parents wouldn't have approved of our being together."

"So it was just a summer romance. It didn't mean anything."

"I got you." Joanna looked from Erin to Kayla. "And this beautiful child, who wouldn't be here otherwise."

In the silence, Erin could hear her heart pounding. "Did he ever ask to see me?"

"Once. He called one day out of the blue and asked if I would bring you to the park. I remember he gave you a My Little Pony and bought you a cone from the ice cream truck."

An image suddenly popped into Erin's mind. "Was it pink? The pony?"

"I don't remember. It could have been."

"How old was I?"

"Four."

"I was four when Gramps died."

Joanna nodded pensively.

"Do you think my father liked me?"

"Oh, Erin. What do you want me to say? He thought you were a cute little girl. He seemed pleased that you had his hair and that you were healthy. He asked if the child support was enough."

"That's all?"

Joanna's eyes were dark with sorrow and regret. "He didn't know you. By that time, he was married and had a child on the way. We were never a part of his life, other than the monthly check." She laughed a little. "You have to admit that he kept up the child support payments."

"Whoop-de-do for him."

"Don't minimize the importance of those checks, young lady."

"So he does his duty. I guess that's something." Erin wished now that she had never brought up the subject of her birth, but there were a couple more questions she wanted the answer to. "Does he still live in St. Paul?"

"Yes. Why?"

"Just curious. And for the record, what's his middle name? I want to fill out Kayla's genealogy sheet accurately, and there's only his initial on my birth certificate."

"He doesn't have a middle name. Just the initial. Andrew J McGee."

Sunday, January 23, 1983
Dear Juneau, and Willadene, and Gabby,

Thank you all for the calls and the cute baby clothes. Buying bigger sizes was a good idea—I already had scads of newborn dresses and sleepers.

I'm finally feeling better. The labor and delivery were really hard. Cory was a great coach, but at the end I gave up on Lamaze and asked for drugs, and I'm not sorry.

Cory cried the first time he held Kayla. He had saved up vacation days so he could be home with me the first week. Bless him. He knew I didn't want his mother camping out at our apartment, so he's been making sure she doesn't stay too long when she comes.

The Women have fallen in love with Kayla, Mom especially. She comes over as often as she can, and we're all getting along better. Cory took the picture I've enclosed—four generations of Larson women: Grams, Mom, me, and Kayla. Definitely one for the genealogy books, especially because Grams looks happy!

Speaking of genealogy, I finally got Mom to tell me about her and my father. I always thought that they had a grand romance, but it turns out they were teenagers having a fling.

Hope everything's going well for both of you and your families. I'm glad to have you as examples of how to be a good mother.

Love and kisses,
Erin

Sunday, February 29, 1983
Dear Gabby, Juneau, and Willadene,

Today Cory blessed our baby girl: Kayla Marie Johnson. He, Steve, the bishop, Skipp, and Grandpa Wagner were in the circle. Yes, the Wagners came up from Florida for the occasion. It's a wretched time of year to visit Minnesota, but they've been to the blessings of all their grandchildren and great-grandchildren, and they didn't want to miss Kayla's.

We were all impressed by the Wagners' commitment to family, even Grams. I think it's likely we may never see them again, they're in such bad health. Linda blames it on her brother, Gerald, for not making sure they take their meds as prescribed.

Guess who else came. Norm and Angie Dunmeyer. I didn't think they would because they aren't churchgoers. Imagine my surprise when they arrived right on time and dressed appropriately, too. (I'd had visions of Angie wearing her tights.)

Cory gave Kayla a beautiful blessing. I could tell Mom and Grams were touched, especially when he blessed Kayla that she would bring joy into the lives of all her family and all those who know her.

I've never seen Grams look as beautiful as she did that day. Her eyes were soft, and her smile was tender. Mom looked beautiful, too. Being filled with love and touched by the Spirit does that, I guess.

> Feeling like there's love and hope,
> Erin

Erin couldn't believe that her body could be so attuned to the little human being that was her daughter. The sound of Kayla smacking her lips was enough to let down Erin's milk, driving her to pick up her daughter and offer a breast. The slightest whimper from the bedroom sent her scurrying down the hall to see if Kayla was all right. Her hunger for her daughter had her rocking the baby long after she was asleep, reveling in the warmth of the little bundle she cuddled against her neck.

She was so tired in the first few weeks after Kayla's birth that she couldn't imagine how she had ever worked at Stefani's, shopped for Finders clients with Colleen, kept the apartment relatively orderly, done her visiting teaching, and taught her Sunday School class. Even after she learned she was pregnant, she had kept up her schedule until Cory and her swollen ankles had convinced her it was time to stop. Her energy then had been amazing, compared to how she felt now.

When Cory had to iron a white shirt before going to work one morning, Erin worried that she wasn't taking care of him as she should. He came home that night to a row of shirts pressed and gleaming, enough to take him through the next workweek at Pillsbury.

"You didn't have to do that," he said.

"Yes, I did. Having a daughter to take care of isn't a reason for neglecting you."

Cory bent down to kiss the top of Kayla's head and then Erin's cheek. "You're doing just fine. I couldn't be prouder of my two girls."

Adoration gleamed in his eyes. It was like a magic potion, giving her strength and confidence in her ability to be a good wife and mother.

The next day, Kayla got sick.

First, she was fussy and nursed fitfully. Then she began crying. Erin did everything she could think of, to no avail. As the day went on, Kayla began running a fever. Her wails rose in pitch and intensity until Erin was beside herself.

"What do you think's the matter with her," she asked Colleen. She always called Colleen first when she needed advice.

"I don't know, but if she's got a fever, you need to call her pediatrician. He'll say what he wants you to do."

Erin dialed with one hand while holding Kayla at her shoulder with the other. It was late in the afternoon, but the pediatrician told her to come right in. Before leaving, Erin called Cory to tell him what was going on.

"I'll call you if there's anything urgent you need to know."

She arrived at the clinic in a panic, but the attentive manner of the nurse practitioners calmed her down. "It's nothing to be too concerned about, Mrs. Johnson. It's probably an earache."

Dr. Thomas confirmed the diagnosis, prescribed ear drops to lessen the pain, and told Erin the dosage of Tylenol she could safely administer. He handed her a sheet of information on earaches, saying, "Don't hesitate to come back in if Kayla starts fussing. Earache pain can bring a grown man to his knees."

When she told The Women what was going on and how tired she was, Ruth said, "I'm coming over tomorrow. I can watch Kayla while you nap."

She arrived a little after nine the next morning. She clucked and fussed over Kayla and then shooed Erin into her bedroom. "You rest, now. You need it."

Erin didn't think she would be able to sleep, but it was noon when she woke up. When she walked into the living room, Kayla was asleep on the couch, and Grams was making tuna sandwiches and tomato soup for lunch.

As Erin sat at the counter watching her, Ruth told her about her sister who had died as the result of an infection, the first symptom of which had been an earache. It was the first time Grams had ever mentioned her family.

"What was her name?" Erin asked, feeling grateful for modern medicine.

"Mary. There were five of us, including her. Three boys and two girls."

"Where are your brothers now?"

Ruth shrugged. "Who knows. My mother was the only one who wrote after we moved here. When she was gone, I heard from my brothers only a few times. Harmon, he was the youngest, came out once with his wife and children. That was when your mother was about seven." She placed a bowl of soup before Erin. "I didn't hear from them much after that. One year I wrote Christmas cards, but they came back. I guess they'd moved."

"Didn't you try to find them?"

"If they were interested, they would have kept in touch."

"What about Gramps's family?"

"He was an only child. When Alfred's railroad job brought us here, we were on our own. Minneapolis is a long way from Michigan."

There was a finality in Ruth's tone that told Erin she was finished with that subject. *How lonely they must have been. How lonely she must be,* Erin thought. It was the first time she had ever experienced compassion for her grandmother. When Grams got ready to leave, saying she would be back the next day, Erin gave her a different kind of hug, one more real and heartfelt.

Three weeks later, Kayla woke up crying early in the morning. Her little face was red, her nose was plugged, and there was a faint whistle when she exhaled. Erin had her back in the doctor's office as soon as it opened.

Bronchitis, Dr. Thomas pronounced. Because it followed so soon after the ear infection, he prescribed antibiotics for Kayla. "I'd rather not have a six-week-old taking them, but I'd feel better if she did."

"I'm not worried about you feeling better." Erin's attempt at a joke drew a smile from Dr. Thomas before he continued with instructions: keep Kayla's nasal passages clear, give her water in a bottle to keep her hydrated, run a cold mist vaporizer in the nursery.

Kayla improved more slowly this time. She was miserable and sleepless, so Erin was miserable and sleepless. She refused to let Cory take the grave-yard shift, however, saying that it wouldn't do for him to go to work tired.

Once again Grams offered to help with Kayla. When Erin told her Cory's mother was bringing supper the next afternoon, Ruth said, "I'm coming anyway."

Later, Erin told Cory about her phone calls with her grandmother while he ate his supper of pork and beans with hot dog slices. He laughed. "The battle of the grandmothers," he said. "I'd like to see that."

"The grand and the great-grand," Erin corrected. "I'm glad you think it's funny. You don't have to be here."

Ruth arrived before noon the next day. Erin was quite willing to hand Kayla over to her. She seemed to recognize her great-grandmother and to do better when Ruth was caring for her.

"You have the magic touch," Erin told her.

Ruth gave her a pleased smile. "It may have been a long time since I had a baby in my arms, but I haven't forgotten what to do."

Grams was still there when Erin buzzed Linda into the apartment building. She hurried up the stairs, carrying a covered casserole, asking an avalanche of questions about her Kayla. Erin barely had time to answer one before the next came. As Linda put the casserole on the counter, Erin blurted out, "Grams is watching Kayla."

"That's nice." Linda headed into the nursery, where Grams stood protectively at Kayla's crib.

"It's so nice of you to help Erin out, Ruth," Linda said, shaking her hand. "How is our little sweetie?"

"Better." Grams glanced at Erin and then stood aside as Linda bent over the crib, talking in low tones to Kayla and smoothing her damp hair back from her forehead.

Erin could tell Grams could hardly stand to have Linda in what she considered her bastion, especially when Linda picked up Kayla, who was still in a light sleep.

"I think we've created a monster," Erin told Cory that evening. "The Great-Gram-Monster. She acts like Kayla's her exclusive property."

"The next time Kayla gets sick, you may have to tell Ruth she can't come every day."

"Don't even think the word *sick*." Erin knocked on wood, just in case.

By the time the chinook arrived in late March, bringing with it the springtime scent of damp soil, Kayla had been healthy for weeks, and Erin was stir-crazy. She ran through her basic chores quickly one morning and then called Colleen. "Do you want to go antiquing? Jake must be wondering where we are."

"I'd love to. I was wondering when you'd suggest it."

They drove east toward Minneapolis, stopping at their favorite shops, finally arriving at Jake's. He was delighted to see them and quite taken with three-month-old Kayla. After murmuring an unintelligible string of baby talk to her, he gave Erin Joy, who was two and a half, equal time. Then he grinned and asked, "What are you dear ladies up to these days?"

Erin made a gesture that included both little girls. "Being moms."

"The best job in the world, I always say."

"Do you have children?" asked Erin.

He nodded. "A son. Kirk and his family live in Nashua, New Hampshire. His mother took him out east when we divorced. Want to see pictures?"

After admiring the pictures Jake showed them, Colleen asked, "Is there anything you'd like us to be on the lookout for?"

"Actually, yes, if you think you're ready."

A half hour later, they were back in business. Colleen was excited, but Erin had doubts.

"I'm still worried about Kayla. I don't want her to get sick because I'm hauling her from pillar to post."

"I know," Colleen said. "I'm not expecting you to go out as often as we did before. I just don't want Finders to wither on the vine."

"Neither do I."

After that, Colleen and Erin went out one or two days a week but never when it was cold or rainy. When Kayla appeared to be doing fine, Erin got out the list of women she and Colleen had done work for and made some calls, telling them that Finders was up and running again.

Three days later, Kayla went from feeling fine to feverish. Erin cancelled her outing for the next day with Colleen and then did everything she had learned to cool her baby and ease her discomfort. As the fever rose and Kayla's breathing became more labored, Erin called Dr. Thomas's office. The next call she made was to Cory, telling him to meet her at the hospital.

Pneumonia kept Kayla in the hospital for a week. The first night she was there, her bed was surrounded by family—Cory's parents and The Women came as soon as they could. They were all subdued, and Grams for once didn't get prickly being in the same room as the Johnsons.

They were talking quietly when Cory said, "Dad, did you bring the oil?"

"Yes."

Cory turned to The Women. "Ruth, Joanna? My dad and I are going to give Kayla a blessing." He explained the power of the priesthood he and Skipp held and what would happen during the anointing and sealing of the blessing. Erin gripped the edge of the crib as he spoke, but Grams and Joanna listened with sober expressions.

When the men went to the head of Kayla's crib, Linda held out her hands to Joanna on her left and Grams on her right. Erin's heart burst with pride and love when, after only a slight hesitation, both women joined hands with Cory's mother. Then Grams reached for Erin's hand. They were all joined together, the women of Kayla's family, at that sacred moment when Cory laid his hands on his daughter's head. He blessed her that she would have health and strength and be a bringer of peace to all those who were around her.

Hearing those words as she stood connected to The Women and Linda, Erin thought, *She already is.*

Mother's Day, 1983
Dear Gabby, Juneau, and Willadene,

Happy Mother's Day! I hope your lovely families told you what amazing women you are.

This is the first time that someone has celebrated me on Mother's Day! It was the most amazing thing to stand in church when the young men passed out roses to all of the mothers. I was already wearing a lovely gardenia corsage from Cory, who was so proud of both me and Kayla. Colleen had a gardenia corsage, too. I think Cory and Steve ordered them at the same time. It's nice to see what good friends they are.

After a nice dinner with Skipp and Linda, Kayla, Cory, and I all had naps before going over to visit The Women.

I was so glad to see them. For the first time ever, I understood how they might be feeling on Mother's Day. All the things I normally complain about just didn't matter. I wanted them to know how much I appreciated everything they did do for me and especially for the wonderful way they helped us out when Kayla was sick. (She's been doing great since then.)

Cory's doing fine and busy as always. He's still teaching the investigators' class, and I'm back to teaching the seven-year-olds. Life is good!

Love,
Erin

Chapter Twenty-Four

WILLADENE

When Roger received his master's degree in education, the whole family celebrated with balloons, presents, cake, and ice cream. For the first time in months Deenie felt she could take a deep breath and exhale without waiting to see what would happen next.

When Roger announced he had been offered a position at Utah State University as a graduate assistant, teaching two nights a week, and that he intended to take it, Deenie dropped the mixing bowl of cookie dough she'd been stirring and went back to holding her breath. She knelt down to clean the sticky mess from the floor. "Hand me the garbage can," she snapped as she scooped with one hand and wiped with the other.

Roger handed her the garbage can and then sat down at the kitchen table and waited. "This is important, Deenie."

"So were those cookies. Now I have to start all over again."

"They can wait."

She sat back on her heels. "So, being gone three nights a week for the last two years wasn't enough for you, hmm? Now you have to find another way to avoid being part of this family?"

"I'm doing it for the family, Deenie. Every move I make toward a doctorate moves us closer to the top of the pay scale."

"Well, you aren't doing it for me! We don't need more money. We need more you. Here. At home."

Roger's expression was mixed irritation and determination. "It's my responsibility to provide for this family, and I think this will help me do it. Can't you trust me to make the right decision?"

"Can't you trust me to know what the family needs?" she countered. "I'm the one who's at home. I'm the one who sees how the kids need more of your time. Do you know Carl doesn't even ask if you're going to be at his pack meetings anymore? Last year he really missed you. This year it's as if he doesn't care. Doesn't that worry you?"

"That's unfair. I might not be around as much as you want, but you have the whole family behind you. Even the ward members are here for you. Where's my support? My advisor in Salt Lake said my master's thesis is good enough to be the foundation for a dissertation. Getting my doctorate is important."

"So are we." Deenie held Roger's gaze.

He shook his head in frustration. "You're not listening," he said. "When you decide you're ready to hear me, I'll be in my study." He left the kitchen in a hurry.

I've heard of mother-deaf, Deenie thought disgustedly as she watched him go. *But I never thought I'd be on the receiving end of wife-deaf.*

WILLADENE

June 10, 1983
Dear Ladies in Triplicate,

School's out, thank heaven. I feel like this whole school year has been about convincing Carl that getting into trouble is not "cool" or "rad" or anything else. Just when I congratulated myself on seeing some results, I got a visit from Grandma Streeter. The twins are coming again, and for the first two weeks their big brother, Stan, is coming along with them. Their mom is coming, too. Forgive me for saying so, but I imagine she's a too-rich Chicago suburbanite who neglects her kids. How Grandma Streeter ever ended up with that kind of a daughter beats me.

Roger is either working hard on the farm or on papers for the assistantship. I am relying heavily on Grandma and Grandpa Rasmussen to fill in the parenting gap. My own mother is busy taking care of Sunny, who is feeling lonely and left behind. Her two best friends from the special needs program have moved to a group home in Salt Lake. Sunny wants to go, too, but she's so frail that Mom won't even consider letting her leave home.

Roger has taken a day off from the farm occasionally to help Jonas with Gabby's grandson Bryan while they work on the Caddie. I don't know how this project started, but Bryan thinks it's cool, and he has even started being a little more pleasant around Gabby. The influence of Jonas, I think. A good relationship can go a long way in saving a troubled boy. I'm going to remember that.

With all that's going on, don't be surprised if you don't hear from me often this summer.

Deenie

A few days later, the new car coming down the street caught Deenie's attention. She opened the living room curtains, thinking that in a town this little anything unfamiliar or unusual was worth a second glance. She was surprised when the car slowed down and stopped in front of her house. A strange woman exited the driver's side and stood staring up the walk. Deenie guessed her identity at once. She had to be Patience Streeter Crafton, daughter of Grandma Streeter and mother to Stan, Ryan, and Reece.

Pat Crafton looked every bit the big-city woman Willadene had expected her to be. She was tall and unusually thin, carefully made up and casually dressed. Casual for Chicago, Deenie amended as the woman approached. Here in Wellsville the linen slacks and smart silk T-shirt would qualify as dress-up for a downtown luncheon with the ladies.

At the edge of the curb, Mrs. Crafton paused and straightened the hem of her shirt and then rubbed her hands up and down on the sides of her linen trousers as though trying to dry them.

Deenie knew that gesture. *She's afraid. Can she actually be afraid of me?* At the absurdity of that thought, most of Deenie's harbored ill will toward her melted away. She opened the door and walked down the front steps to greet her unexpected guest.

They met in the middle of the sidewalk. After a moment of mutual assessment Deenie was the first to speak. She extended her hand and said brightly, "I'm Deenie. You must be the twins' mother. Grandma Streeter has told me all about you."

ERIN

"Work hard, keep the commandments, and say your prayers, and all things will work together for your good." The sacrament meeting speaker's words touched Erin's heart. Never in her life had she imagined a future like the life she was now living. She shut her eyes and said a silent prayer of thanksgiving.

Cory sat beside her, his body pressed warm and solid against hers. Little Kayla lay on her breast, breathing out in small puffs. And after church was over, they would go home to their little nest, a small Cape Cod that had three tiny bedrooms on the main floor, a large paneled upstairs room with dormers, a detached garage, and fenced backyard with mature trees. Her little bit of heaven.

She still couldn't believe they had their own house. They had started looking in May, or rather, Cory had, even though they didn't have enough money saved for a down payment. Now that they had a child, he'd been determined they should have a real home. Erin had gone with him. It was fun to tour different houses, see how they were furnished, and imagine what their life might be like in them.

They found the house following "Open House" signs. Cory was immediately taken with it. Sensing that, the realtor asked what it would take for them to be seriously interested.

Erin blurted out, "A down payment."

To her surprise, he offered to lend them what they needed, with the idea they would pay him back after they got their tax return the next year.

Every part of Erin said No! She dragged Cory out of the house and made him promise to talk to his dad before making any decisions. She had no idea what that would lead to. She'd never before seen Cory use his enthusiasm and certainty to get something out of his parents. Not that he did it knowingly—that was just the way he was. She'd also not understood that his desire for a home echoed his parents' desire for them. Before Erin knew what was happening, Skipp and Linda had agreed to see the house, and if they thought it was a good deal, to lend Cory and Erin the down payment.

Erin felt odd having a house almost as large as the one The Women lived in. They were glad for her, though. Joanna helped scrub and paint, often working with Linda by her side. Ruth watched Kayla while pulling the weeds she could get at without kneeling in the flower garden.

Erin and Cory and Kayla had moved into the house on a hot, muggy July day with the help of the elders quorum. When the furniture from their apartment had been arranged the way Erin wanted, the house looked as if they'd lived in it for months. She'd surveyed the results with satisfaction and then said to Cory, "It's home."

I am so blessed, Erin thought now. She leaned over to Cory and whispered, "I love you."

He smiled and squeezed her shoulder. "I love you, too."

The changes just kept coming. That was the way Cory liked it, Erin realized, when he surprised her one night with the news that he had been offered a job in the mayor's office. It was a move up, he said. He would be doing what he had always wanted to do: organize events from neighborhood coffees to high-profile evenings featuring guest lists that were Twin Cities Who's Who.

"Sounds stressful." Erin was doing the Relief Society Sway, patting a fussy Kayla on the back.

"Yeah, but think of the connections I'll be making. This could be the start of something big."

"Isn't that a song title?"

"If it isn't, it should be. Are you happy for me?"

She gave him a hug and kissed his cheek. "If you're happy, I'm happy."

"Ecstatic is more like it. My office will be in City Hall, so I'll be right in the middle of everything, but don't worry. You and Kayla will always come first."

Right, Erin thought. *After God, church, business, and basketball.* Without warning, she felt hot tears on her cheeks.

Cory took her and Kayla in his arms. "Hey, hey, hey. What's going on here?"

Her voice was muffled against his shoulder. "You're going to be so far ahead of me, I won't know how to keep up."

"You don't have to keep up, not in the way you're thinking. You're doing great with Kayla, and you've made this house into a home for all of us. I couldn't ask for more."

He kissed her and then went out to work on the basketball rim he was putting up on the side of the garage so he and Steve could play horse and one-on-one. She watched him go, a deep ache in her heart. She missed being at Stefani's, talking to her regular customers and seeing Angie every day. She also missed having money she could call her own. The private stash in her lingerie drawer was small, saved for some big occasion.

What's the matter with me that having the home and family I always wanted isn't enough? she wondered. She fervently hoped that Kayla didn't pick up on her feelings while nursing, especially her shame at how much she looked forward to the days that she and Colleen took their girls on Finders outings.

Finders had taken a step upward when Kathleen Parker, one of Erin's former clients from Stefani's, asked them to look for vintage fabrics in yellow and red. Erin began learning about textiles—how to judge their quality, how to care for them, and where one might find interesting examples in the Twin Cities area. It took some time and some rejections before they found exactly what Kathleen wanted: a fabric with a red cherry design on a butter-yellow background and a coordinating red and yellow and green plaid. Erin had also purchased some accent items, hoping that Kathleen might be interested in them, too. Kathleen bought them all.

Still, Cory's delight in his new job made Erin feel left out. She envied his capacity for energy, excitement, and confidence. She listened from the sidelines when Cory mesmerized family and friends with stories of the people he met through his work. Some of them were important people, but Cory always talked about them in a familiar manner. Once Steve said, "You know, Cory, you sound just like that sportscaster on WCCO, Sid Hartman. You both refer to everyone as a 'close personal friend.'" She had laughed along with the others, but she knew that Cory really felt that way.

One day she stopped by his office on a whim, taking Kayla in to say hi to her daddy. It was quite a process, driving downtown, finding a place to park near City Hall on South 5th Street, and then searching out his office. Cory was in an informal conference when she found him. He was delighted to introduce Erin and show off Kayla to his co-workers, and they all clustered around her and the baby for several minutes, asking questions and telling stories about Cory.

Erin stood in the middle of them, embarrassed by the way she looked compared to the sleekly groomed women Cory worked with. In her old peasant blouse and faded jeans, she knew she couldn't compete, didn't belong, and wasn't good enough. By the time she got back home she had conjured up a book of disasters. Cory regretting he had married her. Cory finding someone else to love, someone who was slimmer, well-groomed, energetic, and bright. Maybe someone who was a better Mormon than she.

"No way am I going to let that happen," she said as she unbuckled Kayla from the car seat. "Just you wait and see. I'm going to be the perfect wife, the perfect mother, and a successful businesswoman. Your daddy will be so proud of me. But first," she promised herself and Kayla, "I'm going to lose this baby fat and buy some new, classy clothes."

WILLADENE

August 1, 1983
Dear Ladies,

I had to write. This summer my conscience has taken on the size and habits of a large agitated porcupine. No more judging my neighbor, especially when I don't know her. Pat Crafton (Grandma Streeter's daughter) stopped by the first week of summer vacation to pick up the twins and Stan (an older and very angry version of the twins). They were learning to identify animal spoor in the foothills with Grandpa Rasmussen and my boys.

While we waited for them to come home, we talked. At first things were awkward. I mean, how would you feel if you knew your mother had talked about you from the pulpit during sacrament meeting? But I was surprised by how much we have in common. She's nice. I liked her, and I liked spending time with her. I hope she comes again.

Learning how hard it is on her boys to have their parents separated is making me more patient with them. And knowing how hard Pat and her husband are trying to work out their differences makes me more supportive. The thing is, I should have been patient and supportive from the start.

It was a surprise to discover Pat used to spend a lot of time at the Rasmussens' when she was a teenager. She hung out with Gordon and Keith, Roger's older brothers, and even knew Bert when she was a little girl. I wonder why they never mentioned it?

Miss you ladies a bunch. Gabby, how about dinner next week? It's definitely time for a visit.

Love,
Deenie

JUNEAU

September 7, 1983
Dear COBs,

Life is an unending drama, with the Good, the Bad, and the Ugly all combined. I remember being a bit depressed the first time I read in the Book of Mormon that there needs to be opposition in all things. Little did I guess the truth of that! But as they say, "That's life!" Remember that old schtick we used to say that went like this?

"That's life."
"What's life?"
"A magazine."
"How much does it cost?"
"A quarter."
"I only have a dime."
"That's life."

Anyway, that's life, and I'll try to keep up with it. To quote Agatha Christie, "I like living. I have sometimes been wildly, despairingly, acutely miserable, racked with sorrow, but through it all I still know quite certainly that just to be alive is a grand thing."

Okay. The Good. The bishop called me into his office last Sunday and asked if I'd be Spiritual Living leader in Relief Society. It's something I've never even considered to be in the realm of possibility for me. I mean, Spiritual Living! I've always thought that calling required women who are ready for translation. Women who can quote an appropriate scripture at the drop of a dishrag. Women who know a revelation from a rameumptom. Women who have solved all their problems. Women who are wise. Women who are living spiritually!

I questioned the bishop, but he assured me that I am the one who came to his mind when he prayed for inspiration. Who, me?

I accepted the position, feeling humble but with just a tinge of pride that I was getting the prize of all jobs for women in a ward.

Well, you know the old saying about what pride goeth before. The next day—the Bad—Misty was arrested for shoplifting at the mall. This was just a week after she turned twelve and started in the Young Women's program.

So what do I do now, dear COBettes? Do I resign my new calling even before I lead my first discussion? Do I stand out on Colorado Boulevard and wail out how I've failed as a mother? Do I move?

Stay tuned for the next thrilling episode. I told Marisol yesterday that the guilt fairy has taken up permanent residence at my house. She said she'd check with her church and see if there is a patron saint of guilt I can pray to. Always helpful, Marisol is. She's always on my case, saying that Christ took on the world's guilt and there is no need for me to repeat the process.

Other than the above, things are going pretty well. I sold another story, this time to *Ellery Queen's Mystery Mag*. They don't pay a whole lot, but who needs pay!!!! I feel as if I should pay *them*.

Greg is very supportive of my spending so much time writing. He says it's nice I can make a little spare change to do with as I please. He scarcely glances at my checks (which I've deposited in my own account for the proverbial rainy day!). To help me out, he makes pizza for lunch every Saturday and cooks dinner at least two nights a week, including Thursdays when I go to Mrs. Jarvis's class. He's becoming really quite good at it.

Regina's heart beat wildly as she approached the table, laden as it was with the food he had prepared. Salmon, gently caressed with butter, lay supine on a pale green platter. Potatoes, mashed and massaged into a smooth, lilywhite mound, peeked shyly from a pink bowl. In a tall glass, celery, impertinently upright, challenged her to sit down and partake. Greg, his smoldering eyes devouring her, extended a sinewy arm to draw her to the table, reaching behind with the other hand to swat at Philip Atwater who, bulbous nose undulating eagerly, was poised to gobble the alluring feast all by himself.

Just testing to see if I can still do the purple-prose scene. It's been a while since we shared those romance novels in the corner drug-store back in Provo.

Nicole just came by to tell me that scorpions can't really sting themselves to death. I hadn't been aware that they'd been accused of such a thing. But she has become our Source of Startling Facts. She's in the fourth grade now and always has a book sprouting from the end of her arm (no romance novels as yet!).

Any advice on above problems, especially that impertinent celery, gladly received.

Love,
Juneau

She didn't feel nearly as jaunty as her letter sounded. She hadn't come to grips with Misty's theft. The meeting with the juvenile authorities still loomed ahead, as well as an appointment with the bishop that she and Greg had set up.

They'd learned that Misty hadn't attended the first Young Women's activity night after she turned twelve, even though Juneau had driven her to the church and dropped her off in the parking lot. Instead, they learned later, she'd sneaked off to the home of her girlfriend Capri who lived nearby, and the two of them had walked down to the McDonald's on Foothill where they'd spent the evening talking to some older boys. Which was frightening to think about.

The letters from the COBs in answer to her plea for advice had been comforting but contained no magical incantation sure to work on a rebellious daughter.

Juneau wished she could stop time so that Misty would remain at twelve long enough for her and Greg to change the direction their daughter's life seemed to be taking. It might be possible at twelve. If she still walked this road of belligerence and secrecy when she was fourteen, it would be much more difficult to divert her from disaster.

The meeting with the juvenile authorities helped some. At least it impressed Misty and Capri. Misty responded fairly well to the bishop's counsel during the meeting with him. Sometimes Juneau searched the past to figure out just what caused Misty to turn away from the chosen path. She found hints at things gone awry. Like when Misty, at age nine, learned the facts of life from someone. Juneau had not yet discovered who that someone was. Misty refused to tell, and Juneau had eventually let it lie.

And then one day, a month after Misty's arrest, she found out who it had been. She was putting some of Misty's clothes away after she'd washed them, and she rearranged some sweaters on a shelf in her closet. At the bottom of the pile was a book, slim and bright-colored, with appealing cartoon figures telling everything a young girl needed to know.

She flipped it open, examining the pictures and the text. It was a good book, well done. And on the title page was a little note in familiar, bold handwriting. It said, "Welcome to womanhood, Misty." It was signed "Grandma Paulsen."

Juneau backed up far enough to plop down on Misty's bed. Her own mother had undercut her, had encroached into territory where she didn't belong. Where she had no business being. Where she should have known there was a "No Trespassing" sign.

Juneau was so angry she leaped to her feet and stomped to the telephone, snatching it from its cradle and punching in a number. She waited for her mother to answer but instead got a bored, disembodied voice that announced the number had been disconnected.

So the Peripatetic Paulsens had moved on, leaving yet another mess behind them.

Why hadn't her mother given *her* the book and let *her* decide when to give it to Misty? The book was good. It was the timing that was bad. Irresponsible. Destructive of the relationship between her and Misty. Hadn't her mother realized that?

No, probably not. Pamela Paulsen's mind would have been on the plot of the book she was working on at the time. She'd probably remembered that she'd never informed her own daughter about the mysteries of life, so she'd undoubtedly figured she'd make sure her daughter's daughter got it all before she needed it. Or was it Juneau herself who was wrong? Should she have told the girls about life when they were five? Six? Seven? When should innocence end? There was always an appropriate literary quotation, and Juneau thought of one now, from William Wordsworth. "The world is too much with us," he'd written in the early 1800s. "Hey, Billy Baby," Juneau said to herself, "if you thought the world was too much with you back in your time, you should see what it's like now, in 1983!"

She slammed down the inoffensive telephone, wondering if her mother even remembered giving Misty the book. After all, it had been three years. Pamela Paulsen's memory didn't extend that far back if it didn't involve a plot in one of her books.

Seething, Juneau threw Misty's clothes onto the shelf and then carefully placed the book on the littered desk by the bed. She had to talk to Misty. She's probably make a mess of it, but it had to be done.

Misty came home from school and went to her room without a word of greeting, which was her current modus operandi. Juneau followed, choking down her anger. Anger at her mother. Anger at Misty. Anger at herself, and Philip Atwater, and Greg, and life, and all things that couldn't be controlled.

Leaning on the door frame of Misty's room, she said casually, pointing, "I ran onto that book when I was putting your clean clothes away. I wondered why you didn't tell us three years ago where it was you learned about sex."

Misty, seated at the desk, looked up, and Juneau saw that she had been experimenting with eyeshadow that day. Probably at the back of the social studies room with Capri and her other girlfriends who cared even less than she did if they ever put anything into their heads, even though they all had what could be productive brains, if they were used.

Misty smiled. "Because, Mommie Dearest," she said, "I like keeping secrets from you."

Juneau's reaction was a flash of anger that made her want to stride into the room and swat her daughter's smirking face. But just as quickly came the sure knowledge that it wouldn't do any good, followed immediately by a crushing feeling of guilt. Was it something she'd done that made Misty so rebellious?

Instead of acting on her anger, Juneau forced herself to take a few deep breaths. She remembered Gabby saying, "Every stream has its share of rocks." This rock was big. Boulder-sized. Fortifying herself with one more gasp of oxygen, she walked over and put an arm around Misty's shoulders.

"Sweetie," she said, "can we talk?"

Misty turned her black-rimmed eyes upward. "About what?"

"About anything you'd like to share," Juneau said. "We don't seem to communicate very well anymore."

As soon as she said it, she regretted it, feeling that it might drive Misty further into the sullen separation where she lived these days. But to her surprise Misty said, "Do you care, Mom?"

Juneau considered her answer carefully. She sat down on the edge of the bed next to the desk so that her face was level with her daughter's. "Oh, yes, Misty," she said softly. "Yes, I care. I love you very much."

Misty gazed at her for a few moments. Then a slight smile lifted the corner of her lips. "*How* much?" she asked.

It was an old game she and the girls used to play. *How* much do you love me? An ocean full. A pile as high as a mountain. From here to China, is how much.

Juneau smiled, too. "It would fill the universe," she said.

"No matter what?"

"No matter what," Juneau said.

Again Misty gazed at her. Then, surprisingly, she slid over to sit beside her on the bed, snuggling up close by her side. "Mom," she whispered, "would you sing that old song Nicole and I used to like? The one about 'Hush, little baby'?"

Juneau put an arm around her so that Misty's head was resting on her shoulder. "I hope I can remember."

"I remember," Misty said.

"Then you sing it."

"I want you to."

"Okay. I'll give it a try." Juneau cleared her throat. "'Hush, little baby, don't say a word,'" she sang in a low voice. "'Mama's going to buy you a mockingbird. If that mockingbird don't sing . . .'"

Misty was lost in a dark place somewhere that Juneau couldn't go. Nevertheless, if she could cast out a line that could bring the child back even for an instant to a familiar childhood world, she would sing all the old songs in her repertoire and recall all the near-forgotten childhood games. But even as she treasured the thought, she knew it was only a thread, a link too fragile on its own to bind Misty to the family for good.

Chapter Twenty-Five

ERIN

Cory came home with flowers one day in late September. He handed them to Erin with a flourish. "These are for my girls," he said.

Erin took the bouquet, which featured chrysanthemums and sunflowers. "It's beautiful. What's the occasion?"

"Check the calendar. Kayla was born nine months ago today."

Erin looked quickly at the calendar on the kitchen wall. "You're right." She stood on tiptoe to kiss him. "You are so romantic." She turned to Kayla, who was sitting in her high chair, gumming a cracker. "See what Daddy brought us? Isn't he the most wonderful daddy in the world?"

Kayla grabbed at the flowers, making happy noises.

"I have something else for you," Cory said.

"What?"

"A personal invitation to an award gala for businessmen who have contributed significantly to civic projects and the quality of life in Minneapolis."

"How did you wrangle that?"

"A businesswoman named Paula Craig has been involved in the planning process. I've told her a lot about you and Kayla, and she'd like to meet you." He handed her a heavy cream-colored envelope bearing her name.

"Looks fancy-schmancy," said Erin. She examined the elegant envelope and insert. At the bottom of the invitation there was a personal message. *Please come. I'm looking forward to seeing you! Paula Craig.*

"Signed by the woman herself." Erin felt a shiver of excitement. Or was it anxiety?

"You'll really like her," Cory said. "She's got it all: brains, looks, money. And to top it off, she's nice. She treats everyone with respect. I can't tell you how great that is when you have to work closely with someone."

"Well, I guess I'd better find a dress."

"Uh . . ."

"What?"

"I thought maybe you might like Mom to go with you. She knows what people wear to these sorts of things."

"I'd like that," she said, smiling to hide her disappointment. She had been gradually shifting her fun, funky clothing to the back of the closet, replacing it with more classic items. He had complimented her not that long ago on how great she looked, but apparently he didn't trust her to find something that wouldn't embarrass him.

"Great." He gave her a brief hug and went for the refrigerator. "Better get those flowers in water," he said over his shoulder.

Erin looked at the bouquet she was still holding. The flowers didn't look quite as cheerful as they had when he first presented them.

Linda picked up Erin on Saturday morning. Colleen was watching the girls so Cory and Steve could play basketball at the church cultural hall. "It's a good thing we're starting early," Linda said. "We've got a big day in front of us. I thought we should start out at Dayton's Oval Room and go on from there."

Four hours and many shops later, the packages Erin carried back to the car contained a royal blue two-piece cocktail dress quite similar to but much less expensive than the designer dress Linda had deemed absolutely perfect. She had charged the dress and paid cash for a little black clutch discreetly trimmed with rhinestones and a pair of dressy heels the likes of which had never been on her feet before.

Linda offered to let Erin raid her jewelry box, but Erin declined with thanks. She was determined that her jewelry, at least, would be a reflection of her personal taste. Several days later, she stopped by Jake's to pick up a silver filigree pin accented by spinels that she'd seen in his display case. It was the perfect final touch.

Cory left early on the day of the event, which was to be held in the lobby of the Craig-Bonner building, one of the downtown jewels. He gave her a quick kiss. "I'll keep an eye out for you. If I don't see you when you first get there, just circulate."

Just circulate! How like Cory it was to make it sound easy. She smiled a little, remembering Juneau's advice. "Just think to yourself, what would Regina do?"

Regina stepped down from the carriage, her head held high. She could see curious faces turned her direction and heard a murmur roll through the crowd. She didn't care what they were saying. She knew she was the long-lost daughter of the king. Now if she could just keep from stumbling in her three-inch heels!

Erin found the building easily and took advantage of the valet parking. "Okay, here goes nothing," she said to herself. Squaring her shoulders, she walked through the revolving door, glad that she had spent time learning to walk in her fancy new shoes.

The main lobby of the beautiful building was festively decorated and lit, and the sound of live music and conversation filled the air as she entered. Over it, she heard her name called and turned to see Cory hurrying toward her. "You look great," he said, giving her a kiss. "Better than great." He had her turn around so he could appreciate the total effect. "I especially like what you've done with your hair."

She had tamed her short spiky hairdo with styling gel, easing it into a sophisticated look. "Thanks. How are things going?"

"So far, so good. Come, let me introduce you to Paula."

He escorted her into the crowd, stopping now and then to introduce her to people he knew. Co-workers from his office, Mayor Donald Frazer and various aides, and even some guests she recognized from the wedding reception.

"I can't believe you know so many people," she said.

"It comes with the job. And with having a dad who loves people. Oh, there's Paula." With one hand at the small of her back, he guided her through the crowd to a striking brunette wearing a purple dress. It was very like Erin's in style.

"Cory!" Paula said, closing the gap between them. "I see you've brought your wife to meet me."

Cory presented Erin with a flourish that let her know he was proud of her.

"Cory told me you were beautiful," Paula said. "I see he wasn't exaggerating."

Before Erin could respond, a man approached Cory and spoke to him in urgent tones. Cory turned to them. "Sorry, ladies, but I need to take care of something. Erin, will you be okay for a minute?" Without waiting for an answer, he turned and walked after the man.

"He's very good at this, you know." Paula smiled kindly. "But I get the feeling that you're not so comfortable."

"I don't belong here. I guess that's easy to tell."

"Yes, you do, because I invited you." Paula hooked elbows with Erin as she began to walk. "Come now, it's not so awful. Not everyone is a natural like your Cory. Some of us have had to learn how to do this."

"You? I can't imagine you having to struggle. You look like you belong."

Paula's laughter was clear and light. "I gave up wanting to belong a long time ago. I'm a cliché, my dear, the secretary who married the boss after he divorced his first wife. I took over his real estate empire after he died."

Real estate, thought Erin. *Craig. Craig-Bonner.* "This is your building!"

Paula nodded. "Nobody thought I could manage my husband's real estate holdings, but I learned. Now the papers call me 'formidable,'" she added with amusement.

"I had no idea. I wish Cory had told me more about you before I came."

"What did he tell you?"

"That you were brainy, beautiful, and rich." Erin blushed. "Oh, no. There I go again. I've been wondering how many times in one evening I could put my foot in my mouth. Judging by the last few minutes, the sky's the limit."

"Lighten up, dear," Paula said. "No matter what you do or say tonight, you'll wake up in the morning. Now, tell me what you do besides take care of your handsome husband and your daughter?"

Paula listened as Erin told her about Finders, Inc. "That sounds interesting. Do you have a specialty?" she asked.

"I'm learning all I can about textiles, Retro and Art Deco."

Paula nodded. "Okay, let's make the rounds before the boring part begins." She directed Erin to a group of women. She greeted them warmly and said, "I want you to meet my friend Erin Johnson. She's got a little business called Finders, Inc."

Everyone wanted to know what kind of a business it was, so Erin found herself the center of attention. It was easy to talk about something she loved and natural to pass out business cards to those who were interested. Paula added that Erin's specialty was Retro or Art Deco, saying, "She'll even give you some decorating help, if you ask nicely."

"You shouldn't say that," Erin whispered urgently as they moved on. "It's not true."

"Isn't it? You have found items customers wanted, haven't you?"

"Yes."

"You've decorated your home, haven't you?"

"Yes, but I just put things I like together."

"Then what I said is as true as most of what you're hearing here today."

When Erin began to protest, Paula silenced her with an upraised hand. "What do you think the high-priced decorators do? Most do have degrees behind their name and pages of experience on their resume, but in the end, they put together things they like. And people pay for their services."

Paula introduced her to several other groups of people and then said, "Do you think you'll be okay on your own now?"

"Yes." Erin was surprised to realize she felt quite at ease. "Thank you for taking so much time with me."

Paula kissed her cheek. "My pleasure. You remind me a bit of me at your age. Although I wasn't as stunning."

Erin flushed.

"You really don't know how beautiful you are, do you?" Paula squeezed her hand. "Enjoy the rest of the evening. I hope to see you again soon."

Erin couldn't stop smiling. She was beautiful. She had something to offer. And she belonged. Paula had said so. She circled around the lobby, looking for and finding openings for conversation until a voice over the PA system announced that the awards part of the evening was about to begin.

She was following the crowd into the auditorium when Cory came up beside her.

"There you are, Erin! Sorry I had to cut out on you. I had to take care of a bunch of things." Taking her hand, he looked at her closely. "Are you okay?"

"I'm fine," she said, laughing. "I've been 'working the room.'" And when she saw his astonished expression, she added, "Paula taught me how."

WILLADENE

September 15, 1983
Dear Ladies in Triplicate,

You should see the piles of books Roger brings home to read. Ugh. They look absolutely boring to me, but he seems lit up with enthusiasm. In fact, the more he shines the duller I feel.

Maybe I should go back to school. Dropping out to put Roger through his bachelor's degree has never bothered me until now. But there's not much call for conversation on Popsicle art and child rearing at faculty functions. I think I'll start looking for reading in the not-Shoebox-books section of the public library. Hope I don't give the librarian a heart attack from the shock . . .

I ran up to campus last Wednesday night to take Roger some corrected tests he had forgotten that morning. I heard one of the students refer to me as the teacher's old lady. I thought I was still more of sweet young thing. How did I ever evolve into that?

Deenie

September 21, 1983
Dear Ladies,

"This is the forest primeval. The murmuring pines and the hemlock stand like Druids of eld." I think I'm in love. With Evangeline and Henry Wadsworth Longfellow, that is. Talk about romantic.

Juneau, I am beginning to understand your fascination with words. The librarian has recommended that I read *Giants in the Earth* next. But Grandma Rasmussen sent home a copy of *Trail of the Lonesome Pine*, and I am going to read that first.

Later: I am down one book and one box of tissue. Who would have thought I would find so much to identify with in a book published in 1908? Roger's the engineer and I'm the mountain girl without enough education to hold him. Of course, in my case there won't be any going away to school and returning to sweep him off his feet with longing.

A book away from Pearl S. Buck.

Deenie

JUNEAU

September 25, 1983
Dear COBettes,

What can hurt the heart more than a straying child? What makes one child stray and another stay? How can I keep my little girl away from the things that could hurt her? I'm full of painful questions today. Misty has been sneaking out of the house after telling us she's going to bed. She's already in so much trouble, what with the shoplifting and then being caught smoking, along with her friend Capri, behind the gym at school. It brings up all the old questions of heredity versus environment. Greg and I are not perfect parents, to be sure. But there has always been an abundance of love. And all those wonderful Primary teachers. Her Beehive teacher is a gem, but Misty won't go to Young Women's unless I go, too, and sit with her in class. That's embarrassing to both her and me. The other girls try to be friendly, but she won't respond. I've taken to keeping her home on YW activity night. She spends the time studying, which at least helps her grades remain steady.

So is it heredity that makes her so rebellious? I've tried to find out more about Great-Grandma Letitia, but Mom won't tell. She must have done something dreadful for Mom and Aunt Hattie to be so secretive. Wouldn't it be easier for them just to let me know? I told Greg I want to go to Idaho during his quarter off so I can track down the family history, but he has a chance to teach during the summer, so it probably won't work out.

Discouraged,
Juneau

ERIN

Sunday, October 9, 1983
Dear Juneau, Willadene, and Gabby,

You asked some tough questions in your last letter, Juneau. I don't suppose you really expected us to have any answers, except maybe Gabby. I look at my little Kayla and wonder what she'll be like when she's Misty's age. I have no way of knowing what is in store for me and Cory.

Knowing you, dear friend, I'm sure that you and Greg did everything for Misty that you thought you should. It's scary to think of all the things—and people—that can influence our children when they are outside of our care. I pray that the Lord will watch over all of our children, and us, too! We all need all the help we can get.

I never thought one little girl could keep me so busy. One spoiled little girl, I should say. Grams has spent so much time with Kayla that she expects to be the center of attention all the time. She puts up quite the fuss when she isn't. I spend a lot of time with her on my lap, singing songs and going through picture books. She loves playing with the learning toys her grandmothers have bought her, but she's like Cory, always wanting to go on to the next thing. Even at her age!

I'm having fun fixing up our house. I think I'm a decorator at heart. I love looking through *House and Garden,* and I'm always seeing how I can add a new touch to one of the rooms. I asked Grams to help me figure out what to do with the sad-looking flower garden. We've already plotted where we'll plant tulip, daffodil, and hyacinth bulbs in October and other flowers in the spring.

I understand a little of what you're feeling, Deenie. I bet Cory's gone as often as Roger, what with work, missionary splits, and sporting events. To say nothing of networking—the key to our future, he says. Our guys are ambitious, and they love a challenge. I didn't see at first why Cory needed to change jobs, but he's much happier where he is. Maybe Roger will be so happy to be doing what he loves that it will compensate for all the stress and extra work that ends up on you. We can hope!

> Love to both of you,
> Erin

Chapter Twenty-Six

WILLADENE

The day after Thanksgiving was Deenie's first day of the Christmas season. She couldn't get started soon enough to suit her. She loved it all, from the decorations to the kids' school programs. But Deenie was especially thrilled that Roger would soon have time at home over Christmas break. In anticipation of that treat, she determined she would have every distracting Christmas task completed before vacation days started.

The first Saturday morning in December, Deenie got up very early. She pulled on her furry slippers and lit a fire in the family room fireplace. Then she propped up her list on the mantel. It read:

1. Work up the layout for the Rasmussen family Christmas letter. Call everyone for news updates.

2. Select the cover art for the ward Christmas program. Type in the information.

3. Finish final preparation of Spiritual Living lesson for December.

Even though the last item on the list was the shortest, Deenie knew it would take the most time. So, gathering all the material needed to finish it, she set to work. An hour passed, and then another, and it was time for a breakfast break. She was savoring warm cinnamon toast and hot buttered vanilla milk when the phone rang at 7:30 A.M. Deenie knew it was Sunny before she answered.

"Deenie," the sweet voice commanded, "it's time to come home! You haven't been to see me for lots of days."

"I know, honey," Deenie replied. "But today I'm working on my Relief Society lesson."

"I could go to Relief Society," Sunny insisted, changing subjects without a pause.

"Yes, you could. In fact, I'm inviting you right now to come to my Christmas lesson, if it's all right and Mom can bring you." Deenie heard the phone on the other end of the line smack against a hard surface. Then she heard Sunny call in a loud voice, "Deenie says I can so go to Relief Society, so there."

Suddenly her mother was on the line. Her voice was tired. "Sunny's not up to attending a full three hours of meetings right now, Deenie. I would appreciate it if you would quit putting ideas in her head."

"Morning, Mom," Deenie greeted her quietly. "I didn't realize that inviting Sunny to come to my lesson would be a problem."

"One lesson isn't the problem." Margaret's voice was stern. "The problem is that you never ask permission first. In the future, do." Margaret insisted sternly.

"Yes, Mom."

By the end of the conversation, Deenie's pleasure in the early morning Christmas preparations had dimmed. She tossed out her toast and dumped the rest of her drink down the drain, and then she turned resolutely to the unfinished tasks at hand.

Some time later, Roger, still dressed in his pajamas, crawled over her boxes into the family room.

"Looks like Relief Society Prep Day is already here again," Roger groused, climbing over Deenie's slotted illustration box and empty Christmas file. He piled the pictures from the couch onto the floor and sat down.

"All this isn't for my Relief Society lesson," Deenie snapped. "We're in charge of the handouts for the Christmas program, and if you'd asked before you cleaned off the couch you'd know that those Christmas pictures were set out for you to choose one to go on the family Christmas letter. It's our turn to do it this year."

"Sorry." Roger retrieved the illustrations and started sorting absently through them. "You know, Deenie, you don't have to make this so hard on yourself." He waved his arm to indicate the clutter on every available surface in the room. "You could teach your Relief Society lessons like we do in priesthood, straight from the manual, without any of this stuff."

"The sisters in the Relief Society apparently expect *more* from their teachers than the men do. Maybe the comparison means that they should increase their preparation instead of me preparing less. Hmmm?"

"I wasn't criticizing, Deenie. I was just making a suggestion."

"That wasn't what it felt like." Deenie rubbed the tension lines on her forehead. *Men don't get it*, she thought. *They always praise the finished product but complain about what it takes to get there.*

Roger interrupted her thoughts. "Today is tree-cutting day. I'm taking the kids with me so you'll have the house to yourself until this afternoon."

"Is Bert home?" Deenie asked. "She could help with Bitsy, so it won't be so hard on your mom."

"Yup, we have it all worked out." Roger bent and gave Deenie an absent-minded peck on the cheek. Then he began gathering the kids for the Saturday morning's ritual Sugared Cereal Breakfast.

Later, when the house was empty and quiet, Deenie sat down in the center of her messy family room and thought about what Roger had said. She didn't like the questions his comments had raised in her mind. She had tucked her doubts about her teaching techniques safely away last April. Now they were back, along with her mother's comments about her intent when she taught. *How much of all this stuff has to do with teaching gospel principle and how much of it has to do with me being Deenie Stowell Rasmussen living up to the family reputation?*

Remembering Nathan's suggestion about how to teach with the Spirit, she moved to the recliner, curled up under an afghan, and read through her Relief Society lesson again. *So maybe I do need to cut and paste less and pray a little more,* she acknowledged, *and get suggestions from other Spiritual Living teachers.*

She could think of two immediately. In a flash, Deenie grabbed the phone and dialed. Within moments Juneau answered. Two hours and two conversations later, Deenie had several neat pages of notes. Juneau and Gabby had strong, rich ideas for the lesson, and not a single one had anything to do with handouts, pretty pictures, or treats. "But I'm not giving up the gingerbread cookies!" she insisted as she packed away boxes of stickers, poster board, adhesive letters, and marking pens.

December 12, 1983
Dear Ladies,

Carl turned eleven on December 7. We had a wonderful family dinner to celebrate, and his Grandpa Rasmussen marked the occasion with the gift of a .22 rifle, without asking us first. He assumed that a rifle and an eleven-year-old boy were a natural pairing and there wasn't anything to discuss. You'd think the fact that I'd turned down the offer of a BB gun for Carl when he was ten would have been a clue. But Roger didn't object, and Carl looked like his Gramps had just hung the moon.

The best I could do was get Carl to agree to never take out the gun unless he was with his father and get Roger to promise to be in constant supervision of the boy and gun.

Christmas is coming soon and all the decorations are up. Cooking is next on the list as well as December's RS lesson.

The stress of being a graduate assistant is starting to get to Roger. I wonder what it would take to create the male version of Crusty Old Broads for the men in our lives. How about CODs—Crusty Old Dogs, or COGs—Crusty Old Grouches. Maybe if Roger had listeners like I do he wouldn't be so grumpy all the time. Jonas is good, but he's long distance and we're on a budget.

> Glad I have you,
> Deenie

ERIN

The first year they were in their new house, Erin and Cory went all out to decorate for Christmas. The day after Thanksgiving, they set up a tree so tall the star scraped the ceiling and put garlands around the front door and wreaths with electric candles in all the front windows. High enough to be out of Kayla's reach, they set up the beginnings of a Christmas village, complete with fake snow.

Cory surveyed it with pride. "It looks perfect! What do you think about hosting Christmas dinner this year?"

"For your parents?"

"And The Women."

"You've got to be kidding." Erin started stacking up the empty decoration boxes. "Grams has surprised me with how well she's gotten along with your parents, but you know how she gets this time of year. I don't want our first Christmas in this house ruined."

"The last two years haven't been too bad."

"That's because we spent Christmas Eve with her and Mom and Christmas Day with your folks."

"You don't know that for sure."

"Trust me."

She handed him the boxes and opened the door to the upstairs so he could go first. He stacked the boxes in a corner of the large, unfurnished room and then faced her. "Give Grams a chance, Erin. She's not my favorite person, but she is part of the family. If she's in one of her moods, I'll warm her up. If I can't, Dad can."

Skipp was the grand master of schmooz, but Erin still had her doubts. "I'll only agree to have them if you promise not to blame me if something goes wrong."

"Promise."

She was halfway down the stairs when he said, "I was also thinking about having some people from work over sometime in the next couple of weeks."

She stopped so fast he almost ran into her. "Wait a minute! We're always entertaining your friends. What if I want to have some of mine over?"

"Nothing's been keeping you from it. Invite them."

"Okay, I will."

The minute Erin said she would, a host of reasons why she couldn't do it popped into her mind. First and most disturbing was the question, *Who are my friends?*

Really, she had only three, not counting Gabby, Juneau, and Willadene. Colleen, Angie, and, oddly enough, Jake Ingram. She had felt drawn to the soft-spoken giant from the very first time she met him.

Of the three, she had regular contact only with Colleen. *What does that say about me?* she wondered. She smiled at the answer: *That I'm not Cory!*

Before she could talk herself out of having a party, she called the three of them, extending the invitation to Angie and Colleen's husbands, too. Counting Jake, that left an odd number. On a sudden inspiration, she called her mother at work. "Mom, I'm having some friends over for dinner on Friday night. Is there any way you can come? Without Grams?"

"That sounds fun." The lilt in Joanna's voice told Erin that she was smiling. Then there was a pause, and when Joanna spoke again, the lilt was gone. "I'd like to come, but I'd better not. Grams wouldn't understand why she wasn't invited, too."

"That's too bad. I wanted you to meet Angie and her husband and Jake Ingram."

"The antique man?"

Erin chuckled. "Jake's old, but he's not antique!"

"I wish I could come. If I can think of some way to make it work, I will."

As the evening of the party approached, Erin felt her excitement rise. Cory noticed it. "This is the first time I've seen you eager to have company coming."

"Maybe because it's my company."

She opted for casual, hearty fare: a big lasagna, salad, garlic bread, and apple cobbler with ice cream. She also opted for casual place settings featuring a mix and match of interesting pieces of dinnerware she had begun picking up on Finders trips. For entertainment she had purchased a game that required players to answer revealing questions. The other players had to guess whether the answers were true or false.

Steve and Colleen arrived first, Colleen carrying a large potted poinsettia. Jake arrived shortly after. He looked like a cross between Paul Bunyan and Santa Claus, with his rosy cheeks, woodsman plaid shirt, and ubiquitous red suspenders. After greeting all around, he presented Erin with an antique sled painted with holiday motifs.

Angie and Norm arrived on their heels. Erin hadn't realized how much she had missed the two of them until she was enveloped in one bear hug after the other. Norm handed her an antique pull toy. "Merry Christmas."

"I love it. How did you know I was thinking of collecting antique toys?"

When Cory took their coats, Erin saw that they were wearing matching handmade sweaters. Norm's was normal length, Angie's long enough to cover her backside. When Erin commented on them, Norm joked, "Bet you're glad I didn't wear tights like Angie!"

As Erin had hoped, Norm and Jake hit it off famously, and Angie immediately was drawn to Colleen. Conversation was flowing in the living room when the doorbell rang. It was Joanna.

"Mom! I didn't think you were coming."

Joanna stepped inside and took off her coat. "Grams was in her nightgown watching a movie when I got home from work. When I told her I was thinking of visiting you, she said, 'Fine. I'll be okay.' So here I am."

"You look great."

The fuchsia cowl-neck sweater Joanna wore put color in her cheeks. She hugged Erin and whispered in her ear, "I didn't say you were having a party. I'll tell her when I get home, like I just happened to walk in on it."

"Mom!" Erin was surprised a second time. They giggled like teenagers as they planned how to squeak by Grams. Then Erin grabbed her by the hand. "Come on, let me introduce you."

After the introductions, Erin invited her guests to the table. She seated Joanna across from Jake, who kept them laughing with tales of his varied careers as precocious evangelist preacher, high school counselor, bond salesman, realtor, and finally, antiques shop owner. Norm responded with stories of his travels from small-town football hero and Viet Nam medic to EMT and fireman. He added, "Angie here was going to beauty school and working as a makeup artist at a funeral chapel when I met her. "

"Angie!" Erin said. "You never told me that!"

Angie shrugged. "It paid the bills, and I never got any complaints."

After the laughter died down, Jake turned to Joanna. "What about you?"

Joanna had a twinkle in her eyes that Erin had never seen before. "I started out as a dispatcher in a trucking company. It was the best job I ever had. I got to tell a bunch of tough guys where to go."

Everyone laughed, and Erin thought, *That's my mother?*

"Now I'm office manager at an insurance company. I live with my mother in the house I grew up in." She gave a self-deprecating smile. "Forty years in the same house."

"Continuity. It's not necessarily a bad thing," Jake said.

"Philosophy," countered Joanna. "It's not necessarily a bad thing, either."

Erin had never heard such lively conversation at their dinner table. There was a wonderful chemistry among her guests. They moved easily from the dinner table to the living room, from conversation to playing the game. They stayed until late, when the Harringtons finally had to leave to take their baby-sitter home.

Joanna hugged her hard as she left. "Thank you for inviting me. That's the most fun I've had in years."

The glow of the evening stayed with Erin through the following weeks. The Christmas season had never seemed more magical. She delighted in introducing eleven-month-old Kayla to Christmas stories and songs. She enjoyed shopping and baking cookies with Colleen. She especially loved the late evenings when she and Cory snuggled on the couch, enjoying the colorful Christmas tree lights and the lush harmonies of a Tabernacle Choir Christmas album.

Since The Women were coming for dinner on Christmas Day, Erin accepted Colleen and Steve's invitation to spend Christmas Eve with them.

It was a lovely, low-key evening. There was something special about being with such good friends who were in the same stage of life as themselves. Steve read a child's version of the Christmas story to Kayla and EJ, after which EJ sang "Jingle Bells" in her clear little-girl voice while Steve shook some bells in rhythm. Erin left feeling supremely content.

Erin and Cory spent Christmas morning in the kitchen, getting the ham, sweet potatoes, salad, and dessert ready. Right before the guests were to arrive, they changed clothes, got Kayla into a little green velveteen dress trimmed with lace and ribbons, and put Christmas music on the record player.

Linda and Skipp arrived first with a Fitz and Lloyd Santa Claus as a hostess gift. The Women arrived a little later, Joanna in her fuchsia sweater and Grams bearing a tray of the holiday cookies that were her specialties. The Johnsons ooh-ed and aah-ed over them, making Grams smile.

It's going to be all right, Erin thought, grateful for the way the Johnsons seemed to know how to handle any situation. And it was—until they were in the living room after dinner. Kayla was down for her nap, and they were all feeling mellow from wonderful food.

It started with a seemingly innocent question. Linda turned to Grams and asked brightly, "Aren't you happy that the kids have such a nice house to bring up Kayla in? I just love what they've done with it."

"It was quite a surprise that they could find one this nice in their price range," Grams said.

Erin sat at attention. Grams was setting Linda up.

"We gave them a little assist. Didn't you know?" Linda said.

"You did?" asked Grams sweetly.

You know they did, thought Erin. *I told you. What are you up to?*

"Yes," Linda said in response to Grams's question. "We like being able to help Cory and his family. We're so fond of Erin, you know."

"It must be nice to have the money to do that. Alfred and I had to work and save for many years before we could make it into a house of our own. He was on the railroad, and I was a fry cook in a little cafe. We didn't have anyone to hand us a check."

"It was that way for us, too." Linda smiled at Skipp. "Back when we were starting out."

"You mean, Skipp was on the railroad? And you were a fry cook?"

"No." Linda shook her head, frowning. "I mean we had to work hard, too."

Grams sighed dramatically. "Some of us still have to work hard. Some of us have barely enough money to keep our heads above water." The look in Ruth's eyes was enough to tell Erin what was coming next. "It would have been different if Alfred hadn't died. Twenty-one years ago in December. He was fifty-five."

"Mom," said Joanna with soft intensity, "this is Erin's first Christmas dinner in her new home. Let's not ruin our celebration with old sorrows."

"Some celebration. Erin didn't even come home to go to Christmas Eve service."

"We were invited to Colleen and Steve's for Christmas Eve," said Erin. "I told you that."

"Did you go to services?"

Cory answered her. "Grams, Mormons don't have a Christmas Eve service."

"Why not? Every other Christian church does."

Ruth's voice was a notch higher, and Erin could hear the pressure behind it. *She's going to blow*, Erin thought. *There's no way to stop her.*

"We focus on celebrating the birth of Christ in our families," said Skipp.

Grams made an agitated gesture. Her voice was challenging. "I'm not so sure you're Christians anyway. Joe Smith and his golden plates."

"The Book of Mormon is a strong testimony of Christ, Ruth. If you read it, you would know we worship him as the Son of God."

"That may be so. But if Erin hadn't joined your church, she would have been home with us on Christmas Eve, where she belongs." She stood as if to go.

Cory rose to face her. His actions were marked by deliberate slowness, a sure sign to Erin that he was furious. "In case you've forgotten, Erin is my wife. She belongs here, with me."

"Well, Mr. Cory Know-It-All Johnson, she may belong here, but I don't. You Mormons go ahead and celebrate your Christmas. I'm going home!" Grams took a few steps and then turned to glare at Joanna.

Joanna sank deeper in her chair, arms crossed and feet firmly planted. "I'm not going with you, Mom. If you're determined to leave, I'll call you a taxi."

Erin looked from her mother to Grams and back again. She couldn't believe what was happening. Grams seemed shocked as well. Only moments before, she had been puffed up like a banty hen with justified anger. Now deflated, she looked older than her sixty-eight years. Erin held her breath as the silence stretched.

Skipp came to the rescue. He stood between Cory and Ruth, an arm around each of them, speaking in a low, soothing voice. "Come, Cory. Ruth. This is no way to celebrate peace on earth. We're family, now. There's nothing more important than that we love and support one another."

He gave Ruth a conciliatory and paternal smile, one Erin was sure he used with feuding law clients when necessary. "We don't go to the same church, Ruth, but we all believe in God and his Son, Jesus Christ. The biggest lesson he taught was that we love one another. Let's show we can do that now."

His words were interrupted by a fretful cry from Kayla, wanting to be picked up from her crib.

"For Kayla's sake," he added.

Erin had no idea if Grams had heard Skipp's last words. At the sound of Kayla's cry, she had shifted gears instantly and hurried down the hall.

When she was gone, Skipp smiled at Cory and Erin. "I think Kayla is the key to handling Ruth. She loves her great-granddaughter."

"I'm sorry you had to see that," Joanna said to Linda. "My mother gets distressed this time of year. She hasn't ever gotten over my dad's death."

Or the circumstances of my birth, Erin thought, but she didn't say anything. And when Ruth brought Kayla into the living room, she acted as if nothing unpleasant had happened.

Chapter Twenty-Seven
1984

WILLADENE

The first day of the new year was bright, clear and freezing. The perfect kind of day to be tucked warmly inside, playing. That was how Deenie saw packing away the Christmas ornaments and decorations—as play. Usually the whole family helped, but on this morning Carl and Roger were missing. "Have you seen your father?" she asked Paul as she packed away the nativity scene.

"He went to the farm with Carl," he said, putting the lid on the box of clothespin soldiers.

"When was that?"

"A while ago. I was supposed to tell you, but I forgot."

"Did he say why they were going?"

"No, but they took Carl's new rifle with them."

"Oh, did they?" Deenie headed for the phone and punched in the number of the farm.

When NaVae answered, Deenie asked, "Are my men there?"

"Of course," NeVae said. "It's New Year's Day."

As if that has anything to do with it, thought Deenie.

"Could I speak to Roger, please?" she asked.

"They're still out at the rifle range. I'll have him call you the minute they get back in the house. I'd hate to interrupt them. A boy's first day on the shooting range with his dad and his grandpa is a big thing."

"Tell Roger I called when he gets in." Furious, Deenie hung up the phone as loudly as she dared.

What a lousy thing to do to me on New Year's Day, Deenie thought. *Sneaking out to shoot that gun, when Roger knows I didn't want Carl to have it in the first place! The least he could have done was tell me face to face. How can we solve anything if we don't talk to each other.*

It was forty minutes later when Paul looked out the family room window and announced, "Hey, Dad's pulling in the driveway. Carl's with him, and so are Gramps and Rauf. Are we having a party?"

Deenie sucked in a deep, slow breath, reining in her anger and marshaling her thoughts. "I don't think so."

But any thought of confrontation fled when Deenie saw her white-faced son in his blood-spattered jacket standing stiffly between Roger and Wilford Rasmussen.

"Carl!" she screeched. She dashed to him, touched his face, grabbed his shoulders, and ran her hands over his chest and back, babbling in hysteria, "Where is it? Where is he hurt?"

"Calm down, Deenie," Roger said. "The boy is fine. But he has something to tell you."

Carl looked up at his dad as if for reassurance, and then he faced Deenie and said in a flat, solemn voice, "Mom, I killed a chicken."

"What?"

"I didn't mean to, and Gramps said it wasn't any big deal." Once started, Carl rushed on without a breath. "Chickens end up in the pot sooner or later and it was a clean shot and after we cleaned it Grandma plucked it and put it in a pot and said she was glad to make chicken and dumplings on such a cold day."

"Cool!" Paul said, looking at his big brother with glowing eyes.

"And I missed Rauf," Carl finished as though that made everything okay.

Deenie felt her face numb with shock. "You were shooting at Rauf?"

"No, Mom," Carl said impatiently. "Rauf chased the chicken right in front of the targets just as I was getting ready to shoot. I looked at the chicken when I was pulling the trigger and my arms followed my eyes and bang! It was dead. Because Rauf was chasing it. Because someone left the chicken coop open and Grandma let Rauf out for a run and Rauf saw the chicken . . . I didn't do it on purpose."

"Where's Rauf?" Paul interrupted, suddenly concerned for his pet.

"Still cowering in the van," Grandpa explained in a hearty voice. "He's had quite a shock, but he'll come around."

Carl's face lightened as he leaned toward Paul. "You should've seen him. Man, he took off like he had firecrackers tied to his tail."

"Carl," Deenie said sharply. "You nearly shot your dog. I don't think that makes a funny story. And you did shoot Grandma's chicken."

"And Gramps made me clean it, too. It was so gross. There were guts and everything, and then we had to help pull out the feathers."

Deenie was furious. "Don't change the subject with me, young man. It could have been one of the farm dogs or livestock or one of your cousins."

Carl's attitude switched from storytelling to supplication in a split second. "Aw, Mom," he pleaded, "don't have a fit. Dad said you'd have a fit."

In the momentary silence, Will stepped forward. "For the record,

Willadene, a chicken is a small loss to teach a boy about gun safety. Nobody will ever be more careful with a gun than Carl. And there never was and never will be any risk to anyone on the farm when the rifle range is in use. No one approaches that area unless invited or announced. Especially on New Year's Day."

"Everyone in the family knows it's off-limits except for dads and boys who got guns for presents," Carl said, trying to smooth things over.

Deenie glared at Roger. "Oh, really? I didn't know. Where is your gun?" she demanded, turning on Carl.

"Gramps has it. He thought it would be better if he kept it at the farm for a while."

Roger turned Carl around and helped him out of his coat. Looking at Deenie over his shoulder, he said, "That's enough for now, Deenie."

"More than enough," Deenie agreed. "Roger, why don't you put that coat to soak in cold water." When Roger stepped away from Carl, she gave her son an extra long hug. "I bet you'd like a hot shower." She gave his cap-flattened hair a ruffle with a shaking hand.

"Sure, Mom." Carl hurried from the room.

Deenie hoisted Bitsy to her hip and motioned to Paul. "Grab some doggie treats. Let's see if we can coax poor old Rauf out of the van." When Paul jumped to obey, Deenie took a moment to glare at Will and say shortly, "I bet NeVae has that whole pot of chicken and dumplings ready for you, Will. You shouldn't keep her waiting."

"Deenie!" Roger reprimanded sharply from the doorway of the laundry room where he'd been headed to rinse the blood from Carl's shirt.

Looking shocked, Grandpa Will bellowed, "Roger! Come take me home."

Deenie ignored both of them, heading for the garage to rescue the dog.

Rauf wasn't having any of it, not the coaxing nor the petting nor the treats. He wasn't going to leave the van under his own steam for anybody. So Deenie set Bitsy on her feet and then grabbed Rauf's collar and pulled. The harder she pulled, the harder he resisted. By the time she had bodily hefted the sixty-pound dog to his favorite spot by the family room fire, she had worn off the top level of her anger. But there was still plenty underneath.

When Carl came down, clean and dressed in his sweats, he went straight for Rauf and sat down beside him. Deenie sat next to him.

"I was really scared, Mom," he confided, running his hand repeatedly from Rauf's head to tail as if to make sure he was really all right. "I pulled the trigger and there was the blood and Rauf howling and everything." The hand petting Rauf speeded up. "If Dad doesn't mind, I don't think I want go shooting again for a while." Carl looked down, concentrating on his dog, and Deenie knew he'd said all he would on the subject.

After the children were in bed, Roger found her in the kitchen.

"Let's get it over with," he said. "It's been a long day, and I'm tired."

"You're not the only one," Deenie said. "Where were you when Carl almost shot the dog?"

"Right where I promised I'd be, standing next to Carl."

"You sneaked out without telling me."

"I don't sneak! I left a message with Paul to avoid having a scene like this spoil the day for Carl. I'm going to make sure Carl knows how to handle a gun safely, Deenie. Guns are part of a boy's life in Wellsville, no matter what you think. I'm not going to let you ruin it for him."

Deenie was shocked at the idea of being the family spoiler. "I thought we were partners."

"We are. But that doesn't mean we have to agree on everything. There are times when you're just going to have to trust me."

"I did, and look what happened." Deenie shook her head in exasperation. "It's a moot point anyway. Carl says he doesn't want to go shooting anymore."

"You mean you talked him into it when he was still upset about Rauf and the chicken."

"As a matter of fact, what he said exactly was, 'If Dad doesn't mind, I don't think I want to go shooting again for a while.'"

"For a while, Deenie. Only for a while."

"So what am I supposed to do when he wants to go shooting and you aren't here?"

"Call my dad. He'll make time for Carl."

"Great."

Roger headed for the stairs, leaving Deenie alone with her thoughts. They weren't good company. *Am I in the right, or is Roger? Am I really the family spoiler? What happened to me? When did Roger stop seeing me as Deenie the Wonderful, Deenie the Love of His Life, and start seeing me as the person mostly likely to pitch a fit and spoil the fun?*

All alone, sitting by the burned-out fire in the denuded family room, Deenie longed for someone, anyone, who saw all of her, who knew that Deenie the Wonderful was still inside of her.

In that moment, 1984 became for Deenie The Year of the Dead

Chicken or The Year of the Almost Dead Dog. She feared the events of that day were an indication of the days to come.

ERIN

Late on New Year's Day, Erin and Cory decided to set goals for the coming year—this time, writing them down in a notebook, not just talking about them. They started with their spiritual goals. These were the easy ones to set, because they were so clearly defined in conference talks and Sunday School lessons. The only time Erin felt an inner glitch was in regards to genealogy. *You can write it down, Cory,* she thought, *but I'm not going to do it.*

Finances were more problematic. Erin insisted they needed to trim expenses, cut up their credit cards, work on building up their emergency fund and food storage, and put some money into retirement. "We can't do all that," Cory said, running his hand through his hair. "We don't have enough money."

"We would if we made a budget and stuck to it. We'd have to cut back on using credit cards and eating out. You could take a bag lunch to work once in awhile."

"Those are all directed at me. Are you saying I spend too much?" He sat back in his chair, crossing his arms, daring her to say yes.

Erin hated it when he even seemed angry, and more often than not she let things slide in favor of peace. It took courage to say what she was thinking. "Yes, I am."

"If you think you could do a better job of the finances, why don't you take them over?"

"I'll be glad to." She knew he thought he was issuing a challenge she wasn't up for, but it was exactly what she had been hoping for. "I know you don't like doing them, and I'm good with numbers."

He sputtered, but she stood her ground. Finally he agreed to let her take over on a trial basis, and they went on.

They talked about what they wanted to do with the house and yard, their fitness goals, and career development goals. Cory wanted to expand his network of contacts, and Erin wanted to upgrade Finders from a hobby to a real business.

"What does Colleen think about that?" Cory asked.

"She's up for it." Erin fiddled with the pencil she was holding. "Did you know they've been trying for another baby?"

Cory's eyebrows rose. "It's not the kind of thing guys talk about."

"It's been almost a year, with no luck. Colleen's feeling pretty down about it. She wants something to keep her mind occupied."

"I had no idea." He took her hand and starting kissing her fingertips. "What do you think about another baby?"

She snatched her hand away. "Cory! Kayla's not even out of diapers yet."

"I know." He grinned. "She's such a cutie. I'm crazy about her. I wouldn't mind having another one. Or two."

"Maybe in another year."

When they finished with their plan, Erin rose. "I'm going to fix a cup of herbal tea. Do you want one?"

"In a minute. I want to talk to you about Grams."

He took her hand and pulled her back down on her chair. "I'm really worried about Grams being around Kayla so much."

"For heaven's sake, why? She's devoted to Kayla."

"I know, but the way she acts, okay one day and the Wicked Witch of the West the next, I don't think she's stable."

"She can be prickly, and she gets strange during the holidays, but she's never done anything around Kayla that's been a cause for concern."

"It's more than that. Erin, I know what growing up with Grams did to you. I don't want the same thing to happen to Kayla."

Erin bounded to her feet. "That's not fair. She's been a guardian angel to Kayla ever since she was so sick."

"Really? Who knows what she's already been whispering in Kayla's ears when we're not around to hear? It doesn't take much to plant negative ideas in children's mind. They don't even need to understand the words. They know from the tone of voice."

Erin turned her back to him, so he wouldn't see how his words were affecting her. She remembered as if it were yesterday, hiding under her bed, listening to the sound of angry, tearful voices. How old was she then? Maybe as young as two.

"Erin? Please sit down. I don't want to talk to your back."

Reluctantly, she sat back down, but she didn't look at him.

"If you're honest, you know your grandmother has put me in the same category as That Catholic Boy. I have a gut feeling that one of these days, she's going to start calling me That Mormon Boy when she's talking to Kayla. I don't trust her."

"Cory, Grams doesn't mean half of what she says. She can't help—"

"Don't even go there! You and Joanna have put up with Ruth by telling

yourselves this is just the way she is, but I don't accept that. There's no point
to the gospel if people can't see the light and change their behavior. You
have to talk to her. Tell her we don't feel comfortable about leaving her
alone with Kayla anymore."

"You mean *you* don't, so tell her yourself."

"It's not my place. She's your grandmother."

Erin didn't sleep well that night. If she talked to Grams, Grams would
be heartbroken and angry. If she didn't, Cory would be furious. It was Catch-
22.

She hadn't intended to discuss the issue with Jake when she dropped in
on him several days later while running errands with Kayla. It was a gray
January afternoon, and no customers were in the store.

"It's always slow after Christmas," Jake said cheerfully. "Good thing you
stopped by. You can keep me company for a while." He fetched some sodas
from his office fridge, and they settled in comfortable chairs at the front of
the shop. Erin put a lidded cup and a sack of cheese crackers on a low table
for Kayla.

"I really enjoyed myself at the party," Jake said. "Thanks again for asking
me." He raised his Dr. Pepper can in a toast and then took a swig. "Your
guests were delightful. Your mother especially. You're a lot like her, you
know."

"Really? Nobody's ever told me that."

"It's in your eyes and the way you talk. I hope I meet your grandmother
sometime. Then I could see where it comes from."

Erin made a short sound. "I hope you don't see any similarity between us
and Grams. She's . . . difficult." Without intending to, Erin found herself
telling him all about Christmas Day, Cory's concerns and his insistence that
she talk to Grams. "I haven't done it yet," she confessed. "I can't see how to,
without causing a bigger problem than we've already got."

Jake tugged thoughtfully on his suspenders. Today they were black with
red horizontal stripes. "It won't be easy," he said. "If Ruth loves Kayla as
much as you say she does, she won't understand what the issue is."

"That's what Angie says, but Cory says we can't take the risk that she'll
get off on one of her tangents about how horrible life is and how Mom and
I are responsible."

"That's the way life is, to her."

"That doesn't minimize the effect. I've been trying for years to get
Grams's voice out of my head. I don't want it in Kayla's."

At the sound of her name, Kayla babbled a reply. Instantly Erin rushed to where Kayla was trying to clamber up the side of an old trunk.

"Here, Kayla," Jake said. He handed her an antique pull toy to divert her attention from the trunk and showed her how to make it work.

He and Erin watched her for a moment. Erin said, "Cory isn't saying Grams can't see Kayla. Just that she can't see her *alone*. There's a difference."

"Ah. Supervised visitation with an observer present. How pleasant."

Erin gave him a sharp look. "You sound like you're on her side."

"I understand her a little, I think. Life has dealt her some blows, and she gets back at it by making others hurt as much as she does. It's rather sad."

"You just made my point. We don't want her to hurt Kayla, intentionally or unintentionally."

"Have you or your mother ever encouraged her to get some help?"

"Angie suggested therapy. Fat chance of that."

He tossed his soda can into a wastebasket on the other side of the room. "Three points," he crowed. Then he turned to her, his expression sober. "If there really is a possibility that she's unstable, it's important that you get her some help. Even if she's just a crotchety old lady, it could make a difference."

Erin gathered up Kayla's things silently.

"At the very least, make sure she gets a checkup if she hasn't had one in a while. It's important for people her age. Besides, you can use it as a bargaining chip. She gets the checkup; she can see Kayla."

"That's a good idea." She paused. "How do you know all this?"

"One of my degrees was in psychology. I was a school counselor, remember?" Jake put his arm around her in a friendly—no, *fatherly*—gesture. "You've been thinking that your grandmother is a lost cause. She probably thinks that, too. But what if who she is has been distorted by depression or the trauma of her husband's death? That would explain her going through the same drama every November and December."

"You don't know what it's like."

"You're right, I don't." He stood and gestured toward a display shelf. "Do you want to see the Oven King cookware I got at an estate sale?"

Sunday, January 22, 1984
Dear COBettes, Dear Gabby,

I've started this letter twice and I almost gave up, but you're my buddies, best friends, and confidantes. Who else can I complain to?

Cory's parents and The Women spent Christmas Day with us. Grams picked a fight with Linda and brought up the old story of my grandpa's death. It was the last straw as far as Cory is concerned. He's worried that she'll start filling Kayla's sweet little head with her bitterness. He insisted that I tell her she can't see Kayla without our supervision. Stupid me, I did, and she was utterly heartbroken. The only good thing that came out of it was that Mom took Jake's advice and made sure Grams got a thorough checkup, the first in years. She's on meds now for high blood pressure and osteoporosis, but that's not bad, considering.

As if that weren't enough of a shock to start the New Year with, Bishop Palmer called me to be . . . you guessed it! Spiritual Living teacher. I was still upset from my confrontation with Grams, and when he told me what he wanted me to do, I started to bawl. I blurted out everything I thought I was doing wrong. He just smiled and said everyone has problems and God doesn't expect me to be perfect, just willing.

I am willing but scared to death. I hope you guys will share what you're doing for lessons! One thing's for sure: I'm going to be spending a lot of time on my knees. I've been learning what it really means to pray since Kayla was born.

Remember back at Education Week when I was all upset about the necessity of sacrifice? I understand it more, now that I have something in my life worth sacrificing for: a dear husband and precious daughter.

> Much love to you all,
> Erin

WILLADENE

February 9, 1984
Dear Ladies,

Call me Annie Oakley. Despite my anti-gun stance, I have decided that if guns are going to be important to Carl, I'd better learn all I can about them. I want to be able to take him shooting when Roger can't. I borrowed a .22 rifle from my brother Jerry, and my dad has been going with me to the indoor range in Logan. Even though they think I'm off my rocker, Mom and Sunny are glad to watch Bitsy for me those days. It's all hush-hush for now. I don't want anyone to know until I feel confident I can handle the gun properly. I can't imagine how Roger will react when he finds out. Once Dad outfitted me with protective earmuffs—I hate the loud, sharp noise—I've found this gun thing to be unexpectedly intriguing. I like the feeling of power in the recoil against my shoulder when I pull the trigger. I'm even getting hooked on seeing how many times I can hit the target in succession. (Note that I didn't say the center of the target!)

I have started on my Relief Society lesson for March on joy through repentance. I love the opening quote from Alma where he says in 36:21, "There can be nothing so exquisite and sweet as was my joy." We could use something sweet and exquisite around here, and I'm all for joy. They've been in scarce supply since the fiasco on New Year's Day. We could use a good dose of repentance, too. But who should repent and why are still under debate.

Bert wrote and will be home from her mission in Scotland on April 15. I am so excited. We were getting to be really good friends before she left. Now that she will be a returned sister missionary, she will be more unique than ever in our ward. I am hoping for a spring thaw in the families as well as the fields when she gets here.

Deenie

March 5, 1984
Dear Ladies,

The cat is out of the bag, and I'm the one who did it. Last Saturday Carl was begging his dad to take him shooting, but Roger had already promised the day to Jonas. Carl was disappointed and a little jealous, too, I think. After Roger left, I offered to take him to the range in Logan. He was totally surprised when I told him I'd been practicing with Grandpa John. I was floored when he turned down my offer. He said going with me just wouldn't be the same as going with his dad.

When I told Dad about it, he said to never mind and to keep coming to practice. I think I will. It's pretty cool to have my dad all to myself. Some days we even take time to get a sandwich at the deli before going home. I can't remember us being this free with each other since before Sunny was born.

We have had a little thaw in the extended Rasmussen family, but we haven't reached any forgive-and-forget stage yet. I don't know if I ever will with NeVae. She is so put out because I "scolded Papa and made him feel unwelcome." If anyone was feeling unwelcome in my home at that moment, it was me!

The sisters-in-law, Charlotte and Jenny, have some sympathy for me, but both say I must have insulted Will badly for NeVae to act this way. Sigh.

Gabby, will we see you soon? Roger said he thought you needed a break.

Deenie

Chapter Twenty-Eight

JUNEAU

In the spring of 1984 Misty seemed to have a change of heart and became more cooperative. She even consented to attend the Young Women's activity nights. Juneau was relieved, and now that she was more relaxed, she was able to complete a book for teenagers. Mrs. Jarvis had encouraged her to try writing a novel for young people after she sold two stories to a leading teen magazine.

"You seem to have a natural talent for addressing that age group," Mrs. J had said.

"But I don't know how to write a novel," Juneau had protested.

Mrs. Jarvis had shrugged. "You didn't know how to write a short story when you first came to class."

True. "But a novel is not just a long short story," Juneau persisted.

"You're right," Mrs. J agreed. " We'll guide you here in class."

So Juneau had wrestled with a main plot with subplots and more characters than she was used to dealing with. She made many false starts, but true to her word, Mrs. Jarvis guided her along, aided by the class members, many of whom were excellent critics. The man named Clyde was big on action and delighted the other students by making a sound like air escaping from a balloon when the plot fell flat. On the other hand, he was the first to cheer when she turned in a well-written chapter.

It finally worked out. She wrote a novel.

In the course of writing the book she'd made some discoveries about herself. When she tried to narrow down the story theme to exactly what she wanted to say, she wondered if her life had a theme. When she set up a goal for her character to strive for, she asked herself what *her* life's goal was.

After she sent off the manuscript, Juneau began doing some hard thinking about her own life. She sat down at the typewriter at the kitchen table one afternoon to transfer her thoughts to paper and found that plotting a life was far more difficult than plotting a novel. When Nicole came home from school and pulled up a chair beside her, she was glad for the interruption.

"What's up, Pup?" Juneau asked.

"A lot, Dot," Nicole said.

They'd got into this rhyming thing a few months before. Its genesis had been the "See you later, alligator," and "How are you, kangaroo?" that Nicole had picked up at school. It was something Misty sneered at (what *didn't* Misty sneer at these days?), but Nicole, at age nine, loved it.

"So spill, Jill," Juneau said.

Nicole planted her elbow on the table and fitted her chin into her cupped hand. "Mom," she said.

"Yes?"

"What do you want me to be when I grow up?"

"It doesn't matter what *I* want you to be. What do *you* want to be?"

Nicole stared out of the window. "A long time ago when I was little, I wanted to be an antho . . . anthro . . . anthro-pol-o-gist. Me and Beto were going to go live in Egypt and dig up mummies. But I changed my mind. I want to be a baton twirler."

Juneau wasn't sure just what she'd been expecting Nicole to say. An astronaut, maybe. A pilot. Lawyer. Teacher.

"A baton twirler," she repeated.

Nicole nodded, her face brightening. "What I really want to do is be Miss America, but I need to have a talent to do that, so I want to learn how to twirl a baton. Can I take lessons, Mom?"

"We might arrange that," Juneau said.

"Soon," Nicole said. "Then I'll practice for eight years until I'm old enough to be Miss America." She leaned over to kiss Juneau on the cheek. "Thanks, Mom." She skipped away to her room.

Juneau chuckled to herself. Nicole had her life all planned out and was prepared to do what was required to achieve her goal. Then it didn't seem quite so funny. Wasn't that exactly what Juneau was trying to do?

Turning back to her machine, she typed "Goals" at the top of a blank page. Under that, she typed "Family."

"Too broad," she heard Mrs. J's voice saying.

Under "Family" she put "Greg" and then wrote "Date nights to get to know each other better," and under that, "Temple," "Movies," and "Out with friends." After pondering that section for a minute or two, she went on to Misty ("Save her from herself," and under that, "Bring her back to family"). *This is harder than I figured,* she thought. *Maybe I should join Nicole and be a baton twirler.*

She went back to her task, and soon she had a list three-quarters of a page long, including "Establish better relationship with parents" and "Get in touch with Flint."

She read over the list, realizing they were all personal relationship goals. What about her want-to-accomplish goals? Her writing career? Dared she even think of it as a "career"?

It seemed inevitable. She was a Paulsen, and now she'd actually had some success.

Under "Career" she typed "Start another novel."

The list was too long to tackle everything at once. She remembered being impressed by *The Autobiography of Benjamin Franklin* in which he made a long list of character qualities he wanted to work on and then concentrated on just one each week. She could do that. But some of her goals overlapped. And some couldn't be relegated to some future week.

Well, she'd do the best she could.

First, she wrote a letter to Flint. He was the one who'd been most neglected. "Dear Bro," she typed. "Just because I'm so slow in corresponding doesn't mean I don't love you."

A few days later Flint called in response to her letter. "Hi, sis." His booming Marine drill sergeant's voice rattled Juneau's eardrum. After preliminary greetings he said, "Guess what? I'm being reassigned to Camp Pendleton for a short stint before I'm deployed overseas. Since that's just a short hop of a hundred miles from Pasadena, I'll present my ugly face at your door in about four weeks."

"I'll bake a cake," Juneau said.

Flint laughed. "Mom's recipe? Contents of a box plus a cup of water?"

"I'll let it be a surprise," Juneau said. "I'll absolutely *love* to see you, Old Bro. Are Valerie and the kids coming, too?"

"Just me," Flint said. "This is a six-month assignment, and Val doesn't want to take the kids out of school. See you soon."

A visit from Flint was a rarity, something to look forward to. She was glad she'd have time to write to Willadene and ask for a super-duper, extra-tasty, no-fail chocolate cake recipe.

That evening, to celebrate Flint's impending visit, Juneau took the family to the Acapulco, their favorite Mexican restaurant now that Misty and Nicole had expanded their eating repertoire beyond McDonald's.

The girls were excited at the thoughts of actually seeing their legendary Uncle Flint. Misty faintly remembered his last visit, when she was seven.

She entertained Nicole with tales of his size and his big voice. "He's in charge of teaching all the guys how to march in parades and stuff," she said.

"Parades?" Nicole contemplated that. "Do you think he needs a baton twirler?"

It was a successful family evening, and Juneau felt that she was on the way to accomplishing a goal or two. She felt even better when the first chapter of her new novel was well received by Mrs. Jarvis and her class.

"The story question is clear," Mrs. J said after class, "and you've got your theme set up nicely."

Juneau glowed. "Well, it's all due to your good teaching. I don't think I could have sold a thing without you."

She was still glowing when she left the room. To her surprise, the man named Clyde was waiting outside the classroom door. "Hi," he said. "I just wanted to tell you how much I enjoy your writing. You're getting to be an expert at setting up a good story."

"Thanks," Juneau said. "That means a lot to me. I feel so unsure of myself."

He smiled. "Occupational hazard. Most writers feel unsure, even well established ones."

"Do you?"

"You don't see me producing much of anything, do you?"

"I remember your story about a man wanting to conquer a mountain, but what he really was doing was facing a mountain inside himself."

Clyde nodded. "But I'm not sure enough of that story to send it out." They walked along a few steps. "Want to join me at the coffee shop next door for a little while? We could have a cup of joe and talk about our uncertainties."

Cup of hot chocolate, Juneau amended, surprised at how much she really wanted to sit down over a cuppa and talk with someone who truly shared her writing interests. Then she thought of Jay, the tired man back at the truck stop in Springville who wanted to talk over a glass of Pepsi.

"I have to get home to my family," she said a little too quickly.

Clyde smiled. "Another time maybe."

"Maybe," she said and went home to Greg.

April 7, 1984
Dear COBettes,

Guess what! The Peripatetic Paulsens have peripatetted (I made that up) to California! They need to do some research near San

Diego, so their Airstream is at an RV park in Carlsbad. We drove down to see them last weekend. It was such fun! The girls didn't want to come back home. Especially Misty. She wishes that we'd sell our house and buy an Airstream, too.

Anyway, we talked and played games and walked on the beach, and Mom cooked Hotdogs Herbert, a recipe she got from a guy named Herbert back when we were kids. There's nothing special about it—just boiled weiners on buns, with mustard, ketchup, and pickle relish. But Flint and I always thought it was special because of the name.

They entertained the girls with tales of Flint and me growing up. They remember things even I had forgotten, like the 4th of July when the two of us and Starette, the girl I've told you about, got firecrackers from somewhere and set the trailer park on fire. No real damage was done, but the way they tell it is pretty exciting. The stories especially delighted Misty. She said she was glad to know I was a real human being when I was young. I guess that tells me how she regards me now!

As for me and Greg, I spend most of the hours that the girls are in school writing, and Greg practically lives at the computer lab on campus.

I might say I'm really enjoying leading the Spiritual Living discussions. And as usual, I learn far more than the class members do.

I forgot to mention that I called my brother, Flint, the Marine. He's going to be at Camp Pendleton for a short while. That's about a hundred miles from here, so we'll get to see him. Too bad he wasn't here while the Peripatetic Paulsens were in California.

Nicole and her pal Beto from next door are growing up. A few years ago they were into digging for mummies. Right now Beto is trying to decide whether he wants to be a Catholic priest or a Mormon missionary. Nicole has been taking him to Primary with her. She wants to be a baton twirler so she can take part in the Miss America pageant. And win, of course.

Love,
Juneau

ERIN

Four years after Erin and Cory first had a family home evening with Colleen and Steve, they were still getting together. Now, however, it was only once a month, on the second Monday. The first was for them alone, the third was reserved for Cory's folks, and the fourth for The Women.

In April it was the Johnsons' turn to host the Harringtons for family home evening. Erin fixed a big pot of stew and baked some refrigerator breadsticks and apple pie. The breadsticks were especially for Kayla and EJ. They were favorites of the girls, now aged fourteen months and heading toward four years old.

Steve and Colleen arrived late, EJ rushing before them. "We have a farmhouse!" EJ said, jumping up and down to get attention.

"A house?" Erin asked.

"We signed the papers this afternoon," Steve said. He and Colleen both looked a little stunned at what they had done but excited and proud as well. "For the one on County Road 6," he added.

"Man, that's good news!" Cory pumped Steve's hand, and Erin hugged Colleen.

Once everyone had calmed down and was seated at the table, Steve described their new home. "It's an old farmhouse on an acre lot. We have a shed, a barn, some apple trees, a raspberry patch, and a big garden that's fenced to keep the deer out. The only downside is we'll be in another ward."

"I can't believe it," Erin said. "I know you guys have been talking about getting a place where you could be self-sufficient, but I didn't think you'd really do it. What do you know about orchards and gardens?"

"Nothing," Colleen said. She and Steve both laughed, leaning into each other. EJ joined them. "It's crazy, but it's what we want to do."

"We're going to have chiiickens!" cried EJ. "Mommy and I are going to get eggs from them. We have to be verrrry careful, or we'll get pecked!" She made little pecking gestures with one hand on the back of the other.

"No way!" Cory was shaking his head. "You guys are crazy." Cory passed Steve the big bowl of stew. "Well, it sounds like we won't be seeing much of you guys, especially in the summer." He shook his head. "With a garden, a lawn as big as a football field, and those chickens to take care of, you'll need a forty-eight-hour day just to keep your heads above water."

Steve and Colleen exchanged glances. "I'm thinking of getting my teacher's certificate, so I can have summers off," Steve said.

"Man, you just bought yourself a money pit. Being an accountant pays a lot more than being a teacher."

"I'm not quitting my job tomorrow, bro. It's just something I'm looking at."

They spent the rest of the meal talking about the new property. When everyone had eaten, Erin started gathering up the dishes. Cory's voice stopped her. "I'm thinking about changing jobs, too."

Erin almost dropped the dishes she was holding. "What? You haven't said anything about that to me."

"I thought I'd wait until I had something to tell."

"So, tell." Erin didn't even try to keep the frustration out of her voice. Colleen pulled on her sleeve, urging her to sit down.

"It's not really a *new* job, like Steve's thinking of. I'd be doing a lot of the same things I am now, except for a small company called Behind the Scenes. It handles PR and event planning for companies that don't have in-house capacity. The cool thing is that they're starting to do some work for individuals who want help with things like reunions and weddings. Stuff like that."

"I should have guessed you'd be ready for a change," Erin said. He was always talking about what was next, when she was trying to find her footing and hang on to things the way they were. It wasn't fair that he should spring this on her when they had company. "How serious are you?"

"Pretty serious."

"I thought you liked working at the mayor's office," Steve said.

"I do, but it's getting a little boring. Same-old, same-old."

Erin stood abruptly. "Part of life is same-old, same-old," she snapped. "Some of us are grown up enough to realize that."

In the uncomfortable silence that followed, Steve cleared his throat and stood. "I think it's time for us to leave. We'll pass on dessert, if that's all right." Colleen followed his lead, getting their coats from the entryway closet. Their good-byes were hasty and strained.

When the door closed behind them, Cory turned on Erin. His voice was quietly furious. "Congratulations, Erin. You embarrassed me and made our friends so uncomfortable they had to leave."

"You embarrassed me by dropping the bomb about your new job in front of them. When were you planning on telling me?"

He stood, hands on hips. "I don't know. You don't make it easy for me to tell you what I'm thinking.

Suddenly suspicious, she said, "You haven't just been talking about this job, have you? You've already decided." She read the answer in his eyes even before he spoke.

"I start in three weeks."

"Do your parents know about this?"

"Yes."

"Why did you tell them and not me?"

"Because they're supportive of what I do and excited when I have an opportunity to move forward. The truth is, you don't trust me. Not like Colleen trusts Steve." His eyes were pools of sadness and regret. "I hope that one of these days you'll realize that I'm not your dad."

Cory's words haunted her. Did part of her lump him in the same category as her father? That Catholic Boy. That Mormon Boy. The thought horrified her. How could she? They were nothing alike. Cory had made a commitment to her that was more than "'til death do we part" in the temple of the Lord. He had given her their beautiful daughter. Every move he had made since they got married had turned out to be for their good. Even buying the house when they didn't have enough money to do it on their own.

That doesn't matter. He should have told me about the job! she argued with herself. *He must have known for weeks, yet he said nothing. What's trusting about that?* Remembering what he had said, she sighed. That was her fault. He didn't trust her, because she didn't trust him. She was the one who needed to change, not Cory.

What hurt her most was the unflattering comparison to Colleen. She had always been critical of how willing Colleen was to let Steve make the decisions in their household. Realizing that Cory admired that quality in Colleen was devastating. She saw he was tired of her constant questioning, her need for reassurance and proof that she was safe following his lead.

What would Regina do? When the question popped into her mind, she batted it away impatiently. She wondered instead what Willadene would do. It seemed to Erin that Willadene looked to Roger for leadership and approval. She accepted the order that Church leaders said was right: The husband was the head of the household. When it came to Juneau, Erin was quite sure she didn't defer to Greg the way Willadene deferred to Roger. In fact, it seemed to Erin that Juneau didn't trust her husband to make decisions any more than she herself trusted Cory.

Erin sighed. Of the two, she thought Willadene was the happier. Was letting the man be the head of the household what it took to be a Forever Family? If it was, she was in trouble.

She was weeping quietly into her pillow when Cory climbed in bed.

"Hey, what's this?" He scooched up behind her and put his arm around her middle. "I'm sorry I yelled at you. It's just frustrating not being able to count on you to support me."

That only made her cry harder. "I'm sorry about what happened," she said, turning into his arms. "I want to trust you, but I can't if you're not telling me what's going on. No more secrets, Cory."

"I'm sorry. I should have told you about the job." He squeezed her and kissed her neck. "No more secrets. I promise."

Sunday, April 17, 1984
Hi, Ladies,

Guess who's motoring around on her own two feet? Miss Kayla, that's who. Most of the time, she has more energy than a sack of alligators, but she's been miserable lately, because she has a molar coming in. Grams brought some clove oil to rub on her gums, which seems to help.

She is such a doll. Her hair has settled into a curly reddish-blonde, which goes great with her blue eyes and pixie chin. I love dressing her up. But I'm afraid we're in for trouble when she hits the Terrible Twos. She already knows her own mind and wants her own way.

Cory's changing jobs again. This time he'll be working for a small company named Behind the Scenes that does PR and a little of everything else, including really high-profile event planning. Most of their clients are corporations, but they'll plan anything for anyone who can afford their services. There are plenty who can, it seems.

He's ecstatic about it—and especially the salary increase. The private sector certainly pays better than city government. The first thing he did was go shopping for a new suit and all the accessories to match, which he charged, of course. Juneau, who said "Beware of enterprises requiring new clothes"?

Our Finders business has really picked up. Colleen and I meet with clients and go scouting two or three days a week. Colleen's husband is an accountant. He's been helping us with the books and logistics.

Grams and Cory avoid each other as much as possible. When they can't, they seem to relish arguing. Most recently, they got into it over this AIDS scare that's been in the papers the last couple of weeks. Grams is sure that AIDS is God's way of punishing homosexuals. Cory thinks she's been spending too much time listening to rant-and-rave evangelical preachers.

She's been great helping me get my garden in, although I'm the one doing all the bending and kneeling. We've already planted cold-weather crops, salad stuff mostly. Of course, Miss Kayla was right in there with us. She appears to think dirt is a delicacy. The bulbs we put in last October are starting to peek through the mulch. I can't wait to see my flower garden in bloom.

Aren't I quite the little homemaker?

Looking forward to our Spiritual Living phone call!

Erin

Saturday, May 21, 1984
Dear Juneau, Deenie, and Gabby,

Today we helped Steve and Colleen move out to their new place. The troops were marshaled—the elders quorum, his parents plus one of his brothers, her parents, and various Relief Society sisters. We worked most of the day moving and cleaning and mowing and repairing. I was wiped out when we left, but the place was in pretty good shape by that time.

I am so grateful for what I don't have! No raspberry patch, no apple orchard, no fences to mend, no chicken coop waiting for new occupants. I remember when we were sitting in your orchard, Deenie, and you described all the hard work it takes to keep one producing. Poor Colleen! I can't believe she really wants to be a pioneer, but she says she does.

She's going to have to keep a sharp eye on EJ. She's just shy of four now and fast as a scalded cat. She could be out of sight and into trouble in a flash. If that place were mine, I'd already have some of the back lawn fenced and a lock on the barn.

I love that barn! It's the oldest building on the property, with a stone foundation about five feet tall and weathered red siding on up. When Colleen and I were poking about in it, we found a bunch of old nails, yard and kitchen tools, and even harnesses. I'm surprised that the former owner didn't have an auction before selling—Jake says such things can bring a lot of money.

On the way home, Cory and I agreed that we will never, ever have a place with more than a half-acre lot! That's quite enough for both of us.

> Much love,
> Erin

Chapter Twenty-Nine

WILLADENE

When Bert got home from Scotland in April, the whole Rasmussen clan started into a celebration that lasted until the family dinner after her homecoming talk the third Sunday in May. Deenie had been a part of it all, from the trip to the airport to feeding the whole clan from her kitchen more than once. Although everything ran smoothly, the constraint between Deenie and Roger's parents put a damper on Deenie's enjoyment. She began to believe their relationship would never return to the easy affection of the earlier days of her marriage. It was a Dead Chicken to her, the name she now applied to things she couldn't change. That was opposed to the Almost Dead Dog problems she had some hope of solving.

Carl's behavior fell into that category. Deenie had been called into the principal's office twice to pick him up for getting into some kind of mischief—spit wads the first time and glue on pencils the second. They were harmless pranks, but Deenie read him the riot act and piled on the chores. She didn't tell Roger. Carl expressed his relief by getting back into line.

In June she finally wrote the ladies again, sending a separate and different version of the same letter to Gabby.

June 9, 1984
Dear Erin and Juneau,

I taught my lesson on enduring to the end and had three of the older sisters in our ward tell us what they thought it meant. If I could do it over again, I'd teach it from the standpoint of the single parent. Pat Crafton would be my inspiration.

With the divorce final, she and her two boys have moved in with her mother, Grandma Streeter. I am blown away by the way she is always there with and for them. Pat says the good Lord watches over fools and children, so he must be spending a lot of time looking after her and the boys.

I am in awe of anyone who would even try to raise a child alone. You can tell your mom that for me, Erin.

I feel like I could write a book on single parenting for the married woman, but at least I know Roger is in the same state and I can get him home if there's an emergency.

Carl is learning to drive the tractor this summer. My objections were almost as successful over that as they were over the .22 rifle which, by the way, has found its way home from the farm and back into Roger's gun cabinet.

Grandpa Will offered the Crafton boys jobs on the farm, as well, and they jumped at the chance. Paul is clamoring to go along, too.

He is going to be baptized this Saturday, and I told him I wouldn't even discuss it until after that. We will have The Dinner afterward, this time here instead of at the farm.

I invited Gabby and Jonas as well, but Gabby said she wasn't up to a big celebration. She didn't say anything more, but she sounded peculiar. If Roger knows what's going on, he isn't telling. I can only guess there are more problems with her son, Hyrum Golden Jr., and his family. Maybe we should be all write her separately and let her know how much she means to us. Let me know if you hear from her.

Bert has returned to us a refined and reserved lady. She's home for the summer before she starts job hunting. NeVae is sure she is home forever. "After all," she says, "who's going to hire an anthropologist in Cache County?" She has no idea Bert has bigger plans.

Hope all's well,
Deenie

"Are we friends again?" Roger asked as he put his arms around Deenie from behind as she finished the dinner dishes.

"I hope so," Deenie said. She was weary of the distance between them. "Six months is a long time to live with someone who isn't a friend."

Roger hugged her closer. "Thanks for not saying anything more to Carl about not shooting with me and Dad."

"It's okay." Deenie turned in his arms and hugged him back. "I still don't like it, but I guess there are some things that should be kept between a kid and his dad."

Side by side they walked into the family room and sat on the couch. "Bert told Dad she thought he was wrong to butt in. I know he's sorry. But I can't apologize for him," Roger said. "I can't apologize for you either, Deenie."

"I'll take that into consideration."

"It would be nice if you could consider it before the Fourth of July blowout on the farm," Roger said with a grin.

Deenie smiled back. "I can try." *Maybe there's still hope, thanks to Bert,* she thought. *Maybe my relationship with Will isn't a Dead Chicken after all. Maybe it's only an Almost Dead Dog.*

ERIN

Erin woke up on Saturday to the sound of cartoons and the aroma of bacon cooking.

She pulled on a robe and padded downstairs to the kitchen. Kayla was in her highchair, making quite the mess of a pancake. She kissed the top of her daughter's head and then sat at the table where a glass of orange juice awaited her.

"Good morning, sleepyhead," Cory said. He untied the apron that covered his sweats. "You ready to take over here? I want to go play basketball this morning." He grabbed his sports bag and headed for the door. "Do you want me to stop at the supermarket on the way home?"

"That would be great. I have my Relief Society lesson tomorrow, and I'm not quite ready yet."

"That means you'll be on the phone with Willadene and Juneau. I'm glad you have such good friends."

"Cory, what would you think about me inviting them to come visit in the fall? Would that be all right?"

He grinned. "Sure, why not? I wouldn't mind being around a houseful of ladies."

Once Cory was out the door, Erin got the kitchen clean and Kayla set up in her playpen. Then she sat down in the sunny living room with her Spiritual Living manual with its already broken back and the binder she kept her prep notes in. She opened the binder, turning the pages she had scribbled for each of the lessons. The first lessons had been a review of gospel basics and relatively easy for Erin to prepare. The plan of salvation. The need for faith in Christ. The role of repentance. The covenant of baptism.

The lesson for May had been more difficult. It was entitled "These Things Shall Be for Thy Good," but Erin had thought of it as The Necessity and Value of Suffering. She had wavered between anger and penitence during her preparations. The thought that God allowed terrible things to happen, or worse, visited them upon his children purposely to test and try them, had made her angry. Enough bad things happened to good people without God getting into the fray.

"I can't possibly teach that lesson," she had told Juneau and Deenie. "I don't believe that trials make a person better."

"Not the trials themselves, Erin. The way people respond to them," Deenie had said.

"Does God know how someone will respond?"

"I think he does.

"Then if he knows a person will be dragged down or become bitter and angry, and he still sends the trial, how can you say it's for their good?"

"Maybe being bitter and angry is part of that person's learning process," Juneau had said.

Erin had thought of Grams. "What if they don't ever learn? God's condemned them from the moment he sent the trial because he knew they wouldn't."

After a long silence Deenie had said, "You don't trust God, do you?"

Erin had taken a sharp breath. "Life is tough enough without God giving us trials on purpose. It's not fair. And don't you dare tell me that it is."

"Life isn't fair," Juneau had said. "And God loves his children."

"Erin, dear." Deenie's voice had been kind. "You said once Cory accused you of confusing God with your father? I think you're confusing God with your father, too."

Erin had hung up from that conversation stung by the realization of how little she believed in a benevolent God. Her life was blessed, but she didn't trust that it would continue so. Some part of her was constantly on guard, watching for the first sign of the inevitable troubles. It wasn't a very pleasant way to live.

She had followed Willadene's suggestion that she fast and pray. When she'd told Cory she was fasting because she needed to feel the Spirit, he had fasted with her. They had made time to read scriptures together, and Cory had given her a blessing. The May lesson had been one of her best, because she'd been humble and had relied on the Spirit to do the teaching.

And now here was the June lesson on enduring to the end, the one she privately called First We Suffer and Then We Die.

Juneau called right on time, put Erin on hold, and then connected with

Willadene. Erin could tell they were worried about her, because the first thing they both wanted to know was how she was doing.

"I'm okay, now, but who knows how I'll feel after we talk about Enduring to the End. It makes life sound hard."

"Don't let the terminology get to you," Juneau said. "It only means *choosing* to the end. We're always choosing. We just don't like to think we are, because we don't want to be responsible for our choices."

They spent fifteen minutes going over the lesson, sharing insights and approaches for involving the sisters. Erin's heart warmed as she listened to them talk back and forth. She loved hearing the voices of her two friends. She could see their faces in her mind's eye. They seemed so close that she felt she could reach out and touch them. "I really miss you guys," she said. "I wish you were here, right now. I was going to invite you out this fall, but that's too far away. Do you think you could come this summer?"

"I wish I could," Deenie said. "I've never been farther east than Yellowstone Park. But summer's a busy time of year for us, what with the kids out of school, the orchard, and Roger helping on the farm."

"I'm pretty much stuck in front of my typewriter until I get this manu-script done," Juneau said. "Maybe next spring?"

"I need a COBs fix sooner than that. Did we really mean it when we made our Pact, or was it just something three ten-year-olds would do?" Erin's voice was full of frustration.

"I meant it," Willadene insisted.

"So did I," Juneau said. "Only I didn't give any thought to how we were going to keep it." She paused. "Mrs. Jarvis has been trying to convince me to go to a writer's conference in Salt Lake in August, just to get acquainted with other Mormon writers. She's LDS herself, you know. Anyway, I didn't actually give it much thought because I don't consider myself a serious writer."

"You write, don't you?" Deenie asked.

"Well, yes."

"You're serious when you're at your typewriter, aren't you?"

Juneau chuckled. "Yes."

"Then you're a serious writer. If you come to the conference, maybe you can arrange a couple of extra days. I'm sure I can manage to drive down for a day. Roger might be able to come, too. How about you, Erin?"

Erin could feel excitement rising. "Cory wants to take me to San Francisco some time this summer. He's been talking about having a layover in Salt Lake City so we could go to the temple! How's that for a coincidence? Give me the dates, Juneau, and I know I can make it work."

"Let's do it!" Deenie said. "I need a COB fix myself."

JUNEAU

June 30, 1984
Dear COBs,

You convinced me. I'll come. Both to the conference and (yay!) to a meeting with my fellow COBettes. Or should that be my lady COBs? (Have you ever thought about the fact that we don't have an equivalent of "fellow" in our female vocabulary? A word that indicates a sisterhood of good ol' girls?) When I talked to Greg about my going to the conference, he checked his budget book and pronounced it healthy enough for a plane ticket. I didn't mention that I could pay for it myself now that I'm selling stories. I've told you how he likes to be in charge.

Anyway, he says the investment is well worth it because I'm so cheerful when I come home from a meeting with you guys. You girls. Actually, I'm not sure he'll even notice that I'm gone. He's in love with computers these days. He eats and drinks computers, and when he sleeps, his fingers twitch, and I know he's caressing a keyboard. Sometimes he stays on campus so long that I'm ready to call the police to see if he's been in an accident or something. If I didn't know better I would think he might have become involved with a tasty little coed. Thank heaven it's just a machine.

He says eventually everybody will have a computer at home, including us. I told him that was silly because who has the space? The only computer I've seen was one several years ago when the faculty wives had a tour of the campus, and it took up a whole room! Greg assured me that now they fit on top of a desk, like my typewriter, and that as a writer I would benefit from having one. I told him to forget it, that there would never be anything that could surpass my sturdy IBM Selectric.

Well, let's see, what else do I need to catch you up on? The girls are doing well right now, even Misty. I've been spending a lot of time helping with their studies and taking them shopping or over to the Arboretum and once to the La Brea tar pits. Sometimes just simply playing Monopoly together. Misty never expresses any appreciation for any of it, but at least I know where she is, most of the time.

Nicole is fine, which is typical for her. She's taking baton twirling lessons from Isobel, Marisol's oldest daughter, who is a twirler for the Pasadena High School band. Nicole is all excited about sleep-overs at Marisol's while I'm gone. Misty likes to go there, too. Besides twirling batons, Isobel is an expert at makeup and hair-styling. Besides, Marisol is a great cook. She makes tamales to die for, and of course that flan recipe I made in Provo was from her.

Even Philip Atwater likes to go over to her house because there are more kids to play with him.

Last but certainly not least, I sold another story. That's five so far this year. I sold one in 1981. Then two in 1982. Four in 1983. So I should sell eight this year. If I keep doubling every year, that means in 2005, when we keep The Pact, I will sell 16,777,216 stories. If I do, I'll pay for a week in Paris for all of us, husbands included!

Anyway, I will be seeing you in Salt Lake City next month. I want to stay a day past our meeting so I can attend a session at the Salt Lake Temple.

I hope Greg can come out of his computer coma to watch over the kids and Philip Atwater!

Love,
Juneau

ERIN

Wednesday, July 4, 1984
Dear Juneau and Willadene,

Happy Independence Day. I hope you and your families had as good a time as we did. Angie and Norm had a fireworks-watching party at their place. You remember, that's where I had my tree-house apartment. It's right across the bay from Excelsior, so it's a perfect spot for watching the display.

They invited a lot of people, including us, the Harringtons, The Women, and Jake. We had potluck and grilled bratwurst for supper and then staked out places to sit on the front lawn. Jake brought Grams one of Norm's handcrafted Adirondack chairs and set her up in the place of honor. I think he feels sorry for her, after our talk. Cory and I and the Harringtons sat on a big blanket, Mom and Jake on another. They sat pretty close together, if you ask me.

I'm so excited about getting together in SLC. Cory is all for stopping over. We can meet with you guys one day and go to the temple the next before flying on to San Fran.

Thank you for being patient with me on our phone calls. I thought that belonging to the Church would totally wipe out the old ways of thinking and feeling, but it doesn't. When I'm tired, frustrated, or ticked off at Grams, all those old feelings come roaring right back up. They fade a little when I exercise or read scriptures or play with Kayla, but I still feel them like a humidity in the air.

Willadene, I know how you felt leaving your kids at home when you went down to Gabby's. This trip will be the first time I've been away from Kayla in eighteen months. I get the shivers just thinking about it. Linda is going to keep her half of the time, and Colleen the other half. Grams didn't say anything when I told her the arrangements we'd made, but I know she's disappointed. Both Linda and Colleen said they'd drive Kayla over to visit Grams while we're gone. Isn't that nice of them?

See you soon!

> Love,
> Erin

Chapter Thirty

ERIN

"Erin! Over here!" Erin looked in the direction of the voice to see Juneau and Willadene hurrying toward her. She would have recognized them anywhere, yet they looked subtly different. Juneau, who still had the hairstyle Erin had given her at Willadene's, was dressed in a dove gray pantsuit with a periwinkle shirt. Willadene was wearing a pink dress that was distinctly retro. It had a pointed stand-up collar, a fitted bodice accented by a wide belt, and a circular skirt.

A moment later, they were in a group hug. When they pulled back, Erin said, "Juneau, you look great. Dressed for business, I see."

"I thought this suit might help me pass at the convention," Juneau said with a laugh.

"And Deenie! You look darling in that dress."

"Me and Annette Funicello." Willadene turned in a circle, a shy but pleased smile on her face. "Roger likes the way it looks on me, but I probably won't be grocery shopping in it. What about you? You look like an advertisement for an Eddie Bauer catalog."

Erin posed artfully in her chinos, camp shirt, and leather slip-ons. "This is the new me: wife, mother, and entrepreneur."

Juneau chuckled. "I guess we shouldn't be surprised that we've all changed a little. I wonder what else we're going to discover."

They joined the men just as Cory and Roger were shaking hands.

"I'm so glad you came, Roger. I've been wanting Cory to meet you." Erin turned to Cory. "Roger is the best example of a dad that I know."

"You really impressed Erin," Cory said. "Now that I have a daughter, you'll have to tell me the secret of being a good father."

"I don't have a secret." Roger flashed an appreciative grin at Erin. "I don't remember doing anything particularly special the week you were in Wellsville."

"Maybe not," Erin said, "but I could see how much you love your children and how much they love you."

Roger's pleasure at the compliment shone in his eyes. He put his arm

around Willadene's waist. "That's nice to hear. Our family is the most important thing to both of us."

"Us too," said Cory, taking Erin's hand. "'Course, we're new at the
parenthood part. Kayla is only eighteen months old."

"Do you have photos of her?" asked Juneau.

"Do roosters crow?" Erin reached into her bag. They stood in a huddle
as Erin went through the latest photos of her grinning, mop-headed toddler.
They were still passing them around when another call alerted them that
Gabby, Jonas, and Sophie arrived.

As with Juneau and Willadene, they all looked different but the same.
Gabby was a little thinner, if that was possible, and her face bore a network
of newer or deeper wrinkles, but she still stood straight and tall and her smile
was welcoming. Jonas walked at her side, holding her elbow protectively.
They love each other, thought Erin with a smile. She hoped she and Cory
would be like than when they were old.

Sophie walked on Gabby's other side. She was much taller than she had
been, thin like her grandmother, and slightly awkward in her movements.
She's still growing, thought Erin. *She doesn't know quite what to do with herself.
Bless her.*

Then Erin noticed a handsome young man walking slightly behind the
others. He was familiar, somehow. Where had she seen him, and when? Her
jaw dropped when she realized she was looking at Bryan, the bratty teenager
who had interrupted their dinner at Gabby's wanting the Caddie. He saw
her looking at him and smiled as if he knew what she was thinking.

The group reached them, and there was another round of animated
greetings and warm hugs. Gabby drew Bryan to the center, holding his arm
with pride. "This is my grandson Bryan. You may remember him, ladies."

Erin grinned as she watched Juneau react in the same way she had.
Willadene simply smiled. *She knew Bryan was coming with Gabby,* Erin
thought. Bryan tipped his head in a gesture reminiscent of Jonas, a smile
turning up the corners of his mouth.

"Yes, I'm that Bryan," he said with a chuckle. "I wasn't on my best
behavior when I ruined your dinner a few years ago. Would you accept my
apologies?"

"With pleasure," said Juneau. "What caused this miracle? Just in case I
need some help with my girls one of these days."

There was an awkward pause. Then Bryan said, "Seeing my brother get into serious trouble. Everything Gran was trying to tell me all those years finally made sense."

"Jonas gets some of the credit," Gabby added. "When Bryan and I finally came to an agreement about his using the Caddie a couple of years ago, it had been sitting so long it needed some major repairs. Jonas agreed to help Bryan with them. Roger lent a hand, too."

Introductions complete, they followed Gabby into the Tiffin Room, where Gabby had reserved a private corner. The nine of them were seated at a table that put them all close enough to talk to each other. For the next hour conversation ebbed and swelled, punctuated by bursts of laughter.

"The last time most of us were all together was when you two got married," Jonas said, raising his water glass in a toast to Erin and Cory.

"And life's been good ever since," Cory said. "Marrying Erin was the best thing I've ever done."

Erin leaned against his shoulder. "That's sweet," she murmured.

"Cory and Erin have had a baby since then," said Juneau, "and I'm officially a writer. Willadene, what would you say is the biggest thing that happened to you?"

"To me? Nothing. I'm just the backup person. Now that Roger's busy with his graduate assistantship, I keep the boys out of the emergency room and Bitsy supplied with goodies for her tea parties."

Erin saw a shadow cross Roger's face when Deenie mentioned his degree. *Maybe everything isn't so well in Wellsville,* she thought.

Conversation paused as they enjoyed their dessert.

"I'd like to get us checked into Hotel Utah," Cory said. "How about if we all go over there after we pay the check? The lobby has lots of comfortable seats."

"Sounds good," said Gabby. "You three need some time together," she said looking at the COBettes. "Sophie and I will entertain the men. Why don't you join us in an hour?"

Walking down the corridor with Willadene and Juneau, Erin felt suddenly awkward. The initial excitement and the first round of sharing was past. What was there to say now? "This is odd, isn't it," she said after a few moments of silence had passed. "We couldn't wait to get together, and now nobody knows what to say!"

"We just need to get caught up with the things we don't know about," Deenie said. "The things we don't put in our letters."

"What haven't you written, Deenie?" Erin asked.

"Yeah," said Juneau. "You've been telling us all the things you've been doing, but I'm wondering about you. Are you doing too much?"

"Well, I haven't fainted lately, if that's what you're getting at." Deenie stopped. "I'm doing what I have to do—because Roger's doing what he says he has to do."

"Sounds a little like Cory to me," Erin said. "He can always give a convincing reason for why he has to do what he wants to do."

"Greg, too," Juneau put in. "How do you feel about that, Deenie?"

"It doesn't matter how I feel. As Grandma Streeter says, you do what needs to be done and worry about feelings later."

"In fiction, it's the feelings that keep the plot going," Juneau said.

Erin nodded. "And cause the big confrontation right before the end."

"It's a good thing my life's not a book, then," Deenie said. "If it were, I'd want it to be the kind that would go in the Shoebox. Easily solved problems, a lot of romance, and a happy ending."

In response, Juneau beckoned them nearer. "*Regina paced back and forth in her bedroom. It had been weeks since her husband had jumped on his old plow horse to set out on a quest for the secret of life. Where was he? Why didn't he return? She could feel her innards roiling with loneliness. Suddenly she heard footsteps on the stairs, heavy as a lumbering bear. She flung the door open and there stood . . .*"

" *. . . a lumbering bear,*" Deenie carried on. "*As he enveloped her in a squeeze as tight as iron bands, Regina thought, Well, at least somebody wants me.*"

They all burst out laughing as they turned the corner at the far end of the mall.

"What about you, Juneau? What haven't you been telling?" asked Deenie.

Juneau shrugged. "Not much. I'm working out some problems with the latest story I'm writing. I don't tell you guys about those because I don't want to bore you."

"Who do you tell?" Erin asked.

"Mrs. Jarvis, for one."

Erin picked up on the last part of the sentence. "Do you talk them over with Greg?"

"Nah. He's in a constant computer coma."

"Then who else?"

"Well, there's this man named Clyde in Mrs. Jarvis's class. In some ways, he reminds me a little of Jay, the man who changed my tire when we were at Education Week."

"In what way?" Deenie asked.

"He's nice. And he's lonely." Juneau hesitated. "And came out of seemingly nowhere when I needed help."

"Another flat tire?"

"More like flat plotting." Juneau laughed. "He's not the best writer himself, but he can give really good advice on other people's stories."

"Does Greg know about him?" asked Erin.

"Oh, yes. I tell him all about my class. But by the time I get to Clyde, he's usually snoring." Juneau looked at Erin. "It's your turn to bring us up to date on the untold stuff."

Erin stood to one side and spread her hands out. "This is the new me, but I have to admit, there's still someone inside who'd love to wear a dress like yours, Deenie."

"So why are you dressed like this?" Deenie's gesture included the whole outfit.

"I'm trying to support Cory. These clothes wouldn't have been my first choice three years ago, but it means something to him when I dress in a certain way. He does so much for me, I want to please him."

"Hmmm. What's that going to lead to?" asked Juneau.

"Happily Ever After, I hope."

"I don't think the road to Happily Ever After is the same road as to COBhood," Juneau said. "We know Gabby's life hasn't been storybook, but she still got there."

"So are you saying suffering leads to COBhood?"

"Heavens, no! It's how you deal with it. And if you let it, Happily Ever After can come in between."

They were almost back to ZCMI by then. *What interesting women they are,* Erin thought. *I expect them to show up the way I remember them, but they show up as the new, more interesting version. The more complex version,* she added.

WILLADENE

They found Gabby, Sophie, and the men in a conversation corner in the lobby. Willadene caught Roger's eye, and he pointed at two shopping bags on the floor by his chair, grinning conspiratorially. She mouthed, "Later."

"There you are!" said Gabby. She motioned toward Bryan, who stood in front of the group. "Bryan's telling us about his adventures delivering pizza."

"People say it's an easy job, but it's not," Bryan said. "Let me tell you, it's a tough way to earn money for a mission."

Sophie jumped up and flung her arms around his neck. "You're going on a mission? When did you decide that?"

Bryan smiled at her enthusiasm. "I've been thinking about it for a while. Jonas and Roger fixed more than the engine while we all had our heads under the hood of Caddie. I think it's the right thing to do."

"Have you told Mom and Dad?"

"Only Gran. I wanted to tell Roger and Jonas next, and this seemed like a good time to do it."

Everyone stood to offer congratulations, shaking Bryan's hand and clapping him on the back. Deenie watched as Cory pulled out his wallet and handed Bryan a bill. "I'd like to contribute to your mission fund."

Bryan's eye widened. "Did you really mean to give me *this?*" He held up the hundred-dollar bill.

"Yes. It'll get you some white shirts. You're going to need quite a few."

Bryan hesitated. "Thanks, but Gran and I have talked it over and I want to pay for my mission myself. It's important to take responsibility for my choices." He looked at Gabby questioningly.

"It's a lovely gesture, Bryan, and it will help," Gabby said. "I think you can accept it without going back on your word." She looked at the others. "You may not know this, but Bryan's brother, Kenny, was the driver in a fatal hit-and-run when he was sixteen. He was in the juvenile correctional facility for some time, but that wasn't enough to scare him straight. He's been in and out of trouble with the law ever since. He never admits that he's responsible for the choices he makes. Bryan doesn't want to follow his example."

Cory nodded soberly. "Then I would be doubly honored if you would let me be part of your mission."

"Thanks, Brother Johnson," Bryan said.

In the pause that followed, Roger leaned toward Deenie. "Now?" he whispered.

She nodded. She had been anticipating this moment for weeks.

Roger carefully removed the contents of the first sack onto a nearby table.

"What's this?" asked Jonas. Everyone's attention was riveted on the packages wrapped in hand-stamped brown paper.

Deenie smiled. "You'll just have to wait and see."

Roger picked the first package from the top of the pile, checked the name, and handed it to Bryan.

Bryan accepted the gift with genuine pleasure and surprise. "I guess this is just my day." He opened the card and read out loud: "To Bryan for being one of the good guys." He looked at Deenie. "I don't know what to say."

"'Thank you' works for me," Deenie said with a huge smile. "Your grandmother says we should celebrate every good thing."

Bryan opened the package to discover a seven-inch chocolate torte. He took a deep whiff. "Now that's chocolate!"

After that there was a quick distribution of the gifts on the table. Homemade bread for Jonas. A Dorothy Keddington romance for Gabby. And a young adult novel for Sophie.

"The lady at Deseret Book recommended it when I asked for young adult reading," Deenie explained as Sophie thumbed through a book titled *Trish for President*. "She said this is a popular novel for young ladies. I hope you like it."

"Thank you. I'm sure I will. Hey!" Sophie chirped. "I get to be a young adult and a young lady all in the same day. How about that."

Everybody laughed. Deenie noticed how the laughter was coming more readily as the day progressed, just the way she'd hoped it would.

Roger lifted up the next sack and took out a gift for Juneau. She opened it at once to discover one of the newer, larger journals sporting a hand-quilted and embellished cover. "Oh, Deenie," was all she said as she ran her finger across the careful embroidery.

I love this, Deenie thought. *It's been worth all the extra time and effort, to see their faces. I love them.*

"Where's my present?" Erin joked with a playful pout. Roger handed her a shopping bag all her own. She pulled out a crib-sized patchwork quilt in apple green and berry pink with matching green-checked piping and ruffled eyelet trim. Erin read the label, "To Kayla from Aunt Deenie. 1984." She smiled at Deenie. "I knew you'd do something like this. It's so lovely."

As everyone exclaimed over the bounty, Deenie smiled softly. She felt warm inside, the way she did at Christmas when the family opened their presents. She knew she spent far more time in making, buying, and wrapping presents than other people did, but it was important to her to give the people she loved the perfect gift. The gift that would make them happy.

Deenie's musing was interrupted when Erin and Cory stood. "We'd like to walk around Temple Square and sit a while in front of the window where you can see the Christus statue," Erin said. "Anybody want to come with us?"

"That's a great idea." Deenie turned to Roger, but he shook his head. "We need to start home, sweetie. I've got things to do yet tonight."

Gabby stood. "It's time for us to go, too. It's been a long day."

"But . . ." Deenie began.

Now the rest of them stood and a round of good-byes began. The COBs had a big group hug, Sophie included, and the men shook hands.

Erin turned to Juneau. "See you at breakfast."

Deenie knew that the Johnsons had invited Juneau to attend the temple with them the next day. She yearned to stay overnight and go with them, and she watched hungrily as they headed down the corridor to their various destinations. *This isn't how it's supposed to go,* she thought. *It's happening too fast.* She wanted slow, delicious good-byes. More time, more hugs.

Twilight lit the valley as Roger turned off the main highway onto the road to Wellsville. As he slowed on the winding road, he said, "You're extra quiet tonight, Deenie. Didn't you have a good time today?"

"Yes, I did. I really enjoy those women. But being with them makes me want something . . . I don't know how to describe it. Something more."

Roger glanced quickly at Deenie, his expression puzzled. "More what?"

"That's the thing. I don't have the faintest idea. But it occurs to me that the world outside of Cache Valley is very large indeed, and we live in a very small corner of it." She gave a small sigh.

"Would you like to live in some other corner of it?"

The intensity of Roger's voice surprised her. "Actually, I was thinking more along the lines of reading a big city newspaper once in a while. It would be an adventure to live somewhere new, but where could we go that would give us something better than we have now? We have a home of our own, a great place for our kids to grow up, good neighbors and friends, family coming out our ears, church across the street, and a temple twenty minutes away. What more could we ask for?"

"Maybe not more, but how about different? Different would be an adventure." The way he spoke had Deenie's antennae on alert.

"I like the idea of adding a little adventure in my life," she said, the emphasis on *little*. "Sometimes I feel like I'm living my grandmother's life and her mother's life before that. The only things that have really changed are the appliances and the transportation."

"We don't have to stay in Cache Valley, you know," Roger said eagerly. "With my master's degree there are a lot more places I could teach, maybe even a junior college. What's to stop us?"

Deenie shivered. "Oh, I'd say my father and your mother. And my Aunt Stella and your Uncle Don, etc., etc., etc. Need I go on?"

"I know they wouldn't like it if we pulled up roots, but if it offered a better opportunity for our family, they'd support whatever choice we made."

"It would have to be a fairy-tale wonderful kind of opportunity for that to happen. Besides," she added as they pulled into the driveway, "where else could we find a house with a front end one hundred years old, the back end twenty years old, and the middle only three?"

JUNEAU

The red light on the telephone in Juneau's room was flashing when she got back to the hotel after breakfast. Probably Greg had called to wish her and her friends a happy time. She wished he'd been able to come with her and meet them. She called the front desk and found there was indeed a message from Greg. "Call back immediately," it said. "Urgent."

Her midsection iced with fear and her finger trembled as she punched in her home phone number. *Urgent* was such a terrifying word.

"Hello?" Greg answered immediately, as if he'd been sitting by the phone.

"Greg," she said, "is something wrong?"

"Yes." His voice was tight. "Misty's missing."

"Missing?" she repeated.

"Missing, as in gone."

Now her whole body froze. She could barely breathe. Gripping the handset, she croaked, "Do you have any idea where?"

"No," Greg said. "She told Nicole on the way to school not to worry if she didn't see her for a while, and then she took off. Nicole thought she meant she was going to go walk to school with Capri or something."

"She promised she wouldn't go to Capri's while I was gone," Juneau said.

"She *didn't* go there, that's the thing. Nicole called me an hour ago when the principal asked her if she knew where Misty was. She hadn't been in her classroom, and Capri said she hadn't seen her. Nobody's seen her since this morning."

"Oh, Greg! Have you called the hospitals?"

"She's not in any of the hospitals, Juney."

"Then she must have run away. Is there anything missing from her room?"

"Her backpack. But she always takes that to school, so that's not much of a clue." Greg's voice was ragged, and Juneau knew he was more upset than he wanted her to know.

"I'm coming home as soon as I can," Juneau said. "I'll call and see if I can get a seat on the next plane."

"Let me know what you line up," Greg said.

There was a seat available on a mid-afternoon flight, arriving at the Ontario airport at 5:30 P.M. It cost a lot to make the change and buy a last-minute ticket, but what did that matter? She'd miss the final day with Erin and Cory, but what did that matter, either?

There was a tearful and fearful good-bye with Erin and Cory, and then she took the shuttle to the airport, sick with worry.

Greg and Nicole were waiting when she walked off the plane. "We know where she is," Nicole yelled as soon as she was within hearing distance.

Juneau felt her knees go rubbery with relief. Greg caught her arm and gave her badly needed support.

"She's with your parents," Greg said. "In Carlsbad. They called about an hour ago to say she'd come down on the train."

They drove to Carlsbad from the airport, getting there just as the sun was setting over the ocean, coloring the western sky a rich orange. Juneau tried to enjoy the sight, now that she knew Misty was safe, but she was still worried and angry and, truth be told, feeling a little guilty that she hadn't been home when this happened.

She barely waited for Greg to park the car before she got out and ran into the RV park. Her mother was waiting at the door of the Airstream. "She's fine," she said with a "calm down" gesture. "I'd advise not to make a big thing of it, Juneau. She's a mixed-up little girl, and she needs to be treated gently."

Juneau pushed by her and into the living room, with Greg and Nicole following. Misty was sitting on the sofa beside Juneau's dad. She smiled tentatively as her family came into the room. "Hi," she said.

Greg went on the attack despite Pamela Paulsen's cautioning words. "Misty," he barked, "what the heck are you up to?"

"I'm sorry, Daddy," Misty said with a little wave. She moved a little closer to her grandfather, who put an arm around her.

"Well, you'd better be sorry. What were you thinking? You really . . ."

"We're so happy that you're safe," Juneau interrupted, sitting down beside Misty and giving her a hug. "We were sick with worry."

Misty turned big eyes to her. "I thought you were still in Salt Lake, Mom."

"I came back early," Juneau said. "I couldn't stay there when I knew you were missing."

Misty stared at her silently, and Juneau wondered what she was thinking.

Nicole knelt in front of Misty and reached up to put her arms around her. "I was so scared," she said shakily. "I didn't know where you'd gone."

"I didn't mean to scare you, Nicky honey," Misty said. "Next time I'll tell you." They both began to cry.

Juneau expected Greg to blow up over that "next time." But he didn't say anything, only went over to pat both girls on the back until they finished their crying session and sat hiccupping together, which brought on the giggles. Greg gave both of them a big hug. Juneau could see their faces over his shoulder. To her shock, Misty's wore a self-satisfied smirk.

Before Juneau had a chance to decide what to do or say, her mother announced that everyone would feel better after they'd had something to eat. There was Hamburger Helper with a large green salad and a Sara Lee frozen chocolate cake for dessert. It was like so many other dinners she'd fixed while Juneau was growing up. Juneau thought she should have felt some kind of nostalgia about it, but she didn't.

While they ate, Juneau's dad told how they'd been surprised when Misty called from the train station in Oceanside to say she was there and could they pick her up.

"We called Greg and then went to get her," he said. "We've had such a nice visit."

So was that it? Misty had pulled a thing like that, and it ended up being a "nice visit"?

"What I want to know," Juneau said, "is why you ran away, Misty. Is something bothering you? Did we do something wrong?"

Misty glanced at her grandfather, who smiled benignly at her, and then nodded. "You gave Nicole the apple tree."

The apple tree? The only apple tree Juneau could think of was the one in Nicole's room. The one they'd painted for Max.

Nicole reached out to her sister. "I didn't know you wanted that room, Misty," she said. "Why didn't you say so? I would have let you have it."

"If that's what's making you unhappy, I'll paint one for you," Greg said.

Juneau's mom and dad moved to pat Misty's arm and coo soothing words. But Juneau sat stiffly silent. Misty was asking them all to believe that her bad behavior was due to her not having a choice about which room should have been hers *four years ago*? In a pig's eye!

"Misty," Juneau said, "let's you and me go for a little walk on the beach."

Nicole's eyes lit up. "Can I come, too, Mom?"

"Not now, sweetie," Juneau said. "Just Misty and me this time."

"Juney," Greg began, but she silenced him with a look.

Juneau stood up and offered a hand to Misty. "Come on. Unless you'd rather stay and do the dishes for Grandma." Usually that was threat enough to mobilize Misty.

"Okay," Misty said, "I'd like to stay and help my grammy with the dishes."

She was playing them all like a violin. Like a whole dratted orchestra!

"You come," Juneau commanded

It was a short walk to the beach. When they got there, Misty immediately ran for the water, looking back over her shoulder, saying, "Oh, Mom, look at the little sanderlings!"

Juneau glanced briefly at the small birds that scampered along the edge of the waves looking for food or whatever it was they hoped to find. But she wasn't going to be deflected by such an obvious ploy.

"Misty," she said, "come walk right next to me."

Misty came. "This is so much fun, Mommy," she said.

"You can scrub the playacting with me, young lady," Juneau said. "I want you to tell me right now why you pulled this little running away stunt. Do you have any idea how worried we all were? How guilty Nicole felt because she didn't find out where you were going? How your dad was scared out of his wits and missed a day of work just because you wanted to indulge in a little drama? To say nothing of me! I was practically paralyzed with fear all the way down on the plane, not knowing what had happened to you."

"I'm sorry, Mom," Misty said.

"Sorry doesn't cut it." Juneau stopped walking and faced her daughter. "You planned this, didn't you. You wanted to stir us up a little. You wanted to get attention. Sympathy. Which I can understand. But running away? How could you do such a thing?"

"Grandma and Grandpa were happy to see me," Misty said.

"Of course they were. They love you, Misty. But if you wanted to see them, why couldn't you tell your father and have him arrange for you to come down here? Why didn't you wait until I got home, so I could have driven you? You're going to have to come up with a better excuse than that, Misty."

Misty's thirteen-year-old face hardened. "How about this one? You and Dad have always loved Nicole more than me. I'm always second best. She and Dad are such good friends, but they leave me out. You gave Max's room to Nicole without even asking me."

There it was again, the issue of the room. Maybe that incident *had* been more significant than she'd thought it was. But there was more than that long ago event that had made Misty run away.

"What is it that's really bothering you? Why did you think you had to run away to get our attention?"

Suddenly Misty's face crumpled. "Mom, I don't know why I ran away. I don't know why I do a lot of things. I want to be nice like Nicole, but I don't know how to be. I don't know what's wrong with me."

Juneau's heart went out to her daughter, whose confusion sounded so much like her own. She put an arm around the girl. "Misty," she said, "we love you. We want the best for you. I want you to promise that next time you feel like you have to do something like running away, you'll come talk to me."

"You weren't home," Misty snuffled.

Juneau nodded. "You're right. I wasn't. But there is always the telephone. Or your dad. There's always somebody you can talk to."

"Is there?" Misty asked.

Looking at her, Juneau decided she didn't know her children much better than her mother had known her and Flint.

On the way home to Pasadena, Juneau let Greg chauffeur while she sat in the back between their two daughters. She squeezed the hands of both of them as they sang all the old childhood songs they could remember, including the one about how nice it was to get up in the morning when the sun begins to shine. They repeated old kid jokes and whispered old stories.

Philip Atwater welcomed everybody home with barks and wags, concentrating particularly on Misty. The big mutty dog always seemed to be tuned in to what was going on in the family. Misty responded happily to his enthusiastic greeting, and she seemed content enough to be home. She even invited Juneau to come tuck her in when she went to bed. She hadn't done that in a long time.

"I love you, Mom," she said as Juneau settled the covers up over her shoulders.

"I love you, too, sweetheart," Juneau said. Then, on impulse, she said, "Misty, would you like us to paint an apple tree on your wall?"

Misty considered it. "Not an apple tree. I'd like to paint what *I* want on my wall."

"And what would that be?"

Misty smiled. "Wait and see."

August 25, 1984
Dear COBs and Gabby,

Misty is okay. I wish I could say the same for me. I guess you all heard how she went missing while I was in Salt Lake with you. I'll tell you all about it in a phone call. At the moment I can't cope with putting it down on paper. How's that for a writer?

Love,
Juneau

Chapter Thirty-One

WILLADENE

Early in the morning Deenie was up, dressed, and in the vegetable garden long before the children awoke. She attacked the work with determination, pulling and pinching back until the tomato patch looked like it had been given a crew cut. She used the same enthusiasm tearing down the pea vines she'd ignored. All the while she was thinking about last evening's conversation with Roger. Why had she glossed over his comments about finding a new corner of the world to live in? Why had she ignored the hope and excitement she heard in his voice when he talked about the adventure in change? Why hadn't she asked him the questions that had kept her awake most of the night?

Do you need more adventure in your life? Do you want to find that new corner of the world to live in? Isn't our home enough for you? Aren't I enough? Do you want me to be more like Juneau or Erin?

And what would she do if Roger said, "Yes, I want a more interesting place to live. Yes, you could be more interesting, too"?

Maybe I'm like biscuits, Deenie thought. *They're great when they're fresh and warm from the oven, but they go stale really fast. And as much as most people like them, nobody would want biscuits as a steady diet.*

By the time she had picked enough early green beans for dinner and some extras for Grandma Streeter, Deenie had worked herself into a proper snit. She had imagined so many scenarios, responses, and consequences, that she was angry over things that had never happened. In the end, she decided that if asking those questions could cause so much trouble, it was better not to ask. *If Roger needs a change in his life,* she decided, *he will have to bring up the subject himself.*

For the rest of the morning Deenie took on all her least favorite tasks to keep her worries under control. She washed and scalded canning jars, put whites in the washer in a bleaching cycle, scrubbed the toilets, and washed the dog. She was struggling with one hand on Rauf's collar and the other on the blow dryer when Roger and the boys left for the farm.

When Bitsy woke up from her afternoon nap, Deenie was ready for a nap of her own. Nevertheless, there was the rest of the day to be gotten through. So she bagged the green beans for Grandma Streeter and then slathered Bitsy with sunscreen for the walk to deliver them.

"Ooh, what smells so delicious?" Deenie asked when Grandma Streeter invited them into the kitchen.

"You'll have to ask Patience," Grandma Streeter said, nodding toward Pat Crafton, who was lifting some divine smelling cakes from the oven.

Deenie sniffed. "I smell chocolate. And fruit."

"You're right," Pat said with a smile. "But what kind of fruit?"

Deenie inhaled deeply, relishing the complex blend of aromas. "Blueberries?"

"Close but no cigar. Try again."

Grandma Streeter took Bitsy out onto the porch to keep her company while she snapped the beans, leaving Pat and Deenie to play the ingredient game. After a few more rounds of guessing, Deenie threw up her hands in defeat. "Okay, I give up. What is it?"

"Two cups of the best Bear Lake Seedless Blackberry Jam we could lay our hands on."

"You didn't say jam. You said fruit!" Deenie said with chagrin.

Pat just laughed. "So how did your visit in Salt Lake City go?" she asked. "Did your friends like their presents?"

"I think so. I barely finished the quilt for Erin's baby in time. If it hadn't been for you and your mom, it would still be on the quilting frame in the middle of the living room."

Pat began washing the pots and pans. "Are you finished making gifts for this year?"

"Are you kidding? I have a whole list of Christmas projects to tackle."

"You could try consumable gifts the way the Craftons do. I always thought it was one of their family's better ideas."

"You mean like goodies?" Deenie grabbed a towel and started drying.

"That's part of it. The rule was that whatever you gave had to be something that could be used up, like theater tickets or passes for the zoo or museum. Once Van's mom gave us a coupon she had made that was redeemable for a weekend of baby-sitting so we could get away. It was one of the best presents I ever got. Van's dad always gave him a season ticket for the Chicago Bulls games."

"Did you say a ticket?"

Pat paused while wiping down the work island. "Sore subject."

"Oh. So if you were going to give your mother something like that, what would it be?"

"A movie date in Salt Lake City and dinner at Chuck-a-Rama."

Deenie laughed at the picture those words created. Somehow she couldn't imagine Letty Streeter, one of the best cooks in the valley, wanting to eat at a chain restaurant. "I like the gift idea," she said. "But I wonder what my family would say. My dad always insists you don't monkey around with family traditions."

Pat gave her a quick hug. "Can't hurt to try."

August 24, 1984
Dear Ladies,

I am baking, I have baked, and I will bake!

Pat worked as a caterer in Chicago. She is planning to do the same here. She decided to create a signature recipe from a hundred-year-old seedless blackberry jam cake recipe of Grandma Streeter's. I offered to help, and we are having a blast. For the latest trial we added chocolate, black walnuts, and a touch of orange. Yummmm!

While we're cooking, Bitsy plays with Grandma Streeter. They have become such close friends that Bitsy asks to see her Streeter Lady every day. My "family" is getting bigger all the time. First you three and Sophie, then Jonas and Bryan, and now Pat and Leila Streeter.

Pat has given me a few new ideas in the way of Christmas giving I am going to try. If they work out, I won't end up Christmas-weary by Thanksgiving. Sounds good, doesn't it?

Ryan and Reece are going to the farm daily with Roger and the boys. Carl complains because Grandpa Rasmussen pays them to help and doesn't pay him. "Some things you do just because you are part of a family," Grandpa says.

And some things you don't do if you want to keep your TV privileges for the next month. Roger discovered the boys trying to roll tailor-mades in the barn. They were using some old wrapping papers from a permanent that belonged to Grandma Rasmussen and chopped up alfalfa. Grandma scolded them like they were babies, and Roger laughed at them. I think that hurt more than if Roger had punished them severely. Of course they were all sick as could be, but the laughter was worse. When Paul heard what mischief Carl had gotten into, his comment was, "How dumb can you be?"

Love,
Deenie

ERIN

Sunday, September 16, 1984
Dear Juneau and Deenie,

Thank you, thank you for the wonderful time we had in Salt Lake City. I was so glad to see Gabby and Jonas again. They make such a sweet couple. Gabby looked tired, though. I think she's getting worn down with worry over Kenny. How horrible to have a grandson responsible for the death of someone! At least she's got Sophie and Bryan. What fine young people they have grown into.

If there's one lesson I learned from our visit, it's that you can't judge anyone on the basis of one moment. It's not the whole story and it's not the end of the story. Bryan is a good reminder of that.

On to San Francisco. Cory and I had a fabulous time! There was so much to see and do. The part I liked best was visiting Muir Woods, Stinson Beach, and Sausalito. We ate a different kind of food every night and went to bed exhausted but happy.

Deenie, Kayla is inseparable from her new blankie! She drags it behind her everywhere she goes, kind of like Linus in the Peanuts comic strip. I tried at first to pry it away from her so I could keep it from getting worn out too fast, but she refuses to be parted from it. I think it's because you packed it full of love when you made it.

Juneau, I love your new professional look. I can't wait to read the book that you are working on. Knowing you, it will be full of humor as well as insight. Keep it up, girl!

Now it's back to the routine, but I'm not complaining.

Love,
Erin

JUNEAU

Flint was a production. Everyone looked forward to seeing him, and no wonder. Tall, handsome, and affable, with vitality shining all the way from his Marine-cut blond hair to his size thirteen shoes, Flint took over any situation he was part of.

He was a top-ranked drill sergeant because he was a great believer in the "reproving betimes with sharpness" admonition in the Doctrine and

Covenants but then showing caring and concern afterward, "lest he esteem thee to be his enemy." Sometimes it bothered Juneau that his talents were spent in bringing young recruits into the discipline and teamwork that would make them efficient and formidable fighting units.

Maybe it bothered him, too. Recently she'd suspected that he'd moved on into some other form of government work, but she could get no clue from him about what it was, so she'd stopped asking.

He arrived in Pasadena on a hot September Friday that gave few hints of autumn beyond the fact that the leaves of the liquid amber trees were beginning to turn red. The girls were still in school, for which she was guiltily grateful. Once they got home, they would demand his full attention.

Juneau had lunch waiting—melted cheese sandwiches, guaranteed to make him nostalgic for their Airstream days—with slices of tomato and avocado and red onion for a "build-it-as-you-wish" adventure. Plus she'd made Danish rhubarb pudding, the one and only thing she knew that had come down from Great-Grandma Letitia.

"I love the pudding," he said. "I haven't had it since the last time I saw the folks."

"And when was that?" Juneau asked.

Flint tipped his head back, thinking. "About three years ago, when they were in Texas to do a book centered on the Alamo. Mom made the pudding for me then."

"She made a batch when they were here back in 1980 after Daddy's heart bypass," Juneau said. She sighed. "Not exactly a close-knit family, are we."

Flint chuckled. "But we have volumes of shared memories."

"Not that we get together very often to share them," Juneau said. "That bothers me. I've included descriptions of my two long-distance friends, Willadene and Erin, in my letters to you. One of the things that attracts me to Willadene is her connection to family and her closeness to them and interaction with all of them. We have none of that."

"Then you make your own connections," Flint said, cleaning the last of the pudding from his bowl. "With anybody who might be nearby."

"Easier said than done."

"Maybe. For you."

"What do you mean by that?"

"You were always the observer," Flint said. "Detached. Withheld. Watching rather than participating. Analyzing as you go. All the things that make you a good writer now."

Juneau was glad he'd put in the last comment. Otherwise it all sounded totally negative. "You make me sound like a cold fish, Flint," she said.

He shook his head. "You're a warm and wonderful sister. But you never were really part of anything, were you, Juney? You didn't join clubs. You didn't run for school offices. You didn't carry friendships from one of our homes to the next."

It was true. She hadn't thought it was possible. But *he* had. He'd even been student-body president at one of the high schools they'd gone to. He'd been there for four months by the end of a term and was elected to that office for the next year. Their folks had postponed moving on until he completed his duties the following June.

Would they have done the same for her?

"Do you think I'm still detached and withdrawn?" Juneau asked.

"I don't know, Juney. Are you?"

"I guess I'll have to think about that." It was a *lot* to think about. Was she detached with Greg? Certainly they seemed to be walking their own paths these days and not always together. Was she withdrawn from the girls? Was that why Misty acted out so much?

She got up to put the remaining rhubarb pudding in the refrigerator.

Flit raised his hand to indicate he wanted more. "We're different personalities, Juney," he said. "Don't worry too much about it. We've reacted differently to the circumstances of our childhoods, and we've benefited in different ways."

"And suffered," she said softly.

He accepted his second dish of pudding. "You know the old saying? If life gives you a lemon, make lemonade." He spooned pudding into his mouth. "I don't know what kind of lemonade you make," he said, "but Great-Grandma Letitia couldn't have made a better pudding. This is great."

"Speaking of whom," Juneau said, "Great-Aunt Hattie gave me a picture of said G-G Letitia. Also a photo of the gravestone that bears her name—over an empty grave."

He sat back. "So where is she buried?"

"I don't have a clue. Mom has never told me a thing about her, except that she raised her after her parents were killed."

Flint shrugged. "So? You can still fill in your four-generation forms. Do you have to know anything further about her?"

Juneau imitated his shrug. "The writer in me, you know. Other than this rhubarb recipe, I have nothing that belonged to her. No wonder I'm disconnected."

"Didn't Mom ever give you her letters?"

"Letters? I didn't even know there *were* letters."

"I assume she still has them. She sent me one twelve years ago when Jason was born. It talked about how G-G Letitia felt when *I* was born."

"Would you send me a copy when you get home, Flint?"

"Sure, I will. If I remember."

When Greg and the girls came home, it was party time. Flint took them all out to dinner at the Raymond, a delightful and expensive restaurant in an old house tucked away on a hillside. The next day he drove them all to the top of Mt. Wilson, from which they could see all the way to the ocean. He hiked them around trails they didn't even know existed, and when they got back home, they had a water fight in the backyard.

The girls clung to him when he had to leave. Juneau stood back, marveling at how easily he had won them over. He reached out to people, rather than holding back as she did. Why did she do that? She grinned wryly, thinking how convenient it was to have her heritage from Long-Lost Letitia to blame it on.

WILLADENE

September 18, 1984
Dear Ladies,

Miss Bitsy started school the first of the month. She is so proud of herself. She wakes up on her own, and if I'm not there to help her, she picks out her own clothes for the day. Some of her fashion ideas are rare, to phrase it nicely. But if she puts them on before I get to her, I let her wear them.

My mother about had a coronary when she and Sunny picked Bitsy up from school on a day when she was wearing one of her own combinations. The little stinker had put on her purple pants and a brown and orange plaid cowboy shirt that used to be Paul's. She finished off with red and white Christmas stockings and her Sunday shoes. Mom asked me how I could possibly let her be seen in public in such garish clothes. I said she should be glad that Bitsy hadn't insisted on fixing her own hair as well.

Pat wondered what the big deal was. She said, "She's finding herself. Let her be." I can hear a lot of Grandma Streeter in Pat. She always gives good advice like Pick your battles, not your nose; Don't major in the minors and minor in the majors; and Don't sweat the small stuff. I'm learning to pick my own battles as far as the kids are concerned.

It's another matter where Roger is concerned. His load at the university is bigger this fall, the kids at high school seem less attentive than usual, and his normal easy-going self is living somewhere else at the moment. I keep the kids out of his hair and keep a low profile myself until he emerges from his study for the night.

With Bitsy in school I have time to catch up on a lot. In fact, I am making remarkable headway on my do-it-when-you-have-the-time list. At the rate I'm going, I'll be caught up before the holidays.

Looking forward to it,
Deenie

ERIN

On a crisp October day, Erin drove out to the farm, as she called the Harringtons' place. Colleen met her in the yard, eager to show her what she'd done with the barn. When she unlatched the heavy door, Erin made a sound of surprise.

The barn had been thoroughly cleaned. In the open space at the front were baskets, boxes, and copper water boilers filled with odd assortments of small items. Larger items were lined against the walls. "Were all of these things in the back?" Erin asked.

"A lot of them." Colleen busied herself rearranging kitchen items in a basket. "I've been picking up things on my own. There are always yard sales out here, and I stop at all of them."

"You could have a garage—barn—sale today, if you wanted to. I can't believe all the things you've got here."

"I don't spend that much money, okay?" Colleen's voice was sharp, and she stood in a defensive attitude, chin forward.

"I didn't say anything about spending money."

Colleen sighed. "Steve says I'm getting addicted to shopping the sales, but it keeps me from thinking about what I don't have."

It took Erin a moment to realize Colleen was talking about the baby she and Steve had been hoping for. "Oh, sweetie. I'm sorry," she said, giving

Colleen a hug. "I didn't realize you were feeling so bad about not getting pregnant."

Colleen accepted the hug. "Did you mean what you said about a barn sale?"

"Absolutely. But we'd probably better do it soon, before a big snow comes."

"Great. Let's set a date." Colleen paused. "Erin? Steve doesn't need to know I told you all the things we've been doing to get pregnant. Guys don't understand why women spill everything when they have a heart-to-heart."

They had the barn sale the last weekend in October. They invited everyone they knew, and they encouraged people to bring over the day before any items they wanted to sell. When Erin called to invite The Women, she suggested that Grams bring the broomstick afghans she compulsively crocheted and then stacked in a corner of her bedroom. First Grams had pooh-poohed the idea, but then she said, "I guess I could give some of them up."

When Cory asked why she was going to all the extra work, she said, "It's the garage sale mystique. The more you have, even if it's junk, the more people are inclined to stop and buy." She gave him a sly smile. "It's an event, Cory. You know what it takes to make an event successful."

"And here I was thinking it was just a yard sale."

Erin had put a classified ad in the paper, and Steve and Cory set up signs with balloons at major intersections within two miles of the Harringtons'. The first customers arrived at 7:30 A.M., even though the day was windy and cold, and they kept coming until 5:00, when Cory took down the signs and Steve closed the barn doors.

To Erin's surprise, the day was a success not only as a business venture but as a social event. Everyone who was helping enjoyed talking to everyone who came, friends and strangers alike. Grams became a roving saleswoman, carrying on spirited conversations with customers over old kitchen utensils she had used in her childhood. And Jake and Joanna talked more to each other than to the customers who came to their table for cider and cookies.

Colleen pointed the latter out, wiggling her eyebrows suggestively. "I thought they had something going at the fireworks party. Now I'm sure of it."

"I think you're right." Erin watched them for a while and then turned away. Was this really a budding romance? Could her mother be interested in a relationship after all these years? Why not? She was only forty-four. She thought of how nice Jake had been to all of them—Joanna, Grams, Kayla, and herself. Joanna could do worse.

After everyone had left, Colleen and Erin sat down with the notebook they'd used to keep track of the sales. They separated out into piles the money they owed others who had brought items. When Colleen divided what was left, Erin shook her head. "It's all yours. I didn't bring anything to sell."

"I couldn't have done it without you and Cory. You have to get paid for your time."

"Listen, friend. In this business, you can't pay yourself for your time. This is revenue from the items that you bought or were in the barn. It belongs to you."

Colleen looked at the stack of bills and sank back into her chair with relief. "Thank you. Steve was beginning to bug me about where the money was going. Not the Finders money. My household money. Don't let me get carried away again, okay?"

"I'll help you any way I can, you know that. But what do you want me to do? Go with you wherever you go? Padlock your purse?"

Colleen shook her head. "I don't know."

JUNEAU

Juneau had an addiction. Actually it wasn't as much an addiction as an intense craving, but Juneau was embarrassed about it and preferred to think of it in the more pejorative terminology, just to shame herself into withdrawal.

It was another of her Guilty Secrets. Greg knew about it, but the girls didn't. She didn't want them following in her footsteps, exposing their teeth to constant sugar. Juneau's addiction was lollipops.

She'd been addicted since she was a child, when she'd saved up her allowance from month to month so that when the Peripatetic Paulsens stopped for a while in a town where there was a candy store she would stock up, buying whole bags of the tasty confections and then squirreling them away under her bed in the Winnebago. She hadn't shared them with Flint. Not that she wouldn't have if he'd wanted some. But he'd declared early that it was sissy to go around with a lollipop stick poking from your mouth. Like a baby sucking a pacifier, he'd said. He'd spent his money on comic books and matchbox cars.

Juneau had thought she'd grow out of it, and she did from time to time.

Months might go by without her thinking about it, but it would worm its way back, and she'd feel the craving deep inside her, calling to her, stimulating her taste buds so that all she could think about was lollipops.

So she understood—at least a little—Greg's addiction to computers. She knew how he could crave to gaze at a monitor, to feel his fingertips touching the keyboard, to hear the click-click-click as he typed, magically producing text on the screen. Or at least that's what she'd put together from what he said. She'd never seen the object of his affections.

Then one night he came home from the night class he taught and asked if she thought they might tighten their budget enough so that he could buy a computer of his own. "I'd like an IBM PC," he said. "They're pretty much top of the line. But I checked out a Dec Rainbow 100, and it's not quite so pricey. I'd be happy with it." He named a price that would require not only tightening the budget but stretching it so thin that a night at the movies would snap it.

"I don't think so," Juneau said. "Besides, where would we put it?"

Greg looked around the kitchen where they stood. "It doesn't take much space. Just a desk top."

Juneau glanced around, too. Greg had a small desk in the family room, but it was stacked with toppling piles of books and papers, with barely enough room for a telephone. The kitchen counter wouldn't do. She had to put cooking ingredients and equipment somewhere when she cooked. And her typewriter and paper supply took up the rest of the space except when it roosted on the kitchen table.

Greg scratched his head thoughtfully. "I'll get that room built in the garage," he said. "I'll go to Ole's tomorrow and price the materials."

Wait a minute! Juneau thought. *That's supposed to be my workroom.* All these years, he'd promised that he'd rough in a studio for her in the garage. Now that he was finally going to get around to it (that round tuit, again), he was thinking of his own needs, not hers.

She started to object, but then it occurred to her that she had produced many a story there at the kitchen table. She was not superstitious enough to think the well might dry up if she tried writing anywhere else (wasn't it Hemingway who refused to try to write on anything but his old manual portable?), but why take chances? At one time she'd had the thought that someday she might offer a collection of her stories with the title *From the Kitchen Table.*

Thinking about her stories made a flashbulb go off in her head. "Greg," she said, "I'll give you the money for a computer."

His eyebrows rose. "You?" he said.

She tried not to be offended. "Yes. You remember how you told me to keep the money from my stories?" (What he'd said when she'd offered to deposit the checks in the household account was, "I support this family, Juney. You keep the money from your little stories.")

"I remember."

"I opened a bank account, and I've got it all. Greg, there's enough for your computer. I'll take out what you need."

His eyebrows rose even higher. "I can't do that, Juneau. I can't take money from you."

She felt her face flush. "Why not? I've been taking money from you for all the years we've been married."

"That's different."

"*How* is it different?"

"Well." He paused. "Well, you're *supposed* to take money from me. I can't take money from my wife."

Juneau stiffened, her sudden anger wiping out all of Gabby's wisdom about taking time to craft a soft answer to an aggravating question. "And just how, exactly," she blurted, "would that compromise your cherished manhood, pray tell?"

"Well." He paused again, seeming to fumble with words. "Well, Juney, a man likes to think he can support his family."

She softened a little then. He was a good man who took seriously his responsibility of being head of the household. She didn't want to take that away from him. "You do a fine job of supporting us, Greg. I appreciate it."

"So you can see how I can't take money from you. A man's got his pride, Juney."

She reached up to put her hands on either side of his face. Holding it so that he had to look straight into her eyes, she said, "A woman has pride, too, Greg."

He gazed at her, obviously assimilating her words, examining them, feeling their impact. She sensed that this was an important moment, one that could either calm the rough waters or whip them into a major storm.

Finally he spoke. "Juney," he said slowly, "have you really been paid enough for those little stories to buy a computer?"

She nodded. "That, and more. Will you need anything else, other than the computer and the screen thingie that shows the text?"

"A printer. But I'll scrape up the money for that."

"No," she said. "Get everything you need. I'll pay for it."

For fully a minute he gazed at her, and then his eyes crinkled as a smile spread across his face. Suddenly he swooped her off her feet and swung her around and around. "Whooeee," he yodeled, "have I ever got me a woman here." Setting her back down, he yelled, "Misty! Nicole! Come on out here and take a look at a real honest-to-goodness, living, breathing author!"

They came. Nicole had obviously been awakened from sleep, but Misty, just as obviously, had been experimenting with eye shadow. They stared in bewilderment around the room.

"Where's the author?" Nicole asked finally.

"TA DA," Greg sang, extending his arms in a grand gesture toward Juneau.

The girls continued to stare.

"That's just Mom," Misty said finally.

"She's an author!" Greg announced. "People send her money for the stories she writes."

"How much?" Misty asked.

"Enough that we're going to buy a computer," Greg said jubilantly.

Misty's eyes lit up with interest. "A computer! Wow!"

"Wow!" Nicole echoed. "None of my friends has a computer!" Her forehead wrinkled. "What does a computer do?"

They all laughed, even Misty. "When will we get it?" she asked.

Greg looked at Juneau. "Ask Mom. She's bankrolling this toy."

"Will tomorrow be soon enough?" she said. Then she realized this was an opportunity. "But it doesn't come out of the box until that garage room is ready to put it in."

After everybody else was asleep, Juneau got up and went to the kitchen, where she pulled out the step stool and climbed up on it so she could reach the high cupboard above the refrigerator. It was there she kept her stash of lollipops. It had been awhile since she'd needed one, but the craving was strong. She took out two, a yellow one and a green one, her favorites. Pushing the bag into the far corner, she got down from the stool and sat at the kitchen table, idly touching the keys of the IBM Selectric as she filled her mouth with the green sucker and let it begin to dissolve against her tongue while she pondered the mysteries of life.

Who would have thought that giving in to her obsession to write would lead to keeping Greg closer to home and maybe Misty, too? Who would have thought that the thing she'd feared would damage her marriage and family life if she gave in to it might actually perhaps be its salvation?

November 17, 1984
Dear COBs,

We have a computer. And Greg is applying for permits to build a room for it in the garage and a carport over part of our driveway. He said, "You'll be taking over the computer for your writing soon," but I said, "No way, José." Why should I use a complicated machine like a computer when my lovely IBM Selectric does such a good job?

Misty is totally fascinated by the idea of the computer. She can't wait for Greg to finish the room in the garage so he can set it up. I think it will make for good leverage. If she acts out, she loses privileges, once it's up and running.

We told her after she ran away that she could paint a scene on the walls of her room, since a little envy of the apple tree mural in Nicole's room showed up. She painted one wall dead black, with a few soft yellow slashes through it. I asked her what it all meant, and she said, "You figure it out." So I'm trying. She has also dyed her hair black and spikes it when she gets to school. We've tried to set up some therapy sessions for her, but she says she won't go. So we just continue to love her and hope for the best.

Love,
Juneau

WILLADENE

December 20, 1984
Dear Ladies in Triplicate,

I am delighted to say that I now have two priesthood holders in my family. Carl has been ordained a deacon. When he passed the sacrament for the first time this Sunday, Paul was determined to take the bread and water from his tray. Since Carl was assigned to the other side of the chapel, it created quite a stir! Carl acted angry, but I think he was secretly pleased by the attention.

We had the usual grand family dinner to celebrate the occasion. Carl moved from the kids' table to the grown-ups' table with his older cousins. He's feeling very grown up. After dinner he shunned the kid play in favor of sitting and listening to the men talk. Once in a while I catch a gesture or a tilt of the head that looks exactly like his father. Is it nurture or is it nature? (Thank you to Bert for that phrase.)

I suppose you've gotten the announcement of Bryan's mission call Gabby sent out. If not, I'll tell you he's going to the North Carolina Charlotte Mission. He'll enter the Missionary Training Center on the first Monday in March.

Would you like to go in with us on getting a present for Bryan? Gabby is helping him get all the things he needs, since his parents are only publicly supporting his choice. I'll ask her what would be the most helpful.

We are heading deep into the holidays, putting up wreaths and stringing lights. Mom and Sunny are holed up at home creating surprises. Roger will soon be taking all the kids out to the farm for the ritual of choosing and cutting down the perfect Christmas trees. I'll wrap presents while they're gone.

Pat Crafton is up to her ears in orders for the hazelnut tortes for Christmas and has asked for my help. I said yes. Mom and Sunny are pitching in, too. Pat pays Sunny a little for every cake she boxes. Sunny's proud to have a job—and thrilled to have the paycheck that goes with it.

I have decided to take Pat's advice on gift-giving this year—only consumable gifts. I am giving theater tickets, gift certificates to restaurants, and subscriptions to the *Church News* to family out of state. No more afghans, quilts, fancy totes, or anything else handmade from me. I'll let you know how it all turns out.

> Love to you all,
> Deenie

P.S. Bet you can't guess what you're getting for Christmas!

Chapter Thirty-Two

1985

ERIN

Tuesday, January 1, 1985
Dear COBettes,

Happy New Year. Thank you for the picture Christmas cards.

Juneau, your girls are so pretty! How is Misty doing? I've thought about her a lot lately, probably because I contemplated running away from home many times. I never did, though. It takes courage—even if misdirected—to actually strike out on one's own. Deenie, your boys are really shooting up, and Bitsy is quite the little lady. They've changed a lot since I saw them in person.

Kayla's changed, too. She'll be two this month. Age-wise, that is. Behavior-wise, she's been in the Terribles for a couple of months now—lots of stamping and pouting. Grams can cut her tantrums short with a look, but not me! Cory is interested in having another child, but I can't imagine taking care of a newborn with Kayla on a rampage.

The holidays came and went without any major upset. Glory hallelujah! Want to know the secret? Jake! When he's around, everyone seems to mellow out. I wonder if I could give him a standing invitation to all family functions?

I'm working on my Spiritual Living lesson for January. I wonder if the bishop knew when he gave me this calling that it would be such a struggle. Cory says I'm like Jacob wrestling with the angel. "You bang and bruise yourself trying to get a blessing, when all you have to do is stop fighting and ask." It can't possibly be that simple, can it?

Maybe it is. One of the ladies in our ward sang a lovely song in sacrament meeting several weeks ago. It touched me so deeply, I asked her for the words. It's from an oratorio. *Elijah*, I think.

O rest in the Lord. Wait patiently for Him
And He shall give thee thy heart's desires.
Commit thy way unto Him and trust in Him
And fret not thyself because of evil doers.
O rest in the Lord. Wait patiently for Him.

I hope when I write to you in January 1986, I'll be able to say I did rest in the Lord. At least some of the time.

Love,
Erin

JUNEAU

It took Greg several months to finish building the room in the garage. He'd set his ETF (estimated time of finish) as Christmas of 1984. He almost made it, impelled as he was by the thoughts of having a computer right there at home.

In the meantime, the computer with its monitor and printer sat in huge boxes in the family room, in the spot where they normally put their Christmas tree. Juneau had impressed upon Greg the inconvenience it would be to set it all up in the already crowded space of the family room, which was right off the kitchen, and wouldn't be a good place for a computer anyway because there'd be the noise of the TV plus the clacking of her typewriter and clatter of cook pots and all that other stuff, she said, to say nothing of the presence of all the family members and Philip Atwater. Reluctantly, Greg had agreed to leave it boxed until the room in the garage was ready.

So the Christmas tree sat atop the monitor box, but that was all right because it made it so tall that Nicole, for one, was totally awed. "We have the most beautiful Christmas tree in the whole world," she breathed when they'd put all the lights and traditional ornaments on it, including the flour-and-water ones she and Misty had made when they were in kindergarten. "It goes clear to the ceiling."

It did, indeed. They piled the presents on the other boxes, which Juneau had covered with red tissue paper, and it was a good Christmas. Misty requested money to have her ears pierced, plus some gold earrings. Reluctantly Juneau and Greg complied. Juneau had found that most of the girls her age, fifteen that year, had their ears pierced, even LDS girls. *Maybe*

I'll have mine done, too, she thought. Nicole wanted her own boom box, smallish compared to the ear-busting units some of the kids hauled around. Philip Atwater didn't express his wishes, but he got a pair of antlers, which Nicole attached around his head. He seemed so embarrassed when they all laughed at him that Nicole put them on her own head, where they stayed most of the day.

As for Greg and Juneau, they'd told each other they didn't want anything, but Juneau had bought a lovely set of cherrywood paper trays for Greg's desk in the garage room, when it was finished. And Greg gave Juneau a small portable typewriter, which he confessed wasn't new but had scarcely been used. "For when you go visit your friends and want to write," he said.

She was pleased. It was a thoughtful gift.

She fixed a prime rib roast with a pepper rub for dinner, a recipe she'd found in the food section of the *Los Angeles Times*. Her family was impressed.

So the year ended well, and 1985 began. And Greg finished the garage room. He bought an inexpensive computer desk, and at last his coveted machine was up and running. When he wasn't on campus, he lived there in the new room.

Juneau couldn't understand his fascination with the computer. He'd showed her how it operated, but it seemed enormously complicated, and she wasn't tempted by it. However, she *was* tempted by the room. It should have been hers. For years it had been promised to *her.* True, the kitchen table had worked out all right. But the books she needed regularly, like *Roget's Thesaurus,* and *English Usage,* and the one on synonyms and antonyms, were in the garage now, residing in the new bookshelves Greg had built. She yearned for the compactness of the middle bedroom when it had been her office, with all she needed for her writing within easy reach.

One morning after Greg and the girls had gone to their various schools, she went out to the garage room. It wasn't a particularly inviting room, with its cement floor and cold white wallboard walls that were taped and primed but not yet painted. But the room had a nice new window and was sunny and bright. It was also larger than she'd realized. If she moved the bookcases over to *that* wall instead of where they were . . .

Juneau had an idea.

She immediately drove to Penney's, where she bought some curtains and the necessary hardware. Nothing frilly. Just straight panels in a luscious shade of pale orange that matched one of the colors in the fake but pretty 6' by 9' Oriental rug she also bought.

She went to the paint store next and finished up at a secondhand furniture shop, where she bought a typewriter table and a small bookcase to hold her paper supply.

By the time Greg and the kids came home, she had the curtains up and the rug down. She'd painted the window wall a warm cream color, and as an afterthought painted the typewriter table as well. She'd also cooked a spaghetti dinner, something she was good at and that her family loved. As a grand finale, she'd baked a chocolate cake.

It wasn't until they were finished eating that Greg noticed something was different. "Where's your typewriter?" he asked.

"Guess," she said.

"You got frustrated with a plot and threw it out," he offered.

"Guess again."

Now Misty and Nicole got into the game. "Philip Atwater has decided to be a writer and moved it to his doghouse," Misty said.

The big dog, sprawled on the floor beside the table, raised his head at the sound of his name and then laid it down again with a sigh when no food or pats were forthcoming.

"Guess again," Juneau said.

Nicole wrinkled her forehead. "An alien came swooping down and beamed it up to Ugug."

Misty giggled. "What's Ugug?"

"That's where the alien lives," Nicole said. "It's a planet way out past Pluto. Haven't you heard of it?"

Now they all giggled, and Juneau was grateful for a rare moment of family togetherness. Misty had been fairly docile, for her, since her running away episode.

"Okay, we give up," Greg said. "Where *is* your typewriter?"

"In the studio," Juneau said. "In the writing room. The computer room. The garage room."

Greg's eyes widened. "You took over my room? What did you do with my computer?"

Juneau bit back a sharp retort that it was *supposed* to be *her* room.

"Your computer is residing happily on your desk," she said. "And my typewriter is living just as happily on my new typewriter table."

Greg continued to stare and then turned and stalked to the door that led to the garage. The girls followed him, with Juneau bringing up the rear. Greg switched on the light and stood surveying the room.

Nicole was the first to speak. *"Neat-*o," she said softly. "This sure doesn't look like a garage any more."

Even Misty was impressed. "If you gave me a choice of which room I wanted now, it would be this one," she said.

Greg was silent, and Juneau feared she'd overstepped some kind of bounds.

Finally he said, "Juney, I have one thing to say."

She waited.

"I'm betting that you will eventually want to take over my computer— which you paid for. When that happens, I get dibs on it for evenings after I get home from campus."

She was still tentative. "You don't mind my taking part of the room?"

Greg reached out a hand and took hers. "It seems to me I promised you a long time ago that I would make a room for *you* here. It kind of slipped my mind, but I've finally kept my promise."

"You got a round tuit," Juneau said.

"What?"

"Never mind. I love you, Greg."

"I love you, too." He turned to Misty and Nicole. "And I love these weird alien munchkins who are invading our space here." He gathered all of them into a big hug.

It was one of the best evenings that Juneau could remember, topped off by a second piece of chocolate cake, which had turned out to be quite delicious.

Juneau wrote to the COBs about the whole adventure, which brought a phone call from Gabby.

"You probably weren't in Relief Society yet when the course of study for the literature department was called 'Out of the Best Books.'"

"No," Juneau said, "but I remember my mom talking about that."

"There was a story titled 'The Revolt of Mother,' by Mary Freeman, in the second volume. It's about a wife who for forty years asks her husband to build them an adequate house, but he never gets around to it. Then he builds a snug and beautiful barn. While he's gone one day, the wife moves all the furniture into the barn and makes it into their home. When he comes home, she feeds him a favorite meal, and he capitulates without a squawk. Sounds like you accomplished the same thing in the same way."

"I'd like to read that story," Juneau said.

"I'll photocopy it and send it to you," Gabby said, "and the comments at the end as well, which include a statement that 'a lifetime of nagging would not have worked.'"

"That's true," Juneau agreed.

"Let me read you one of the last lines of the story," Gabby said. "It says the husband 'was like a fortress whose walls had no active resistance and went down the instant the right besieging tools were used.'"

They chuckled together.

"If you learn a thing a day, you come up smart," Juneau said. "I think it was Festus on *Gunsmoke* who used to say that. If I live long enough, I may have a particle of your wisdom someday."

Gabby chuckled again. "Good-bye, Juneau," she said. "May you produce many fine books in your new writing room."

February 1, 1985
Dear COBettes,

I finally have my writing room. Or half a room, that is. But that's not why I'm writing.

When my brother, Flint, came to visit last September, I learned that he has a letter written by Great-Grandma Letitia on the occasion of his birth. Mom gave it to him. Right off, I wondered why she didn't give me a similar one on the occasion of my birth. Those violins signaling the start of a pity party were mighty loud.

I asked Flint to send me a copy of the letter, which he finally remembered to do. It's in G-G Letitia's own handwriting. It's short and rather cryptic, but it's a connection! Move over, Willadene. I'm staking out a spot on the family history shelf!

Want to know what G-G said? These are her words: "Thank goodness you produced a boy who will have some control over his own life." That's it. I've written it into my notebook of Clues About Letitia, which is all that's in there except the fact that she's not in her own grave.

Mysteries abound!

Love,
Juneau

WILLADENE

The children were snuggled all deep in their beds, but it wasn't Christmas, and Deenie was sure that no one was dreaming of sugar plums. Not after the fiasco with Roger's papers after dinner.

He had set a pile of corrected tests on the edge of the table, where they were a perfect target for Rauf's curiosity, especially after Bitsy spilled her milk on them. He blew up when he saw the resulting soggy, chewed-up mess. Then he left for his night class at the university, leaving a dark cloud behind him.

We can't go on like this, Deenie thought. They were on a steep slide down from Almost Dead Dog, and she wasn't going to let it go unchecked right down to Dead Chicken. While she waited up for him, she baked a small version of his favorite spice cake and put milk for hot chocolate on the stove. She timed everything to be at its best when he came home. But when he arrived later than his usual late, he wasn't interested in the cooling cake or the mug of hot chocolate that had already skimmed over.

"Let it be, Deenie!" he barked when she brought up his after-dinner explosion. Then he marched into his study and slammed the door.

Deenie was too wired to sleep. She rocked in her favorite chair at a furious pace, wondering how she was going to make life all right again for the boys and especially for Bitsy who had fallen asleep in tears, repeating, "I'm sorry, I'm sorry, I'm sorry."

When no answers came, Deenie sought distraction in the pile of books the librarian had set aside for her to read. Maybe she could bore herself to sleep. The top volume was the second in a series of the collected works of Shakespeare. Deenie opened the book at random and began to read. "Now is the winter of our discontent . . ." *I sure don't need to read about discontent,* she thought and slammed the book shut.

Determined to have something good come out of the evening, she cut the cake and bagged the individual pieces for the children's school lunches tomorrow. She dumped the chocolate down the drain and touched up the kitchen. When that activity wasn't enough to calm her whirling thoughts, she decided to write a letter. There was only one person she could think of who could give her the advice she needed.

Dear Gabby, she wrote. *Do you think Jonas had any idea of what he was getting this family into when he suggested that Roger get his master's degree and encouraged him to take the assistantship at the university? I have to wonder.*

Things around here are downright miserable at the moment. Then she went on to describe exactly how miserable they were.

Gabby's letter came by return mail. It was filled with comfort and solicitude. Nevertheless, the ending held neither. *Jonas was saddened to learn things are going so poorly for you,* Gabby responded. *However, the choice was Roger's, and Jonas is not to blame for that. It was a grown-up choice that has created these grown-up problems and it's going to take—guess what—a grown-up to deal with them. Who will that be? You? Roger? Best case would be both of you together.*

If we can be of any help, feel free to call. Love, Gabby.

Not likely, Deenie thought, crumpling the letter and tossing it into the trash. Whether intended or not, she'd found two lessons from that letter to take to heart. First, to avoid further criticism, she would keep her mouth shut, no matter how serious the problem. Second, it was her job to keep both her children and her husband content and happy no matter what the circumstances. Once she had identified the tasks, Deenie promised herself to do them both to perfection.

Chapter Thirty-Three

WILLADENE

February 12, 1985
Dear Ladies,

I am totally and completely out of the chocolate cake, cookie, and candy business. In fact, I have banned chocolate from the house for at least a week.

Pat has a new landlord for the bakery and has taken a business partner. She has rented the upstairs of my dad's store, so he's the new landlord. The business partner is my mom. I'm in a tizzy over the whole thing.

With all the help she's getting, Pat should be up and running in no time. Mom is setting up the bookkeeping like she used to do for Dad. She seems to have taken a new lease on life. She even dresses differently. And even when Sunny is too tired to take part, she never tires of watching everything unfold. She says it's like magic. Mom is still watching Bitsy one afternoon a week so I can play Annie Oakley with my dad. I am getting quite good at it, too.

As much as I didn't want to be Pat's partner, I am feeling left behind. And I used to worry how I could help Sunny so she wouldn't feel that way. Isn't that an odd one! Sounds like a pity party, doesn't it, and me with no chorus.

Roger says he's glad the house won't smell like a candy factory. He wants the smell of meat loaf or fried chicken or beef stew when he gets home from work, especially in this freezing weather. The kids, too. Besides, there is only so much extra mess and chaos a family like mine can take without meltdown.

We are still hopscotching (and a losing game it often is) our way through the minefield of trying to fit family life into Roger's busy schedule. I guess I should be grateful for the fact it isn't spring with fields to till and sheep to lamb.

I have started on my lesson for March on the Atonement. I am on the section on Adam and Eve. Some days staying innocently in the Garden sounds like a right fine idea to me.

Deenie

ERIN

March 25, 1985
Dear Gabby, Juneau, and Deenie,

News flash! I'm pregnant again. I'm feeling pretty well, once I get the mad morning dash over and done with, but I could sleep twelve hours at a time. Cory wants to drive down to Nauvoo the week before Memorial Day. That's where Harold and Trina are on their second mission. I want to go, because I've never been to any Mormon history sites except Salt Lake City. Cross your fingers that I'm feeling better by then. If not, all those rolling hills in southern Minnesota could be a real problem.

I felt funny telling Colleen. She and Steve have been trying to get pregnant for so long, and here Cory and I get pregnant at the drop of a hat. Colleen wants to be happy for me, but I can tell she's heart-sick. When we're together, I catch her looking at my still-flat tummy. When she catches me catching her, she's horribly embarrassed.

It's so sad. She's been my very best friend for ages, and now she can hardly stand to be around me. I don't know what to do. I can't get un-pregnant, and she can't get pregnant, so there we are. Cory says to pray for her, but what do I pray for? That she get pregnant? How do I know that's the right thing for her and Steve?

I guess I'll pray that she will be comforted and that the Lord's will will be done.

Mom and Grams are thrilled about the baby. Mom is already planning to take a week off to help me when it's born, and Grams is crocheting a crib blanket in mint green and butter yellow. I'm going to have to be careful that The Women don't squeeze out Linda. Sometimes I think she feels like she's not needed or wanted, especially when Grams is around.

Nothing's changed on the Grams/Cory front. She brings out the worst in him, and he brings out the worst in her. For the last year, I've been asking the Lord to soften their hearts. That's 352 on-my-knees prayers, not counting the ones I say as I go about my day. So far, I can't see any change, but I still hope.

Love,
Erin

WILLADENE

April 1, 1985
Dear Ladies,

The snow is beginning to melt in Cache Valley. Finally! It has been a longer winter than usual, and a twelve-year-old boy with cabin fever is a completely different animal from an eleven-year-old—as Carl has demonstrated to us all. With the help of the Streeter twins and the boys in the ward, he's discovered a thousand new ways to irritate his father, bug his mother, and drive his little brother and sister to violence.

As soon as it dries out enough, all four boys will be spending time helping on the farm. Roger's dad guarantees that will work some of the mischief out of them. I can hardly wait!

Erin, I was delighted to hear about the newest Johnson on the way. You have my sympathies over the close relationship with the toilet bowl.

Roger's schedule is winding up, with finals both on campus and at the high school. The whole family is missing him. It doesn't look like that is going to improve any time soon. He has taken on teaching some summer classes, and the farm work is always there.

He's rigidly faithful about the farm work, and rightly so. It was part of the deal that helped us get this house as an inheritance after he gave up his place on the farm for a teaching career. So I'm missing him, but there are snowdrops blooming in the garden, and I am looking forward to crocuses any day. That perks me up.

Deenie

ERIN

Erin and Cory planned their Nauvoo trip for the week before Memorial Day. Cory's grandmother had assured them over the phone that the weather would be absolutely gorgeous, not too hot or humid, and the flower gardens an explosion of color. "I can't wait to see you two. On our day off, Harold and I will give you a VIP tour."

They took Kayla out to the Harringtons' Friday night, so they could leave early on Saturday morning. Erin had never been on a road trip before, so she was thrilled to be setting out with her husband in their recently purchased gray minivan. She chattered away as Cory drove south on 35S out of the city and into a landscape of rolling fields dotted with farmsteads set off by windbreaks and ruled over by tall silos.

As the miles went by, Cory entertained her with stories of the summer vacations he'd spent with his Johnson grandparents at their lake cabin. She told him about her summer jobs at the counter of a dry cleaner's, waiting tables at a hospital coffee shop, and working as a gopher in her mother's office. He gave her blow-by-blow descriptions of basketball games he'd starred in. She told him of hours-long games of Holy Fours with the neighborhood kids, a version of the dice game 10,000.

At Albert Lea, just shy of the Iowa border, Cory found a small park where they ate lunch and walked around a bit before setting out again. Once on the freeway, Erin fell sound asleep, her head resting against a pillow wedged between her shoulder and the window.

She woke up slowly an hour later. Looking at him through sleepy eyes, she was jolted into alertness by an expression on his face she had never seen before. She made no sound as she tried to understand what was written there. Anxiety? Grief? Despair? The planes of his face were stark, and his mouth was clamped in a narrow line as if to hold something in.

Not wanting him to know she was awake, she took in shallow, soundless breaths while eyeing him from under almost closed lids. *What is weighing him down so?* He had given her no hint of trouble at work. They hadn't argued over anything recently, at least not anything important.

Well, that isn't true, she admitted with sinking heart. They argued over everything, and it was all important.

Over finances. Although Erin was getting the bills paid on time and they hadn't had any overdrafts at the bank, they had a bigger credit card balance than she was comfortable with, mostly run up by Cory.

Over the discipline of Kayla, who already knew the buttons to push when she wanted something. Over who spoiled Kayla the most, Linda with her frequent gifts or Ruth with her attention and indulgence.

Over the division of household chores, the frequency of lovemaking, and Cory's overscheduled weekends.

But didn't everyone have the same disagreements? Women were always writing letters about them to one or the other of The Dears, Ann and Abby. Women's magazines were full of articles on them.

Erin felt a growing queasiness, and it wasn't car sickness or her pregnancy. There was something Cory wasn't telling her, and she was too afraid of what she might hear to ask him what it was. She closed her eyes tightly, hoping that when she opened them again, she would know this was a dream.

Cory touched her shoulder when he stopped for gas at Cedar Rapids. "You awake?" He was grinning, looking like himself again, and Erin was all too glad to imagine she had dreamed the whole thing.

The last leg of the trip was long and exhausting. Erin was grateful when they arrived at Mississippi Memories and were escorted to the delightful room reserved for them. She soaked in the big tub while Cory finalized plans for meeting his grandparents in the morning. Then they went to bed, snuggling in the middle of the king-size expanse.

Harold and Trina met them at the Visitors' Center the next morning. A handsome couple with gray hair and dressed in their Sunday best, they looked like the other older missionary couples Erin and Cory had passed on their way to the center. Their smiles were wide, bright, and confident, the kind of smiles Erin loved seeing on Cory's face.

As she did now, she saw with relief.

It was the beginning of a perfect day. Harold and Trina gave them a personal tour of all the displays in the Visitors' Center, after which they spent some quiet moments in the Monument to Women sculpture garden. Erin was enchanted by the sculptures, especially one entitled *In the Family Circle*. It depicted a little girl taking her first steps from her mother to her father, both of whom held arms out protectively to catch her should she fall. "Makes me think of Kayla," Cory said.

They visited the Mansion House, the Red Brick Store, and other historic buildings. They drove to Carthage, where Erin held Cory's hand tightly as they climbed the stairs to the upper room where Joseph and his companions had spent their last hours. She was deeply moved by the evidence of industry, faith, and sacrifice she saw everywhere she looked. Her heart was full when she said her prayers that night, kneeling next to Cory.

They were looking forward to seeing more of the sights the next day and watching a musical performance in the evening, but early in the morning, Skipp reached them at the B&B to tell Cory that his Grandpa Wagner had passed away.

The trip back to the Twin Cities was grueling. Cory drove over the speed limit and stopped only when absolutely necessary because he wanted to get back to his mother as soon as possible. His fingers had the steering wheel in a death grip, his posture was stiff, and his mouth set in a tight line, shutting inside everything he was feeling.

At least I understand what he's feeling now, Erin thought, remembering how she had tried unsuccessfully to fathom his odd expression on the trip down to Nauvoo.

When they arrived at his parents' home, another shock awaited them. Grandma Wagner had followed her husband in death while they were on the road. "I guess she couldn't let Frank go on without her," Skipp said.

Erin had never been in the presence of such grief as the Johnsons were experiencing. She sat with one arm tucked through Cory's as he and his parents tried to talk themselves through the shock of both grandparents going within hours of each other.

"Go home, dears," Linda finally said. She stroked Erin's check. "You need to get some rest. We can make plans to go to the funerals tomorrow." She paused. "You will both come to Florida with us, won't you? If Steve and Colleen can watch Kayla again?"

Of course they went. They stayed in a hotel, but they spent most of their time in the home of Linda's brother, Gerald. Erin often sat to the side watching Linda, Gerald, and their spouses deal with the aftermath of death. But mostly, she watched her husband. She caught glimpses of his normal ebullient self, but he was uncharacteristically subdued, especially when his Uncle Gerald started telling the group about how Grandma Wagner had kept every letter Cory had sent them from his mission.

Cory accepted the packet of letters tied with string. At the request of the group, he picked several at random to read aloud, pausing at times to keep his emotions in check.

"What was the best thing about your mission?" one of Cory's cousins asked.

Cory looked at Erin. His chin trembled and he gripped her hand tightly as he answered. "The advice my mission president gave me to get married as soon as I got home. My wife and daughter are the most important things in my life."

Erin thought he seemed more himself the day of the funeral. Back in their hotel that evening, he said he wanted to rest a little, so she took a romance novel into the bathroom and filled the tub with hot water. She was about to climb in when she heard a strange and awful sound from the bedroom.

Cory was crying in the painful way of a man who rarely cries. Erin was terrified by the harsh and ragged sounds he tried to muffle but couldn't. She knelt before him in her bathrobe, comforting him the way she would Kayla, with nonsense murmurs and soft strokes and kisses. If only she knew how to kiss this wound and make it better!

"Your grandparents are happy now, dear." She took his face between her hands and looked into his red-rimmed eyes. "It's all right. They're together."

He said nothing, just clung to her as if to a lifeline. Even when she awoke during the night, his arm was still around her waist, holding her to him.

They flew home the day after the funeral. Erin was relieved to be back in her home, surrounded by familiar things. She hungered to hold Kayla and savored the smell of her daughter's neck when she was sweaty with play.

Slowly, life settled back into the old rhythm. Being busy was especially good for Cory, who seemed more like his normal self once he started back to work. The day he came home full of excitement about a citywide celebration he was in charge of, Erin sighed with relief. The morning she opened a package delivered to their door to find a replica of the statue *In the Family Circle* and a card from Cory saying, "Thank you for giving me my daughter," she knew they were going to be okay.

WILLADENE

May 15, 1985
Dear Ladies in Triplicate,

Summer has started with a blast . . . of water balloons hitting cars along the state highway that passes the Rasmussen farm. And a bang . . . the sound of Carl slamming every door he can in the house since he got grounded.

He was picked up by the county sheriff along with Reece and Ryan for the balloon incident. It looks like Carl was the instigator of the whole episode. All three boys were defiant until Grandpa Rasmussen got hold of them.

He gave them the plain and pure word, from what I hear. He made it clear that being trusted and being a rabble-rouser do not go together, especially when heavy farm equipment is involved. He said he wanted men he could count on working for him and not foolish boys.

Grandma Streeter has been my stalwart backup. She is largely responsible for the baby quilt you should have received by now, Erin. When I mentioned you were expecting again, she set up the quilting frame in her living room and had the yellow squares put together before I even had time to think about it. She's determined to be mother for me since my mom spends so much time helping Pat at the bakery. It's nice to have the backup.

Speaking of Mom, she and I had a date for my birthday—our first time alone in ages. We went to lunch at the Copper Kettle and saw the movie *Amadeus*. It's the kind of movie that fascinates and repels you at the same time. I always thought geniuses, especially in fields like art and music, had to be outstandingly honorable and moral to have such talent. That movie was an eye-opener. You get talents whether or not you deserve them, just like you get trials.

I have another date to look forward to, a dress-up date. Roger and I will soon celebrate our fourteenth wedding anniversary. I have already made the reservations and have romantic plans in motion, ones I defy even Regina and Reginald to duplicate. It promises to be a night to remember.

Love,
Deenie

Chapter Thirty-Four

WILLADENE

The mantel clock bonged the half hour as Willadene put the finishing touches on her going-out-for-the-evening makeup. Roger should be arriving any minute to change clothes so they could be on their way. It was their fourteenth anniversary, and they had promised each other that it would be a new start as partners and lovers. To celebrate, Deenie had made dinner reservations at Gias and purchased tickets to a performance at the Eccles Theater. She had also arranged to have the children stay the night with their Rasmussen grandparents.

Deenie smiled in anticipation. It was going to be a wonderful evening, their first alone in many years. She smoothed her hands down the sides of the new sleek black dress and admired how the fashionably wide shoulders accented her now slightly trimmer waist. She checked the clock once more and then slid on silky sheer nylons in midnight black and slipped into a pair of spiked heels.

Come on, Roger, she thought. *It's time.* She picked up her beaded evening bag, a gift from Roberta Jean, and walked downstairs and into the living room to look out the front window. There was no flash of headlights coming up the road, and she tapped her foot impatiently.

When the phone rang, she hesitated answering, afraid it was Roger calling to say he would be late. But it was Sunny.

"Deenie, it's time to come home. Mommy is a grumpus, and Daddy's still at work. Can you come be my friend?"

As always, the sound of Sunny's voice touched Deenie's heart. "I'd love to come, sweetie, but tonight is date night for Roger and me. Remember I told you we're going out for our anniversary? I'm wearing the fancy black dress you helped me pick out."

"With the shiny black stockings and the pointy shoes?"

"Umhum." Deenie grinned, thinking Sunny had just described an upscale Halloween witch.

As Deenie hung up the phone, the clock bonged seven times. Still no Roger. At 7:30, Deenie sat weighing her fear against her anger. Fear won out. She called Roger's school. There was no answer, but she hadn't really expected one at this hour. She called the Rasmussens. They hadn't heard from him.

Now Deenie began pacing. *Where could he possibly be? Probably squirreled away in the history reference section of the Utah State University Library with no idea of what time it was.*

Deenie punched in the number. The girl at the desk said she couldn't look for him but promised if he passed through checkout she would tell him to call home.

When eight o'clock came and went silently, Deenie took off her pointy shoes and shiny black nylons. They wouldn't be going to dinner. They wouldn't be seeing the show.

When the phone did ring at quarter to nine, Deenie snatched it up. "Roger!" she said without waiting to hear who was on the other end of the line.

"He's not home, then?" Wilford asked.

"No."

"He's probably all right, but if you don't mind, I'd like to come over and wait with you."

"I'd appreciate that, Will."

At ten o'clock, when they still hadn't heard from Roger, Will called the sheriff and then the hospitals. There was no news about Roger. Sick with worry, Deenie listened to her father-in-law's end of the conversations. As she did, she took off the delicate pearl-and-silver bracelet that had been last year's anniversary present and set it on the dining room table. Then she slipped off the matching earrings Roger had given her for Christmas and added them to the pile.

She was pacing the room, nervously twisting the rings on her left hand when a car came roaring up the drive. Headlights flashed past the living room window. The garage door opened and closed. Then Roger tromped through the back door. "Sorry I'm late," he said "but those reference books I've had on reserve at the university finally came available—" Roger stopped mid-sentence and stared at Deenie and his father. Deenie could almost see the cogs in his brain turning as he took in her dress and his father's stern expression.

"Oh no, our anniversary!" Roger dropped the books on the dining room table and came toward her, arms held out. "Oh, honey. I'm so sorry. I'll . . ."

"I don't want to hear it." Deenie didn't care that her voice was cold. Almost without knowing what she was doing, she pulled off her engagement ring and wedding band and dropped them on the table next to the bracelet. With all the dignity she could muster she walked quietly, stiffly from the room.

Her heart was pounding as she climbed the stairs. *What would Regina do,* she wondered bitterly. She paused for a moment on the upper landing and then locked herself in the guest room.

When Deenie woke from a heavy sleep early the next morning, she was surprised to find she was still in the guest room. That wasn't the way it was supposed to go. Roger was supposed to have pounded on the door and begged apologetically for her to forgive him the way she had imagined he would. He hadn't, and she had spent her whole anniversary night alone behind a locked door.

For the first time, she realized what a horrible thing she had done when taking off her engagement ring and wedding band. Worse still, she had done it in front of Will. She and Roger had promised each other the day they married never to threaten each other with divorce. But that was exactly what she had done. How else could Roger interpret her action?

She heard the phone ring and then Roger's voice. A few moments later there was a knock on the door. Deenie unlocked it in a rush, ready to fling herself into his arms, to do whatever she could to make things better, but they were folded stiffly across his chest.

"My mother called and offered to keep the kids another day if we wanted," he said, his voice cold. "I told her that would be a good idea. We need to talk."

Deenie got dressed swiftly, her hands trembling in anxiety. What was he going to say to her? What was she going to say to him? Before going down to the kitchen, she got on her knees and prayed fervently for help and guidance.

Roger was sitting at the kitchen table crumbling a piece of toast on his plate when she entered. When he looked up at her, the anger in his eyes was shocking. The only thing she feared more than Roger's absence was his anger, and she had never seen him this angry before. She wanted to run away and hide, but she knew she had to see this through.

"This has got to stop, Deenie," he said.

"I agree," Deenie said, enormously relieved that he recognized the negative effect his absences were having on their family and especially on their relationship.

"I'm glad you do. Because I don't want you ever to get my father involved in our personal problems like you did last night. In case you've forgotten, I'm the head of this family."

"What?" Deenie stepped back in shock. They weren't on the same page after all. He didn't have a clue as to why she had done what she'd done.

Feeling the acid of conflict begin to roil in her stomach, she wondered if they were even on the same planet.

"Oh, I remember that you're the head of this family," she said bitterly. "I think you're the one who's forgotten."

Roger pushed away his plate in a gesture of disgust. "How can you say that? Everything I do is for the family."

I will be calm. I will be Gabby, Deenie repeated, as if it were a mantra against her anger. "I know that's what you believe. But you're providing us with what you think we need, not what we really we need."

"And what is that, exactly?" Again, his crossed arms seemed like a barrier to Deenie.

Okay, Deenie thought, *here goes.* "How about being home regularly for family home evening?"

Roger snorted. "This is all about family home evening? I'm here every Monday night I can be. And when I'm not, my folks help out."

"Yes, they do. But this is our family, not theirs. You should be presiding here, not your father. We should be the ones teaching them about the gospel. Our children should be bonding with each other and with us, not with stand-ins."

Roger stood up abruptly, scraping his chair noisily on the floor. "Are you saying that I'm not close enough to my own children?"

"Yes, I guess I am."

"That's not true! You know I love this family."

"I know you love us. And we love you. But a lot of things happen while you're away. The boys are changing daily. Carl is turning into a young man and boiling with questions he'll never ask me. And he sure as shootin' won't ask your father, either. He's going to turn to someone else. Who do you want it to be?"

Roger started to protest, but she forged ahead. "This is Bitsy's first year of school. She comes home every day with something new she's learned that she wants to tell you about, but by the time you get home, she's gone to bed. We can't schedule life's important moments around your studies. You have to be here!"

"You've gone a long way from being mad because I messed up last night."

"That was just the last straw."

Roger leaned against the counter. She could tell that under his anger, he was deeply hurt. "That's how it felt to me when you took off your rings and walked out on me. In front of my father. *And then you locked me out.*"

"I know I shouldn't have taken off my rings," she said, her voice contrite. "I *am* sorry about that. But I needed some way to get you to pay attention."

"Oh, it got my attention all right. What I don't understand is why you seem more angry over where I was than what I did. Like my career is some kind of threat to you."

"You don't understand it? Well, let me tell you. When you are home, you're in the study counting the minutes until you can leave again. It's like you save everything for the hours you spend at the university, even your conversation. What happened to you and me as a team, sharing how our days went? Working together around the house? Story time with our kids . . ." Deenie sputtered, at a loss for words.

Roger walked toward her, his arms outstretched. "Ah, Deenie girl. I had no idea you felt that way."

She stepped back, a warding hand keeping him at bay. "Are you joking? Are you nuts? *I've been telling you this for the last three years.* Haven't you been listening?"

"Apparently not." Roger looked at Deenie as if he had never seen her before. "But I'm listening now."

He might have been listening, but Deenie often thought in the next several hours that he still wasn't getting the message. Every time she tried to explain a point, he took it as an attack and immediately defended himself. Then she would protest and he would counterattack. They wore themselves out getting nowhere. They skipped lunch, and the argument continued. Finally, Roger sat down and said, "What do you need me to do that I'm not doing?"

"I need you to be home when you're home."

"What does that mean?" Roger was clearly at the end of his patience. "Tell me specifics."

"Okay. When you come home, put your briefcase and books in your office and don't go near them until the kids are in bed and you and I have had some time together."

"What if I have a deadline?" he asked.

"Then tell me, and we'll renegotiate. Unless it's on Monday nights. Then family home evening comes first."

"There's something I need from you, too. Don't expect me to guess what it is you want. Just tell me."

"Okay, from now on, I'll be precise about what I expect."

Roger ran his hand through his hair. "As long as we're clearing the air, Deenie, you ought to take a look at those expectations, especially the ones you have for yourself." He forged ahead, not giving her a chance to interrupt. "There have been plenty of times when I've wanted to talk to you, but you were too busy trying to perfect some project or another. How do you think that makes me feel?"

Deenie's eyelids stung. She had been so caught up in her own complaints she hadn't stopped to look at the situation from Roger's viewpoint. She was as responsible as he for the mess they were in.

As they talked sincerely and candidly to each other for the first time in years, they created a picture of how they wanted their family life to grow and change in the coming days and months. Deenie kept notes. By the time they finished, they were sitting on the couch. Roger's arm was around Deenie, and her head rested on his shoulder.

"Thank you so much for this," she said. "I'm sorry about last night."

Roger smiled down at her. "Then do you think it's time to put your rings back on again?"

Chagrined, Deenie fetched her rings and returned to his side.

"Do you want to do the honors?"

Gently he slid her wedding ring on her ring finger and then the engagement ring. Her heart overflowed with love. This renewed commitment was a sweet reflection of the first tender promises of forever they had made in the Logan Temple fourteen years ago. She had been so young, had known so little, and hoped for so much. Now she felt that hope reborn by his tender gesture. Deenie hugged him tightly. "No matter what's happened, I never stopped loving you."

"I love you, too," Roger said. Then he hesitated.

Deenie's heart sank. "What is it? What haven't you told me?"

Roger took both of her hands in his. "I was going to tell you last night at dinner, but I got sidetracked and then everything got so messed up. I've been accepted as a doctoral candidate at Utah State University." He paused. "I think I can make it work. I want to make it work."

Roger's expression was so sincere and hopeful it hurt Deenie to look at him. "Do you know what you're asking of all of us?"

"I can only guess. But I'm asking it of myself, too. And I'm willing to renegotiate anything that we agree isn't working. Okay? Are you willing to give it a try?"

She nodded, willing but afraid of what the future might bring.

Chapter Thirty-Five

JUNEAU

June 29, 1985
Dear Gabby, Willadene, and Erin,

If you've been worrying about why I haven't written, rest easy. It's just that I'm involved in another road show. Our Unbeatable Team is producing another winner, I think. My script this year is titled *The Pits*. It came about because I heard some seminary students wishing that a pit would open up in the parking lot so they could drop into it and sleep in the early morning. So guess what? That's what my show is about, a boy who wanders into The Pits and encounters . . . I'll leave that to your imagination.

A friend of Brother Waite wrote original music for all the songs, and Sister Waite designed fabulous costumes for the ghouls that our hero encounters. All the boys and a couple of the girls want to be ghouls. Of course it all works out okay in the end when our hero is challenged by the ghouls who say he's a chicken if he doesn't join up with them, but he tells them he'd rather be a chicken than a turkey. The last scene is him sitting happily in class in, what else, a chicken suit.

There is a lot of dancing, and Misty is proving to be a really good teacher. She isn't quite up to doing the choreography, but Sister Williams does that, and Misty takes it from there. I'm so pleased she's interested. I think it's the ghouls that she likes!!!!

I have another book in the works that Clyde, the man in Mrs. Jarvis's class, says will be a winner.

I've had a couple letters from my parents recently. When they left the San Diego area, where their last book was set, they went to Maine. Quite a difference. They said they hankered for the North Woods, so off they went. I prefer staying in one place most of the time. Some days The Wanders come to roost on my typewriter, but I seem to have conquered some of the restlessness I had in abundance in 1980 when we were in Provo. I should be grateful that it afflicted me then. Otherwise I would never have met you! Isn't it strange how things work out! At present I am quite happy in my half of the room Greg built. He's still trying to talk me into giving the computer a try, but so far I've resisted.

Wish us well with the road show. I enjoy doing that kind of thing so much that I'm wondering where it might lead me . . .

Love,
Juneau

ERIN

Thursday, July 4, 1985
Dear COBs,

Happy Independence Day!

I'm sitting on the couch with my feet up, watching fireworks on TV. We just got back from a picnic hosted by Cory's boss, Peter, and his wife, Barbara. It was more than a picnic; it was an event. I shouldn't have been surprised, given that he's the big kahuna at Behind the Scenes. They'd even hired high school girls to play games with the kids, so the adults could enjoy themselves without riding herd on their children.

I'm feeling good these days, but I get tired easily. I don't remember being this worn out when I was pregnant with Kayla, but I didn't have a two-and-a-half-year old to chase after. I'm wondering how I will manage when the baby's here.

No, I'm not doing too much. Colleen and I are focusing on getting ready for the Big Barn Sale in October. It's one thing we can do to build awareness of Finders that doesn't require much more time than we're putting in now.

Jake is going to bring some of his things out of storage for it and send out a mailing to his clients. He's such a nice guy. Last year when we had the sale, Colleen thought that he was interested in Mom. I thought so, too. He pays a lot of attention to her when-ever I invite them both to something, but I don't think they see each other in between. Neither has said anything to me, and I'm not going to ask!

My eyes are getting droopy. I'm going to pack it in.

Much love,
Erin

Cory came home for work one evening with an odd look on his face. He sat at the kitchen table and motioned to another chair. "Come sit beside me, Erin."

She hesitated a moment, during which a line of possible horrors crossed her mind. "In books, they always ask people to sit down for bad news."

"This isn't bad news. Just unexpected." He waited for her to pull up a chair beside him. "I wasn't going to tell you, but I guess it's the best thing to do. I met your father today."

Erin heard the words, but she couldn't make sense of them.

"He's a bigwig at an architectural firm Behind the Scenes is doing some work for. He was at a planning session I went to."

She still stared, speechless.

"He's a pleasant man, easy to talk to. His hair's red, but he's got a little gray, too, so it's not as bright as it probably was."

"Di . . . did you talk to him?"

"Sure. That's what I was there for. His firm got a big grant for an urban renewal project, a neighborhood of mid-range houses only a short drive from downtown Minneapolis. It will probably be in the paper one of these days."

"Does he know who you are?"

"You mean, does he know I'm the husband of the daughter he had with Joanna Larson? No. I could hardly introduce myself that way." He paused. "I met his other daughter. She's doing an internship at Dwyer Homes."

"His *other* daughter?" She knew she sounded stupid, but that was how she felt, as if she had lost her capacity to hear and understand.

He nodded. "Her name's Caitlin. You two look quite a bit alike. She's about your height and weight, and she has your coloring."

She started to rise. "I don't want to hear this. Why did you think I would?"

"He is your father. She is your sister."

"*Half* sister. I doubt if she knows I exist."

"What should I have done? Lie to you?"

She put her elbows on the table and rested her forehead on her hands.

"You should meet him, Erin. He's not a villain. No black hat anywhere in sight."

"Really?" She tipped her head to grin at him. "No horns?"

"Not a one. Come here." He took her hand and drew her onto his lap.

"I probably should meet him and get it over with. But let me do this in my own time, please."

So the next few days she scanned the newspaper every morning for an article about Dwyer Homes and the project. She found it in the business section on Sunday. She didn't have to read the caption below the black-and-white photograph—she knew instantly which face belonged to her father. It was a familiar face. She had seen the same square jaw and straight eyebrows every time she looked in the mirror.

"Who are you?" she asked the man in the photo. "What else do I have from you besides my face and hair?"

At that moment, Kayla came bounding in the kitchen and climbed up on a chair. "Hi, hi!" She reached for the colorful comics. "I read the paper, too. See?"

When Erin didn't pay any attention to her, she grabbed the paper Erin was holding and tore it right through the article and accompanying photograph.

"Kayla! Let go of that." she cried, prying the piece from her daughter's fingers. She tried to smooth it out, but Kayla was blubbering and Cory was yelling, "What's going on?" from the bedroom. In frustration she wadded both pieces up, threw them in the recycle box.

Late that night when Cory and Kayla were sleeping, she pawed through the box for the torn pages. She gently spread them as flat as she could and then ironed them between two sheets of white typing paper. When she had flattened them as much as possible without scorching them, she carefully matched the edges and taped the pieces together. The tear had missed her father's face, but it went right through his name. Although she was excruciatingly careful, she couldn't line it up the way it had been.

WILLADENE

September 14, 1985
Dear Ladies,

School has started again. This year the Streeter twins will be attending high school while Carl finishes his last year in middle school.

Even though they are in different schools, they still find time to hang together. Roger says that shows what good friends they are.

Bitsy is in second grade. I can hardly believe my baby is such a grown-up girl. She is doing so well in reading that she has been put in the fast group.

I am going to be a reading mentor for Bitsy's class and help with social studies in Paul's. I'm out of the loop where Carl is concerned. They hire teaching assistants in middle school. If I stay on the PTA board, maybe that will give me more access.

Roger and I have been married fourteen years! We've been looking at what changes we can make that would improve our family relationships. Scheduling is a big issue now that the kids are older and busier and Roger's been accepted as a doctoral candidate at the university. We've made family home evening and Friday date night our first priorities. The kids don't think we'll stick with it. I tell them to sit back and watch.

We'll have Thanksgiving at the Rasmussens' this year and Christmas Day at the Stowells'. I am hostess for Christmas Eve and that suits me fine. The Streeter clan will be joining up for the Christmas events. They have become a regular part of this family. I think I am even beginning to like Reece and Ryan. To the surprise of us all, they have taken Will's advice and are seriously hitting the books.

Roger is really missing Bert, now that she's off to UCLA to pursue her master's (and maybe more) in anthropology. Of all the Rasmussens, she's the one who understands his love of education, probably because she has it herself. He could use a visit from you, Jonas. And I'd love to see you, Gabby. The Harvest Festival is coming up the first week in October. Will you come?

Deenie

JUNEAU

September 20, 1985
Hi, Willadene,

Your mention of Bert being at UCLA prompted me to track her

down through the anthropology department and invite her to dinner. The campus in Westwood is only about thirty-five miles from here. It's right close to the temple, and since Greg and I try to go there at least once a month, we may be seeing her a few times before she finishes. I'll be really happy to meet her.

Love,
Juneau

ERIN

September 22, 1985
Dear COBettes,

We had our second annual Big Barn Sale, and it was absolutely fabulous. Between the ad in the classified section, our mailing, Jake's mailing, and the signs we put up, the place was a madhouse. There were people parked all up and down the road and on Colleen's lawn from 7:30 to 5. It was a smashing success.

I don't know if I told you that Grams has been working all year for the sale. She's been crocheting and knitting like mad. Afghans, mittens, hats, and scarves, all in really pretty colors. Mom sewed aprons and placemats. I think it's been good for them to have something to look forward to. Angie's husband, Norm, brought some of his carvings and Angie some of her stained glass. Paula Craig brought some of her framed photographs. It seems like everyone I know is so talented! My contribution to the day was running the cash register.

It took two days for Colleen and me to get all the finances figured out. After all was said and done, we each made a nice little pile of Christmas money. Paula says that even if we don't do anything but have the sale once a year, we can still consider ourselves successful.

Love,
Erin

P.S. You're probably wondering what is going on between Mom and Jake. When I know, I'll let you know.

JUNEAU

November 4, 1985
Dear Willadene,

Bert is such a delight! She came to dinner yesterday, and we had such a good time. The girls, especially Nicole, were dazzled by her anthropology stories. Nicky is back to wanting to be an anthropologist. She still wants to be a baton twirler (and she's pretty good at it now), but she says maybe she can be both since Miss Americas like to impress people with what they are studying.

In return for Bert telling us her great stories, Nicole offered a few of her Fascinating Facts. She asked if we knew that screech owls don't screech. They moan. Also that in the olden days, as she says, false teeth were kept in place by springs and that sometimes they sprang right out of people's mouths!

Well, anyway, she and Bert have become great friends. Thanks for having such an interesting relative.

Love,
Juneau

ERIN

November 18, 1985
Dear Ladies,

Thanks for your calls, dear friends. I hope I didn't say anything weird. I was still a little out of it. The labor was hard and fast. Mark Aaron Johnson was born just a couple of hours after we got to the hospital. He is an odd-looking little fellow. Long and skinny with white-blond hair and a funny old man look about him. But he's as good as gold, which is a blessing, because I'm feeling a little overwhelmed.

I guess that's understandable. I'm home alone all day with a totally dependent baby boy and a rambunctious toddler. Miss Kayla is almost three and very independent. She's into everything that's not nailed down or locked up, and she wants what she wants when she wants it. If it's not one of them howling for attention, it's the other. When they both howl at once, I want to hide.

Cory is in seventh heaven. He would have been happy with another little girl, but he's crazy about Mark. I know he's thinking ahead to playing ball and doing all the guy things men do with their sons. I saw a dad at a restaurant once who was teaching a little boy not more than one to give him a high five! That'll be Cory.

He wanted to take a week off after I got home, but his company is doing the Thanksgiving and Christmas parties for a couple who live on Wayzata's Gold Coast. Old flour-mill money, Pillsbury or General Mills, I think. He feels a bit over his head, but he's loving every minute of it.

The Johnsons are thrilled to have a boy to carry on the family name. Grams thinks the baby is sweet, but he hasn't captured her heart the way Kayla did when she was sick.

Cory will bless him the second Sunday in December. Harold and Trina will get off their mission to Nauvoo in time to be here for it. It's kind of sad that the Wagners aren't here. I hope they are looking down from heaven on Mark. Maybe they're his guardian angels. Except Mormons don't have guardian angels, do they?

Hope you have happy holidays,
Erin

JUNEAU

November 27, 1985
Dear Erin,

I think Mormons must have guardian angels. On the day after Thanksgiving, Abby, a good friend of Nicole's, invited her to go to the movies. Since we live less than a mile from one of the big theaters, they asked if they could walk there and then have Abby's mother pick them up after the movie was over. They are twelve now, and it was a bright sunny day, so we gave permission.

About twenty minutes after they left, a woman called to say the girls were at her house and we should come get them. We drove down the hill to get there faster. A police car arrived just after we did, and we all hurried inside—me, Greg, and the policeman.

We found two very frightened girls. A man in a van had pulled up alongside them and got out to ask if they'd seen a lost puppy. They'd had warnings about such things many times so they started to hurry away, but the man grabbed Nicole's arm and began pulling her toward the van.

Both girls screamed and fought, and fortunately a man who lives on that street was in his garage fixing his car. He came running out with a wrench of some kind in his hand and not only scared the guy off but also got his license number. He yelled for his wife to come take over the girls while he called the police. The upshot was two very frightened but safe little girls and one arrested slimy predator.

So I do believe Mormons, as well as others, have guardian angels. Some of them are right in our own neighborhoods!

I send loads of congratulations on your new little guy. I'm envious, but I guess I'd better forget about such things now that I'm pushing forty. Then again, they say life begins at forty. Who knows what's around the bend?

Love,
Juneau

WILLADENE

December 20, 1985
Dear Friends and Family,

Roger and I have taken our Christmas message this year from Doctrine and Covenants 42:45. "Thou shalt live together in love." We are striving to learn the habits of a godlike love as suggested in our Relief Society lesson for November. It is the kind of love, the lesson says, "that brings peace between people as well as peace of mind." It is a love without reason. Given freely. Pure, needing no justification other than it is the love the Master shows us. What better place to start practicing than with our families and in our homes.

As we have looked for ways to let the Spirit into our lives and love more, things have been getting better and better for our family this year.

Bitsy took part in her first spelling bee and placed second. Paul has been invited to attend a math camp at the university in the spring, and Carl is president of his deacons quorum. Roger has been accepted as a doctoral candidate at the university and is moving through his required classes with ease.

But more important than those achievements is our family's achievement in learning to put Christ in the center of our lives.

We are thankful for all the friends and family who have contributed to this change in our lives. You are a blessing to us, and we know it.

We would also like to share our testimony with you this Christmas season of the power of the word of God in our lives to help us be kinder and more loving. We also testify that the Word of God was made flesh and it is his birth we celebrate this day.

Thinking of you and all you are,
The Roger Rasmussen Family

Chapter Thirty-Six
1986

ERIN

January 2, 1986
Dear Ladies,

Belated Merry Christmas to you all. Enclosed you'll find some photos of the Cory Johnson family in our Christmas PJs. I got the idea from a sister in our ward who makes new PJs for her whole family every year. I bought ours. I'm afraid I created a monster, because Cory says we should do something similar every year.

The holidays are past, hurrah! I've been anxious and irritable ever since Mark was born. Grams and I were a pair this year. I had no interest in cooking or shopping, and I thought the idea of putting up the decorations just so we could take them down was ridiculous.

Cory was determined to celebrate in spite of me. He put up a tree and bought plain sugar cookies and supervised Kayla while she "decorated" them. He did the shopping and got all the packages wrapped before he left the stores. He turned on every TV holiday special he could find to see if he could cheer me up. (No, I didn't watch *It's a Wonderful Life!*)

Taking care of a new baby is tougher when you have a rambunctious toddler getting into everything. Cory says things will be slow at work from January to March, so he should be able to spend more time at home. I'm glad. I think I have a case of the baby blues, because I'm not very enthusiastic about anything, except maybe sleep.

Did any of you go through something similar?

Love,
Erin

Erin knew there was something wrong with her, but she didn't know what. Physically, she was fine, but emotionally and mentally, she was a mess.

Mark's birth before Thanksgiving had awakened all the old questions about her own birth—and all the old longings and insecurities. Who was she, really, deep in the blood and bones? What genes from her father nudged her toward certain behaviors without her even knowing it? What genetic propensities to disease were lurking in her body and now in the bodies of her children?

Christmas had poked other questions awake: Why did her grandmother resent her so? Why did her mother put up with Grams, when Grams was constantly complaining? Why was Grams compelled to top off Christmas celebrations with the accusation that her husband's fatal heart attack was Joanna's fault—and by extension, Erin's, too?

The three questions that the gospel was supposed to answer—Who am I? Where did I come from? and Why am I here? plagued her, and they never failed to bring up thoughts of her father. Images of him haunted her, floating like wraiths down the hallways of her mind, appearing when she least expected them.

When that happened, she felt like the truth of her life was that she was the illegitimate daughter of a man who didn't care about her, born to a mother who didn't protect her and a grandmother who hated her. She was neither wanted nor loved, simply tolerated.

The grown-up Erin knew that this was not true—at least not all of it, but at the beginning of 1986, the grown-up was not in charge. The self in charge was very young and wanted nothing more than to hide under the bed.

The bitter winds and dangerous roads the first two weeks of the month often made travel unwise, especially with a new baby. Erin seldom ventured out, alone or with the children—not even to church. With no place to go, there didn't seem to be any reason to get dressed for the day; she often was in her nightgown and bathrobe when Cory came home late in the evening. Not getting dressed made it seem as if the day really hadn't started, so she did her tasks in a desultory manner, curling up on the couch between taking care of Mark and pulling Kayla off the counter or away from the TV and VCR controls. Cory often came home to a messy house, no dinner, and Kayla tearing around the living room with wild hair and a dirty face, also still in pajamas.

When Colleen offered one day to pick up some things at the grocery store for her, Erin was more than glad to give her a list over the phone. She didn't say no when Colleen offered not only to bring the sacks of groceries in but to also help put them away and clean the kitchen.

"Are you okay?" Colleen asked. "I'm worried about you."

"I'm doing fine. I'm just a little tired." Erin looked away, not wanting to see in Colleen's eyes that her house was a mess and she herself was unkempt.

When the Relief Society president called to see if Erin would like the sister who had taught her Spiritual Living lessons since November to keep on for a while, it was an invitation to say yes—so she did.

Why did I do that? she wondered after hanging up. She had been looking forward to immersing herself in preparations, longing for the presence of the Spirit. It seemed so long since she had felt it. She reached for the phone and then hesitated. What if this was just a nice way of telling her that the sisters didn't want her to teach any more? Of course, that was it. She dropped her hand. They didn't want her. They didn't miss her or even care whether she was there or not. So why bother going to church at all?

And why bother go antiquing when she and Colleen didn't have any current requests? Jake, the antiques dealer who had encouraged them to start Finders, had warned them that January and February were slow. Going on hiatus until March seemed like a good idea to Erin.

Colleen didn't think so. "Even if we don't have any clients, getting out of the house would be good for you."

"Maybe, but I'm not really up to it."

"Erin, you're my friend, and I want to help you. Please tell me what I can do."

"Nothing, unless you can make me not be me."

"What does that mean?"

"I don't know. Forget it."

Erin hung up the phone and then went into the bedroom where Mark was asleep in his crib, his little bottom up in the air and his hands curled into fists. She smoothed his white-blond hair and kissed the back of his neck. *Who are you, little man?* she wondered. *How much of me do you have in you? And how much of that comes from my father—the unknown Mr. McGee.* Mr. McGoo, she almost said, which made her laugh as the image of the cartoon character came to mind.

A cartoon character. That's really what Andrew J McGee was—someone drawn in broad strokes with an exaggerated feature. The Red-Haired Catholic Boy.

Oh, Mark, she thought. *I hope you will be glad you were born. I hope you won't hate me.*

One night Cory came home after the children and Erin were all in bed. She woke to see him silhouetted in the light from the hallway as he hung up his suit jacket and took off his tie.

"Hi," she murmured.

"You awake?" There was something odd in his voice.

She sat up and turned on the bedside light. "Yes. Why?"

"We need to talk." He sat down on his side of the bed. "You've been kind of squirrely ever since Mark was born." He paused. "Have you got the baby blues? Or a holiday hangover from that thing you and The Women get?"

She felt her defenses rise. "That 'thing'?"

"You know what I mean. You may think it's normal, but it isn't."

"So?"

"I'm worried about you, and I don't know how to help you."

She turned away from him. "There's nothing you can do."

He didn't leave; she could hear him breathing. Finally he said, "My mom has been asking me when she can come see the kids. It might be a good idea to let her come over. Kayla needs some attention."

"If she needs attention, I'll give it to her."

The next morning, Erin forced herself to move. She was up and dressed before Cory left in the morning. She had a casserole in the oven by four o'clock so that he would have a decent meal when he came home. For several days she kept the dishes washed and the toys picked up. Then she started sagging. Each day she did less and less, until she was back where she was before.

In late February, Erin crawled out of bed in response to Cory's angry voice. "Hey, Erin! Get in here! I'm gonna be late for work."

"I'm coming, I'm coming." Erin pulled on her bathrobe and dragged herself into the kitchen. He stood by the door, impatiently shifting his weight from one foot to the other. Kayla held up her hands, begging to be released from the high chair.

"Sorry," she said. She took Kayla out of the high chair and held her up to Cory's height. "Give Daddy a kiss good-bye." She could see Cory relax as Kayla leaned toward him with puckered lips. "Bye, bye, baby," he said, chucking her under the chin. "Be a good girl for Mommy." He turned to go and then turned back. "Try to pull yourself together, Erin. We can't go on like this much longer."

"What do you want me to do?"

"Are you kidding? Look around you. The house only gets cleaned when your mother or I do it. I can never find a clean shirt when I need one, and the kitchen is always a mess. You never go anywhere, not even to church. You don't read your scriptures or say your prayers." She could see condemnation in his eyes. "And what's worse, you neglect our children."

A cry escaped her lips. She started to protest, but Kayla's wild curls and dirty sleeper stopped her words.

"Something has to change, and soon, or . . ."

Fear clutched Erin's heart. "Or what?"

He shook his head, disgust distorting his handsome features. "I don't know." He slammed the door behind him when he left.

He's going to leave me! thought Erin wildly, the sound of the door slamming reverberating in her ears. *He's going to get a divorce and take the children. What can I do?*

She walked back and forth in the kitchen, sobbing and wringing her hands. Then it occurred to her that if she cleaned the house and had supper waiting for him, he wouldn't be so mad. *Yes!* she thought. *That's what I'll do.* She looked up to see Kayla standing in the doorway and changed her mind. *No, I have to take care of Mark and Kayla first. He can't think I neglect them.*

She got Mark fed, changed, and dressed in a clean sleeper. She washed Kayla's face and tried to tame her curls. In frustration, she dampened Kayla's hair and trimmed it, Kayla howling in protest through the process. Then she tackled the house. She cleaned like a mad woman, sobbing as she worked, muttering to herself under her breath as her thoughts went down a destructive slide.

No wonder he wants to leave me. He doesn't love me; nobody ever has. My father doesn't care. Grams hates me. Mom probably didn't even want to have me, but she didn't have any other choice. I don't know why I'm doing this. A clean house won't make him love me.

But fear kept her moving forward. Noon came and went. She caught up with the laundry, folding load after load. She made a pot of chili and let it simmer while she made corn bread to go with it. In between these tasks, she cared for Mark and tried to keep Kayla from fretting. Exhausted, she took a shower and dressed. Everything was ready. Now all she had to do was wait and pray.

Then she looked at herself in the mirror. Her eyes were red and puffy, and her sweat suit strained over the rolls of baby fat. *No wonder he can't stand me*, she thought. *I can't stand myself.* She wasn't even sure what she was doing when she dialed her mother's number at the heating company where she was office manager. When Joanna answered, she said simply, "Mom. I need you."

She didn't answer the door when Joanna knocked. She was curled up in a blanket on the couch. Mark and Kayla were napping in their room.

Joanna opened the door. "Erin?" she called.

"In here."

"What happened? What's wrong? Where are the kids?"

"The kids are fine," Erin said in a tired voice. "But I'm not." She choked on a sob. "Cory doesn't love me anymore."

Joanna dropped down on the couch beside her. "Whatever gave you that idea?"

"He said so."

"I can't believe that. What did he say exactly?"

"He said I was neglecting my children and myself. He said something had to change or else." She looked pleadingly at Joanna. "Can't you see? He was trying to tell me that he's thinking of getting a divorce."

"No, he wasn't honey. He loves you; I know he does. He's just worried about you. So am I." She reached out to touch Erin's cheek. "Erin dear, something's been different ever since Mark was born, and I don't mean the difficulty you've had keeping up with the house. What is it?"

Erin snorted. "Cory says it's 'that thing you and The Women get at Christmas.' Isn't that funny?"

"Is that what's bothering you? The family Christmas crisis?"

Erin shrugged. "You tell me."

"Erin, you called me because you needed me. Don't play games now."

"That's part of it, I guess," Erin said, her head turned so she wouldn't have to look in Joanna's eyes. "I don't know why, but I always feel so sad and guilty during the holidays, like I'm to blame for everything that goes wrong. And I get nervous, like something awful is about to happen." She took a deep breath. "But the worst is knowing that I don't deserve my husband and family. I'm not good enough."

"You are good enough," said Joanna fiercely. "You deserve to have a wonderful life."

"How can that be true when I made Gramps die?"

"What?" Joanna forced Erin to look at her. "What did you say?"

"I made Gramps die. How did I do that, Mom? I don't remember, but I must have done something, because Grams always says it's my fault."

"It's not your fault!" Joanna paused and then said simply, "It's my fault."

"But how . . ."

"You remember when we went to the park when you were four?"

Erin nodded. With her eyes closed, she could see in her mind's eye the dark leafless trees standing in stark contrast to the white snow. As if she were there, she could feel her cheeks tingling, hear the sounds of people having fun, smell the hot dogs grilling at the concession stand. Then, for the first time, she could see her father standing there, his hands stuffed deep in the pockets of his plaid wool coat. He had sober blue eyes under straight eyebrows, a wide mouth and strong jaw. His hair was like her own, bright and unruly, and permanent freckles stood out on his cold cheeks . . .

Suddenly Erin's eyes popped wide open. "Was that when . . . You mean while we were at the park, Gramps . . ."

"Yes." Joanna's voice was clogged with emotion. "That was when he had the massive heart attack that took him away from us."

Now memories flooded her mind. Erin was happy she was on the way home, admiring her pink pony, not minding that her mother was oddly silent. Then they turned the corner onto their street, and her mother let out a cry and began running. Frightened, Erin tried to keep up, her boots slipping on snow and ice.

When she caught up with her mother, she was sucked into a maelstrom of fear and anger. Men were pushing some sort of cart down the walk with Gramps on it. Grams was running behind it, shrieking, trying to follow when they put the cart into the ambulance. A uniformed man told her mother to follow in her own car to University Hospital. Then the ambulance driving off with lights flashing, siren howling.

But Grams was shrieking even louder. Her wild eyes frightened Erin. She clutched onto Erin's mother's coat tightly. "Where were you? Why did you leave him alone?" Grams cried.

When her mother didn't answer, Erin said timidly, hoping to make things better, "We went to the park. A nice man gave me a present. See?" She held the pony out proudly.

Grams turned to Joanna, hate blazing from her eyes. "It was him, wasn't it? You were with that boy when your father had another attack. He was lying on the floor when I came home, lying on the floor in pain while you were . . ." She was trembling with fear and rage. "If anything happens to your father, I'll never forgive you."

Slowly, Erin told her mother what she had remembered. "Is that right, or am I just making it up?"

Joanna nodded. "Pretty close, especially the last part. Your grandmother never has forgiven me. Or you. In her mind, our going to the park to meet Andy caused Gramps's death." Joanna sighed, and her shoulders slumped. "She may be right."

"What do you mean?"

"If I had been home when he had the attack, the paramedics would have gotten there a lot quicker. Every second counts in situations like that. And while he was lying helpless on the floor, you and I were drinking hot chocolate. With the Red-Headed Catholic boy."

Erin reached for her mother. "It was an awful coincidence, Mom. You can't blame yourself."

"But I do. I've let Grams torture us Christmas after Christmas, hoping one day she would have her pound of flesh and forgive me. Then I could forgive myself. Now I see that will never happen." She looked at Erin, her eyes brimming with tenderness and regret. "Listen to me, Erin. None of this is your fault. I made some choices, and I've had to live with the results. But you're not to blame for anything that happened then. Do you hear me? You were a sweet, innocent little girl who got caught in the middle."

She drew Erin into her arms and rocked her as if she were a child. "There's nothing wrong with you, my sweet girl," she crooned. "You are wonderful just as you are. I love you so much. I am so glad you came to be my daughter. You deserve all the good and wonderful things in life, and you don't have to be perfect to have them. There, there."

There was a sound at the door. Erin looked up to see Cory standing there.

"Do you still love me?" she asked. "Are you going to leave me?"

"Oh, Erin." He traded places with Joanna, cradling her in his arms. "I'm sorry I yelled at you this morning. I didn't understand what was going on until I heard what you and your mother were talking about. I'm not like your father. I love you. I want you. I'll never leave you. You don't ever have to worry about that. We're a family, and we will be, now and forever."

Chapter Thirty-Seven

JUNEAU

In January of 1986 the space shuttle *Challenger* blew up on takeoff from its launch pad in Florida. The entire crew, plus Christa McAuliffe, the first schoolteacher to be shot into space, died.

Juneau, along with all other citizens of the world, was horrified, and Nicole was totally devastated. Her science class in junior high had been closely following the program Mrs. McAuliffe had planned to present while circling the earth. She came home from school red-eyed and weepy.

"Mama," she wailed, "why would God let such an awful thing happen?"

Juneau had been wondering the same thing. So many people had been praying for the safety of the *Challenger* crew. So much planning had gone into the mission. The crew had trained for months. Thousands of scientists had been involved in checking every aspect of the flight. What, then, had happened? Despite all the precautions, something had gone wrong.

"I don't know, sweetie," she said.

Nicole snuffled and sobbed. "Remember when Ronnie Parker's puppy got lost, and he prayed and asked God to find it? Then they were looking in the park, and it came running out from some bushes. If God has time to find a puppy, how come he didn't have time today to take care of the *Challenger?*"

Juneau remembered the discussion she and Willadene and Erin had had in the cemetery in Logan a few years before. "Bad things happen," she told Nicole. "We don't know why."

"But where was God when they needed him?" Nicole cried.

Philip Atwater got up from his place on the floor and came over to put his muzzle up near Nicole's face, as if to comfort her. She wrapped her arms around his neck and buried her face in his fur.

Feeling her way, Juneau said, "Honey, he was there, and I'm sure he felt bad that the *Challenger* blew up. But a long time ago he gave us our agency, which means we can make mistakes. We don't know yet what happened with the *Challenger*, but very likely somebody made a mistake in something that made the booster rocket blow up."

When Nicole didn't answer, she went on. "We all need God to help us get through this. He'll help you, if you ask him to, Nicky."

Nicole shook her head. "I don't like him very much right now. I don't want to ask him for anything."

For a week she stubbornly refused to say her prayers or to take part in the family prayers, during which she went to her room. Greg said she'd get over it. But Juneau was worried. And feeling guilty again. Why wasn't she better prepared to explain why bad things happen to good people? On the other hand, could anybody explain it any better?

February 12, 1986
Dear COBS,

I have decided that when I came to earth somebody forgot to give me the manual. There must be some kind of instruction book for life, isn't there? I'm sure you're as wiped out about the *Challenger* disaster as we are. It hit Nicole especially hard, and she blamed God for it all and said she didn't want anything to do with him. But she came to me yesterday and said she missed him too much and wanted to know if it was all right if she apologized. She said, "He knows how bad we feel. He had to watch his very own Son die." Sometimes I think she did get a manual when she came.

I couldn't help but think of one of the Spiritual Living lessons we all gave back in 1984 titled "Humility: Key to Spiritual Progress." I feel so humble right now that I think I must have progressed a baby step!

I hope all is well with you. Things are kind of okay here. Misty has been sneaking out of her window again, after we thought she was safely in bed. She was grounded and denied access to the computer for two weeks, which brought her to her senses a little, I hope. I can't help but wonder what her next transgression will be. We try so hard to keep her in line, but somehow we just don't seem to connect.

Speaking of the computer, Greg talked me into trying something on it last week. It was fun to just type away without worrying about throwing the carriage, but it all seemed so very complicated. I don't plan to get that close to it again.

Please pray for Misty. Please pray for me. Pray for us all.

Love,
Juneau

WILLADENE

The Christmas snow in Cache Valley was soft and fluffy, drifting wonderland high and frosting the trees. But when the February winds swept down the hills, the snow turned to stinging beads cold enough to burn the face and snatch away breath.

"It's mighty cold this year, but not as cold as it could be!" claimed Wilford Rasmussen.

Grandpa Stowell said it wasn't really cold until your spit froze before it hit the ground. And Nana Lewis had always maintained that if the burp in your throat turned to ice it was time to stay inside. Everyone had a distinctive definition of what was "too cold."

For Deenie "too cold" meant the snow squeaked when you walked on it and crusted over rather than drifted, and pipes froze unless you left water dripping all night. When that happened, she waited for the bus with the kids inside the van and the motor running to keep them warm. The bus stop was at the end of the block.

Today was that kind of day and more. With the winds whipping the snow through the air, visibility was minimal. Roger made sure the van would start for Deenie and then left early for work. Deenie, knowing he would be fighting the slippery roads and the blinding snow all the way, checked the car emergency kit and sent him off with a thermos of hot chocolate in case he got stalled.

When Deenie returned home from seeing the kids from warm car to bus, she noticed the front steps and porch hadn't been shoveled. Determined to finish the job she could tell Roger had started, she went inside, double-layered socks and gloves, pulled Roger's ski hat down over her head, and tied Carl's old neck scarf up over her mouth and nose. She was well protected but could barely see where she was going.

Sweeping off the sheltered front porch wasn't too bad, but the stairs filled with drifting snow as fast as she cleared them. Deenie grumbled as she forced the unwieldy snow shovel back and forth across each elevation. "Stupid weather, stupid snow, stupid shovel!"

Her eyes were watering from the cold, she missed seeing the bucket of rock salt wedged in the corner of the stairs and caught her pants on its torn edge. Thrown off balance, she tumbled down the stairs, landing in an awkward pile with one leg bent beneath her.

"Dang it," came first. "For Pete's sake," came as she struggled to get her footing. Then, when she tried to put weight on her right ankle and fell again, out came all the words she forbade the children to use.

Biting her lip against the pain, Deenie crow-hopped into the house. The sharp tingling of her fingertips and toes as they warmed added to the agony of pulling the boot and sock off her hurt ankle. Silent tears rolled down her cheeks as she took the maximum aspirin she dared, packed the ankle with ice, and elevated her foot.

As she sat there, she became consumed with the fear that if she didn't get the walk completely clear, someone else would take a bad tumble. So after her ankle was numb enough to move with minimum pain, she wrapped it in an Ace bandage, bundled up again, and finished the job. Then she hobbled, huffing, puffing and muttering, back in the house for another round of ice-aspirin-ice.

She couldn't sit and do nothing, however. So she prepared stew while she iced her ankle, peeling vegetables at the kitchen table, her foot elevated and layered with a package of peas and a package of corn from the freezer. By three o'clock everything was simmering in beef broth, and it was time for her to warm the car and pick up the kids.

When Bitsy noticed her shuffling gait, Deenie told her it was "Mommy's cold-weather walk." The men in the house were oblivious. So Deenie went about her daily tasks, hobbling on an ankle that protested every step she took. Apirin held the pain down some but not enough. Twelve days passed before Deenie finally admitted to herself that her ankle wasn't going to get any better unless she simply got off her feet.

She hobbled to the fridge and opened the freezer, longing for the relief numbness would bring. But there was no ice. After a moment's thought, she assembled what she needed: snow-filled towels rolled into tubes, a plastic mat, and a bucket.

She put the bucket atop a plastic mat in front of her favorite chair, grabbed a Shoebox book, and lit the fireplace. Once in the chair, she settled her now snow-packed ankle over the bucket to catch the melting snow. She figured by the time it melted completely, her ankle would be happily numb. Relaxing deeply into the cushions, Deenie yawned. The book slipped from her fingers. She snuggled under an afghan and drifted off to sleep to the crackling of the fire.

Regina was magnificent in her defiance. She stood straight and tall before the tribunal. Her bare feet were blue with cold, her belly rumbling with hunger. Her hands were tied together so tightly, her wrists were bleeding from the force. She longed for freedom, but she refused to tell them her secret. Without deliberation they condemned her to the flame.

Out in the courtyard the crowd gathered for the spectacle of a noble woman embracing such a searing death. As the fire crackled and smoked, a resounding howl of "Noooooooo!" stilled the yelling of the peasants.

Through the crowd he came, seated on his raging stallion, Fabio. Reginald, the hero of her heart and of the rebellion. He swept her into his arms and away from the inferno.

"Really, darling," he whispered as they raced for freedom. "When I said I wanted you to burn for me, this isn't what I had in mind."

Deenie awoke shivering and wet to the sound of someone kocking on the door. It opened, and Pat Crafton called, "Deenie, you home?"

"In the family room," she answered.

"Sweet heavenly days," Pat gasped as she walked into the room. "What have you done to your foot?"

"It looks worse than it is."

"Then it must feel absolutely rotten! What on earth are you doing?" Pat demanded as Deenie struggled to her feet.

"I've got to get these wet jeans off and pick up the kids."

Pat looked at her as if she were crazy. "Don't be ridiculous. You're not going anywhere."

By the time Deenie had changed clothes, taken another dose of aspirin and made new ice rolls, Pat was back with the kids. Deenie could tell by the looks on their faces that they had received a talking to from "Aunt" Patty about helping their mother. Bitsy laid her head on Deenie's shoulder and started to cry. "I'm sorry, Mommy," she sniffled. "I didn't know you were hurt."

"But now that you all know," Pat countered briskly, "let's see what you can do to help out."

With Pat in charge, Deenie allowed herself the luxury of dozing. She woke up almost two hours later to hear Roger hollering from the back door.

"Hey, what's going on here?" His voice was friendly. Deenie could hear him stomping the snow off his shoes.

"Deenie's in bad shape with that ankle of hers."

"What ankle, what's wrong?" Roger came into the living room. When he saw her ankle resting above the bucket, he burst out laughing.

"It's actually not funny," Pat said, coming up behind him. "Just look at this." Against Deenie's protests, she unwrapped the ankle to show him the sickly greenish-yellow old bruising and the brighter maroon new. "She's probably reinjured it several times since she sprained it," she said.

"Deenie! When did this happen?"

"Almost two weeks ago. When I was shoveling the steps during the big snow."

She looked at him for sympathy, but what she got was anger. "You've been walking on this ankle for two weeks?"

"I didn't know what else to do. You were in Logan. I didn't want my mom driving on those slippery roads, or your mom either. The Relief Society was already overextended, helping older sisters who couldn't get out in the bad weather. I did what I thought was best for everybody."

"Not everybody, Deenie." He sat down beside her and took her hands in his. "I wish you would have told me. Keeping secrets isn't a good idea, especially when it comes to your health."

"It wasn't that much of a secret." Her voice was sharper than she had meant it to be. "Bitsy noticed I was favoring this leg. Why didn't you?"

He didn't defend himself, as she had expected. He knelt down by the recliner and wrapped his arms around her. "You're right, Deenie girl. I should have noticed. I've had my nose to the grindstone lately. Can't see much from that position." He paused. "I'll make some phone calls and line up some help. And first thing in the morning, we're going to the doctor."

"He'll just say to stay off my feet."

"Well, maybe if he does, you'll actually do it. Deenie. Promise that if anything like this happens again, you'll tell me."

Deenie hugged Roger tightly in response and lifted her face for his kiss. She loved that he apologized, that he cared, and that he was willing to share the burden at home. But she didn't promise, and he didn't notice. Even as he tucked her in, she was still convinced staying silent had been the right choice.

WILLADENE

March 12, 1986
Dear Ladies,

I have lived through—and recovered from—a four-point landing at the bottom of a snowy stairway and my first honest-to-goodness sprained ankle. Like an idiot, I walked around on it too long before admitting I was hurt, but once Roger found out, he took over managing the house and kids.

Miss Bitsy has the makings of a fine nurse, but I think I'll keep that a secret for a while. If my Aunt Stella found out, she would be jumping at the bit wanting to start training Bitsy as a midwife. We can't have that.

Roger is pushing hard on his research as well as his classes. He plans to track down early school records on-site in the Four Corners area this summer if he can get the time. I said that sounded like a vacation to me and we should all go. He didn't answer, but he smiled so I'm not giving up!

That's all for now.

> Hope all is well east, west, and
> south of us,
> Deenie

P.S. If you haven't heard, Bryan has been made assistant to the president and has been transferred to the mission home in Charlotte. Gabby says Bryan loves working with the mission president, but he misses being in the field and teaching the gospel. He isn't the boy we first met at Gabby's house. Neat, huh!

JUNEAU

April 19, 1986
Dear Willadene, Erin, and Gabby,

You know the old thing about "life begins at forty?" I'm about to see how much truth there is to that. I don't know if I can handle it, if it gets more intense than it is right now!

Not that there's anything new to report. Well, yes, there is. Flint's wife, Valerie, called to say that he was in Tripoli when the U.S. bombed it a few days ago in retaliation for the Libyan terrorist bombing of that disco in Germany where there were a lot of U.S. military men. Flint got a small nick from shrapnel or something, but he's okay. I'm worried, though, because now I know for sure he's not just a drill sergeant. I wish he'd tell us what he's doing. But maybe he can't.

Take care of your dear selves.

> Love,
> Juneau

ERIN

Mother's Day, 1986

Hello, COBs-in-the-Making and Grand COB Gabby,

I bet you didn't know that Mother's Day and the start of fishing season are on the same day in Minnesota. I wonder how many women end up by celebrating themselves while their men are out on one of the ten thousand lakes trying to snag a fish to bring home for supper!

This Mother's Day, I had twice the reason to celebrate. Mark and Kayla are both doing fine, and so am I. Thanks for the calls, all of you. I guess a long silence after the letter I wrote at New Year's wasn't such a good idea. I should have known you'd be worried about me. I had a bad time after Mark was born, but I'm much better now. It's taken lots of determination, prayer, and hard work to climb out of the pits. Some days I still would rather pull the covers over my head, but I don't ever want to get as low as I was. It's too difficult to get back up.

Mom and I had an incredible conversation that helped turn things around. And Colleen told me that back when I was visiting after EJ was born, she was going through the baby blues herself. I had no idea. By the way, she's pregnant and due in October! Isn't that wonderful news?

One thing I've learned through this is when you get into a funk, you lose your connection to the Spirit. I knew I was getting better when I had that unmistakable warm glow in my heart for the first time in a long time. I'd let someone take over teaching Spiritual Living for several months, but I'm going to teach the lesson in June. I love the time I spend reading the lesson and the scriptures with Mark cuddled to my shoulder.

Well, that's the news from Lake Wobegon, where the women are strong, the men are good-looking, and all the children are above average. (I think that's the way Garrison Keillor says it at the end of *The Prairie Home Companion*.)

I love you guys,
Erin

Chapter Thirty-Eight

WILLADENE

Deenie hadn't had a single problem that she could refer to as a Dead Chicken or even an Almost Dead Dog since the sprained ankle incident early in the year. She knew it was because she had accepted that Roger's increasing absences were just the way things were going to be for a while and not an unsolvable problem. The incidents she would normally find maddening were all tempered with her delight in planning the first Rasmussen family vacation that wouldn't take place at the Rasmussen cabin near Bear Lake.

It was going to be a real vacation, with takeout food and motels to sleep late in. It was still a jeans and T-shirt kind of vacation, but Deenie ironed those T-shirts and jeans, got a shorter, easy-care haircut, and bought a new bright lipstick to honor the occasion. Everyone seemed excited by the prospect of such a rare treat, except Carl.

June 1, 1986
Dear Ladies,

Guess what? We are going on vacation! It's a working vacation for Roger, who will be checking out some early Mormon records for his research. The rest of us will get to see all the sights in the Four Corners area, a lot of color country, and ancient Native American dwellings like Mesa Verde and Hovenweep. It's the first time we've gone away for any length of time as a whole family.

Except, as of today, it's not exactly the whole family. Carl is staying on the farm to work.

It was hard to take when he first announced he'd rather stay and spend time with the twins and his gramps than go with us. I'm still a little leery about him spending time with the twins, especially while we're gone. They've become more reliable workers, but they play as hard as they work, and getting into trouble is just a game to them.

He'll be okay, I guess. Pat and Grandma Streeter both say they'll watch out for the boys while we're gone. Grandma Rasmussen, too. Maybe this is just the first step in letting him grow up.

My mailman is starting to worry about the way I look at his bag with longing. So grab a pen and paper and bring me up to date.

Deenie

The Rasmussen family vacation passed swiftly. It was everything Deenie hoped it would be, but she learned soon enough to think of those lovely two weeks away as the calm before the storm.

When they arrived home, an Almost Dead Dog problem loomed at every corner. NeVae had fallen on the cellar steps and broken her wrist.

Though the wrist fracture itself was more inconvenient than serious, any fall for a seventy-two-year-old woman was cause for concern. Deenie found NeVae with her right arm strapped across her chest to stabilize her wrist, every one of her seventy-two years written on her face. Deenie thought she had never seen a sorrier sight.

Bert had flown home to help, but her announcement that she had been selected to go on a two-month research trip to Africa was a bigger blow to NeVae than the broken wrist. And the cold Deenie's own mother had been nursing before the trip had turned into a nasty case of bronchial pneumonia.

"She's doing much better now," her father assured her. "Sunny's been quite the little nurse, and the Relief Society has been bringing over food. But they can't match you for a good meal, Deenie. We sure would appreciate it if you'd bring over something. A couple of times this week would do."

Deenie immediately added that to her to-do list. It didn't seem any imposition, really, since she was making chicken and rice for her family and NeVae's as well. Another cup of rice and two more chicken breasts wasn't much trouble at all.

That's two, Deenie thought as she worked. *If trouble comes in threes, what's next?*

She was sliding the casserole dish in the oven when Roger charged into the house dragging Carl behind him. Seeing Roger's face, she knew she was about to find out what trouble number three was. "Another dead chicken?" she asked with an attempt at lightness.

"Nothing so easy." Roger said shortly. "Carl and the twins have had quite a time while we were gone. They set off a bunch of firecrackers under

Leila Jeffrey's bedroom window at four o'clock in the morning and broke into the Wilsons' barn."

"Carl!"

"It's not that big a deal, Mom," Carl said, his expression pleading for understanding. "We were just goofing off after work. We worked really hard. Even Gramps said so."

"How did you get in it? The Wilsons haven't used that barn for years. It's locked up tight, doors and shutters."

"How do you think?" Roger's fury made him rude. "They broke in." He shook Carl by the shoulders. "Disturbing the peace, malicious mischief, and breaking and entering. You're heading for real trouble, young man." Roger turned to Deenie. "When Dad went to pick Carl up at the station, Fenton laid it on the line to him and Pat. He said he had a real job that didn't include babysitting the boys and if we didn't get them under control, the state would."

Deenie gasped. "What did he mean by that?"

"It's possible that if the Wilsons and Sister Jeffrey hadn't been willing to work this out with the boys personally, all three of them could have spent a night behind bars."

"Carl!" Deenie sank to the nearest chair. "What were you thinking!" Then she saw from Roger's face that there was something more. She was almost afraid to ask, but she did. "What else."

"Dad has banned the twins and Carl from the farm. Until they can show they are trustworthy, he doesn't want to see hide nor hair of them."

Dealing with Carl's misbehavior made Deenie feel as if they were back to square one in the summer of the Dead Chicken. Paul sided with his older brother, dismissing his misdemeanors as "no big deal." Bitsy heightened the tension by deciding that boys were nasty and refusing to have anything to do with either of her brothers, and Roger was unexpectedly swamped with work at the university.

Deenie felt swamped, herself. She felt she should be doing something for NeVae and Margaret, but their situations paled in comparison to the mess Carl had gotten himself into. She was his mother; he needed to be her first priority.

She went down to talk to Pat, thinking that since their boys were in trouble together, they would be allies in solving the problem.

She couldn't have been more wrong. Pat greeted her coolly, opening the door only partway and leaving Deenie standing awkwardly on the porch.

When Deenie suggested that the two of them could work together disciplining the boys, Pat's response was quietly furious. "I've listened to all the criticism of my sons that I can take. Everyone thinks it's all their fault. We both know that's not true."

Hurt, Deenie blurted out the first thing that came to mind. "Carl never got into trouble until they came along."

"Must be nice to be a perfect family," Pat said, speaking through the screen door. "And so willing to help out those of us who are less than perfect. But that's pretend, isn't it? If your family was all that worried about helping the twins out, Will wouldn't have banned them from doing the one thing they took pride in."

Before Deenie could respond, Pat quietly but firmly shut the door.

Deenie could hardly think as she drove out to the farm to talk to Will. He was glad enough to see her when she found him turning water from a ditch onto a bean field, but Deenie could tell he was worried about his wife and overworked, now that he was shorthanded on the farm.

He shook his head wearily when she told him of her concerns for the boys. "I've got too much on my plate right now to ride herd on those boys, Deenie. That's up to you and Roger. And Pat."

When she asked him what the boys had to do to come back to work, he restated his conditions: offer formal apologies to everyone they had harmed or offended and make any restitution their victims might deem necessary.

Deenie watched him turn back to the field, knowing that she would be the one who had to make sure Carl followed through.

Several days later, she asked Roger for more help supervising Carl. He leaned back in his office chair and said, "I've already told him we'll be having father-son talks every Sunday evening, and I'll be checking during the week to see if he's doing what you tell him to do. But as far as the day-to-day goes . . . Honey, I'm sorry, but this is one of those times you're going to have to do it on your own. You know I have to get this work done before the school year starts."

Deenie leaned against the door frame, wondering if this was Roger's idea of negotiation. There wasn't anything she could say, so she did what had worked for her in the past. She buried her feelings as deep as she could and got on with it. She kept Carl loaded with chores and monitored him from sunup to sundown until he capitulated to Will's demands. She stood by him when he apologized to Sister Jeffrey and drove him to Dry Lake to face the Wilsons and oversaw the process of reboarding a third of their barn door.

During this time, either Reece or Ryan called every day, trying to convince Deenie to let them talk to Carl. She remained firm in her refusal. "You're not allowed to talk to him until you apologize and finish the Wilsons' barn door," she repeated time and time again.

If the twins were pestering her, Pat was avoiding her. There were no phone calls, no walks around the block, no sharing of laughter while rocking on the front porch.

Shortly after another round of phone calls from the twins and refusals from Deenie, Deenie got a call from her mother.

"Dear, I know how hard this has been on you. But it's been as hard on Patience. I see it every day at work. Each time you come down on her boys, they act out with her. Couldn't you ease up just a bit for her sake?"

Deenie closed her eyes and bit down on her tongue to keep from blowing up. "Sure, Mom," she said sweetly. "I can give it a try."

I've added lying to secret keeping, she thought as she hung up the phone. *What kind of a person am I becoming? A secret-keeping, lying, resentful, paranoid person, that's what! And I'm so afraid for Carl, I can hardly stand to have him leave the house. What if something worse happens and we lose him altogether?*

ERIN

Erin sat on the tiny patio in the backyard of their St. Louis Park home watching her children play. Kayla was helping ten-month-old Mark push his plastic trucks in a game only they could understand. She smiled contentedly. She loved those two little creatures more than she had ever thought possible.

The moment was especially sweet, because everything in her life was working. The house was clean, and the laundry caught up. She had begun work on this month's Relief Society lesson in plenty of time to prepare it the way she felt she needed to. She was happy with how her relationship with Cory was going. They didn't have enough time alone, what with two young children, but Cory always knew how to make her feel loved—a surprise night out, flowers delivered to their doorstep, his coming home in time to eat supper with her and the kids.

She closed her eyes and said, "Thank you, Lord. Thank you." Then she crossed her fingers, hoping that this moment of contentment might last.

Two weeks later, Cory came home early with a gleam in his eyes. He set down his briefcase and gave Erin a resounding kiss.

She was smiling as she turned back to stirring the spaghetti sauce that was supper this evening. "What's got you going?"

"Hold onto your hat. Dad's found us a new house!"

Her breath caught, and she stopped stirring. "What?"

"He says it's everything we've ever wanted, and it's in their neighborhood."

"What are you talking about?"

"You know Dad and his connections. He heard that this place was going on the market at a fantastic price—it was repossessed by the bank or something like that. We're supposed to meet the realtor there at 7:00 tonight. Come on, let's get the kids fed so we can get there on time."

When she didn't move, he put his arm around her. "Hey, where's that smile? This isn't tragic, you know."

"Cory, just because your dad suggested we look at this house doesn't mean we have to."

"I know. But I want to."

When Cory pulled up in front of a house on a gracious, tree-lined street five minutes from downtown Edina, Skipp and Linda were already standing on the steps with the realtor, a stout older man impeccably dressed.

"What are your parents doing here?"

"Dad wanted to see the place himself, since it was his idea, and Mom's going to entertain the kids so we can take our time." He craned his neck so he could see it from the car. "It is beautiful, isn't it?"

Erin nodded. She knew this house. It was only blocks from the Johnsons' home, and she and Linda had gone by it when taking the kids for walks. A classic Prairie design with detached garage, the house sat on its lot like a hen on its nest, settled and protective. It was larger than the house they were currently in, but not extravagantly so, and the exterior and yard were in immaculate condition.

Now Linda was at the car door, reaching for Mark. "Isn't this exciting?" she gushed. "Imagine us being just around the corner from each other. When the kids are older, they'll be able walk over to visit their grandma and grandpa. Won't you, Markie?" She chucked Mark under the chin. "Come on, Kayla. Let's go see your new house."

"This isn't our new house, Kayla," Erin said sharply.

Linda shot her an odd look and then herded the kids toward the house.

"Your mother seems to think this is a done deal," Erin said as she and Cory walked up the sidewalk. "You haven't done anything you haven't told me about, have you?"

"You know as much as I do."

Skipp introduced the realtor to them as they stood on the steps. "You have a rare opportunity here," Mr. Ebowitz said, shaking Erin's hand. "Technically, this house isn't on the market yet, so you're the first to see it." He stepped back and waved them into the living room.

He began pointing out the features of the house, but the minute Erin stepped into it, she stopped listening. The house spoke for itself. She knew she could move into it just as it was, and that frightened her.

To the right on the main floor was the living room with a fireplace flanked by built-in bookcases. French doors on the east side opened into a three-season porch. To her left was the dining room with a built-in buffet and china cupboard and a lovely window seat. Both rooms had wood floors, high ceilings, and wonderful Arts and Crafts detailing in the woodwork. They were decorated with deep, cushy furniture and tables and cabinets whose clean lines were reminiscent of Frank Lloyd Wright. Between the rooms was a hall leading to the kitchen area and a handsome staircase leading to the second floor.

When Erin followed the parade into the kitchen, she drew a quick breath. She could imagine herself in this room cooking Sunday dinner for the family and the Harringtons. Cory walked up beside her as she looked out the sliding glass doors to the deck and backyard. "Isn't this a great place? Don't you just love it?"

"It's perfect. And maybe we can afford it in ten years."

When the tour was over, Mr. Ebowitz lead them back into the living room, inviting everyone to sit. He looked at Erin. "I don't know if Skipp told you, but there's the possibility of buying some or all of the furnishings."

She nodded numbly, but she snapped out of her daze when he next addressed Skipp. Skipp, not Cory or her. "Well," he said, rubbing his hands together, "are we ready to talk business?"

"I think so," Skipp said heartily. "It's a great investment, and a wonderful place for my grandchildren to grow up in. What do you think, son? Do you like the house?"

"It's fantastic," said Cory.

"And you?" the realtor asked Erin.

"It doesn't matter whether I like it or not. It's out of our league." She reached for Kayla. "Come on, sweetie. It's time to go home."

"I don't want to go!" Kayla dug in her heels. "Grandma says this is our house."

Erin picked Kayla up more roughly than she had intended, and when she spoke to Linda, her voice was sharp. "Why did you tell her that?"

Clearly upset, Linda turned to Skipp. "I told you we needed to talk to them first."

"I can see I've made a mess of this," Skipp said ruefully. "Erin, dear, Linda and I have been wishing for some time that you and Cory lived close enough to us that the children could stop by whenever they want to. When I heard this house was for sale, I knew right away that it was just what we had been hoping for. But with the asking price, I knew it would go fast. That's why I put earnest money down on it without consulting either you or Cory."

Erin was about to speak, but he held up his hands in a wait-a-minute gesture. "Just to hold it until we could all see if it was as lovely a place as I'd been told. And if you thought you could live here."

"I appreciate what you're trying to do for us, Skipp, but whether or not I can live here isn't the point. Getting into a house like this is a bigger stretch by far than getting into our little house. We aren't ready for it."

"Then there's something else you need to know." Skipp put his arm around Linda. "Whatever we have will go to Cory and you and the children through him. Linda and I would like to give you some of it now, in the form of a substantial down payment on this place. One sizeable enough to make the monthly payments an amount you can handle."

Cory's mouth gaped in surprise. Then he jumped from his chair to hug his father and then his mother. "Dad, Mom. That's unbelieveable. I don't know what to say." He looked at Erin. "Isn't this fantastic, Erin?"

The excitement on his face pained her heart. Kayla was jumping up and down, saying "Isn't this fantastic" in imitation of her father's joy. Skipp and Linda waited for her answer with expressions of yearning and hope. Erin smiled weakly.

"So, we're agreed?" Skipp asked.

He was going to make her say it, Erin realized. She shook her head no, but the word that came out of her mouth was yes.

WILLADENE

August 19, 1986
Dear Ladies,

We have survived yet another summer. At first I didn't think we were going to make it through. Carl turned to Paul for company since he's restricted to home and the farm. That's the silver lining to Carl's troubles, I guess.

The Crafton twins finally came around and were welcomed back on the farm last Monday. While they see Carl at work, they are still banned from the house until school starts. Luckily for me, my relationship with Pat is slowly mending. She is more forgiving than I am on my best day.

Roger has been a trouper overall. Even though he has been putting in long hours at the university and on the farm, he never misses a family home evening and makes time for one-on-one interviews with each of the kids.

Bitsy loves the interviews. She always tells Roger she thinks boys are nasty, but she loves him. She's quite a handful, but if you really want to know what out-of-control is like, rent a teenager for a day! Better yet, I'll send you mine.

Gabby says Elder Farnsworth is happily back in the field again, after his stint in the mission home. He has been made a zone leader and tells his grandma his main job is to whip the greenies into shape. Teaching the gospel isn't for wimps, especially in the South.

Roberta Jean will soon be home from Africa. NeVae won't rest easy until her daughter is back on native soil. This absence has been harder on her than even Bert's mission. She can't seem to get over her worry.

But then who am I to comment? I worry about my kids even when they're home tucked into bed. I think I need a tune-up. COBs, dear ladies, where are you?

Deenie

ERIN

Wednesday, September 3, 1986
Dear Gabby, Juneau, and Deenie,

Guess what my in-laws did? They bought Cory and me a house without asking us.

OK, I'm exaggerating, but not by much. They're the ones who found the house and put enough money down that we can afford it. They're the ones who bought all the living room and kitchen furniture and a bunch of other things, so I wouldn't have to shop. We only have to live in it.

Remember back when I said I felt like I'd been swallowed by a whale named Johnson? Well, now I feel like I've been digested and absorbed! Our lives are taking on the shape of Skipp and Linda's dreams.

Angie says I need to decide what my boundaries are and make sure the Johnsons understand where I draw the line. That's a hard one. I think I wanted to be asked, not told, not squashed by a steamroller. (By the way, Angie and Norm are so cute. She calls him Mr. Allnut and he calls her "Old Girl," like Bogart and Hepburn in *African Queen*.)

When I told The Women, Mom said she was proud of everything Cory and I had accomplished since we got married. I made the mistake of saying how blessed we were. Grams shot back with something like, "Do you think if your mom and I joined your church, we'd get blessed, too? Do you think we'd be able to get a new house?"

I get so mad at Grams, but when I complained to Colleen about how we got the house, she said I was just like Grams! She said I was making myself miserable by always finding the worm in the apple. Is it possible that she's right? She's certainly given me something to think about.

Love,
Erin

October 25, 1986
Dear Ladies,

This isn't a Good News letter. My friend Colleen had her long-awaited baby, a little boy she and Steve named Richard. He has Down Syndrome.

Steve was devastated when he called to tell us, and so was Cory. I've never seen Cory grieve like this except when the Wagners died—within twenty-four hours of each other. He and Steve had talked a lot about all the things they would do with their sons if the baby turned out to be a boy. Now, Steve has to come to grips with the fact that things won't turn out quite the way he'd imagined.

Remember back when I said I didn't know what I should pray for regarding Colleen wanting a baby? Well, I prayed that she would. If God did hear my little prayer, why did he answer it in that way?

Ricky is healthy in most respects, which is a blessing, but he will need an enormous amount of extra help learning to do things that are automatic for other kids. Dear Colleen is so determined to do whatever necessary so that he'll have a life as close to normal as possible. I just hope she won't be disappointed.

It's a good thing Jake's been helping us get ready for the Big Barn Sale. It's just around the corner, and Colleen won't be in any shape to help.

I think it's time to go put on some Tabernacle Choir music. I need to stop thinking.

Love,
Erin

Chapter Thirty-Nine

WILLADENE

Deenie considered the spectacular fall that followed as her personal reward for having survived the summer. Everything appeared intensified to her. The colors in the canyon were brighter. The patchwork fields of winter wheat and straw were lighter. Although she had lived there all her life, she never tired of it. So whenever opportunity arose she took the quick drive to Mantua and back through Sardine Canyon as her own special treat.

Today, she busied herself with bottling jam and baking bread. When the bread was resting on the cooling racks, Deenie rubbed the top of each loaf with the inside of the paper the butter came wrapped in. It made the loaves gleam alongside the bottles of fruit and jam that waited to be put away in the storage room. She loved looking at them. They were visible proof of who she was and what she could do for her family.

She looked contentedly around her home. She was feeling very satisfied with life when an errant thought interrupted. *Would you be as grateful if you had less? Well, of course,* she answered herself automatically. *But what if . . . ?* The question repeated itself unexpectedly in the next days, adding a shadow to even the most innocent moments.

Like when the whole family was raking leaves. The boys were mostly horsing around, having fun together in a way that made Deenie smile.

Carl sneaked behind Paul, scattering his collected pile of leaves. "You're not getting away with that," Paul bellowed, pelting his brother with handfuls of rakings.

"Says who?" Carl asked gathering up an armload.

Bitsy shrieked and jumped on her brother. "Says me!"

Deenie couldn't resist, and soon all four were engaged in the battle.

Roger emerged from the open garage at the sound and joined the group wrestling on the lawn. "Is this any way to spend a Saturday afternoon?" he asked with a smile.

"You bet it is," Paul crowed, stuffing leaves down the back of Bitsy's shirt.

"Daddy, save me!" Bitsy tussled with her brother until Roger came to her rescue.

Deenie was laughing as she brushed down each of her children in turn. "Come on, kids, let's get this mess cleaned up."

"Afraid you're on your own," Roger said. "Carl and I have general priest-hood meeting tonight, and we have to get ready."

Deenie watched her two priesthood holders walk away shoulder to shoulder. Carl was gaining on his father in height. He looked more like Roger every day. They even walked alike. And at the moment they were at peace with each other. Deenie relished the truce, though she knew it could be easily broken by one of Carl's confrontations or questions: "What about evolution? Why didn't God stop the concentration camps?"

As Carl and Roger reached the house, she heard a burst of laughter and saw her husband throw his free arm around their son. It was a good moment. *But what if . . . ?*

Later that evening Deenie was tucking Bitsy in bed when the phone rang. "Gotta get that, sweetie." She kissed her daughter on the forehead and flipped on the night light.

"You're positive sure?" Bitsy asked, halting Deenie at the door to con-tinue the conversation they'd been having.

"Yes, Pumpkin, I'm positive sure nobody's ever drowned at their bap-tism!"

When she answered the phone, Aunt Stell was on the other end of the line.

"I need a favor, Deenie," Aunt Stell said in her usual brusque voice. "Leila Jeffrey's daughter, Ellen, is staying with her for the weekend. She's four months pregnant and feeling some discomfort. I need you to sit with her and calm down Sister Jeffrey. I'll get there as soon as I can."

"I thought you weren't taking any new clients." Deenie twisted the tele-phone cord nervously.

"I'm not. Ellen talked to an on-call doctor. He said there was nothing to worry about, but you know Leila. She needs reassurance, so she called me. Can you go? Jeffreys' house is just past the tabernacle."

"I know where the Jeffreys live, Aunt Stell, but I can't leave the kids." Even as she said the words, Roger walked in the door, taking away her excuse. "Oh, all right. But what if . . . ?"

Stella hung up without saying good-bye.

At Jeffreys' Deenie found Ellen resting comfortably in the living room and Leila darting to and fro like an agitated barn swallow.

"Honestly, Mother Jeffrey," Ellen protested, "I really am fine. The doctor said these twinges were likely my tummy muscles stretching to allow for the baby's growth."

"Yes, yes." Leila sat down and stood up. "But I can't help worrying. Are you sure there isn't something I should be doing?"

"You're doing fine." Deenie put her arm around Leila and led her to an armchair next to the couch. "It's good for every young mom to know that her mother-in-law cares about her. Let's get you settled here, and then I can chat with Ellen." Deenie helped Leila to the armchair next to the couch and then gave her a lap robe and a drink of water.

Maintaining a light running dialogue, she slipped easily into the routine she had started to learn at the age of ten as if Aunt Stella were right there coaching her. *Keep the patient relaxed and warm. Check her pulse, ask about her due date, if she's been taking her vitamins . . .*

They had reached possible baby names in their conversation when Stella arrived. "That's what I like to see," she said in a hearty voice. "Everyone all comfy and relaxed. Everybody all right?" They all nodded in response. "Good!" she continued. "You stay that way, and I'll see Deenie to the door. She needs to get back to her children."

Once outside Stella stopped Deenie with a hand on her shoulder. "You did just fine," she said.

Deenie brushed her hand away. "There wasn't anything *to* do. But you knew that, didn't you. So why did you call?"

"Leila needed help. She needed to calm down before she had another stroke. I knew you would do that as well as I."

"You could have told me that in the first place. I wouldn't have panicked about something really being wrong with Ellen."

"I know. That's why I didn't tell you. It's high time for you to face your fears and get over them."

"Not like this, Aunt Stell."

"Then like what? It's been years, and you're still letting what happened to you when you were twelve determine how you live your life."

"Is that what you think I'm doing?"

"What else can I think, Deenie? You're not using the talents the good Lord gave you. And he doesn't give his gifts lightly. Where much is given . . ." She let the rest of the sentence trail off.

"And you're so sure there is such a gift?" Deenie asked angrily. "All your training and the supposed Stowell Sight couldn't save Sunny from brain damage. Maybe my mother is right. Maybe it all is just Stowell family mythology."

"No, Deenie." Stella reached out to caress Deenie's cheek. "I am so sorry for all the pain that your family has gone through because of Sunny's birth. But did it ever occur to you that things happened the way they were meant to? Who would we be without having Sunny in our lives just the way she is?"

Deenie gave her aunt one horrified look and ran down the porch steps. The question kept pace with her footsteps as she hurried home. *What if? What if? What if?*

ERIN

Erin stood in the middle of the kitchen in the new house, trying to figure out what needed to be done next so that the turkey, mashed potatoes, garlic green beans, and rolls would all be ready to go on the table for Thanksgiving dinner shortly after the guests arrived at 2:00.

"I hate holidays!" she yelled.

"I love holidays!" Cory called back from the dining room where he and Kayla were setting the Stickley-style table.

Erin wiped her hands on her apron and stood for a moment in the doorway to the dining room, watching Cory and Kayla discuss the placement of the paper turkeys with the fanned tails and the painted wooden pilgrims in their black and white costumes.

Cory is such a good daddy, she thought, marveling at how he could make almost any task into a game.

Kayla put the last figures in the center of the table. "Do you like it, Mommy?" she asked, jumping with delight.

"Yes, dear, I do." The table was beautifully set with the china and silver that Cory and Erin had received when they got married. There were nine places at the table and two highchairs set at corners. "You've set one place too many," she said, reaching for the plate. "Two for us, two for your parents, and two for Mom and Grams makes six."

Cory slapped his forehead. "Rats! I forgot to tell you I invited Paula a couple of days ago. Her daughter decided at the last minute not to come home. I didn't think one more person would be a big deal."

Erin set the plate back down. "It'll be interesting to see how Grams reacts to Paula."

"I want Grams, I want Grams," Kayla chanted.

"She'll be here soon," Erin said. "Grandma Linda and Grandma Joanna are coming, too."

Cory smiled as Kayla ran through the kitchen and into the living room, yodeling "Graaamy, Graaamy." He turned to Erin. "Who would have thought Ruth and Kayla would turn out to be a pair?"

The guests arrived in a cluster, bundled up against the cold. Introductions were made, and then Erin and Joanna started putting the food on the table. Cory poured the sparkling grape juice, and Skipp poured the water. When everything was ready, Erin called her guests to the table. They were in the middle of the meal when conversation turned to Christmas plans.

"I don't do much at this time of year." Grams was looking at Paula as she spoke. "My husband dropped dead of a heart attack twenty-five years ago this December. He just couldn't bear up under the troubles we were having."

Oh, joy, thought Erin. *Cory should have known better than provide Grams with a new audience.*

Skipp cleared his throat. "You know, Ruth, Mormons believe that husbands and wives can be together after death. It's quite a comfort to know that there's continuity of the family unit." He leaned back in his chair as he spoke, his mellifluous voice capturing the attention of all around the table.

Cory was explaining the significance of temple ceremonies to Paula when Kayla burst out, "I'm a Mormon girl. Mommy's a Mormon girl. And Daddy's That Mormon Boy."

Paula laughed with delight, hearing only a little girl's pride in her identity. She was the only one who laughed. Everyone else was devastated by hearing "That Mormon Boy" come out of Kayla's mouth in a cadence she could only have learned from one source.

Erin was about to say something, but Cory gave her a look that said, "It's okay. Let it go."

If Paula felt any awkwardness at the moment, she didn't let it show. When Erin helped her with her coat late that afternoon, she had nothing but compliments. She even said she hoped to see The Women again sometime.

Skipp and Linda left shortly after Paula, but when Ruth started for the door at the same time, Erin caught her arm. "Wait. We have to talk." She set up Mark and Kayla in the family room with their favorite Disney movie and then went back into the living room, where Cory, Joanna, and Ruth sat in silence.

"You know what this is about, don't you?" Cory asked Ruth. "Kayla called me 'That Mormon Boy' during dinner. There's only one person she could have learned it from. You."

"I didn't mean to say it." Ruth's voice was soft. "It just came out."

"Kayla doesn't know it was meant to be mean," Erin added in Grams's defense. "As far as she's concerned, it's a description."

"Is it?" Cory challenged. "This is exactly what I was afraid would happen. It's why I had Erin tell you you couldn't be trusted alone with Kayla." His expression was stern. "I've put up with a lot over the years, Ruth, but you've gone too far."

Erin saw her grandmother stiffen at his use of her given name, and her heart went out to the older woman. "Cory," she said, touching his arm to get his attention.

He ignored her. "I hate to have to say this, but I'm not sure I want you around Kayla or Mark, even when we're there."

"You can't do that." Ruth clasped her hands over her heart in an unconscious gesture. "I love Kayla."

"Do you have any idea how it feels to be talked about in the same tone of voice and the same way as Erin's father?" Erin could see from his expression that he was not only angry but deeply hurt. "I know how much you hate 'That Catholic Boy.' Do you hate me as much?" Erin saw an amazing parade of expressions cross her grandmother's face, from recognition to remorse and finally to understanding.

"I don't hate you," Ruth said. "I just got into the habit of thinking of you that way. When you think something often enough, sometimes you say it."

"Sometimes, what a person says is the truth, whether she wants to admit it or not," Cory said.

Ruth reached for the back of the nearest chair and lowered herself into it. "I don't hate you," she repeated. She turned to Joanna. "I didn't even hate Andrew. I was angry and scared, and then when your father had that bad heart attack at such an early age . . ." She held out her hands in supplication. "It was easier to blame That Catholic Boy for everything that was going wrong." Her inflection was softer, her voice held regret.

Now Ruth looked at Cory. "I am sorry I hurt your feelings. I've never said this before, but . . ." She paused as if to marshal her resolve. When she spoke, it was as if she were making a declaration. "I think you are a fine man, a good husband, and a good father. Please accept my apology."

Cory ran his hand over his forehead and muttered something under his breath. He blew out a great sigh. "We've made a real mess, haven't we? You shouldn't have said that in Kayla's hearing, but I shouldn't have made a federal case out of it. I just can't stand thinking that you'll say the same things to Kayla and Mark that you said to Erin. I don't think you realize how they affect her, even now."

Ruth shrugged, her hands held out, palms up. "I felt sorry for myself. I wanted everyone else to hurt like I hurt." She paused. "Erin?"

Erin knelt at her grandmother's knee.

"I'm sorry for everything I ever said or did that's made life hard for you. I love you. I love you, too, Joanna. You've stayed by me all these years. If it weren't for both of you, I'd be all alone." She steadied herself against Erin's shoulder as she stood and faced Cory. "I'm a crotchety old woman. I complain and find fault. I can't promise that I'll turn into Merry Sunshine, but I can promise I will never do or say anything that will hurt your children. And I'll never use those words again. Is that good enough?"

Cory shook his head. Erin could see him struggle with accepting the apology—and the extended hand—offered by Ruth. Finally he said, "Good enough." He took her hand, and they gave each other an awkward hug.

When The Women left some time later, Cory flopped down on the couch with a groan, draping his arm over his forehead. "I hope Grams keeps her promise," he said. "I've had enough of the Larson family tradition."

Erin sat on the floor beside him. "It may have started out the same as always, but, Cory, I think Grams learned something tonight. Maybe the tradition *has* changed."

WILLADENE

Christmas 1986
Dear Erin and Juneau,

Merry Christmas from the frozen West! We are housebound and right now loving it. The kids don't have to go to school, and Roger doesn't have to go to work. We are so ready for Santa to come down the chimney.

I had a deal with Mom and Pat and Grandma Streeter. Instead of each of us making a whole bunch of goodies for the holidays, we are each going to make big batches of one or two varieties and then share the wealth. So even the goodies are ready. I don't know how long I can keep from sneaking some!

Some of those goodies are boxed and ready to mail to Bryan. This will be his last Christmas in the mission field. I am glad he is in North Carolina and not overseas. This way we can be sure he will get what we send. He has requested enough Utah-style treats for him to share with his families. If you're inclined, I put address labels in the envelope already filled out for each of you.

The Craftons are joining us for Christmas Eve. Reece and Ryan are now always polite and squeaky clean in their attitude and language when they are here, but I keep thinking about last summer and what a disaster it could have been. I wonder if Pat thinks of Carl in those same terms. Although we are spending more time together, that is one subject we've left alone.

I've discovered what has been bothering our dear Gabby. Her grandson Kenny has been arrested again, this time for assault. He'll almost certainly see jail time. HG Jr. and Cecelia are so humiliated and angry (they're sure Kenny's innocent) that they've withdrawn from anyone who thinks he possibly might have done it. They keep Sophie housebound, except for school. She doesn't even get to visit Gabby.

Gabby is devastated. She asked for our prayers on behalf of herself and her family. I promised her we would all take a day to fast for that family. Don't make a liar of me, ladies.

> Holiday Best to you all,
> Deenie

P.S. Congrats on the new house, Erin. It's sounds like Santa found you early this year.

Chapter Forty
1987

ERIN

Sunday, January 4, 1987
Hi, Friends,

The kids are down for their naps, and Cory is watching TV, so I thought I'd get my trusty typewriter out. Juneau, do you think it's worth it to buy a computer just to write letters on? Probably not, but this carbon paper routine gets old.

Thanks to Juneau and Deenie for the cards with the pictures on them. (Gabby, why didn't you do a photo card?) It sure is clear how time flies when I compare your photo cards to those from previous years. The kids are growing up and we're growing . . . wiser! (I wish.)

I thought the staircase in my new house made such a great stage for the family Christmas photo, I'll probably do something similar every year. Didn't Kayla look quite the big sister, with Mark on her lap? (Yes, Mom and I made red PJs for the kids again!) Kayla's four and Mark's about fourteen months. They are both doing well. Remember how sick Kayla was when she was little? She's had nothing but the sniffles and chicken pox since then!

We had another holiday brouhaha, but this time with a different ending. There was some give-and-take on both sides and—get this!—Grams actually told Cory she thinks he's a good man. I never thought I would hear her say that. But Grams is still Grams. You never know when she'll come out with a barb.

The goals Cory and I set for 1987 aren't much different from what they've been the past few years, at least not in the basics. If I could make a wish for the New Year and have it come true, it would be that my dear friends Colleen and Steve are inspired regarding little Ricky's care. Steve still looks really down, but Colleen has tapped into a source of strength that's amazing.

There's not much news to tell, I'm happy to say. Cory isn't looking for a new job, and I'm not pregnant!

When are we going to get together next?

Much love,
Erin

WILLADENE

January 17, 1987
Dear Ladies,

Even though we are still under three feet of snow, the spring cleaning bug has bitten me hard. I am boxing and tossing like a crazy
woman. The storage room at the top of the stairs was my first vic-
tim. That's where I've hoarded all the baby things since Bitsy was
born. But no more! Bitsy will be baptized in May (and insists that
from then on we're to call her Beth), so that makes eight years of
hoarding. That's at least one year too many.

I've kept only a few of the baby items for sentimental reasons and
the crib because it's such a beautiful old thing I couldn't bear to
part with it.

I am starting on the kitchen next. Grandma Streeter warned me
to be careful and not throw out anything I would have to repur-
chase. She is probably right. But it feels so good to get rid of things
like cookbooks I haven't used for years—and old Tupperware without lids.

Crafton Catering is no longer just a novelty but a thriving business. Pat has hired some college kids to help out, and Mom now
keeps regular office hours. Sunny stays home more often when
Mom's at work, unless there is a big order to box. She calls frequently now, and I'm glad.

Carl helps the twins scrub down the premises on Saturdays, just
like the twins help on the farm. The funny thing is, this time Carl
is the one getting paid and the twins are the ones working gratis.
Because, Grandma Streeter says, and she is very much of a mind
with Grandpa Will, that's what you do in a family—you help
where it's needed.

I ran into Dave Fenton in Logan. He's the guy who dumped me just before the senior prom. He's also the county sheriff who's been involved in all of Carl's misbehavior. He informed me that he was visiting all the parents in the area who have delinquent kids in an effort to track gang activity in Cache County.

I can't tell you how thrilled I was to hear it. So I saved him a trip to Wellsville and answered his questions right there. I told him he would find absolutely no gang-related activity in our neighborhood. Roger said I had spoken uninformed. What did I know about the private lives of the other boys in the area? That comment shocked me more than anything. I worry all the time when Carl isn't in sight. And what if Paul is looking for a thrill? How young do boys get involved in gangs, anyway?

Jonas called to give us an update on Gabby and her family. He said Kenny will see a year in county lockup and a long probation. HG Jr. is threatening to leave Provo with Cecilia and Sophie rather than face the shame. Gabby is afraid this time he will live up to his threats. She is worried that even the leverage of the money HG Sr. left won't be enough to keep them from taking Sophie away from her.

Sunny now talks of Sophie as if she were one of her imaginary friends. It's been two years since she has seen her. We all had hopes for that relationship to deepen over the years. But Sunny still gets great pleasure watching the cakes coming out of the oven at the bakery and loves having money that she has earned by herself. She is very careful of it and keeps a little notebook to write down where every penny goes. Roger says I should be as thrifty.

Hope you're all well and happy.

Feeling way too distant,
Deenie

ERIN

In February, Erin started to do some freelance work for Margie Boxwood of Boxwood Design Services. Paula had given her the lead, saying, "She's looking for someone to scout for the perfect accessories. Sounds right up your alley."

After talking the idea over with Cory, Erin made an appointment with

Margie. A petite bundle of energy balanced on high heels, Margie wasted no time on chitchat as she laid out what she needed from a freelancer. She then asked Erin a few pointed questions about her experience. "Okay," she said, seemingly satisfied with what she had heard. "Here's how we'll do it."

Erin found a nursery school in a church close to their home, and with Cory's blessing, dropped Kayla and Mark off Tuesdays and Fridays. "It's good for them," she said when explaining the new arrangement to Linda. "They'll get socialization being with other kids."

She started out doing the preliminary legwork on upcoming jobs, including verifying the measurements of the rooms to be decorated. After that, she scouted for the items Margie's designs called for.

"That part's like getting ready for the Big Barn Sale," Erin said to Colleen when they were doing Finders business at the farmhouse kitchen table. "I'm learning tons, but I'm also seeing where taking some basic courses at the Minnesota College of Art and Design would really help."

"When would you have time for that?" Colleen asked. "You're already taking on too much with this Boxwood Designs thing."

"I don't know. It's just a thought."

The sound of laughter came from the corner of the kitchen that was set up as a play area. Kayla was "reading" a book to Mark. In the portable crib near them, Colleen's Ricky lay on his back, cooing to a soft mobile.

"How's Ricky doing?"

Colleen's smile was determined. "Good. He's behind in all the developmental stages, but that's to be expected. I do exercises with him and read to him every day. EJ plays with him, too. He seems to like that."

"Having you guys for a family makes a big difference for him. You're amazing."

"We're not amazing. We're coping." Colleen looked from Ricky to Mark. "They aren't too far apart in age. I wonder if they'll be friends when they get older."

Erin remembered Willadene writing about the twins calling Sunny a retard and Carl saying, "She is!" Who knew how kids would act when they were older?

She put her arm around Colleen. Giving her an encouraging smile, she said what she hoped was the truth. "We're friends, so they'll be friends."

When Erin took on doing some work for Margie Boxwood, she didn't intend to end up being so busy. At first, she fit in assignments here and there, giving Margie two or three days every few weeks or so; however, her tendency to say yes when she should have said no made life increasingly hectic for the whole family.

When Cory complained about the house showing neglect, she started staying up late to throw in a wash, do other catch-up chores, and put a casserole together for supper the next day. On the days that she went downtown and the kids went to day care, she had to get up extra early to hustle Mark and Kayla through breakfast so she could drop them off on time.

Erin knew she was doing too much when Finders forays, previously the highlight of her week, were becoming burdensome. She was beginning to resent the time commitment, feeling she could be doing something else more productive. Colleen picked up on it but didn't say anything until the day they drove out to Buffalo, a small town west of Minneapolis.

They visited several shops and local garage sales and then stopped to eat bag lunches at a picnic table on the banks of Buffalo Lake. Kayla and Mark, whom Erin took along when she wasn't working for Margie, were more interested in feeding the ducks and Canada geese than they were in eating. "Don't feed the ducks," Erin scolded. "Eat your sandwiches."

Colleen was giving Ricky a bottle, supporting his head carefully. She looked up at Erin and smiled. "I was thinking we should go down to the Bluff Country on Friday," she said. "We haven't been to Lanesboro for a while."

Erin slapped her forehead. "I meant to tell you. I have to meet with Margie on a new job."

"Wait a minute. Fridays are supposed to be reserved for Finders."

"I know. I blew it when I told her I could come in then. Maybe we can make up the time next week."

"What is this project?"

"There's a really neat new development starting near downtown Minneapolis designed to look like a 1950s neighborhood. Margie says I have a real affinity for the kind of furnishings that will complement the model homes. She asked if I was up to taking on decorating all three. With her help, of course."

"It sounds like a lot of work."

"It will be, but it's also a huge opportunity."

Colleen didn't respond immediately, and Erin could tell she was angry, disappointed, and maybe a little sad. "I've got a question for you. If you do this job, how am I supposed to keep Finders going? I can't handle it on my own, not with the extra time I have to give Ricky."

Erin remembered Cory's complaints and her mother's concern. "That's three," she said.

"Three what?"

"Three times someone has said I was too busy with Boxwood Designs. My writer friend, Juneau, says that if you mention something in a story three times, it has to mean something."

"It means you *are* too busy, that's what. If you aren't willing to give Finders the time it needs, I think we should tell our clients we're going on hiatus." She paused, her expression serious. "Or do you want to quit altogether?"

"No! But I don't want to cut back on the time I give Margie, either." Erin dashed to snatch Mark and Kayla before they were surrounded by a gaggle of hungry geese. She felt as if all of her obligations were like those geese, surrounding her, pecking at her. But she'd called each of them to her when she said yes.

Colleen was waiting for her when she got back to the table. "Listen, Erin. Steve says we're at a crisis point. I'm busy with Ricky, and you're up to your eyeballs with work for Margie. Either we both make a no-kidding commitment to Finders, or we let it die a natural death. Which is it?"

When Erin didn't immediately respond, Colleen said, "Well, that's that." Colleen rose and started packing up the picnic leftovers.

"No, wait." Erin touched Colleen's hand. Her mind darted here and there and then jogged loose the memory of what Paula had once said about Finders being a success even if all they did was have the once-yearly sale.

"How about we stop working with clients and focus only on the Big Barn Sale? We can go out every other week or so, and in between, we can both pick up things on our own. Of course, we'll need to block off three weeks before the sale to get ready and a week after to settle up and clean up, but we can do it."

Colleen's expression was doubtful. "I will only work if you're serious about blocking off a month where you won't do anything for Margie."

Relieved, Erin said, "I will. Cross my heart."

Sunday, April 26, 1987
Dear COBettes,

I hate those magazine articles that tell women they can have it all—if they're willing to do it all! And they make it sound easy. Well, friends, I'm here to tell you it's not. Mrs. Over-achiever 1987, that's me. I've been trying to juggle family, home, church,

Finders, and more. There aren't enough hours in the day, and I'm always tired and often grouchy.

I've been short-changing Finders, which has really frustrated Colleen. The other day, she was actually ready to let it go right down the drain. After a good talk, we agreed to phase out the client part of the business and focus on doing the Big Barn Sale every fall. We'll still have to go on shopping trips, but I hope that they'll start being fun again.

Cory is still happy with Behind the Scenes. I think he has finally found a job that gives him everything he wants—excitement, variety, challenge, and acknowledgment for the hard work he does. Meeting Paula was a real stroke of luck for him. For both of us. We wouldn't be doing what we're doing now, if she hadn't mentored us.

The kids are doing fine. They both love going to day care. I know Mormon mothers are counseled to stay home with their children, but I honestly don't think Mark and Kayla are suffering because I'm a working mom. I can't imagine me at home all day—I'd be going crazy looking for something to do if I were. I'd probably start a home business, like making fancy soaps.

That's all for now, folks. I need to read my scriptures before I hit the sack.

                              Erin

Chapter Forty-One

WILLADENE

May 1, 1987
Dear Ladies,

Happy May Day. We are knee-deep in meadow flowers here, but no one is feeling like weaving wreaths or dancing around the Maypole. Roger's dad was in a bad accident on the farm. He slipped coming down from the hayloft and hurt his back. NeVae clucks over him like a mother hen and is driving him nuts. He's scaring her sleepless by doing everything the current pain level will allow, even things against the doctor's advice. She has never quite gotten back to her usual in-charge self since her fall last summer, and the situation with Will is wearing on her.

The Rasmussen brothers are so busy. Roger says he notices something new every day that needs to be done, chores he always figured his brothers took care of. His brothers say the same thing. It turns out that all those chores were covered by Will. They are all three repentant of ever thinking he has not been carrying his weight these last few years. They move around their dad like three little boys who have learned a hard lesson in the woodshed. I guess emotional shock can do that to you.

Paul has been recruited to help on the farm. To think that I fussed when Carl was driving a truck at twelve. Carl will be getting his learner's permit in December. He thinks he's pretty grown up and enjoys lording it over Paul, but he keeps him on his toes where farm safety is concerned.

Reece and Ryan are still as mischief-oriented as ever, although there have been no more run-ins with Sheriff Fenton. I worry anyway, because I know whatever they are up to, so is Carl. Roger says I should have more faith in my son. Be grateful for every good day, he says. I know he's right.

Grandpa Rasmussen doesn't complain a bit about his back. When

I offered my sympathy, he said, "It could have been worse." Then he went on to tell me all the worse things that could have and had happened to other ranchers and farmers in the area. I never realized what a dangerous place the farm can be. On top of everything else, I now have visions of scythes hidden in haystacks and tractors going out of control. To think I've been letting the kids run wild out there!

I was grateful Grandpa Will was able to attend Bitsy's (Beth's) baptism. When Roger confirmed her, it felt like we had passed a milestone in our lives. We didn't have the usual hoopla we've had in the past, but we had a nice dinner and pleasant afternoon. Beth didn't seem to notice the difference. As long as she has her Aunt Sunny to herself, she never complains.

Roger has almost finished his classwork for his doctorate and is deep in the "construction," as he calls it, of his dissertation. Between that and his added responsibilities on the farm, he has little free time. I miss the closeness we developed last year. I know it's still there, but it feels a little hidden these days. I can't even think of a Regina scene that would fit.

At least the boys get time with him since they are together at the Rasmussens' during the day. Hey, maybe Annie Oakley should take up driving a tractor. What do you think?

Love,
Deenie

The quilt top that covered Deenie's bed was worn soft with washings and being dried in wind and sun. It was the perfect place to rest a tired head. That's what Deenie did every morning when she finished praying. After closing her conversation with her Father with an amen, she would add her regular postscript. "And please, Lord, help me make it through today." Then she would fold her arms above her head and rest her cheek on the soft comfort of the old cotton, going over her to-do list for the day in her mind. That routine, except for the postscript she added when Roger started working on his Ph.D., had served her well through nearly sixteen years of marriage.

Today, she acknowledged needing something more. For the last six months, even after praying, she often felt as though there were some unknown threat just out of sight. She would find herself, in unguarded moments, checking over her shoulder, and then whispering with relief, "So far, so good," when nothing was there. Indeed, that sense of unease had grown to such proportions Deenie had assigned him a gender and a name: Griff—The Great What If.

This morning, while the kids were in school, she decided to spend a few hours at the temple. After attending a session and resting peacefully in the celestial room, Deenie felt her distress lightening. She also felt a yearning she hadn't allowed herself to feel for many years. "I want my mommy," she whispered to herself as she dressed in her street clothes.

Deenie's childhood home was only a short drive from the temple grounds. In moments she was pulling into the driveway of the two-story brown brick house where she had been raised. The cream painted portico that extended over the driveway was starting to peel and the spring flower gardens had not yet been planted for summer, but to Deenie it was still the most beautiful house in Logan.

She announced her arrival with a knock on the door and a "Hello, any-body home?" as she entered.

"Up here," answered her mother from the top of the stairs. "I just got Sunny settled in for a nap."

"I smell cookies." Deenie sat down on the landing in the curve of the stairs to wait for her mother to appear. "Coconut oatmeal cookies. They smell so good."

Surprisingly, Margaret Stowell came down and sat on the step next to Deenie. "I always liked to come home to the smell of them when I was little, too," she said.

Deenie leaned tentatively into her mother. "Do you remember when Sunny was a year old and I came down with a bad sore throat and you sent me to stay at Nana Hunter's? You were worried about Sunny getting sick."

Margaret nodded.

"When it turned out to be rheumatic fever and I had to stay four months, it seemed like forever. I wanted my mommy and my daddy and those coconut oatmeal cookies." Deenie slid down a step, rested her head in her mother's lap and burst into tears. After a moment she could feel the rare comfort of her mother smoothing her hair.

"Sweet girl," Margaret said softly. "Can you tell Mother what is hurting you?"

With those words, time slipped away, and Deenie was a little child again with her mommy all to herself, before Sunny and before the wall had grown up between them. She cried all the harder.

"I don't know, Mom." She gulped back her sobs.

Margaret gently lifted her chin and gazed into her eyes. Then she smiled. "Deenie," she said, "I think you're pregnant."

Deenie sat up abruptly and clutched her mother's hands. "I can't be pregnant!" she gasped. "I gave away all my maternity clothes."

At three o'clock that afternoon, a stunned Deenie sat facing her obstetrician, Dr. Slater, in the consulting room of the doctor's office. She was pregnant! Unexpectedly pregnant at thirty-five, in the middle of early menopause. Pregnant with a twist.

Dr. Slater had discovered Deenie had developed a heart murmur since her last exam. A loud heart murmur. A murmur that made her heart say lub-*whoosh*-dub, instead of the usual lub-dub, lub-dub.

Dr. Slater looked her chart and said, "Let's talk about that heart murmur. Have you ever been diagnosed with it before?"

"No, absolutely not. Except for the regular childhood stuff I've been healthy all of my life."

"Tell me about your childhood illnesses." Dr. Slater picked up a pen and opened Deenie's chart to a blank page.

"You know," Deenie answered. "Sore throats, colds, flu, chicken pox when I was about three years old, and rheumatic fever when I was thirteen."

Dr. Slater made some quick notes in Deenie's chart. "The rheumatic fever could be significant. Anyone in the family with heart disease?" she asked.

Deenie answered, and the questions went on. By the time she had reviewed the health and death causes of four family lines, she was exhausted.

Dr. Slater finally handed her a prescription for prenatal vitamins, a paper on heart murmur in pregnancy, and reminded her to make her next appointment before she left.

"We'll keep a close eye on the heart murmur," she said. "Watch for the symptoms on this list, and call me immediately if any of them occur."

At the door, Dr. Slater handed her the familiar prenatal packet of information. "There is some new information in here I'd like you to go over with Roger. It explains the prenatal tests we recommend for mothers over thirty. You can decide what, if any, beyond the regular blood work you would like to pursue."

Deenie left the office faint with worry, combining *what if* with words like *amniocentesis, spina bifida, Down Syndrome,* and *heart valve defects.* By the time she had buckled herself into the driver's seat of the van, turned on the ignition, and pulled into traffic, she was submerged in worry.

How would the boys respond, she wondered. How would Roger feel about starting over again after all these years? The Great What If grew until he filled the back seat of the car, and Deenie could feel his hot breath on her neck all the way home. By then her fear was tinged with anger.

"Well, that's one more shovelful of dirt to bury the myth of the Stowell Sight with," Deenie said to herself as she slammed the kitchen door and slapped the pregnancy pack on the counter. If there was ever a time when she wanted the Stowell Sight to be the real thing, this was it. But she hadn't had a clue about what was happening in her own body.

Telling Roger was the easiest. Since it was after classroom hours, Deenie called the high school and had them page her husband to the phone. When he answered, she said, "Honey, would you pick up a case of 7-Up, some mint tea, and a couple bottles of cola for me? I'm going to be needing them for the next few months."

After a prolonged silence on the other end of the line, Roger asked, "Are you sure?"

"Mom guessed it, and Dr. Slater confirmed it this afternoon." Deenie's deliberately calm voice hid how she really felt.

"Wow!" Roger said. After another moment of silence he said, "Wow!" again.

"Could you please plan a family council for tonight after dinner?" Deenie asked. "I'd like us to tell the kids together."

"Anything for the little mother."

At the family council Beth was as delighted with the news as Deenie had thought she would be.

Paul looked first at his father and then at Deenie, nodded his head, and said, "Cool."

Carl asked, "When?" and then left the room mumbling something about population control and knowing better at that age.

The rest of the extended family responded to the phone-dispersed news with the expected enthusiasm and jokes about what happens to women who give away their maternity clothes.

The Griff made all the things Deenie dreaded about being pregnant worse—the fatigue, the nausea and the forgetfulness, to say nothing of the roller-coaster emotions. At the same time, all the things she had loved about being pregnant with the other children seemed to be missing. She passed her second checkup with flying colors but still hadn't unearthed the packet on prenatal testing to share with Roger, nor had she mentioned the term heart murmur.

She was pleased when Jonas offered her the use of his condo in St. George for a getaway. "I bet you could use a visit with the COBs about now," he said. "I'm sure Gabby would like to come down, too."

The next day Deenie wrote:

Dear Gabby,

I'm sure Jonas has shared our UNEXPECTED news with you and his offer of the St. George condo for a getaway. Please keep our news a secret until our visit to St. George. I'd like to surprise the other ladies.

Love,
Deenie

P.S. If Jonas thinks a free week in St. George is going to make me nicer about Roger driving him to Denver for the jurisprudence panel, he's right!

When Deenie reached the third-month mark without any complications, she broached the topic of a trip to St. George with Dr. Slater.

"You know the rules. If you take your time on the trip down, get plenty of rest, pay attention to your body, and promise me you'll start gaining some weight I see no reason for you not to go." She paused and wrote something on a slip of paper. "Here's the name and address of an associate of mine in St. George just in case you have any concerns."

Deenie left the office pleased at the thought of the trip. She was counting on a visit with the COBs to put everything in perspective. She was certain they could help her shoulder the burden of the choices she had made on her own, the choice not to pursue any prenatal testing beyond the blood work for chromosomal disorders already done, and more importantly, the choice not to muddy the experience of this pregnancy for Roger or the children with the news of her heart murmur. The COBs might even be able to tell her how to get rid of The Griff.

ERIN

In late May, Margie sat down with Erin, a pile of papers between them. "You'll be working with Sabrina Platt at Dwyer Homes," she said. "She was going to be here this morning, but she had to cancel."

"Dwyer Homes. Where have I heard of them before?" Erin wondered aloud. The vague sense of familiarity bothered her all morning as they talked over various design approaches and the logistics of the job. On the way home, something clicked. Dwyer Homes was where Cory had met her father.

She told Cory about the strange coincidence when he came home that night. "I'm wondering now if I should tell Margie to find someone else," she said. "There's the possibility I could run into my father or Caitlin."

"What will you say if you do run into him?" Cory said when she told him that night.

"I don't know." Erin sighed. "I feel like I'm asking for trouble, but I really want to do this job."

"Then go for it. Just be ready for anything that happens."

How do I do that? Erin wondered. Again, she thought of Juneau's writing. At night, she lay awake in bed, plotting a romance novel in which the heroine meets her long-lost sister and father. She created conversation after conversation, but they were melodramatic and not very informative.

Feeling adrift and needing something to hang onto, she got out of bed, padded downstairs, and snuggled up on the sofa with her scriptures. She didn't read them, however. She held them next to her heart, and it seemed to her that comfort radiated from the pages of the book. The words and melody of the hymn "I Need Thee Every Hour" began running through her mind. She sang it softly as if it were a prayer. But she still didn't know what she would say if she ran into Caitlin or her father.

It took Erin three weeks to come up with initial plans for the three model homes that met Margie's expectations—Summer Cottage, Minnesota Farmhouse and Traditional—with some unexpected touches of chrome and Art Deco. Colleen, who was much better at sketching than she, helped her put together the final boards.

With butterflies in her stomach, Erin walked into the offices of Dwyer Homes. Would anyone see the similarity between her and Caitlin, or had Cory exaggerated it? That question was answered when the receptionist glanced up at her briefly with a "Hi, Caitlin" and went back to her work.

Erin stood at the desk until the receptionist looked at her again. The woman started to say something and then stopped, surprise widening her eyes. "You're not Caitlin!"

"I'm Erin Larson, here to see Sabrina."

Flustered, the receptionist said, "Yes, she's expecting you. I'm sorry

392   T H E   C O M P A N Y   O F   G O O D   W O M E N

about that. I really thought you were someone who works in the drafting department."

After her encounter with the receptionist, Erin was a little more prepared when Sabrina Platt said the same thing. Erin summoned her most professional self, but it was difficult to present her ideas when the woman kept looking at her with a frankly speculative gaze. The meeting went well, however. Sabrina complimented her on the treatments she had come up with, saying, "I'll run these by the powers that be sometime this week. Then I'll get back to you."

Several days later, Margie called. "They liked your ideas at Dwyer. There's a few changes, but nothing big. You're on your way, Erin."

All summer long, Erin focused on the job for Dwyer Homes. Much of the work was done from her home office. It wasn't until the actual assembling of the items in the model homes that Erin was on-site. She half expected to see Caitlin or her father—this *was* a Dwyer Homes project—but neither one of them came while she was there. When she neared completion, she didn't know whether to be glad or mad or sad that they hadn't come. She could have sought them out, but she had left it to fate to bring them her way—and fate, it seemed had been against it.

The day before the model homes were opened to the public, Erin drove to the village to walk through the rooms one more time. She was very pleased at the results she had achieved—they were worth all the time she'd had to be away from the kids. *I'll bring them down on Saturday so they can see what I've been doing,* she thought. *Cory, too.*

She was standing in the living room of the last house when she heard a sound at the door. A young woman was standing in the doorway, staring at her.

"I didn't believe it when people told me I had a doppelganger," she said.

Erin guessed that *doppelganger* meant double, because the girl looked like a copy of herself. She had to be Caitlin, the half-sister Erin had never met. Her heart was pounding, but she smiled. "I heard that, too, when I first came to the offices of Dwyer Homes."

"My name's Caitlin McGee," the girl said, stepping into the room and extending her hand.

"Erin Larson. Johnson."

They shook hands, staring at each other. Then they broke into laughter, each pointing at the other, touching the other's hair, standing side by side to compare heights. When Erin caught her breath, she said, "I don't know what's so funny about this."

"I don't, either."

That set off another round of laughter. When it had subsided to intermittent chuckles, Caitlin said, "I love what you've done with the models. I told Dad I could happily move right into any one of them."

"What did he say to that?"

"He'd rather have me stay where I am, in the guest apartment. I'm his only daughter, and he's very protective of me. Only child, actually. Did you meet him when you were at Dwyer Homes?"

"No." Erin's heart was pounding. "Who is he?"

"One of the partners. Andrew McGee." Caitlin chuckled. "If you saw him, you wouldn't have to ask who he is. He looks like me. Like us. Or rather, we look like him."

Erin wondered if Caitlin had recognized the import of her words, but her pleasant expression didn't change. "I'm not likely to meet him," Erin said. "I won't be going to the office anymore, now that my work is finished."

"Then we should go over right now and surprise him. He's heard the rumors, too, but he didn't believe them."

"I don't think that's a good idea." Erin looked at her watch. "My kids are waiting for me."

"How many do you have?"

"Two. Kayla is four and a half. She's a fireball with red hair.

"Does she look like you?"

"More like me than her daddy. Mark takes after Cory, though. He's edging up on the Terrible Twos." Erin smiled briefly. "I'm sorry to break this off, but I really do need to go," she said.

They walked out onto the porch, Erin locking the door behind her. As she turned, one of the workmen walking down the street called to Caitlin, "I see you found your sister!"

Caitlin smiled and waved. She turned to Erin. "Wouldn't it be fun if we *were* sisters?" she said.

Erin could only shrug helplessly.

A shocked expression crossed Caitlin's face. "Are we?" she asked.

"Ask your father," Erin said. "Ask Andrew J McGee if he remembers Joanna Larson and her daughter, Erin."

That night Erin got a phone call. "Is this Erin Johnson?" a deep voice said. "Erin *Larson* Johnson."

She knew immediately who was calling, and a riot of conflicting feelings made her catch her breath. "Yes."

"This is Andrew McGee."

"What do you want?"

There was a pause on the other end of the line. He seemed taken aback by her abruptness. "I understand you met my daughter, Caitlin, at the urban village site. While you were doing some work for Dwyer Homes."

"Yes." Erin's heart was thumping. She couldn't believe that she was speaking to her father. It had been eighteen years since she had made the phone call when she was eleven.

"Caitlin said that you said you were her sister."

"I didn't say that. I said she should ask you."

"She did. She's very upset."

"Because of what you told her, or because of what you've kept from her all these years?"

There was a pause, and then he said. "There were reasons."

She couldn't keep the bitterness from her voice. "Really? Do tell."

"I don't think there's anything to gain by going into that now. I only called because Caitlin wants to get to know you. I'm not sure it's a good idea, but she has a mind of her own."

"Don't worry. I won't contaminate her."

Another pause. "One more thing. My wife isn't doing well these days. She doesn't need any upset. I would appreciate it if you don't come to the house, even if Caitlin gets it into her mind to bring you."

He hadn't asked a single question about her, Erin realized. He hadn't asked how she was, who her husband was, or even if she had any children. His grandchildren. Furious, she said, "I wouldn't dream of it."

Erin was shaking when she hung up the phone. She stomped through the house into the kitchen, swearing under her breath. *What did I expect?* she asked herself. *That he would say he loved me and wanted to see me? That he had been secretly keeping track of me all these years and was proud of what I had accomplished? I should have remembered that he was That Catholic Boy!*

She walked out into the cool of the backyard and sat in one of the swings, the conversation echoing against the walls of her mind. At first, all she could hear were his words. Then she began to hear her own words, abrupt and unwelcoming, delivered in an icy tone.

No wonder the conversation had gone as it did. She had been rude, and that had made him reticent. Who knew what he might have said, if she hadn't made it seem as if she hated him.

She had done it all wrong. The words she had said and the tone of voice she said them in had sent a clear message. Only that wasn't the message she had really wanted to send.

Chapter Forty-Two

WILLADENE

July 1, 1987
Dear Ladies,

I am happy to announce that Grandpa Will is on the mend. He's back to being top dog on the farm. He's a hard man to keep from doing too much, and that is too much for NeVae to handle. Bert is coming home for an extended summer visit soon, and we hope that will cheer NeVae up. She has been blue for the longest time. If Bert would show up with a man on her arm, I think NeVae would cheer up on the spot. It's like she feels she's failed as a mother and grieves that she will never hold a child of her daughter in her arms.

The family officially cancelled the Fourth of July bash at the farm. It's the first time the homestead hasn't been open to the community for those festivities since I've known them and probably longer. I think it will be nice to have family only for a change.

Pat has taken the twins to Chicago to see their older brother Stan off to army boot camp. It seems the boy has turned his life around. The whole family is grateful for his positive influence on the twins. We are, too.

Now for the excitement. Jonas has invited Roger to join him on a trip to Denver where he will be a speaker on a jurisprudence panel. As you recall, he's a retired judge. When the invitation came, I realized Roger hasn't been away from home without us for years. The twins will be back in harness by then, and if Will keeps on at the rate he is going, Roger will be able to take a little time away from the farm with no problem. The break will be good for him.

Jonas sweetened the deal by offering me (as in you and you and me, and maybe Gabby) a week in his condo in St. George.

Sounds like a good idea to me. I think we should take him up on it. July's already here. How about August?

Looking forward,
Deenie

JUNEAU

Dear COBs,

Deenie, yes, yes, yes. August is fine. Our road shows will be over by then. Did I tell you I'm involved yet again? I think now that the bishopric has found out that our "team" loves to do them, they don't even look for anybody else! We'd probably be offended if they did.

Also, did I tell you that Greg is the new Scoutmaster in our ward? I predicted that some time ago, when he was still in the bishopric. I think he'll probably be teaching them computer stuff rather than camping skills, but he'll be good.

The girls are both involved in the road show and enjoying it. Misty sneaks out when she's not on stage, but I think she doesn't go farther than the parking lot. Then again, remember The Pits that I installed myself in the parking lot!

See you in St. George in August.

Love,
Juneau

Juneau was deep in road show rehearsals at the time Willadene's letter came. Once again, as before in '85 and '83 and '81, she was the scriptwriter and assistant producer. They had their usual unbeatable team working together again. This present batch of teenagers had complained as loudly as the previous casts about Brother Waite's long rehearsal hours, but somewhere along the line they'd caught fire.

Even Misty. She'd remembered how much she'd enjoyed being one of the "horrifying pit dwellers" in that 1985 show titled *The Pits* and had consented to be in this show, too. In fact, Misty was teaching some of the Beehives and Scouts the basics of tap dancing, which she'd learned how to do way back in the 1983 show, when she'd just turned twelve.

This new show was somewhat of a takeoff on *The Music Man,* the difference being that the flimflam man was selling tap shoes, not musical instruments. Juneau had titled it *Seventy-Six Tap Shoes*, and it entailed the daunting task of teaching about thirty-five kids to tap dance for the finale. Not seventy-six of them, but there hadn't been seventy-six trombones in *The Music Man*, either. When Juneau had first got the idea for the show, she'd expressed doubts that the kids, boys included, would put in the work required to learn to tap, even the basic steps, which was all they'd need to do to sound good. But Brother Waite had declared the kids could do *anything* and had made them believe it, too. To Juneau's surprise, the teenagers had responded enthusiastically, and even gangly Rocky Hartwell had learned to handle his big feet enough to shuffle and ball-change. Juneau had been surprised when Misty consented to help teach tap dancing, at Brother Waite's request (bless him for having faith in her). She'd done some teaching for the '85 show but not tap. She'd asked for lessons after the first show she'd been in and had attended classes faithfully for more than a year. Until her new friends had convinced her that lessons of any kind were not cool.

Now, although she often retreated into sullen withdrawals, Misty seemed to enjoy her role as tap teacher and had been unfailingly patient with her giggling young students. Juneau had great hopes that this would spark her interest in something constructive that would turn her life around and pull her up out of her own version of *The Pits*.

It was something to look forward to. And so was Willadene's invitation to join her and Erin in St. George.

On the night of the first performance of the road shows, Brother Waite spoke to the entire cast in their holding room as they waited to go on. They were all costumed (Sister Waite had designed and masterminded the construction of the delightful turn-of-the century clothing) and brightened with makeup (under Sister Locke's expert direction). The kids were abuzz with excitement and confidence because they could see how good they looked. And they knew how well rehearsed they were.

"You know what?" Brother Waite boomed, getting everyone's attention. "I don't care whether we win or lose. That's not important. We've already accomplished the best thing of all about doing a road show."

He paused, giving the kids a chance to ask what that "best thing" was.

"What would *you* say it is?" he countered.

They eyed one another. "Friendship?" ventured a Laurel girl.

"Teamwork!" declared one of the older boys.

"Good," Brother Waite said. "You're thinking. But you're not yet where I want to go."

Juneau looked around at the kids, taking pleasure in what she saw. Even Misty was giving Brother Waite her full attention. And Nicole, sitting happily amidst her group of Beehive girl buddies, was totally captivated.

There were a couple other guesses, and then Brother Waite said, "Look around the room. Remember our first rehearsal? How drab we were? How clumsy? How awkward?"

"I didn't believe we'd ever really have a show," one girl murmured.

"Exactly," Brother Waite exclaimed. "And what made the difference in what we were then and what we are now? What brought about the change?"

"Teamwork!" shouted the boy who'd said the same thing a few moments before.

"Correct," Brother Waite admitted. "But I want to emphasize the *work*. How much work did it take to get from there to here? How much work on the part of everybody involved? Did you ever think you'd all learn to tap dance?"

The kids laughed.

"Years from now," Brother Waite said, "when you're faced with some of life's challenges, I hope you'll look back and remember what hard work can accomplish, how it can totally change you, help you grow, expand your life. Isn't that what it's all about? To have a goal and work toward achieving it? To change ourselves from the dull and drab to the confident and polished? What does it take?"

"Work!" the kids shouted.

Just then one of the stake leaders stuck her head in the door. "You're next," she announced.

The show was a resounding success. The tap dance finale, featuring thirty-three kids, raised the audience to its feet, and there was such prolonged applause that the kids did an unprecedented encore. They won the dancing award, the costume award, and not surprisingly, the certificate for Best Show.

It was a heady night for the kids. And for Juneau and the other leaders. A positive experience for all concerned. Yet Juneau was troubled. Was it also positive for the kids whose shows had not won awards? The also-rans? How were they feeling? Juneau knew. Since she'd never lived in any one place long enough to make herself known, she'd always been an also-ran. It was good to be a winner, but how could they include *all* the kids who'd worked hard?

There was talk of doing away with the awards the next time they did road shows. Juneau wasn't sure how she felt about that. Would people work as hard if a carrot wasn't dangled out there somewhere? Wasn't it competition that drove football teams, basketball teams, even TV game shows forward?

Wasn't it the competitive spirit that drove *her* forward to excel in writing? She was sure it was what had inspired Misty to put in all the hours of rehearsal for the show. Misty had always been competitive, which was probably why her grades had remained high even through her worst rebellions. Not so for Nicole. Nicole was happy to sit within the warmth of her friends in complete anonymity. And mediocrity. But she was well loved and popular.

It was another of those imponderables. "I'll think about it tomorrow," Juneau said to herself, like Scarlett at the end of *Gone with the Wind*.

Overall, Juneau was happier than she'd been in a long time. She seemed to have found her niche and balance, not only in being one of the road show team but also in her story and novel writing. She'd been thrilled when her first young adult novel had been accepted for publication and had immediately finished another—fate unknown as yet. But she'd discovered she had a real affinity for writing for that age group. Which was probably why she enjoyed working with the teenagers on the road shows so much.

Things were going well. When she inventoried her life, she found that her cupboards were full.

Then, a week after the final performances of the road shows, Misty came in from school and told Juneau that she needed to talk to her.

"Sure, honey," Juneau said. She'd been in the computer room, which is what they called the room Greg had built in the garage, sitting at her typewriter making notes on a new book. If the one she'd sent out was accepted by an editor, she wanted to have another waiting in the wings to send to show the editor that she wasn't a one- or two-book author.

She invited Misty to sit down at Greg's computer desk.

Misty hesitated. "Could we go into your bedroom where we could shut the door—in case Nicole comes home?"

Juneau felt a little twang, as if someone had plucked some tight string deep inside her. She stumbled over the leg of her chair as she got up.

Misty led the way into the bedroom and closed the door. Before they even sat down, Misty blurted, "Mom, I'm late."

Juneau frowned. "Late?" Late to school? Late to . . . what?

"Late," Misty repeated. "Two months."

Juneau processed that like an equation. Added together, the words equaled only one answer.

"Misty." She tried to control the sudden tremble in her voice. "Are you pregnant?"

Misty nodded. "I think so."

"*Think* so?" Juneau peered at her daughter's troubled sixteen-year-old face, devoid of her usual defiance. "Have you been . . ." She couldn't bring herself to say the words and was ashamed that she couldn't. She changed it to say, "Have you been with a boy?"

Misty nodded again.

"Who is the father?"

Misty shook her head.

"And what does that mean?"

Misty's voice fell to a whisper. "I don't know which one."

"How many?" Juneau rasped.

"Just two."

Just two? Juneau thought she would faint. She reeled to her bed and sat down. Misty came to sit beside her.

"Mom?" she said. "Mommy? I'm so sorry."

Juneau put her arms around the girl and pulled her close. "Oh, honey, so am I," she said. She wanted to shout recriminations, ask Misty how she could do such things when she'd been raised to know better. But that would do a lot of good now, wouldn't it? Now was the time for a cool head. For understanding. For *wisdom.* She wished Gabby were here to guide her. But she couldn't help but think of the irony of it all. She and Greg had not been able to have another baby after Max, even though they both wanted one. And now Misty was *having* a baby nobody wanted. No, no, no. That was not true. This baby would be wanted and loved and cherished, if not by Misty, then by somebody else.

"What do you plan to do?" Juneau asked softly.

Misty was silent for several seconds. "I thought at first I'd just go get an abortion. That's what one of my friends did. It's legal now, you know. Since *Roe v. Wade.*"

Juneau stiffened, and Misty said hastily, "But I won't do that. I remember Max and how sad we were when he wasn't born."

Thank you, Max, Juneau whispered silently inside her head.

Misty was quiet again and then said, "Maybe we could name this one Max, since Max never really used the name. Or Maxine, if it's a girl."

Juneau wanted to cry out, not only for Misty but also for herself. She had forgiven herself for the Max chapter of her life, but she hadn't forgotten. She wasn't sure she wanted a constant reminder of it.

"It sounds as if you plan to keep the baby," she said, fighting to sound calm.

"I'm thinking about it," Misty admitted. Then she said, "Mom, don't tell Dad."

"Don't tell him?" Juneau had a hard time keeping her voice down. "How can we not tell him? It will be obvious in a couple of months."

Misty groaned. "And Nicole. I don't want her to know. She won't want me for a big sister anymore, if she knows."

Juneau wished fervently that Misty had thought about this before anything happened. The only positive thing she could think of was that if Misty cared what her father and little sister thought, there might be hope for her yet.

Of course Greg and Nicole had to be told. Greg first, that same night, after Nicole went to bed. He immediately started yelling. "How could you do this?" he bellowed. "Who's the father, Misty? I'll call him up right now and beat the tar out of him."

Juneau braced herself for what would come when Misty admitted she didn't know which boy was the father. But Misty said nothing. Juneau was relieved. That could come later.

Greg put his hands on Misty's shoulders. "Well? I'm waiting!"

"Oh, Daddy," Misty moaned. Suddenly she twisted away and ran from the room.

Greg whirled to glare at Juneau. "How could you let this happen?" he yelled. "Haven't you been keeping track of what she's been doing? Have you been buried so far in your fiction world that you just let her run loose?"

"Hey, now." Stinging words of defense sprang to Juneau's mind. Like *Who exactly is it who's been buried in their work?* And *If you would just once break off your affair with your computer, maybe you'd* . . . But in her mind she saw Gabby's finger wagging at her. "Number one rule in an argument," Gabby had said. "Cool head, soft words."

"Greg," she said, "right now let's think of Misty."

Before either of them could say anything more, Nicole appeared in the doorway of their room. "I heard yelling," she said, rubbing a hand across sleepy eyes. "What's the matter?"

It was time to tell her, too.

Nicole brought them all back to rationality. She and Juneau and Greg went to Misty's room where Misty, once again defiant and belligerent, informed her little sister that she was going to have a baby.

"A baby!" A smile spread across Nicole's face.

Juneau was reminded of how Nicole and her fourteen-year-old friends loved to serve as surrogate mothers to the babies at church when their mothers needed a break. Nicole loved babies.

"It can have my room," Nicole said. "I'll move back in with you. Oh, I hope it's a boy, like Max!"

She was the only one who'd looked at the baby as a blessing, the miracle it was, despite its beginnings.

"No," Greg said. "It won't be staying."

Nicole looked bewildered. "Why not? Where's it going to go?"

Greg shook his head. "I don't know, honey. But Misty can't take care of it."

"I'll help her," Nicole said.

"You'll go to school," Greg stated, "and so will Misty."

Misty got up from the bed where she'd been sitting. Things were heating up again, and they were all only a few words from meltdown.

"We'll think about it tomorrow," Juneau said hastily, replaying Scarlett O'Hara. "Tomorrow night we'll have a family council."

"Isn't it my place to call family councils?" Greg said caustically.

Again hot words sprang to Juneau's mind. But again she saw Gabby's wagging finger. "So," she said, "are you going to call one?"

"Yes," he said. "Tomorrow night, right after dinner."

"Okay," Juneau agreed. "Got that, girls?"

They both nodded.

"First thing tomorrow I'll call Willadene and tell her I can't come to St. George next week," she went on.

Misty's eyebrows went up. "Why not?"

"Why *not*?" Did the girl think life would just go on as if nothing had happened? "Because I need to stay here with you."

"Why?" Misty asked. "I can't get any more pregnant than I already am. Besides, Nicole and I will be off to girls camp."

"You're still going to girls camp?" Juneau failed to keep the gasp out of her voice.

Misty shrugged. "Of course. I thought you wanted me to go."

"I do, dear," Juneau said. "But . . ."

"We won't tell anybody about the baby," Nicole said. "Not yet. It will be okay, Mom." The words put her unmistakably on Misty's side. She had become her big sister's defender.

Juneau was not at all sure Misty would be allowed to go to girls camp under the present circumstances. She didn't know what would happen.

Greg had been watching this whole scene silently. He remained silent when they all went to bed until finally he said, "I want you to go meet with your little friends in St. George next week, Juneau. You always feel better after you've been with them."

Juneau mulled over the "little friends" part long after Greg fell into a restless sleep. It depressed her. It was as if she'd made no progress at all from that day back in 1981 when he'd told her he was glad he had his "little wifey" back.

They didn't solve anything at the family council the next night. Greg remained totally implacable about allowing Misty to keep the baby. And Misty refused to give any indication of who ("which one") the father was. The only thing they came to agreement on was that Juneau should keep her appointment in St. George.

Chapter Forty-Three

WILLADENE

August 5, 1987
Dear Ladies,

I am sorry to report Gabby will not be joining us in St. George. She says she doesn't dare be away from home even for a day. Sophie might need her. Drat H.G. Jr. and his manipulation! Drat Kenny and all his demands from jail for visits and money.

I have the keys and the papers for the condo. Everything is in place for our getaway. All I need is your travel info and we're a go.

See you in Salt Lake City, Erin. I'll pick you up at the airport.

Safe travel, Juneau.

Deenie

P.S. When Grandma Streeter said never throw away anything you'll have to replace, she was right.

JUNEAU

Juneau had plenty time to think as she drove I-15 north from Pasadena. It reminded her of that first time she'd set off alone, back in 1980, to go to BYU Education Week, where she'd met Erin and Willadene and Gabby, who'd changed her life. Or maybe not changed it as much as added to it. She'd needed something that time and the other times she'd gone to meet the COBs. She'd always received the help that made things better. Now she was in need again.

Misty was pregnant. The words hung there in front of her, almost obliterating the freeway. She had to concentrate to see the far right lane in which she traveled, mainly because she didn't trust herself in the faster lanes. She still wondered if she should have come, if she should have left her family behind at a time like this, even though they had insisted. It was for her own good, they said.

They were right. She really needed to be with the COBs right now. As she neared St. George, she had to admit she was looking forward with great pleasure to seeing Willadene and Erin. Willadene, all soft comfort and consolation, would have soup bubbling on the stove, she was sure, since it was already dinnertime. And Erin would be lighting up the room with her spiky red hair and quick smile.

But that wasn't the way it turned out. There was no bubbling-soup aroma to welcome Juneau as she announced herself with a shave-and-a-haircut knock—dum de-de-dum-dum, DUM DUM!—and then pushed open the unlocked door. As she dragged her suitcase and typewriter through the entry hall, she glimpsed Willadene asleep in one of the bedrooms.

Erin was there in the living room, but as far as her lighting up the room, her fuse seemed to have blown.

"Hi, Erin." Juneau consciously made her voice bright. "I'm *so* glad to see you." Leaving her suitcase and typewriter in the entry hall, she hurried over to where Erin sat flipping through a stack of brochures.

Erin rose to hug her. "Welcome to paradise," she said. "Is this a great place or what?"

Juneau looked around the big room that flowed into the dining area and kitchen, all decorated in soft earth tones. There was a fireplace in one wall and to the right of it a tall grandfather clock, ticking softy to itself. "Just gorgeous." She turned to look at Erin. "What's with Willadene? Is she okay?"

Erin frowned. "I don't know. She's been asleep ever since we got here."

"Do you think she's sick?" Sick was not a word Juneau would have thought was in Willadene's vocabulary. Except for that worrisome time in Wellsville when she'd fainted.

"She didn't look well when she picked me up at the airport. And she was so quiet that I began to wonder who it was driving me down here."

Juneau felt a niggle of concern as she looked toward the bedroom area. "That's not like her at all. I've never known her as anything but bustle and take charge."

"I don't know what she had planned for dinner," Erin said. "She brought a lot of boxes and bags of stuff."

"We'd better wait until she gets up, I guess." Juneau headed for her baggage.

"Your bedroom is the one on the end." Erin pointed and then sat down again at the table and went back to examining the brochures.

Juneau unpacked quickly. Picking up her typewriter, she took it out to the dining table and plugged it in. "I had a couple of good ideas as I drove, and I'd like to get them down," she said as she began to type.

WILLADENE

Deenie awoke to a bursting bladder and the sound of voices drifting from the living room. *Good! Juneau's here. I hope she's started dinner.* With that thought she crawled out of bed and padded her way to the private bath attached to her bedroom.

Erin had mentioned something about dinner when they arrived, but Deenie had been too tired to pay attention, just as she had been too tired to do anything more than toss the groceries for three days of menus into boxes and sacks before she left home. There were no pre-packaged Deenie Dinners, no homemade bread for this trip.

She brushed her teeth and then ran a comb through her hair, peering closely in the mirror at her puffy eyes and rounding face. "I look like an irritated blowfish," she said to her mirror image. She dressed quickly and hurried into the great room, where she was surprised to see Juneau sitting in front of her typewriter on one side of the dining table and Erin with brochures spread out on the other side.

"Deenie!" Juneau cried, standing and reaching out. Deenie walked into a good, hard hug. "It's so good to see you." Juneau stepped back to give her a thorough scan and then hugged her again. "We've been talking about what we could do to help you get dinner going."

"Hey," Deenie said as she backed quickly away. "I'm not cooking this trip. I made the plans. I bought the groceries, and I drove the car. Someone else can cook. I'm on vacation."

Juneau and Erin stared at Deenie as if she had suddenly grown an extra head.

"But you always do the cooking," Erin said.

"Not this time, ladies. The kitchen is all yours. "

"What kind of meals did you have in mind?" Erin was still looking at Deenie as if she were an unidentified specimen.

Deenie listed the items she'd packed. "There's stuff for a tuna salad, fixings for spaghetti, hamburger, and two boxes of macaroni and cheese." She saw the shock on their faces. *What had they expected, game hens every night?* "The only ready-to-eat item is one of Pat Crafton's famous Chocolate Hazelnut Tortes. If you can't manage mac and cheese, I suppose we could have dessert for dinner."

"Works for me," Juneau said too brightly. "I'll get the plates."

Erin jumped in. "I'll cut the torte."

Deenie started for the door. "I'll sit on the patio in the front and watch the sun set until you call me."

After the unblessed and uncertain dinner of chocolate torte and milk, Deenie excused herself again. "I'm still tired from the trip. I'm going to read in the tub and go to bed early. See you tomorrow morning."

As she undressed she noticed how easily her jeans fit over her belly. That was not necessarily a good thing, especially since Dr. Slater had emphasized her need to gain weight when they had discussed this trip. One look in the mirror told her that she was retaining water, also not a good thing.

She gently prodded the puffy bags under her eyes and sucked in her cheeks, trying to minimize their roundness. *I look like I'm gaining weight, but I don't think this is what Dr. Slater had in mind.* She rummaged in her makeup case and pulled out the little card the doctor given her. It listed the seven warning signs of heart trouble. The presence of any one of them could mean that what Dr. Slater had heard was more than the simple heart murmur that could accompany pregnancy.

Deenie checked the list carefully. Her puffy face was a little iffy but still within acceptable limits. Her hands and feet were still fine, and none of the other symptoms had surfaced. *I'm okay so far,* she thought.

She climbed into bed, but sleep didn't come as quickly as she had hoped. On the drive down, she had wondered when she would tell Juneau and Erin about the new baby. Now the question was not when but if. They no longer seemed the cozy confidantes she remembered. If she couldn't safely tell them about her little one and the heart murmur and the choice she had made not to tell Roger about her heart, there was no way she could tell them she was being haunted by The Griff.

ERIN

When Erin got up the next morning, it was early. She pulled on a sweatshirt, laced up her tennis shoes, and went out on the patio. The early sun was turning the red rocks behind Jonas's condo fiery, a dramatic contrast to the startling blue sky. This was country like none she had ever seen before, and she itched to go for a walk on the path that went from the back of the condo up into the hills.

She waited a few more minutes to see if anyone might stir, but when the doors to the bedrooms occupied by Juneau and Deenie remained closed, she wrote a note telling them were she had gone and slipped out into the fresh morning air. She walked for half an hour, finding something new and interesting wherever she looked. When she came upon a large rock, she lay down on it, warming herself in the morning sun like a lizard, thinking about what had happened the night before.

Everything about that evening felt slightly off. Every time Erin had tried to say or do something to recreate the closeness they had felt at other times, it had felt wrong. It was like having distorted vision, she thought, so that when you intended to land on a certain step, you missed and had to catch yourself to keep from falling.

She sighed her disappointment. *Why am I even here?* she wondered. She had so looked forward to this week. She wanted the closeness, the understanding that she had come to expect when they got together. She wanted Willadene's attention and Juneau's humor and insight. Last night, she had felt as if they were strangers.

Later, when she was almost back to the condo, she pulled out of her pocket the key Deenie had given her. She didn't need to use it, though. As she climbed the steps to the door, she could hear the sound of typing. At least Juneau was up.

Juneau looked up as she came through the door. "Morning. Been for a walk?"

"I took the path behind the condo. It leads up to this huge rock. We should have lunch up there one of these days."

"Sounds good." Juneau was looking at the top sheet of a stack of papers.

"What are you working on?"

"A book about a teenage girl who goes to visit her grandparents on the family farm in Idaho. She discovers that there is something about her mother's past that she has never been told, and—"

Erin raised her eyebrows. "Sounds like me, except I wasn't a teenager and there's no family farm in my story."

Juneau offered a chagrined smile. "I *was* thinking of you when I got the idea but also of my Great-Grandma Letitia. And there's really no similarity in what the secret is."

"Any enlightenment yet on Lost Letitia?" Erin asked.

"Nope. But I hope to make a trip to Idaho soon and do some personal snooping. I'd like to have my brother, Flint, come with me. He's good at snooping."

"How is Flint?"

"Alive and well, last I heard." She stood up. "It's breakfast time. Let's see what we can find in the kitchen."

"I saw eggs when we unpacked yesterday," Erin said. "Why don't we make omelets?"

Juneau nodded. "You cook. I'll set the table."

They fell into an easy partnership as they did the preparations. After Juneau set the table for three, she put bread in the toaster as Erin chopped onions and beat the eggs.

"Back to that story. Does it have a happy ending?" Erin asked.

Juneau nodded. "Young readers prefer happy rather than just satisfying or reasonable."

"Who doesn't? It must be fun knowing ahead of time what's going to happen to your characters."

"You'd think so, wouldn't you," Juneau said with a chuckle. "But I don't always."

"Why not? You're the writer."

"That's an odd thing about writing. If you let your characters speak for themselves, they sometimes go places and do things you hadn't counted on." A shadow crossed Juneau's face. "Characters are kind of like kids in that way. You think you know who they are and what their future holds, and one day, right out of the blue . . ."

Something's wrong, thought Erin. She had never seen Juneau look so sad, not even at Willadene's after losing Max. "Has something happened to one of your girls?"

Juneau didn't pause in buttering the toast. "Misty's pregnant."

"Oh, no." Erin swallowed hard. "When did you find out?"

"Just before I came."

"And you came anyway?"

Juneau shrugged. "The damage is done. As Misty puts it, she can't get any more pregnant than she is. Hovering over her won't change anything."

"Oh, Juneau. What are you going to do?"

"Beyond the fact that Misty will have the baby, I don't have a clue. We're still in shock. It really hit Greg hard. He says no way can she keep it."

A scene flashed into Erin's mind of Misty breaking the news to Juneau and Greg. Then the scene changed to her own mother standing before Grams and Gramps, breaking the same news. Erin knew from old photos what her mother had looked like the summer she met Andrew J McGee: bright, laughing, hopeful. In this imagined scene, all the brightness was replaced by anxiety and shame.

But at least her mother had kept her baby.

Juneau seemed to pick up on what she was thinking. "How old was your mother when she got pregnant?"

"Seventeen. A little older than Misty."

"What did your grandparents do?"

"Shipped her north to Brainerd to live with an aunt until I was born. You know what their biggest fear was? That Mom and Andrew would run off and get married, and their grandchild would be raised in the Catholic Church. I guess to them the only thing worse than having an illegitimate grandchild was an illegitimate Catholic grandchild. Can you imagine that?"

"No. But when emotions are high anyway . . ."

Juneau didn't finish her sentence, and Erin wondered what she was thinking. She poured the omelet mix into the frying pan, swirling it twice to distribute it evenly. "Do you know anything about the father of Misty's baby?"

"Not a thing."

"So Misty's been keeping her romance a secret, just like Mom did."

"Romances. Plural. She says there are two possibilities."

Erin stood motionless a moment thinking of what Juneau's words implied. Then she lifted one edge of the omelet to check the doneness and sprinkled the green onions on half before closing it. "Maybe that's worse than knowing your father's name but realizing that he doesn't want to have anything to do with you."

Juneau sounded exasperated. "You're so certain about that, but how do you know for sure? That your father doesn't want anything to do with you?"

"Isn't it obvious? I've only seen him once in twenty-nine years, and when he called after I met Caitlin, he asked me specifically not to come to the house."

"Did he say flat out that he didn't want to see you? What if he does, really? What if there's a part of the story you don't know?"

Hot anger flashed through Erin. "What else could there be?"

Juneau raised her hands in a "cool down" gesture. "I'm just being the writer, Erin. Writers always have to consider the What If? That's how the plot keeps going forward."

Erin put the plate with the finished omelet on the table. Hands on her hips, she said, "Okay, what if?"

Juneau thought a moment. "What if his parents were as prejudiced against Lutherans as your grandparents were against Catholics? What if they blocked Andrew at every turn, making it impossible to have any contact with you without paying an enormous price?"

"They did, actually. Mom told me."

Grinning, Erin struck the Regina pose. *"He looked out the window of his Maserati, watching the upstanding Lutheran family walk to church. Regina, the love of his life, held the hand of a little girl with hair the color of his own. His innards were crawling over each other like snakes. He wanted to grab Regina and his child in an embrace as strong as a tight rubber band. He opened the car door and started to call her name, but a question stopped him. 'If I claim them, I lose my inheritance. How will I pay for the gas for this beast?' He slammed the door and drove away."*

Juneau laughed softly. "Another one to put in the ongoing saga."

"I suppose there is another side of the story," Erin mused. "I've stuck to the one I've known all my life."

"There's a way to find out, and it isn't by asking what if." Juneau said. "Get him to talk to you. Make him answer every question you ever had."

"I don't know how to do that."

"Oh, for heaven's sake. You're not a little girl anymore! Insist. Make a big enough stink that he doesn't have a choice."

Erin grinned. The idea had a certain perverse appeal.

Juneau touched Erin's shoulder. Her expression was sober. "One more thing. I promise you that no matter what, I won't do to Misty what Grams did to your mother. I won't crush her spirit with recrimination and guilt. And if I have anything to say about it, I'll make sure her baby will never think he wasn't wanted or loved."

Erin hugged her tight. "You'll never know how much that means to me."

Juneau was pouring milk as Willadene walked into the kitchen. "Something smells terrific," she said. "I'm starving."

She sat down, unfolded her napkin, and looked at them expectantly. "What have I missed?"

"Oh, we've just been playing a game of What If," said Juneau.

An image of The Griff popped into Deenie's mind. "That doesn't sound like a game I'd want to play. *What if the sky falls? What if the river floods? What if the world ends?* What's fun about that?"

"We weren't talking about cosmic What Ifs," said Juneau. "We were talking about What Ifs in our own lives."

"Like what?" Deenie took a drink of milk.

"Like what if there's another side to the Andrew J McGee story," Erin said.

Deenie choked in the middle of a swallow. When she could speak, she said, "Good grief. Is Andrew J McGee still stuck in your craw?"

First Erin looked surprised, and then she looked angry. "Some things do stick, because they're important. I've got my father. You've got Sunny."

"What do you mean?" Deenie demanded. She couldn't see how Erin could put Sunny in the same category as her father.

"Well, there could be another side to Sunny's story. What if your Aunt Stell and the failure of the Stowell Sight aren't to blame for what happened to Sunny? What if she was supposed to be born the way she is?"

"That makes as much sense as saying Ricky Harrington was supposed to be born with Down Syndrome!"

"Wait a minute." Erin set down her fork, but before she could speak further, Juneau touched her arm. "Calm down, Erin."

"Don't tell me to calm down." Erin voice was sharp. "Here's a What If for you: What if Misty was supposed to get pregnant?"

Juneau leaped to her feet. "Why did you have to blurt that out?"

"Misty's pregnant?" Deenie had always felt especially close to Juneau. She was hurt that she was the last to hear the news. "Juneau, you didn't tell me."

"I was going to, before Erin ran her mouth."

"I'm not the one who started this." Erin looked accusingly at Deenie.

"Don't look at me," Deenie said. "I walked in on the same old song and dance I've been hearing for years. It would be nice if there were something new to talk about."

Erin shoved her chair back and stood, arms akimbo. "If there were, I wouldn't share it with you."

"That goes both ways, sister."

They glared at one another while a miserable silence stretched on and on. Deenie cleared her throat. Erin sighed. The grandfather clock ticked. Then Erin and Juneau sat down again, and they all ate a few mouthfuls of omelet.

"What are we doing here," Juneau asked suddenly. "Did we come because of The Pact, or because we really wanted to be together?"

"I wanted for us to be together," Deenie said defensively. "I was the one who arranged it, remember?"

Juneau nodded. "But why? What did you think would happen?"

"I thought we would have a St. George version of the cemetery talk, only this time, it would be my turn." Deenie looked at her hands. "I thought I would get some comfort and support."

"How are we supposed to know that?" Erin challenged. "You never said anything in your letters. And so far, you've spent most of the time here in your bedroom with the door closed."

"I only wrote what you wanted to hear."

"What you thought we wanted to hear," Juneau countered.

"Fiction works for you; why shouldn't I give it a try? Really, Juneau, people don't quote *Out of the Best Books* every time they pick up a pen. And they don't take their typewriters with them when they go to visit friends."

Juneau stared at her. "You know what? I don't even recognize you, Deenie."

"Well, I recognize you. You're still making choices that leave you hobbled with guilt. First it was Max you were feeling guilty about, and now it's Misty." Deenie turned to Erin. "As for you and all your cosmic whys, some questions just don't have answers. Get over it."

Erin bristled. "Excuse me! Are you saying you don't ever question anything?"

"Of course I do. But you make it a Broadway production with a one-hundred-piece orchestra playing a pity song. You know how you complain all the time that Grams is into suffering? As far as I'm concerned, you're just like her. For her, it's all about her dead husband. For you, it's all about That Catholic Boy. You let him rule your life."

"I do not!"

"Actually, you do," Juneau said. "I'm surprised Cory doesn't object to having the phantom father as third party to your relationship."

Erin shot back, "You should talk. Everything you want in your life is some reaction to having the Pathetic Paulsens as parents!"

"Peripatetic," Juneau corrected. Her voice was icy. "What if we just don't do this anymore?"

"You mean call it quits?" Deenie asked. "The COBs?"

"That's about it."

"Maybe that's a good idea." Erin pushed back her plate and stood up. "I've got to get a breath of fresh air," she said."

Deenie stood, too. "I have to make a pit stop."

JUNEAU

Juneau glowered down at her eggy plate and half-eaten slice of cold toast. Her mind was a jumble from the tensions that had been released as if from Pandora's box. She wished she hadn't come. Deenie was right that she felt guilty about leaving Misty at this particular time. So was that her personal identification—guilt? She'd carried a load of Guilty Secrets to BYU Education Week back in 1980; she was still hefting just as big a burden, if not bigger. She'd brought it along with her, just as surely as she'd brought her typewriter. Had nothing changed in all these seven years?

She looked up when she heard Deenie coming back down the hall and was shocked to see how pale she was. Swallowing the resentment that had stockpiled inside her from the earlier argument, she said, "Deenie, are you all right?"

Deenie shook her head. "The eggs didn't sit too well."

Her face was puffy. She'd been in the bathroom how many times since she got up? And there was that cryptic statement at the end of her last letter, something about Grandma Streeter saying you should never give away anything away that you'd have to replace. Had Deenie written earlier about giving something away?

Yes.

Then Juneau knew. Was this the way the vaunted Stowell Sight worked? You put together a few clues and it all added up to an unavoidable conclusion? What Juneau knew was that Deenie was pregnant.

She remembered that back in 1980 Deenie hadn't said anything about what *she* suspected until she, Juneau, had announced it. Okay, so she would honor this secret now, but she hoped Deenie would confess soon because another thing Juneau knew was that Deenie needed help.

Deenie went over to sit on the sofa just as Erin stomped back into the room, her eyes rimmed with red. She stood apart from them, a defiant look on her face. "I don't know what you're thinking," she stated, "but I didn't invest seven years of heart and soul into the COBs to have it all go down the drain like this. We don't see each other face to face all that often, but I think about you two all the time. I feel closer to you than anyone else I know, even Colleen. We've been like sisters. How can any of us even think of calling it quits?"

Juneau opened her mouth to respond, but Erin wasn't through. Her eyes blazing now, she said, "So what if we don't think alike, and we say stupid things, and we mess stuff up? That's what families do, and if there's one thing I've learned, it's that you don't give up on family."

Juneau felt every one of Erin's words in her heart. "You're right. You two are the only sisters I've ever had. And sisters take care of each other." She looked at Deenie, who sat with knees up to her chin, her face paler than before. She squatted down in front of her so they were eye to eye. "Deenie, sweetie, you've helped us so many times. Let us help you now. Something's really wrong, isn't it?"

Deenie looked up, her face haggard.

"Deenie?" Juneau prompted.

Erin sat on the sofa beside Deenie and put an arm around her.

Deenie took Juneau's hand and leaned into Erin. Taking a deep breath she said, "I'm pregnant. I'm in serious trouble. And I'm scared."

She told them about the heart murmur, her doctor's concerns, and her decision not to tell Roger about the murmur. Once she started talking, it seemed as if she couldn't stop.

"I haven't told any of my family," she said. "I'm just not strong enough to worry about them worrying about me. Sometimes I think I'm losing my mind." She turned to Juneau. "You say asking 'What If' is part of plotting a novel. Well, Juneau, I don't have just a What If. I have The Great What If." She grinned without humor. "He's that lumbering thing that follows you in the shadows, making you second-guess every decision you've ever made." She made a noise that was part laugh, part sob. "We're the Three Gs, you know." Pointing at Erin, she said, "You've got your Grams. Juneau, you've got your Guilt. I've got The Griff."

Juneau shuddered. "The Griff?"

"Short for The Great What If. The Griff is always with me. He's the voice inside that makes me stop trusting myself. He stands behind me and whispers, 'What if Carl is late because he's lying dead by the side of the road? What if Roger isn't really at the library studying? What if one of those sweet young things has her hooks in his heart?' I hate the Griff. His whispers in my ear make me afraid almost every hour of almost every day."

"That's horrible," Erin said.

Juneau saw a look of pure fear cross Deenie's face. "Here's a What If for you," Deenie said. "What if he drives Deenie around the bend?"

Juneau squeezed her hand. "We'll just have to make sure that doesn't happen." She looked squarely into Deenie's eyes. "We'll head him off at the pass."

Deenie gave her a slight smile. "So you're Wonder Woman now, eh?"

Juneau smiled back. "Not yet. Just one of the COBs."

Erin nodded, her expression earnest. "There's something far more powerful than The Griff, Deenie. The Spirit. Don't forget that. We may not be able to give you a priesthood blessing, dear, but we can offer up a pretty powerful prayer." She looked at Juneau, who said, "Would you like us to do that, Deenie?"

Deenie nodded. "Please."

"You're the senior member of the COBs," Erin said to Juneau. "I think you should say the prayer."

Juneau realized that all the anger and tension of the morning were gone. In their place were the love and concern that had begun at Gabby's so long ago and had survived the morning's crisis. She reached out her free hand to take Erin's, and Erin gave her other hand to Deenie, so they were connected in a circle.

Juneau bowed her head. "Our Father in Heaven," she began. She prayed humbly but fervently and at some length. She asked for a special blessing on Deenie and included supplications for Erin and herself as well.

When she finished, they sat silently but still connected for several minutes. Finally Juneau said, "I don't know about you, but I feel as if I just grew up a whole lot. I came expecting us to play the same roles as we have in the past, but that doesn't work any more."

"You're right," Erin said. "I've been making the two of you into what I wanted you to be. I haven't been willing to be myself with you or see you two as you really are and love you that way. The truth is, we've all been dinged and battered by life since 1980. We've changed."

"In a novel," Juneau said, "the main character has to change by the end of the book. I guess that applies to real life after seven years, too."

Willadene looked pensive. "Have you read *The Velveteen Rabbit* to your kids?"

"Yes," Juneau said, "and I'll bet I know exactly what you're thinking of. The old skin horse."

Deenie nodded. "The old skin horse is battered and shabby and missing an eye from being so much loved by a child, but he says that's all part of becoming real. He says you become real bit by bit. I think we COBs are on our way to becoming real now that we are dinged and battered. And we've loved one another a lot."

"What a nice way to put it." Erin patted Deenie's arm. "Your Griff is no match for three COBs on the road to becoming real. You're going to make it through, Deenie. We all are."

Juneau and Deenie nodded their affirmation, but even as they did, Juneau sensed that beyond the closeness and warmth, the Great What If still lurked in the shadows.

The next morning they greeted one another with the giddy relief of children who have passed an important test. *Maybe we have,* thought Juneau.

Maybe this is what COBhood is all about—being willing to hang in there with each other, no matter what.

The rest of the week was filled with the fun, intimacy, and sweetness Juneau had prayed for when she left Pasadena, her heart bruised over Misty and her pregnancy. The three of them enjoyed long mornings on the deck in the cool, fresh air, OJ, or herbal tea in hand. They visited Snow Canyon and played like schoolgirls in the rusty sand. They watched comedies, relishing the release that came with laughter. And they visited the lovely St. George Temple one evening, sitting for a long time under the spell of the gleaming structure and the spirit surrounding it.

The morning they were to check out, they lingered in the kitchen reluctant to say good-bye despite the luggage stacked around them.

"I know what I'll be doing this coming year," Deenie said, patting her belly. "I have a baby hatching. And you," she pointed to Juneau, "have a book."

"And a grandbaby," Juneau added.

"What will you be up to?" Deenie asked Erin.

"Well, for sure not a book, and there's no plan for a baby. I guess what I want to do is really get to know the family I have. Grams, Caitlin, and maybe even my father." She stopped, a look of recognition on her face. "Do you realize how impossible it would have been for me to say that when we met in 1980?"

"Oh, yes," said Juneau. "A lot has changed since then. For all of us."

Juneau looked at them, thinking how much she loved these women, brought into her life seemingly by chance. "What about it, ladies?" she said. "Are we up to renewing The Pact? Making a no-kidding commitment to be together in 2005 no matter what?"

"Where?" asked Deenie. "So I can plan ahead. And make my lists." She grinned as she said it.

"Wherever we decide, I'll be there unless I'm in traction or dead," Erin said.

Juneau held out one hand, and one after another, they layered hand upon hand as if they were in a team huddle. "Remember the Three Musketeers?" Juneau asked. "We're like them: All for one, and one for all."

"All for one, and one for all," Deenie and Erin repeated, pumping the stack of hands up and down.

It was a little silly, but Juneau had the sense it was the kind of silliness that carried hidden meaning and strength. She felt it deep inside her as she headed out of St. George on the road to Pasadena, where her family waited.